Identity and Experience

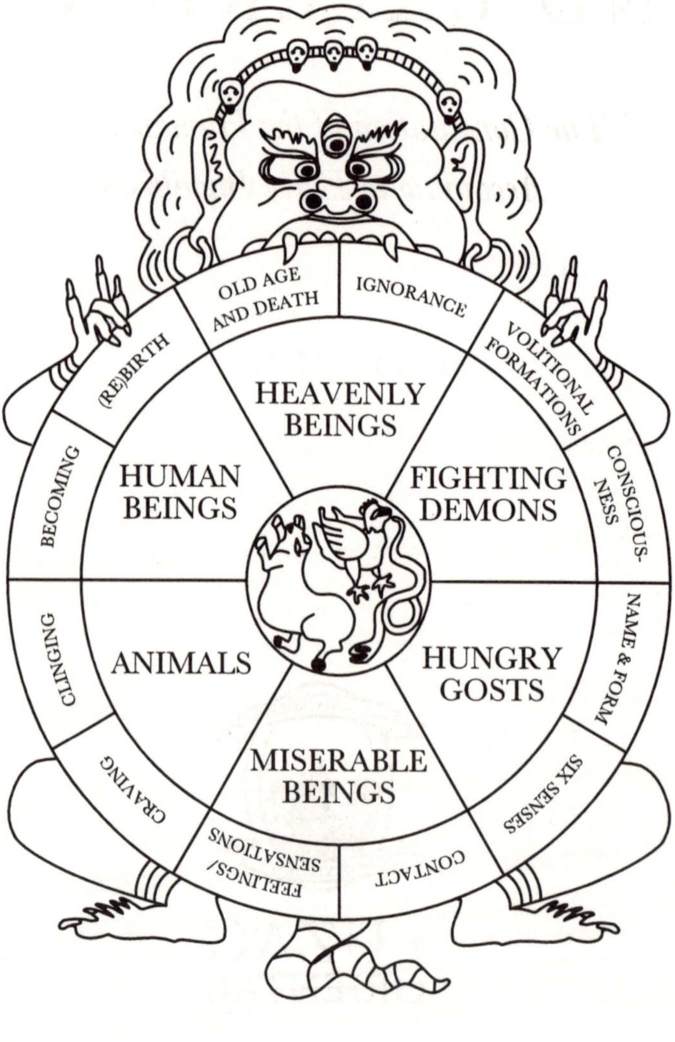

Frontispiece : the demon of Dukkha

IDENTITY AND EXPERIENCE

The Constitution of the Human Being According to Early Buddhism

SUE HAMILTON

LUZAC
ORIENTAL

LUZAC ORIENTAL
46 Great Russell Street, London WC1
1996

ISBN 1 898942 10 2

Printed and bound in Great Britain by
Bookcraft (Bath) Limited,
Midsomer Norton, Avon

For Ma, with love and thanks

CONTENTS

Foreword

"WHAT ARE LITTLE BOYS MADE OFF?", asks the nursery rhyme, and religious traditions ask the same question. Though the Buddha apparently denied that the human being contains something called a soul, what he meant by the denial, or by the word in his language which we translate "soul", has rarely been scrutinised.

In ancient India the Buddha's teaching was commonly summed up in a verse which says that he taught "the cause of things which arise from a cause, and their cessation too." He explained life as a causal process which normally leads to suffering; salvation can only come from reversing that process.

The Buddhist texts assert that a human being – indeed, any being living in our world – has five constituents, one physical and four mental: feelings, apperceptions, volitions, consciousness. The word for these constituents is "bundles", to show that they are plural. So it looks at first glance as if the Buddha was offering two analyses: the static, synchronic analysis of a person into "bundles", and the dynamic, diachronic analysis into a causal chain of events.

Sue Hamilton began by asking the nursery rhyme question and analysed what the texts have to say about the "bundles". She has found an exciting answer: they are bundles of experiences. On close scrutiny it turns out that the Buddha did not ask "*What* is a man?" but "*How* is man?". For objects he substituted processes. And his analysis of the human condition was an integrated whole.

This book is a breakthrough in our understanding of the earliest Buddhism and offers a firm foundation for future research.

Richard Gombrich
Oxford, March 1995

Acknowledgements

This book is a slightly revised version of my Oxford D.Phil thesis. Though I hope it will be of interest to as wide a readership as possible given its specialised topic (a brief glossary is given for the assistance of the more general reader), it is primarily intended to be a contribution to Buddhist studies. To this end, I hope it will not only answer some questions and clarify some areas of ambiguity but also stimulate further questions and on-going research, for myself and for others. As my work on this subject proceeded, I became only too aware of the size of the task I had undertaken, and there is considerable scope for adding to the material gathered together here. This reflects not just the extent of textual references to this topic but also the centrality of it in the context of the teachings of the Buddha.

I would add that this book was already tied into publishing schedules by the time I recently became acquainted with certain relevant issues in the Western philosophical tradition. An earlier acquaintance with these might well have clarified my mind and/or prompted me to write (sometimes very) differently on certain points. But the fact that I was not familiar with them does mean that what is contained herein has not had any Western philosophical thought projected onto the Buddhist material: I was not 'looking for parallels'. (That might happen later.) So while any reader with knowledge of Western philosophy will therefore have to bear with my ignorance, the parallels that there are can the more eloquently speak for themselves.

It is a happy custom that writers of books have an opportunity to thank those who have made a notable contribution, in one way or another, to its production. In my case, thanks are owed to many. Alexis Sanderson was an inspiring teacher in the early part of my graduate studies at Oxford. Richard Gombrich, who supervised my D.Phil, was an invaluable source of advice, thought-provoking comments and constructive criticism. The examiners of the thesis, Lance Cousins and Paul Williams, made useful criticisms and suggestions, some of which have been incorporated in this book: any omissions or errors that remain are entirely my own. During the years of my graduate studies I was fortunate enough to be a member of

Wolfson College, Oxford, which provided an incomparable environment for such an intellectual undertaking, for which I am most grateful. Whilst there I had the benefit of so many useful and stimulating discussions and suggestions that the people concerned are too numerous to mention, but I nevertheless acknowledge my indebtedness.

To two people I owe more than words can say. My daughter, Tanya, learned a great deal about *dukkha* when she was uprooted in her early teens to move to Oxford. She subsequently lived with me not only through the demands and preoccupations of preparing the thesis in a limited amount of time but also a further move to London. She has my deepest love and thanks. My mother, Muriel Anderson, supported me financially, emotionally and intellectually with generosity, understanding and selflessness. For me, this has exemplified the beauty and profundity of the Buddha's teachings and she has my gratitude and respect.

Sue Hamilton
London, 30 March 1995

Abbreviations

Abh.K.B.	Vasubandhu's *Abhidharmakośabhāṣya*
Ait. Up.	*Aitareya Upaniṣad*
AN	*Aṅguttara Nikāya*
As	*Aṭṭhasālinī*
Bṛ. Up.	*Bṛhadāraṇyaka Upaniṣad*
Ch. Up.	*Chāndogya Upaniṣad*
CPD	Critical Pali Dictionary
DA	*Dīgha Nikāyaṭṭhakathā (Sumaṅgalavilāsinī)*
DhA	*Dhammapadaṭṭhakathā*
Dhs	*Dhammasaṅgaṇī*
Dialogues	*Dialogues of the Buddha* (translation of the *Dīgha Nikāya*)
DN	*Dīgha Nikāya*
ERE	Hastings (ed) *Encyclopedia of Religion and Ethics*
Further Dialogues	*Further Dialogues of the Buddha* (SBB translation of the *Majjhima Nikāya*)
GS	*Gradual Sayings* (translation of the *Aṅguttara Nikāya*)
J	*Jātaka*
JPTS	Journal of the Pali Text Society
KhA	*Khuddakapāṭhaṭṭhakathā* (*Paramatthajotikā*)
KhP	*Khuddakapāṭha*
KS	*Kindred Sayings* (translation of the *Saṃyutta Nikāya*)
K. Up.	*Kauṣītakī Upaniṣad*
MA	*Majjhima Nikāyaṭṭhakathā (Papañcasūdanī)*
Miln	*Milindapañha*
MK	Nāgārjuna's *Madhyamakakārikā*
MLS	*Middle Length Sayings* (translation of the *Majjhima Nikāya*)
MN	*Majjhima Nikāya*
Mt. Up.	*Maitrī Upaniṣad*
Muṇḍ. Up.	*Muṇḍaka Upaniṣad*
Paṭis.	*Paṭisambhidāmagga*
PED	*Pali English Dictionary*
PTS	Pali Text Society
Pug	*Puggalapaññatti*
Pv	*Petavatthu*
PvA	*Paramatthadīpanī* Vol IV (commentary to *Petavatthu*)
RV	*Ṛg Veda*
SA	*Saṃyutta Nikāyaṭṭhakathā (Sāratthapakāsinī)*

Śat. Br.	*Śatapatha Brāhmaṇa*
SBB	Sacred Books of the Buddhists Series
SBE	Sacred Books of the East Series
SN	*Saṃyutta Nikāya*
Sn	*Sutta Nipāta*
SnA	*Sutta Nipātaṭṭhakathā* (*Paramatthajotikā* II)
Śvet. Up.	*Śvetāśvatara Upaniṣad*
Tait. Up.	*Taittirīya Upaniṣad*
Vin	*Vinaya*
Vism	*Visuddhimagga*
YS	Patañjali's *Yoga Sūtras*

Introduction

Buddhism has often been said to complicate the attempts of scholars of religious traditions to find common defining characteristics of 'religion'. One of the difficulties is that unlike all the other major religious traditions Buddhism does not accept the existence of a creator God. Nor, as is frequently pointed out, does it accept the existence of an individual self or soul. Because Buddhism is sometimes described more in terms of a way of life, some have even asked whether it is simply a philosophy or an ideology. It is, however, defined as a religion because its central concern is to offer to human beings salvation from the cycle of earthly existences (*saṃsāra*), which is characterised by suffering (*dukkha*). The non-acceptance of a creator God in a system which offers salvation to human beings is not too problematic: it can readily be accepted that salvation is achieved through one's own efforts. The apparent denial of the existence of an individual self or soul has, however, been found less easy to reconcile with such a notion of salvation. If there is no self, what is it that is saved?

The apparent denial of the existence of an individual self or soul is contained in what is known as the doctrine of *anattā* (Sanskrit: *anātman*), a teaching which appears, if in somewhat different guises, in all forms of Buddhism (save perhaps for a few modern hybrid forms). The focus of this book is a collection of texts known as the Pali canon, the textual basis of Theravāda Buddhism, the only surviving school of the early forms of Buddhism. The importance and traditional meaning of the doctrine of *anattā* for this school is indicated by Malalasekera, a distinguished modern Theravāda Buddhist, as follows:

> This is the one doctrine which separates Buddhism from all other religions, creeds, and systems of philosophy and which makes it unique in the world's history. All its other teachings … are found, more or less in similar forms, in one or other of the schools of thought or religions which have attempted to guide men through life and explain to them the unsatisfactoriness of the world. But in its denial of any real permanent Soul or Self, Buddhism stands alone. This teaching presents the utmost difficulty to many people and often provokes even violent antagonism towards the whole religion. Yet this doctrine of No-soul or *Anattā* is the bedrock of Buddhism and all the other Teachings of the Buddha are intimately connected with it … Now, what is this 'Soul' the existence of which the Buddha denies? Briefly stated, the soul

> is the abiding, separate, constantly existing and indestructable entity which is generally believed to be found in man … it is the thinker of all his thoughts, the doer of his deeds and the director of the organism generally. It is the lord not only of the body but also of the mind; it gathers its knowledge through the gateways of the senses … Buddhism denies all this and asserts that this belief in a permanent and a divine soul is the most dangerous and pernicious of all errors, the most deceitful of illusions, that it will inevitably mislead its victim into the deepest pit of sorrow and suffering.[1]

This description of the doctrine of *anattā* reflects the way it is consistently propounded by Theravāda Buddhists, and also the fact that it is traditionally considered to be the central doctrine taught by the Buddha. Such a description, however, might prompt one to add two other questions to that posed above: if there is no thinker of thoughts or doer of deeds, how does a human being experience suffering? What, indeed, *is* a human being according to the Buddha's teaching? The latter of these is the central question with which this book is concerned. And it is limited to the human being because it is with the human being that the texts are concerned: though other living beings such as animals and *devas* are sometimes mentioned, they are never discussed.

Perhaps because, as Malalasekera points out, it presents the utmost difficulty to many people, other scholars writing about the human being in early Buddhism have approached the texts with the aim of understanding the doctrine of *anattā*. In his much-acclaimed book *Selfless Persons*, Collins, for example, writes that it is his aim:

> … to elucidate how it [the *anattā* doctrine] appears in the texts, what it asserts, what it denies, and what it fails to assert or deny; and, perhaps most importantly, I shall wish to study what role or roles it plays in the varieties of Buddhist thought and practice, what function or functions it might have for those who profess allegiance to it and whose religious activity is patterned on it.[2]

In his"The Mind-body relationship in Pāli Buddhism: a philosophical investigation", Harvey states that his intention is to attempt to "understand the full meaning and actual implications of the teaching that 'all *dhammas* are *anattā*'".[3] Harvey's thesis is that consciousness (*viññāṇa*) is in effect a conventional self. Both these scholars write about the Theravāda Buddhist tradition as a whole, using as their primary sources not only the early part of the Pali canon, the *Sutta Piṭaka*, but also the later, scholastic *Abhidhamma Piṭaka*, the commentarial tradition and the *Visuddhimagga* of Buddhaghosa, a highly influential Theravāda Buddhist who lived in the fifth century CE, and many other traditionally Theravāda texts. Other scholars have sought to establish that the early texts implicitly teach that there is an absolutely transcendent non-empirical Self. A recent example of such work is Pérez Remón's book *Self and Non-self in Early Buddhism*, in which he seeks to make "a systematic and complete study of the *anattā* doctrine in the five *Nikāyas*".[4]

Another approach in modern scholarship is exemplified by those who have concentrated on establishing that the early Pali texts teach an elaborate psychology. For example, this is the aim of Johansson, in his book The *Dynamic Psychology of Early Buddhism*.[5] He states his work is "a psychologist's attempt to understand what the Buddha meant by 'dependent origination'".[6] Similarly Reat, in his *The Origins of Indian Psychology*, attempts to understand the human being in terms of a "theoretical psychology".[7] For such scholars, it is the content of the mind that as it were explains the individual human being, and, incidentally, the external world. I will be returning to the subject of the status of the external world shortly.

In attempting to answer the question "what is the human being according to the Buddha's teachings?", I decided, unlike the authors referred to above, to focus on the *Sutta Piṭaka* of the Pali canon, principally the four main *Nikāyas*. These represent the key doctrinal treatises of the earliest Buddhist material we have. A comprehensive comparison between the earlier *Sutta* material and the elaborated and systematised material of the *Abhidhamma* and commentaries would undoubtedly be most interesting and would be a fruitful area for further research, but as a single work it would necessitate an extremely lengthy book. Perhaps more importantly, I also wanted to see what the earliest Pali material had to say on the subject before it was significantly adapted or elaborated as the Theravāda tradition developed. This approach is not so much intended to suggest that there is a pre-Theravāda form of Buddhism as to look at the primary texts without reference to how the tradition has interpreted them in later material.[8] In some circumstances, particularly in chapter i, I have also drawn on the later *Abhidhamma* and commentarial material, and on Buddhaghosa's *Visuddhimagga*, but this is the exception rather than the rule. Such references to the later texts are usually by way of confirmation or contrast in interpreting an ambiguous point. In chapter i, however, it was the notable shortage in the *Sutta Piṭaka* of references to the subject matter of the chapter, the *khandha* of the body, that prompted my consulting the later material. Chapter viii draws on later material, particularly that represented by Buddhaghosa's *Visuddhimagga*, specifically to illustrate a divergence of interpretation as the tradition developed.

My approach to the subject was prompted by the Buddha's own concern with the human condition or the human being itself, an orientation which suggests that understanding the human constitution is important in the context of following his teachings. Three of the key teachings contained in the early *Suttas* illustrate this orientation. The first is perhaps the most well-known of the Buddha's teachings, the Four Noble Truths. These are given in terms of understanding the human condition in *saṃsāra*. In them the human condition is diagnosed (the first Noble Truth states that *saṃsāric* existence is unsatisfactory (or suffering) – *dukkha*[9]); the cause of the condition is identified (the second Noble Truth states that the arising of *dukkha* is because of desire or craving – *taṇhā*); a prognosis is given (the third Noble Truth states that the condition is not terminal – the cessation of unsatisfactoriness (*dukkhanirodha*) is possible); and finally a prescription for achieving *dukkhanirodha* is given (the fourth Noble Truth teaches the Eightfold Path which leads to Nirvana,[10] a synonym for *dukkhanirodha*).

The second key teaching is known as the formula of dependent origination, *paṭiccasamuppāda*. This states that an individual is dependently originated, the most common version of the formula being given as follows:

> Ignorance is the condition for [the arising of] the *saṃkhāras*[11]
> The *saṃkhāras* are the condition for [the arising of] consciousness
> Consciousness is the condition for [the arising of] *nāmarūpa*[12]
> *Nāmarūpa* is the condition for [the arising of] the six senses
> The six senses are the condition for [the arising of] contact[13]
> Contact is the condition for [the arising of] feeling
> Feeling is the condition for [the arising of] craving
> Craving is the condition for [the arising of] attachment
> Attachment is the condition for [the arising of] becoming
> Becoming is the condition for [the arising of] (re)birth
> (Re)birth is the condition for [the arising of] old age and death.[14]

This formula gives us a synthetical explanation of how a human being comes to be born in *saṃsāra*. Describing how the human being is dependently originated, one might call it a formula of existential mechanics.[15]

The third key teaching is given by the Buddha in contexts when he is asked about individual identity: when people want to know 'what am I?', 'what is my *real* self?'. The Buddha says that individuality should be understood in terms of a combination of phenomena which appear to form the physical and mental continuum of an individual life. In such contexts, the human being is analysed into five constituents – the *pañcakkhandhā*. The five *khandhas* are body (*rūpa*), feelings (*vedanā*), apperception and conception (*saññā*), volitional activities (*saṃkhārā*) and awareness (*viññāṇa*).[16]

The importance of the first two of these three key teachings is emphasised by their formulaic form: formulas were often used as a mnemonic device in the oral tradition in which the Buddhist teachings took root. The third teaching is the standard analysis of the human being in a large number of *Suttas*. And though the *khandha* doctrine has usually been associated with the doctrine of *anattā* in the specific sense that human beings *have* no self but only five constituent parts (an interpretation to which I will return in the conclusion), its importance is more positively emphasised by the Buddha's identification of the five *khandhas* together – in effect the earthly life of an individual – with *dukkha*.[17] Thus the fundamental characteristic of the human condition as stated in the first Noble Truth is given not just in descriptive terms but is intrinsic to being human, indicating that the need to understand the constitution of the human being is crucial to achieving the goal of Nirvana, given as the cessation of *dukkha*. Above all, these teachings indicate that however central the doctrine of *anattā* is, the Buddha's concern is most undeniably with the human condition as a whole, and though consciousness is mentioned in two of them it is given no more elevated a place than the other parts of the respective teachings. I therefore chose to approach a study of the human being by looking at the way the texts describe the *khandha* analysis, with frequent cross-references to the *paṭiccasamuppāda* formula.

In all cultures there is some kind of common sense view of what a human being consists of. In the West, for example, we tend to treat the human being dualistically, as consisting of body and mind. There is no consensus, however, about how these relate: major branches of philosophy, psychology and medicine consist of discussing and investigating how body and mind interact, and even physicists and mathematicians have joined the general debate. The situation becomes more complex because Christianity and other Western religions traditionally believe that in addition to body and mind, individual human beings have souls, thus making the question of how each part of the human being relates and interacts more problematic. Furthermore, many cultures, including popular British culture, allow for the existence of ghosts, which have human form but do not obey the laws of matter as they are normally understood.

In view of such diversity just in the contemporary Western understanding of the human being, one cannot assume *a priori* that any culture will have a consistent or coherent view of what constitutes a human being. And it would be particularly inadvisable to make such an *a priori* assumption of the Pali canon since it is a body of oral literature which is generally thought to have come together over time. Accurate oral preservation of literature had been crucial in the pre-Buddhist Brahmanical tradition in India for many centuries, and it is not uncommon the world over for the essential parts of important teachings to have been incorporated into stories, songs, chants, and so on, in order to preserve them accurately. There is clear evidence in the Pali canon of such a process of preservation, and we can thus be fairly sure that much of the *Sutta Piṭaka* is of a very early origin. Nevertheless, it would have been impossible for any one person, or even one close-knit group of people, to have preserved all the extant material, and there is textual evidence that different groups were given the task of preserving certain sections of the teachings. The Theravāda tradition records that there were periodic councils at which the teachings as a whole were recited. It was at these councils (*saṅgītis*) that the teachings were, over time, codified. But it is also probable that the teachings were more widely disseminated in this way: after hearing a complete recitation, a group of *bhikkhus* might have spread topics which it was not strictly their duty to preserve. So there was much opportunity for variations to be included in the material. Though the Pali canon as compiled from all its different sources was written down in approximately 25 BCE, scholars accept that even after that date changes are likely to have taken place.[18] This process of preservation applies to the *Vinaya*, in which the *bhikkhus*' code of discipline is recorded, and the *Sutta Piṭaka*, which contains the doctrinal teachings. The *Abhidhamma Piṭaka* is a later scholastic compilation which deals systematically and minutely with a wide range of issues in the Buddha's teachings. It aims to give definitive views on points which might not have been clear in the earlier material.[19]

My study of the *Sutta Piṭaka* was undertaken with the initial view that where various interpretations of apparently inconsistent passages are equally possible, it would be faulty methodology not to attribute to the texts the strongest interpretation, that is the most coherent and intellectually powerful one, given their common doctrinal background. In view of the way the canonical material was compiled, I nevertheless had little or no expectation of finding a coherent understanding of the human being and anticipated that a large part of this work would consist in relating its inconsistencies. But I found that in the main the inconsistencies lie in relatively minor matters such as the use of terms. In many instances a term is used in different contexts with different meanings. Sometimes the difference in meaning is only subtle and not easy to detect, and sometimes there is a wide variation in meaning. In his *History of Indian Philosophy*, Dasgupta makes the following comment on the fact that terms are used with different meanings in different contexts:

> The Buddha was one of the first few earliest thinkers to introduce proper philosophical terms and phraseology with a distinct philosophical method and he had often to use the same word in more or less different senses. Some of the philosophical terms at least are therefore somewhat elastic ...[20]

In discussing this point, I. B. Horner has suggested that this indicates a certain insufficiency of terms rather than an unsettled state of philosophical and psychological terminology by the time the *Nikāyas* came into being.[21] But philosophy and psychology were in a far from settled state at the time of the Buddha's teaching. The philosophical enquiry in the Brahmanical religion, as recorded in the *Brāhmaṇas* and the early *Upaniṣads*, was a relatively recent phenomenon, seen as merely supplementary to the ritualistic sacrificial system. The development took place gradually, and this is reflected in the early *Upaniṣads* which were perhaps extant at the time of the Buddha. In them we find both the ritual of the *Vedas* and the speculative beginnings of a psychology based upon the new idea of salvation as a special kind of knowledge. The systematic use of philosophical and psychological terminology is far from established, and terms are used to mean different things in different contexts in much the same way as they are in the Pali canon.

Another reason for the different use of terms in different contexts is the fact that the texts are a compilation, as mentioned above. And it is not unlikely that as the years went by and the Buddha's teachings were given to an ever wider range of people with different backgrounds, so they had to be explained slightly differently in order for them to be understood by those people.[22] We know, for example, that there were many different speculative teachings being propounded in the milieu in which the Buddha lived.[23] In particular the Ājīvikas and Jains are referred to in the canonical texts, and others are mentioned in relevant Jain texts. When teaching such people, the Buddha might well have adopted their terms in order to communicate with them. And in so doing, it is possible that the terminology was on some occasions used in what appear to be different ways but in fact with the same meaning.

So the contexts in which terms are found have to be taken into consideration when attempting to ascertain whether or not their meanings are different. I have accordingly tried not to explain a term in one context by taking out of context what is said about it elsewhere and thus arriving at an inappropriate definition. In order to understand what a given term means when it is being used in connection with one of the *khandhas* it is sometimes necessary also to understand what it means in other contexts. In these cases I have not hesitated to discuss the other contexts in detail. In spite of this, I found that in the majority of cases the contexts differ only superficially, and terms are used with a considerable degree of coherence.

The Buddha's understanding of the constitution of the human being is best introduced in the light of a brief description of the way the doctrines and concepts he taught fit into the background in which he was teaching. I have stated above that the religious milieu in which the Buddha was teaching was a complex one and that the terminology he used was sometimes varied to take this into account. But the dominant religion was that of the Brahmans, including both the older *Vedic* sacrificial religion and the relatively new *Upaniṣadic* teachings, at least some of which were known to the Buddha. Others have written about the emergence of Buddhism from its Brahmanical background in considerable detail,[24] and in several places in this book I too will discuss at some length the background to a particular subject in order to gain a better perspective of the way it is understood in Buddhism. Here, I will suggest in more general terms how those aspects of the Buddha's teachings that are most crucial to the human condition in *saṃsāra* correspond to or are different from the Brahmanical religion.

In this respect, the most central doctrine of the Buddha's teaching is based on his interpretation of the law of karma, a word which literally means 'action'.[25] The notion that karma, or action, brings results was deeply embedded in Indian religion by the time of the Buddha. In the classical *Vedic* sacrificial religion, karma is the *sine qua non* for individual well-being, for the well-being of society and for the maintenance of the universe as a whole. The rationale of the entire sacrificial system is the efficacy of (correctly performed) actions bringing about desired, and desirable, results. Sacrifices are performed for specific personal benefit in the short, medium or long term. Such sacrifices can have as their desired results things such as good health, the birth of a son, good fortune both in this world and in the next, or the benefit of one's ancestors already in the next world. Personal ritual duties are also, and more commonly, performed simply for general wellbeing, again both in this world and the next. Sacrifices are also performed for the prosperity of the community as a whole: the performing of the sacrifices serves to please the gods, who not only grant individual desires but also maintain the universe.

According to the *Vedic* tradition, sacrificial, or enjoined, actions are completely self-validating, whether or not a given action has any *prima facie* purpose or expected result. Furthermore, the sacrificial rationale works automatically: the correct performance of ritual actions is as it were a mechanical device. Though it is said that if the gods are 'pleased' they will maintain the universe and grant one's desires, in fact their reciprocal contribution is as enjoined upon them by the performance of the sacrifice as the performing of the sacrifice is enjoined upon the individuals in the community. The ritual actions of the sacrifice can, therefore, be regarded as a mechanical and automatic device for bringing about desired results.

In the early *Upaniṣads* karma is also of central relevance in the doctrine of transmigration they espouse. In the earlier *Vedic* material, life after death could be in one of several different *lokas* or worlds, the most important of which are the *pitṛloka*, the 'world of the ancestors', and the *devaloka*, the 'world of the gods'.[26] Which of these is attained depends on whether or not sacrifices have been correctly performed, though attainment of the *pitṛloka* also requires a man to have performed public services and almsgiving.[27] Gradually this belief developed into a system whereby individual existence was seen in terms of a series of lives. And in the *Bṛhadāraṇyaka* and *Chāndogya Upaniṣads* we read that the kind of deeds performed in one earthly life will determine the nature of the next earthly life: good deeds are rewarded with rebirth in a high status and bad deeds result in a correspondingly unattractive rebirth.[28] Though in these passages there is the suggestion of a difference between the ritual and ethical dimensions of actions, this differentiation was never developed in the Brahmanical religion; good and bad deeds are ritual actions which are correctly or incorrectly performed.

The Buddha took for granted the concept of rebirth in a series of lives, but revolutionised the concept of karma by teaching that karmic consequences accruing to any particular individual are entirely dependent on his or her mental volition.[29] He defined karma as follows: "O *bhikkhus*, I say that volition (*cetanā*) is *kamma*. Having willed, one acts through body, speech and thought".[30] The ethical implications of such a radical interpretation of a well established principle condition the Buddha's teaching about how salvation is attained: spiritual progress is frequently described in terms of moral development, for example, and anything which helps or hinders progress is described as wholesome and unwholesome *(kusala/akusala)* respectively. The Buddha's reinterpretation of the law of karma was also unlike the ideology of the sacrifice in that it involved the body, or corporeal faculty of the human being, with the mind, or mental faculties, in an unprecedented way: *having willed*, one acts through body, speech and thought. Though the ritual actions of the Brahmanical religion are said to bring about *desired* results, 'will' and 'mind' nevertheless have little or nothing to do with the efficacy or quality of the action, which depend entirely on the accuracy with which it is performed. The Buddha's version of the law of karma also had the profound effect of making the individual human being responsible for his or her own spiritual progress. Priests, gods and scriptural injunctions were bypassed by the Buddha and his teaching was centred on the moral condition (in its broadest sense) of individuals themselves and how they could bring about their own liberation. Once again this teaching suggests the importance of understanding how the human being works.

The contemporary developments in the Brahmanical religion, as recorded in the *Brāhmaṇas* and early *Upaniṣads*, include the new teaching that the soteriological path is epistemological. It arose from speculations about the sacrifice which posited a correspondence between microcosm (man) and macrocosm (the universe). According to the *Upaniṣads*, the culmination of the path, *mokṣa*, is achieved when one knows experientially that the essence of one's self is identical with the essence of the universe: *ātman* is Brahman. In the Buddha's teaching, the goal of the path to liberation, known either as Nirvana or as Enlightenment, is also an epistemic condition. But in spite of certain similarities, the two traditions are inherently and crucially different in a way which fundamentally affects the way they respectively understand the human being.

In stating that liberating knowledge is the realisation that the transcendent Reality, Brahman, is identical with the individual self, *ātman*, the *Upaniṣads* are ultimately concerned with being, *sat*. One can see, therefore, that the question they are thus concerned with is "*what* is man?" This would no doubt be the common sense approach to understanding the constitution of the human being; it was, indeed, the question I myself formed when I started my research. But though the Buddha's teachings also stress the need to 'know thyself', in contrast to the transcendent self of the *Upaniṣads* he taught liberating knowledge in terms of insight into 'things as they are', *yathābhūtaṃ*. Most importantly, the macrocosmic/microcosmic correspondence was expressed by the Buddha not in terms of an ontological identity, but in the fact that all things are dependently originated. By extension, this is applied to his teaching on the law of karma: one has to understand how one's existence is conditioned by (dependently originated in) one's volitions. For the Buddha, the important thing is to understand the *nature* of the human condition and we see that he emphasises not what things are but how they operate. Given that all things are dependently originated, he states that it is not fitting to think in the separative (independent) terms of "This is mine, this am I, this is my self".[31] So he does not give us a different answer to the same question "*what* is man?" but asks an altogether more sophisticated question: "*how* is man?" And he sustains this approach systematically throughout his teachings. The Buddha thus substitutes processes for objects. Primarily, he teaches the process of attaining Enlightenment as a goal which is achievable if one understands, and thus is able to overcome or reverse, the mechanics of that which is preventing it. Descriptions in the *Sutta Piṭaka* of the Buddha's own Enlightenment describe it precisely in such terms: and there is no mention of his experiencing *what* he is. And just as this ultimate experience involves understanding the nature of the human being and how he or she exists in *saṃsāra*, so, my research has found, the Buddha also teaches that the analysis of the human being into five *khandhas* is not an analysis of what the human being consists of, but of those processes or events with which one is constituted that one needs to understand in order to achieve Enlightenment. Knowing what the body is, for example, is of relevance only insofar as such knowledge contributes to an understanding of how it operates in the overall process of human existence. And we shall see in chapter 1 that contrary to what one might expect given that we have 'sense organs', the senses are not explicitly included in descriptions of the *khandha* of the body, an omission which serves to highlight the importance of understanding them in terms of the process in which they are involved rather than as organs of the body in the physical sense. Perhaps because our everyday commonsense world consists very much of what we think of as objects, and our tendency to want to know *what* things are, this important point has frequently been missed even within the Buddhist tradition itself.

One might suggest that the consistency of the Buddha's concern with processes rather than substance is reinforced by his dismissal of questions concerning ontological issues. He states that he is only concerned to give whatever information will assist the individual in attaining liberating insight, the process whereby one becomes free from the cycle of lives in *saṃsāra*, and that ontological questions are irrelevant and/or misleading.[32] When asked questions which he did not think would be conducive to the attaining of insight, he refused to answer them. Classically, there are four 'unanswered questions': whether or not the universe is eternal, whether or not the universe is finite, whether or not that which is the vital principle (*jīva*) is different from the body, and whether after death a *tathāgata* (an epithet of the Buddha and the implication is that it means any liberated being) exists or not, whether s/he exists and does not exist, or whether s/he neither exists nor does not exist.[33] In similar vein, a long list of all sorts of ontological views are refuted by the Buddha in the well-known *Brahmajāla Sutta*. Here the implication is that all such views are not just erroneous in the sense of holding to the wrong ontological view, but erroneous in the sense that holding to an ontological view is simply the wrong approach to the solution of the problem of bondage to *saṃsāra*. This point is further supported by the fact that the having of 'views' (*diṭṭhi*) is sometimes stated to be one of the *āsavas*, the most binding and deeply entrenched of all misplaced tendencies needing to be 'rooted out'.

All of this suggests that questions about what cannot be experienced as part of the empirical human condition are considered to be speculative. In refusing to answer such questions the Buddha has left the way open for what one might call the nihilists and eternalists of all times and places, Buddhists and scholars alike, to continue to speculate about whether or not there really is a soul, and whether it is extinguished at death or persists on some transcendent, non-empirical, level. But in the context of the early Buddhist texts such speculations are pointless. First, they are destined to remain speculative. In common with most religious texts, there is much in the *Sutta Piṭaka* that is open to subjective interpretation. Thus both nihilists and eternalists of every persuasion can find what they believe to be support for their theories. Second, and more importantly, in running directly counter to the Buddha's teaching that it is *not* conducive to insight, ontological speculation does not assist in one's attempt to understand the teaching he gave, which *was* intended to be conducive to insight.

However, the question of ontology continues to arise in the scholarship of early Buddhism. In particular, several ambiguous passages in the Pali material have been interpreted as suggesting an idealistic ontology, like the one formulated by the much later Buddhist school of Vijñānavāda. This development perhaps corresponds to the fact that there are passages which suggest idealism in the *Upaniṣads* and this ontology was later attributed to them wholesale by Śaṅkara and other Advaita Vedāntins. The debate about canonical passages which are ambiguous in this way recurs several times in this book, and we shall see that in every case much depends on how a passage is interpreted. An example of how differently a passage can be interpreted can here be drawn from the *Dīgha Nikāya*. In translating the Pali *ajjhattaṃ rūpa-saññī eko bahiddhā rūpāni passati*,[34] Johansson gives: "When somebody experiences forms inside himself, he will see forms outside..." and writes of it: "The objective world, according to Buddhism, is no different from the experienced world: it simply consists of the subjective world projected by our mind...".[35] But the passage can be translated and interpreted differently, as follows: "One who apperceives a visible feature of himself [likewise] sees visible features of others". This translation follows the convention found in some contexts in the *Sutta Piṭaka*, usually those concerned with meditation, of using the terms *ajjhattaṃ* and *bahiddhā*, 'internal' and 'external', to refer to oneself in contrast to others. In the *Satipaṭṭhāna Suttas*, for example, which contain descriptions of key meditation exercises to be practised by *bhikkhus*, these terms are used to indicate that the meditation exercises are to be practised both on one's own physical and mental faculties and also on those of others.[36] The purpose is to realise that one's nature is the same as the nature of anyone else. Even if in the *Dīgha Nikāya* passage the term *bahiddhā* is interpreted simply as 'external', so far as I am aware there is no convention in the *Sutta Piṭaka* of *ajjhattaṃ* being used as part of a psychological term to indicate an 'internal picture'. So in my opinion it is unlikely that this passage was intended to have the implications which Johansson reads into it. Rather, it suggests to me that one sees that both one's own and external (be they of other individuals or not) visible parts are of like nature. This is the more likely because the context of the passage is one in which the various insights which come with meditation are described. One of the most important insights for a *bhikkhu* to achieve is that all things are of like nature, not whether or not the external world is a projection of his mind.

Another frequently found term, *loka*, which literally means 'world', is similarly ambiguous. This is a very important term and its use warrants careful consideration. The nature of the human being is so fundamental to the Buddha's teaching that a common metaphor for the life of an individual is 'the world', *loka*. Failure to understand this metaphor has led some to conclude that 'the world is not real', 'the world only exists in our minds', and so on. But what appear to be ontological statements in fact metaphorically relate to the subjective experience of the individual, and it is invalid to extend the metaphor into a statement that the world *is* that subjective experience.

The metaphorical use of the term *loka* pre-dates the Buddha's teaching. Though in both Sanskrit and Pali the term *loka* does have the conventional meaning 'world', even in the earlier sacrificial religion of the Brahmans its meaning was not limited to the external world. According to Gonda, the Sanskrit word *loka* has an "inherent vagueness".[37] It does not necessarily indicate a spacial location but often means a state of happiness or stability. Gonda traces the changing meaning of the term, and states that its earliest meaning is a "free, open space" or a "safe, sacred space".[38] This concept was of particular importance to the early Aryan settlers in India because of the religious significance in early Indo-European culture of clearings, forest glades and so on. Thus in the sacrifice a sacred space is constructed to represent the desired *loka* in this world and the next. In this way the term also became associated with cosmological planes (desired *lokas*), which tend to be interpreted spacially.[39] But the association of security and happiness with the sacred space becomes extended metaphorically so that in fact the desire to 'gain a *loka*' in this world (through sacrifice) and/or the next does not just refer to the spacial location but to the individual's state of security and happiness. So there are two principal meanings of *loka*, the one spacial and the other psychological.

The way the term *loka* is used in the *Sutta Piṭaka* is perhaps an extension of this meaning of *loka* in the Brahmanical religion. Here, too, it is used to indicate cosmological levels. But metaphorically it is intended to indicate the individual's subjective experience in *saṃsāra*. This is most clearly indicated in the *Khandha Saṃyutta*, which is primarily concerned with the analysis of the individual in terms of the five *khandhas*. Here we read that the five *khandhas* together comprise a "phenomenon which is a world in the world".[40] The context is one in which the Buddha states that he has no quarrel with the world (*nāhaṃ lokena vivadāmi*) or with some of the teachings of other teachers in the world (*loke paṇḍitā*). But he wants to establish a teaching which is not given by those other teachers, that of the five *khandhas*, which he has thoroughly penetrated and realised (*abhisambujjhati abhisameti*). There is no suggestion in this passage that in associating the term *loka* with the *khandhas* the Buddha wishes to deny the existence of the external world. Rather, he is unconcerned with its status and concentrates on passing on his understanding of the *khandhas*.

This metaphorical sense of *loka* is also suggested by the fact that it is used in similar contexts to the term *dukkha*. As we have seen, the Buddha taught that *saṃsāric* existence is characterised by *dukkha*, unsatisfactoriness. And that *dukkha* refers to the individual's *saṃsāric* experience is confirmed by the Buddha's definition of *dukkha* as being the five *khandhas* of which the individual is comprised, as we have also seen. Frequently, teachings are said to lead to the "ceasing of this entire mass of unsatisfactoriness".[41] This means to the point where the individual, who persists with five *khandhas* being reborn in *saṃsāra*, achieves liberation. And that *loka* is being used in the same way is illustrated in the *Nidāna Saṃyutta* of the *Saṃyutta Nikāya*, where two consecutive *Suttas* are the same save for the fact that in the second *Sutta loka* is substituted for *dukkha*.[42] In the *Suttas*, the Buddha states:

> I will teach you, *bhikkhus*, how *dukkha/loka* arises and how it ceases... Visual consciousness arises because of sight and (visible) objects (and so on through all the senses); contact is the combination of the three; feeling is conditioned by contact; craving is conditioned by feeling. This, *bhikkhus*, is the arising of *dukkha/loka*.

The cessation of *dukkha/loka* comes about when the craving which is normally conditioned by feeling no longer occurs: when craving utterly fades away and ceases, then grasping, becoming, birth, and cyclic existence in *saṃsāra* cease.[43]

If one takes the first part of these passages out of context they can be construed to be stating that both *dukkha* and the world arise as part of one's psychological experience of perception. In other words, an idealist might conclude from this that the world has no external reality, that it only exists in our perception. But if one considers the context in full, the terms *dukkha* and *loka* are in fact associated with the life of an individual and the *Suttas* are describing the process by which craving (*taṇhā*) brings about continued becoming, rebirth, and so on, and it is through the cessation of craving that continued rebirth ceases. It is this individual 'world' (*loka*) of the individual, sometimes called *dukkha,* that is the subject of these passages, not the arising of the 'world' in general terms.

A similar passage in the *Aṅguttara Nikāya* states: "It is these five types of sensual desire that are called the world in the discipline of the noble one".[44] The five types of sensual desire are identified with five corresponding senses, and the passage continues by stating that a *bhikkhu* is to become detached from sensual desire and practise appropriate meditation. When he eventually sees that his *āsavas* are completely destroyed, he "is said to have come to the end of the world, he lives at the end of the world, he has overcome attachment in the world".[45] In stating that the five types of sensual desire *are called* the 'world' of the noble one, this passage indicates that *loka* is a verbal convention to indicate *saṃsāric* existence which is fuelled by desire. When the *bhikkhu* has achieved the destruction of the *āsavas*, this, for him, is the end of the cycle of rebirth, the end of 'his world'.

As a final example of this meaning of *loka,* I will draw on a passage in the *Saḷāyatana Saṃyutta*, where we read:

> *Bhikkhus,* I declare that the end of the world is not to be learned, seen, or attained by going to the end of the world. Nor do I declare, *bhikkhus*, that the end of *dukkha* can be made without attaining the end of the world.[46]

Here one does not 'go to' the end of the world, but 'attains' the end of the world. *Loka* has no spacial connotation, as it would if it referred to the 'external' world, but is a designation for the ending of the individual's *saṃsāric* existence, *dukkha*. Later in the same *Sutta*, the individual's 'world' is again defined in terms of the senses. It is because of the craving that we have for sensual experience that our 'world' has continued existence: this is how the individual continues, not what the external world is.

Two points arise from the foregoing discussion. The first point is that these passages and the possible interpretations I have shown illustrate the need for ambiguous passages to be interpreted in the light of the material as a whole. Those of us whose work lies primarily in attempting to understand questions of a philosophical or doctrinal nature have to ask ourselves which of the possible translations is the more likely given the doctrinal background of the Buddhist teachings. With regard to ambiguous passages which have potentially ontological implications, we have to ask ourselves the *prima facie* question of whether it is likely that the Buddha would have made such ontological statements. If we answer no to this question, then we have to consider both whether a passage has an alternative meaning and whether the ontological statements of others are incompatible with his teachings. The second point is that I am in no way attempting to refute an ontological position that other scholars have adopted because I wish to adopt another one. I merely think that in view of the fact that the Buddha clearly dissociates his teachings from anything to do with ontology, it is a mistake to project any ontological significance onto the text.

I would like to make one further comment here about the fact that my research has shown that the Buddha's teaching on what comprises the human being is consistently focussed not on the substance of the constituent parts but rather with what their function is and how they contribute to the complex of human functions. In considering what are usually called 'body' and 'mind', this important point has to be borne in mind. The words body and mind have substantialistic connotations in English. Though corresponding terms are used in the early Buddhist material we will be considering, I shall suggest that such terms are a convenient verbal convention and that they carry no substantialistic or ontological implications. Returning to a brief example given above, this point is particularly important when considering the *rūpakkhandha*, which refers to the living body. It is analysed in terms of four 'elements', earth (*paṭhavī*), water (*āpo*), fire (*tejo*) and air or wind (*vāyu*). Though in the West one might tend to think of the human body as what we would call 'matter', according to the Buddha's teaching these elements are, rather, intended to signify that it is analysed according to certain abstract qualities which characterise how the body manifests. The characteristics of solidity and extension (the primary characteristics of 'matter') are signified by the element earth. Fluidity is signified by water, heat by fire, and mobility by wind. We shall see more comprehensive descriptions of the elements in chapter 1, but my purpose in commenting on this subject here is to alert the reader to the implications of an analysis of the human being which is given not in terms of what he or she consists of but in terms of how he or she operates.

A large part of the third volume of the *Saṃyutta Nikāya*, itself entitled the *Khandha-Vagga*, consists of the *Khandha Saṃyutta*, which exhaustively discusses the five *khandhas*. Used in this way, the term *khandha* is distinctively Buddhist, not being found in the earlier *Vedic* literature except in the sense of 'trunk'. Most frequently, the *khandhas* are referred to by name without giving any explanation as to what the name means or implies; where descriptions are given, these are sometimes so brief that it is difficult definitively to ascertain the precise characteristics and functions of each one. Nevertheless it is possible to extract from the material as a whole a coherent picture of each of the *khandhas*. No reason is given for the order of the *khandhas*, which is virtually always in the order in which I will discuss them below: *rūpa*, *vedanā*, *saññā*, *saṃkhāra* and *viññāṇa*.[47] With regard to the first of these, the *rūpakkhandha*, this presents certain organisational complications in that cross-references between material relevant to understanding it and material relating to the other four *khandhas* are not necessarily self-explanatory until the later chapters have been read. For this reason, some readers may find it helpful to delay reading the first chapter until they have read chapters two to five.

Having discussed the five *khandhas*, I will then go on to discuss two other key concepts with regard to the constitution of the human being, *nāmarūpa* and *manomaya*. The former frequently occurs in association with *viññāṇa* and is one of the links in the *paṭiccasamuppāda* formula. The latter is one of the most obscure terms found in the *Sutta Piṭaka*, but consideration of what it means throws light on the manner in which the human being exists as he or she progresses on the spiritual path to liberation. It also illustrates the power of the mind according to Buddhist teachings. In the light of this, in my final chapter I shall show that there is no justification for holding the body to account for originating the volitions which bind one to the cycle of rebirth.

Notes

1. Malalasekera, 1957, p.33f.
2. Collins, 1982, p.5.
3. Harvey, 1981, p.xi.
4. Pérez Remón, 1980, p.2.
5. Johansson, 1979.
6. Ibid., p.7.
7. Reat, 1990, p.8.
8. Though I am aware this approach is somewhat controversial (cf., for example, Collins, 1990; and it is also an unwelcome approach in other religious traditions), it can nevertheless produce interesting, and in my opinion valuable, results.
9. *Dukkha* is notoriously difficult to translate literally into English. 'Suffering' is often used, but can be misleading if understood in a narrow sense. 'Unsatisfactoriness' is more appropriate in that it conveys that all things are ultimately unsatisfactory because they are impermanent – and therefore if one is seeking the permanence of ultimate bliss (or the ultimate bliss of permanence) then the human condition is, by contrast, suffering. cf. the Glossary entry and Rahula, 1985, chapter 2.
10. The Sanskrit word Nirvana has been integrated into the English language so I shall not italicise it. When translating direct from Pali, I will use *nibbāna*.
11. The meaning of *saṃkhāra* is discussed in chapter iv.
12. The term *nāmarūpa* is discussed in detail in chapter vi.
13. This means contact between the sense organ and its corresponding external sense object, together with consciousness. It is discussed further in chapter ii.
14. *Avijjā-paccayā saṃkhārā, saṃkhāra-paccayā viññāṇaṃ, viññāṇa-paccayā nāmarūpaṃ, nāmarūpa-paccayā saḷāyatanaṃ, saḷāyatana-paccayā phasso, phassa-paccayā vedanā, vedanā-paccayā taṇhā, taṇhā-paccayā upādānaṃ, upādāna-paccayā bhavo, bhava-paccayā jāti, jāti-paccayā jarāmaraṇaṃ.* e.g. SN.II.25 and throughout the *Nidāna Saṃyutta*. All translations are my own unless otherwise stated.
15. I will discuss this purpose, and the varieties, of the formula more fully in chapter iv.
16. These translations are all discussed in following chapters.
17. *Saṃkhittena pañc' upādānakkhandhā dukkhā*: e.g. SN.V.421; MN.I.48; AN.I.177. cf. also SN.III.158: *Katamañ ca bhikkhave dukkham? Pañc' upādānakkhandhā ti 'ssa vacanīyaṃ*. This question and answer in SN.III.158 is referred to again in chapter viii below. cf. also Gethin, 1986, p.41.

18. On the subject of the compilation of the Pali canon see Frauwallner, 1956; Lamotte, 1958; Zürcher, 1962, and Cousins, 1983.
19. The precise chronology of all parts of the three *Piṭakas* is unknown, and there appear to be small areas of possible correspondence of style in late sections of the *Sutta Piṭaka* and early sections of the *Abhidhamma Piṭaka*. But in general terms the *Abhidhamma* is later.
20. Dasgupta, 1975, p.86, n.1.
21. Horner, MLS, Vol. I, p.xxv.
22. Manné (1990) has analysed much of the material in the *Nikāyas* and shown that different passages have a different, usually didactic, purpose.
23. See, for example, the *Poṭṭhapāda Sutta*, the *Brahmajāla Sutta* (both DN, Vol I), etc.
24. For example, Gombrich, 1988, chapters 2 and 3; Collins, 1982, Part I; Reat, 1990, *passim*.
25. Again, the Sanskrit word karma has been integrated into the English language so I will not italicise it. When translating from the Pali, I will use *kamma*.
26. cf. Collins, 1982, p.45ff on existence after death in the *Vedas*.
27. Ch. Up. V.10.3.
28. Bṛ. Up. IV.4.5; Ch. Up. 5.10.7. This teaching is repeated in later *Upaniṣads* such as K. Up. 1.2; Kaṭha 5.7; Śvet. Up. 5. 11–12.
29. Gombrich (1988, p.67ff) places the Buddha's ethicising of the law of karma in its historical context.
30. AN.III.415: *Cetanā'haṃ bhikkhave kammaṃ vadāmi. Cetayitvā kammaṃ karoti kāyena vācā manasā.*
31. For example, MN.I.232f: *Etam mama, eso 'ham asmi, eso me attā ti.*
32. cf., for example, SN.II.223, V.437; MN.I.395; DN.III.134ff.
33. MN.I.157. cf. also the *Cūḷa-Māluṅkyasutta* (MN.I.426ff), the *Avyākata Saṃyutta* (SN.IV.374ff) and the *Aggi-Vacchagottasutta* (MN.I.483ff) (much of the last two are phrased as a series of questions and answers).
34. DN.III.260.
35. Johansson, 1979, p.83.
36. MN.I.55ff; DN.II.290 ff.
37. Gonda, 1966, p.110 and *passim*; cf. also Collins, 1982, p.45ff.
38. Gonda, 1966, pp.1–41.
39. Collins (1982, p.45 ff) discusses the three principal *lokas*: the *pitṛloka*, the *devaloka* and the *sukṛtāṃ loka*.
40. SN.III.139: *Loke lokadhammo.*
41. *Evam etassa kevalassa dukkhakkhandhassa nirodho hotīti.*
42. SN.II.71 ff.
43. *Dukkhassa/lokassa bhikkhave samudayañca atthaṅgamañca desissāmi ... . Cakkhuṃ ca paṭicca rūpe ca uppajjati cakkhuviññāṇaṃ tiṇṇaṃ saṅgati phasso phassapaccayā vedanā vedanāpaccayā taṇhā. Ayaṃ kho bhikkhave dukkhassa/lokassa samudayo. Taṇhāya asesavirāganirodhā upādānanirodho ... .*
44. AN.IV.430: *Pañca'ime ... kāmaguṇā ariyassa vinaye loko ti vuccati.*
45. AN.IV.431f: *Bhikkhu ... paññāya c' assa disvā āsavā parikkhīṇā honti. Ayaṃ vuccati ... bhikkhu lokassa antaṃ āgamma lokassa ante viharati tiṇṇo loke visattikan ti.*
46. SN.IV.93: *Nāham bhikkhave gamanena lokassa antaṃ ñātayyaṃ daṭṭhayyaṃ pattayyan ti vadāmi. Na ca panāham bhikkhave apatvā lokassa antaṃ dukkhassa antakiriyaṃ vadāmi ti.*
47. They are found with *saṃkhāra* and *viññāṇa* having changed places at SN.I.112: *Rūpaṃ vedayitaṃ saññaṃ viññāṇaṃ yañca saṃkhataṃ ...* . This is, however, the first two lines of a verse, and the change in order (and the use of *saṃkhata* rather than *saṃkhāra*) is in order to conform to the *śloka* metre. The interchangeability of *saṃkhata* and *saṃkhāra* is discussed in chapter IV.

CHAPTER I

The Rūpakkhandha

Introduction

IN THIS CHAPTER, MY CONCERN is with the body of the human being, referred to as the *rūpakkhandha*. Having selected the earliest part of the Pali canon, the four main *Nikāyas* of the *Sutta Piṭaka*, as my source material for this study of the *khandhas*, however, an immediate problem presents itself which needs to be dealt with at the outset. In this early stratum of the texts there is a notable lacuna in the information we are given about the human being, a lacuna that at first sight appears to lie in the descriptions of the *rūpakkhandha*. From the two types of definitions of the *rūpakkhandha* that we are given one can draw out an overall view of how the *khandha* is meant to be understood. Though relatively brief, this overall view is in some crucial respects very informative, as we shall see. But as one proceeds to reading canonical descriptions of the four *arūpakkhandhas* (*arūpa* refers to the four that are not *rūpa*) one sees with hindsight that an important and frequently mentioned feature of the human being has not anywhere been explained. This feature is the senses. All the *arūpakkhandhas* are subdivided according to the senses, thus stressing their important role, but they are neither considered actually to be part of the *arūpakkhandhas* nor are they mentioned at all in descriptions of the *rūpakkhandha*. When later Theravāda Buddhists realised the importance of the senses, and attempted to redress the lacuna in the descriptions of the *khandhas*, they included the senses in the *rūpakkhandha*. In view of this, it seems appropriate to discuss the senses in this chapter, and where necessary I have drawn quite extensively on commentarial texts and parts of the *Abhidhamma*, notably the *Dhammasaṅgaṇī* and its commentary the *Aṭṭhasālinī*, and the *Vibhaṅga*. In so doing, I have been guided (perhaps limited) by a desire not to arrive at a definitive view of the *rūpakkhandha* as understood by the (later) *Abhidhamma* tradition, but to suggest an overall picture of how the *rūpakkhandha* and the senses might be understood that is compatible both with the brief definitions found in the *Sutta Piṭaka* and with other aspects of the human being described in later chapters.

To this end, my discussion of this *khandha* will be structured as follows. In the first part of the chapter, the definitions of *rūpa* as given in the *Sutta Piṭaka* will be discussed, including a consideration of the terms 'primary' (*no-upādā*) and 'secondary' (*upādā*) as used in this context. The discussion will also cover the so-called 'elements', the *mahābhūtā*, as briefly referred to in the *Sutta Piṭaka* and more elaborately in later material. The second part of the chapter will concentrate on a specific discussion concerning the senses. Recognising their importance, the Theravāda tradition as a whole (that is the *Abhidhamma*, commentaries, Buddhaghosa's *Visuddhimagga* and the writing of modern Theravāda Buddhists) singles out the senses and their corresponding objects (collectively referred to as *āyatanas*) in defining the 'secondary' level of the *rūpakkhandha* (which itself is not defined in the *Sutta Piṭaka*). In spite of this, the attempt here to gain a meaningful understanding of the senses has not been an easy one. As we shall see, even the *Abhidhamma* is inconsistent in its descriptions. Though it defines them at times as *rūpa*, at other times it describes them in a way which suggests they are not *rūpa*. In the light of such ambiguity, I shall question just what it is that is being referred to when the senses are mentioned in the *Sutta Piṭaka*. Not only do descriptions of each of the four *arūpakkhandhas* state that the senses (or their objects) determine the different kinds of activity the *khandha* represents, as I have said, but the senses are also one of the links in the chain of the *paṭiccasamuppāda* formula which describes how the functioning of a human being is dependently originated. I also referred in the Introduction to passages which state that the ongoing existence of the individual, his or her *loka*, is caused by desire based on the senses. The Theravāda Buddhist tradition, and many scholars of Buddhism, have understood that where the senses are said to determine the different kinds of activity of the *arūpakkhandhas*, they are the physical bases of the corresponding mental activities. But I find this unsatisfactory: if the physical sense organs are meant, one might expect them to be included in a description of the *rūpakkhandha* in the *Sutta Piṭaka*, particularly in view of the fact that they are subsequently mentioned, but *not* classified, in the descriptions of each of the *arūpakkhandhas*. I shall suggest a way they might be understood to be neither *rūpa* nor *arūpa*, thus explaining why they are not included in the *khandha* analysis in the *Sutta Piṭaka*.

In Buddhism, and in other Indian religions also, it is common that the senses include the five which are common to us in Western culture and also a sixth sense, *manas*, the corresponding object of which is *dhammā*. The term *manas* literally means 'mind', and as such appears qualitatively different from the other senses. Perhaps because of this, it remains uniquely ambiguous as a sense, throughout the Pali material. Nor is it immediately obvious what *dhammā* refers to. Neither is explained in the *Sutta Piṭaka*, but in the *Abhidhamma* and commentaries they are classified as *āyatanas*, a term which covers all the senses and their objects (thus giving a total of twelve *āyatanas*).

But in spite of the fact that the other (five) senses and their corresponding objects (that is, those ten of the *āyatanas*) are clearly defined as 'secondary' *rūpa*, neither *manas* nor *dhammā* is defined as being *rūpa*, or at least not consistently so. The lack of clarity is compounded because the *Aṭṭhasālinī*, the commentary on the *Dhammasaṅgaṇī*, contains what one might call a 'theory of sense' (if an imperfect one) in the context of a description of *rūpa*, but it omits *manas* and *dhammā* from this theory. In fact both terms have a multitude of meanings in the Pali material and, in my opinion, they have never been adequately understood in the context of sense and corresponding object, either by the Buddhist tradition or by modern expositors. In view of the role of all six of the senses as determining the sixfold classification of each of the *arūpakkhandhas*, it is important to establish how *manas* and *dhammā* might best be understood and what the function of *manas* is before we go on to consider those *arūpakkhandhas*. The concluding part of this chapter will therefore be a discussion of these two terms.

The *rūpakkhandha*

Apart from the specific context of the *rūpakkhandha*, the term *rūpa* is found in two other contexts in the Pali canon which are relevant and need brief mentioning here. First, it is the term which refers to the sense object (*rūpāyatana*) which corresponds to the sense organ 'eye'. Here the criterion of visibility dominates and it has the general meaning of 'visible object'. In such contexts the literal meaning of the Pali word *rūpa*, 'form', which in common usage usually means shape or appearance, is most relevant. Second, it is also frequently found in the compound *nāmarūpa*. This literally means 'name and form', but has also been interpreted as 'mind and body'. The meaning of *nāmarūpa* is discussed separately in chapter VI. When used in the expression *rūpakkhandha*, *rūpa* is often understood through its literal meaning (form) to refer to the shape or appearance of the human being, that is the physical body. In this way the terms *rūpa* and *arūpa* have usually been understood to imply a distinction between 'body' and 'mind' respectively. We shall see, however, that though *rūpa* refers to the body, this is not just in physical terms, and its shape or appearance, while clearly relevant as visible object, *rūpāyatana*, is not an important factor in understanding the *rūpakkhandha*.

In the *Sutta Piṭaka* there are two main kinds of description of the *rūpakkhandha*: the simple and general description, which gives us minimal information, and the detailed and specific description, from which we get a more comprehensive account of what the *khandha* comprises. The simple descriptions are just two, both being found in the *Khandha Saṃyutta* of the *Saṃyutta Nikāya*.[1] The first occurs, so far as I am aware, only once. But it is picked up repeatedly by the later commentarial tradition. The second constitutes a common formula used throughout the Pali material to define *rūpa*, and is of considerably more interest to us here. We shall see in the comprehensive descriptions of it that the term *rūpa* also refers to a general category, described as 'external', suggesting an overlap between the 'form' characteristics of the body (*rūpakkhandha*) and those of visible objects in general (*rūpāyatana*). But both types of analysis of *rūpa* indicate that the term primarily refers to the body, in accord with the Buddha's central concern with the human being.

The context in which the first simple analysis is given in the *Khandha Saṃyutta* is when the Buddha is teaching that none of the five *khandhas* constitutes anything that should be thought of as a permanent, unchanging 'self', in this life or in any previous life. Each of the *khandhas* in turn is briefly defined, and then each is discussed in a way which illustrates their impermanence. The *rūpakkhandha* is defined as follows:

> And why, *bhikkhus*, is it called body? It suffers, *bhikkhus*. That is why the word 'body' is used. Suffers from what? Suffers from cold and heat, from hunger and thirst, from contact with gnats, mosquitoes, wind and sun and snakes. It suffers, *bhikkhus*. That is why it is called body.[2]

The verb I have translated here as 'suffers', in order to draw out the meaning of this passage, is *ruppati*. It is because of the use of this verb here that this description is repeatedly referred to by the commentarial tradition, and by Buddhaghosa in his *Visuddhimagga*. *Ruppati* is taken by the tradition as a pun on *rūpa*, though etymologically *ruppati* has absolutely no connection with *rūpa*. And in spite of a similar lack of etymological link the punning is also extended to *nāma*, which, as mentioned above, is frequently found twinned with *rūpa* in the compound *nāmarūpa*.[3] So in Pali the play on words reads as follows: *Namanalakkhaṇaṃ nāmaṃ … ruppanalakkhaṇaṃ rūpaṃ*.[4] Discussing *ruppati*, Woodward, the translator of the *Khandha Saṃyutta* for the Pali Text Society, suggests that *ruppati* as a pun on *rūpa* could be taken to mean that body is embodied, form is in-formed, shape is shaped.[5] Literally, however, *ruppati* means 'to be destroyed', 'to be vexed' or 'to be oppressed'. In Sanskrit, *rupyate* means 'to suffer violent pain', and by the *r*/*l* alternation it is closely related to *lupyate*, 'to be broken' or 'to be destroyed'.[6] By extension one can understand *ruppati* simply as 'suffers', being analogous with *dukkha* (so the definition might better read: "It is characterised by unsatisfactoriness (*dukkha*)"). This, surely, is the point that is being made by the use of the verb: such etymologising was, typically, for didactic reasons. This point has been completely missed by Mrs Rhys Davids, who suggests translating *ruppati* as 'affected'. Woodward follows this, though he points out in a footnote that he prefers 'afflicted'.[7] The latter is surely more appropriate, being in accord with the fact that *rūpa* is associated with *dukkha*, which in turn is in accord with the Buddha's definition of *dukkha*, representing the individual's existence in *saṃsāra*, as the *khandhas*. And though it is the *rūpakkhandha* which is defined in terms of affliction, the *Sutta* goes on to state that one identifies mistakenly with each of the *khandhas* as part of *saṃsāric* existence and that one is to become detached from each and every one of them. The explicit association of *rūpa* alone with affliction is primarily because *rūpa* lends itself to this pun. But an individual's life in *saṃsāra* also tends to be predominantly associated with the body. Not only is it the physical presence of an individual, but as such it is the vehicle, so to speak, of his or her experience in a given life. It is therefore disproportionately associated with *saṃsāric* existence to the point where it is seen to be 'responsible' for the affliction of *dukkha*. This point is more comprehensively discussed in chapter VIII.

The second and perhaps the simplest analysis of *rūpa* is frequently found in the Pali material and represents the standard simple analysis not only of the *rūpakkhandha* but also, as we shall see, of *rūpa* in general (that is, whether the body of the human being or of any other visible object). The context in the *Khandha Saṃyutta* from which I am quoting is another in which the Buddha is teaching that the human being should be understood in terms of five *khandhas*, and that none of these constitutes a permanent, unchanging self: one is to become detached from each of them. Here *rūpa* is analysed into the four great elements and whatever is derived from them: "And what, *bhikkhus*, is the body (*rūpa*)? It is the four great elements and whatever physical thing is derived from the great elements: this, *bhikkhus*, is called the body".[8] The four great elements (collectively known as the *cattāro mahābhūtā(ni)*, or less specifically as *dhātus*) are: earth (*paṭhavī-dhātu*), water (*āpo-dhātu*), fire (*tejo-dhātu*) and wind (*vāyo-dhātu*). In some contexts a fifth element, 'space' (*ākāsa*), is mentioned,[9] but in contexts where *rūpa* is specifically being defined only the *cattāro mahābhūtā* are mentioned. In the commentarial tradition, these are explicitly understood to have the abstract meanings solidity, fluidity, heat and motion. In the *Sutta Piṭaka*, such abstract meanings are only implicit, though in the more detailed descriptions of each of the elements the implication is quite clear. It is the abstract meanings of the elements which suggest how they are applicable both to the *rūpakkhandha* of the human being and also to anything else that has form, explicitly described as the 'internal' and 'external' dimensions of *rūpa* in canonical passages which explain each of the four elements in turn.[10] The abstract meanings of the four elements also serve to indicate that the notion of 'matter' is purely conventional here. Rather, *rūpa* refers to the occurrence of various states or processes, collectively referred to as the 'body' (or visible object), which are characterised in a certain way.[11] It is only by virtue of a state or process having the characteristics of solidity or extension that it can be described as 'matter', and the *rūpakkhandha* is not limited to this single characteristic.

In the *Sutta Piṭaka*, the four elements are said to be 'primary'. The term used for this is *no-upādā*, which has two literal meanings: 'underived' and 'not clinging or grasping'. The former does not in any way compromise the teaching that there is nothing in *saṃsāra* that is unconditioned. Indeed, we read in a passage about Nirvana, which *is* referred to as the unconditioned, that it is *without* the four elements, a confirmation of the conditioned nature of the four elements themselves: "Monks, there exists that condition [Nirvana] wherein is not earth nor water nor fire nor air...".[12] Anything to which analysis in terms of the four elements is applicable, therefore, is part of conditioned existence. The meaning 'underived' refers, rather, to the fact that these four elements cannot be further broken down or analysed in the way that, for example, a foot or a hand, both of which are complex organs with more than one function, can be broken down or analysed to the point where it is seen that they consist of an aggregate of elements. Put abstractly, a complex organ is an aggregate which has characteristics that are signified by more than one type of element. In this unaggregated sense *no-upādā* means 'underived'. The latter meaning, 'not clinging or grasping', suggests that *rūpa* has an underived state that is not the product of grasping. In the context of the *rūpakkhandha*, this is not explained any further, but the similar term *anupādā* is regularly found in other contexts in the *Nikāyas* in the sense of not having any more of the fuel (grasping) necessary for rebirth, not clinging to the world. It is grasping, more usually called volition, which leads to continued rebirth, continued human existence. In the light of this, *no-upādā rūpa* means 'primary' in that it has not (yet) been *further* conditioned by intention.[13] In the *Aṭṭhasālinī*, the commentary on the *Dhammasaṅgaṇī* of the *Abhidhamma Piṭaka*, this point is made explicitly: "*Upādā* means 'it grasps'; this means grasping the [four] great elements; not letting (them) go, such (secondary/derived forms) exist depending on them".[14] This all suggests that the *cattāro mahābhūtā* are as it were the potential states from which the body, conditioned by one's karma (intention), is derived; or, put differently, they represent the potential characteristics of the body.

As well as *no-upādā*, *rūpa* is also described in the *Sutta Piṭaka* as 'derived' or 'secondary' (*upādā*). In the simple analyses of the *rūpakkhandha* there is no mention of what *upādā rūpa* comprises, and we shall see that the situation is not clear in the comprehensive description of the *rūpakkhandha* either. Though the commentary on the particular canonical passage we are discussing makes no comment on what *upādā rūpa* means,[15] the Theravāda Buddhist tradition has generally understood the term *upādā rūpa* specifically to refer to the senses (usually taken to be the physical sense organs) and their corresponding sense objects, collectively called *āyatanas*. A typical definition of *upādā rūpa* is given in the *Dhammasaṅgaṇī* of the *Abhidhamma*, where it is stated to refer to ten of the *āyatanas* (that is excluding the sixth sense, *manas*, and its corresponding object, *dhammā*).[16] In the *Vibhaṅga* the same ten *āyatanas* are in turn described as the four great elements which are derived,[17] which amounts to the same thing put differently. In the *Aṭṭhasālinī*, *upādā rūpa* is discussed at length in terms of the *āyatanas*, so much so that the translator of the text for the Pali Text Society has entitled an entire chapter "Derived Material Qualities".[18] In addition to such definitions, where the *Abhidhamma* categorises *upādā rūpa* more extensively, so that it is said to comprise twenty-three different phenomena, the *āyatanas* are included.[19] Likewise, in the section on the *rūpakkhandha* in his *Visuddhimagga*, where Buddhaghosa lists twenty-four kinds of *upādā rūpa*, he includes the *āyatanas* in the same way as the *Abhidhamma* and the commentaries.[20] Modern Theravāda Buddhist writers also define *upādā rūpa* as the senses.[21]

That *upādā rūpa*, undefined in the *Sutta Piṭaka*, eventually came to be defined in this way might be because of the fact, mentioned above, that in contexts in the *Sutta Piṭaka* where the five *khandhas* in turn are being defined, and where the *rūpakkhandha* has been defined according to the simple analysis of the four elements and their derivatives, the different *arūpakkhandhas* are each said to be of six types according to the six senses or their objects. This repeated reference to the *āyatanas* in such classifications might account for the fact that they became singled out for mention as *upādā rūpa*.

Given such prominent mention of the senses in the *Sutta Piṭaka*, and given that it is obvious to us that there are physical organs corresponding to at least five of the senses (so one might equally obviously assume that they are part of the *rūpakkhandha*), it is also conversely notable that nowhere in the *Sutta Piṭaka* are the senses, or their corresponding sense objects, explicitly stated to be part of the *rūpakkhandha*, and none of the passages which is specifically describing the *rūpakkhandha* includes any of them as *upādā rūpa*. It is this omission that prompts me to question whether the consistent references in the *Sutta Piṭaka* to the senses or their objects determining the types of mental activity necessarily implies that it was intended that either the senses or their objects, or all of them, should be classified as part of *upādā rūpa* within the *rūpakkhandha*, as later defined in the *Abhidhamma* and understood within the Buddhist tradition.

The question is prompted not just by the omission but also by the fact that compared with what is found in the *Sutta Piṭaka*, the later tradition's understanding of the senses becomes, on the one hand, more complex, and, on the other hand, more 'physical'. Dealing with the first of these first, the *Abhidhamma* gives a more comprehensive classification of the twelve *āyatanas* collectively than is found in the four main *Nikāyas* of the *Sutta Piṭaka*. In the *Sutta Piṭaka*, there is more of a distinction between the senses and the sense objects, and the term *āyatana* is more frequently said to be sixfold.[22] Where *saḷāyatana* appears in the *paṭiccasamuppāda* formula given in the *Sutta Piṭaka*, for example, only the senses are included in the definition, not the sense objects.[23] And though the senses and objects are at times referred to as separate groups in the same classification, that is as *āyatanas*,[24] the point is that the senses and objects are more clearly delineated from each other, each as separate 'sixes', than in the *Abhidhamma* where the senses and their objects are all referred to individually and equally as *āyatanas*, giving twelve in all, and are grouped together in definitions or descriptions of *upādā rūpa*.[25] This inclusion of the objects of sense in a definition of something that is subject to 'grasping' is not, as might at first be thought, in itself problematic. These objects are not necessarily external to the human being: eyes and visibility, nose and smell, tongue and taste (and so on) are all aspects of the human body. But this development represents a more complex way of attempting to understand the senses than is found in the *Sutta Piṭaka*, a complexity that is compounded by lack of consistency.

By way of example, in the *Dhammasaṅgaṇī* we read that whatever *rūpa* is 'internal' (that is personal to the individual) is *upādā*, but whatever *rūpa* is 'external' is sometimes *upādā* and sometimes *no-upādā*.[26] External (*bāhiraṃ*) *rūpa* seems here to refer specifically to aspects of *rūpa* which are experienced subjectively oneself.[27] What is external in the sense of being part of other beings is referred to in this text as *bahiddhā*, and is also referred to as *dhammā*.[28] Though the *āyatanas*, whether internal or external (*bāhiraṃ*), are usually collectively classified as *upādā rūpa*, *poṭṭhabha*,[29] *manas* and *dhammā* are often excluded from the classification, though no reason is given for this.

With regard to the increasingly 'physical' understanding of the senses, not only does the later tradition explicitly classify the senses as *rūpa*, but the later texts also give long and elaborate physical descriptions of the sense organs. The Pali terms used to refer to the senses are *cakkhu, sota, ghāna, jivhā, kāya* and *manas*, and following a physical interpretation of their meaning, these are usually translated eye, ear, nose, tongue, body and mind. But none of the meanings of the term *āyatana* suggests that a physical organ is meant.[30] In the *Sutta Piṭaka*, the senses are also sometimes referred to as *indriyas*, 'powers' or 'faculties'.[31] Though in such contexts they are also usually translated as sense organs, the term *indriya* does not suggest that physical organs are implied any more than does *āyatana*. Similarly, they are also called *dhātus*, elements, which again need not imply physicality.[32] This suggests that the later attempts to classify the senses as *upādā rūpa* might be placing an inappropriate emphasis on their physical aspects. And as a further complication, we shall see in the next part of this chapter that even in this respect the later material appears inconsistent.

The nearest the *Sutta Piṭaka* comes to associating the senses with *upādā* is in a passage in the *Sutta Nipāta* where there is a reference to the fact that the five sensual pleasures plus *manas* are the grasping (*upādāna*) which afflicts the world.[33] This does not, however, refer specifically to *rūpa*, nor to the senses themselves, but to the fact that sensual desire, the arising of which is based on the senses, represents the fuel of continued *saṃsāric* existence: *loka* here meaning the 'world' of the subjective individual rather than the external world as a whole, as discussed above.

In the *Sutta Piṭaka*, all five *khandhas* are sometimes referred to as the *upādānakkhandhā*,[34] and they too are *upādāna* in both senses of the word: they are both derivatives and conditioned by grasping. Another passage in the *Khandha Saṃyutta* describes both the *pañcakkhandhā* and the *pañcupādānakkhandhā*. The term *pañcakkhandhā*, it explains, refers to the five *khandhas*; *pañcupādānakkhandhā* means that each and every one of the five *khandhas* is subject to *āsavas*.[35] I referred to the term *āsava* in the Introduction. It is a notoriously difficult word to translate into English, but it refers to the strongest and most deep-seated of the factors ('graspings') which cause bondage to *saṃsāric* experience. There are said to be either three or four *āsavas*: the three are the *āsava* of sense desire (*kāmāsava*), the *āsava* of desire for continued becoming (*bhavāsava*), and the *āsava* of ignorance (*avijjāsava*), and the less common fourth is the *āsava* of holding views (*diṭṭhāsava*). The *āsavas* are to be eradicated; but so profoundly are they rooted in the human psyche that such eradication represents the very experience of Enlightenment, the goal of the path to liberation. Thus any reference to the *āsavas* being present indicates an association with the *saṃsāric*, pre-Enlightenment life of an individual, when he or she is conditioned by grasping. Ñānavīra, a modern Theravāda *bhikkhu*, suggests that this passage distinguishes between an *arahant*, in whom the *āsavas* have been eradicated, who comprises the *pañcakkhandhā*, and an unenlightened individual, who comprises the *pañcupādānakkhandhā*.[36] The point Ñānavīra is making is that an individual only arises as a result of continued grasping (the mechanics of which will become clearer in chapter IV), and after Enlightenment the individual will not arise (be reborn) again.

If the senses were to be classified as part of the *rūpakkhandha*, then of course it follows from the foregoing that they would be *upādā rūpa*, requiring further discussion here. But in view of the ambiguity about precisely what the terms used for the senses (*āyatana*, *indriya* and *dhātu*) are referring to, and the fact that in the *Sutta Piṭaka* the *āyatanas* are neither defined as *upādā rūpa* nor included in any of the definitions of the *rūpakkhandha*, it seems more appropriate to defer such a discussion. Accordingly, I will return to them in the second part of this chapter after discussing the detailed analyses of the *rūpakkhandha* found in the *Sutta Piṭaka*. At that stage more attention can be directed towards their important role.

The more detailed and specific analysis of the *rūpakkhandha* is found in three places in the *Sutta Piṭaka* where the *cattāro mahābhūtā* are being explained.[37] This analysis gives us much more information about *rūpa* as the body of the human being, though it is here that the term *rūpa* is explicitly stated also to refer to *rūpa* that is 'external'. In each of the contexts in which the comprehensive analysis is found, it is given for the purpose of teaching that the individual's body is merely an aggregate of the elements and that it should not be thought of in terms of selfhood or identity. In one place, descriptions of the impermanent nature of the 'external' manifestation of the elements are given in order to emphasise that the internal elements are equally impermanent. For example, the external element of motion, wind, is at times too strong and can blow down whole villages and at other times there is no wind at all and people have to fan a spark in order to make a fire burn.[38]

The descriptions of the elements of *paṭhavī* and *āpo*, solidity and fluidity respectively, with regard to their 'internal' manifestation as the body of a human being, consist of various parts of the body. We read of the 'internal' aspect of the element of solidity:

> And what is the 'internal' element of solidity? Whatever is internal to the individual and is hard and solid, and the product of grasping; that is to say hair of the head, hair of the body, nails, teeth, skin, flesh, sinews, bones, bone-marrow, kidney, heart, liver, membranes, spleen, lungs, intestines, mesentery, stomach, excrement, and whatever other thing is internal to the individual and is hard and solid [and which is] the product of grasping: this is called the 'internal' element of solidity.[39]

Similarly, the 'internal' element of fluidity is described as follows:

> And what is the 'internal' element of fluidity? Whatever is internal to the individual, is liquid or fluid, and the product of grasping; that is to say bile, phlegm, pus, blood, sweat, fat, tears, serum, saliva, mucus, synovic fluid, urine, and whatever other thing is internal to the individual, is liquid or fluid, [and which is] the product of grasping: this is called the 'internal' element of fluidity.[40]

Though both these passages include actual parts of the body, I suggest that the point they are intended to make is to establish that the body includes elements which are characterised either by hardness/solidity or by liquidity/fluidity. In neither case are the literal meanings of the elements, earth and water, directly applicable: it is their abstract meanings which are of central relevance. Similarly, the fact that the list is manifestly not comprehensive suggests that such descriptions are not intended to be understood as definitive lists of what the body is made of; rather they indicate examples of the characteristics being described.

The passage continues with a description of the 'internal' element of heat:

> And what is the 'internal' heat element? Whatever is internal to the individual and is heat, heated, and the product of grasping; that is to say that by which one is warmed, by which one ages, by which one is exhausted [lit: burned], that by which one properly digests [lit: transforms] what one has eaten, drunk, consumed or chewed, and whatever other thing internal to the individual which is heated or warm [and which is] the product of grasping: this is the 'internal' element of heat.[41]

I. B. Horner states that *tejo* includes cold as well as heat since both vitalising energy and decay are due to this element.[42] Though it may be appropriate to refer to it as the element of temperature rather than just of being hot, it unclear whether this extends literally as far as being cold. In a passage elsewhere in the canon, we read that it is heat, life and consciousness that vitalise the human being (though the Pali word for heat in these contexts is *usmā*) and without them there is only a dead body, thus dissociating heat and the processes associated with it from a dead body.[43] But the concern of this passage is to establish the impermanence of the vitalising factors, not the extent of the activity of heat: *usmā* and *āyu* are said to be mutually dependent,[44] and *viññāṇa* is associated with the senses.[45] The three are also described as *saṃkhāras*,[46] which both indicates their constructed nature and implies that they are the result of past karma.[47] I. B. Horner's suggestion is supported by the description of the 'external' aspect of *tejo*, which refers to fire:[48] it might be that it is in its external aspect that this element is involved in the decay of a dead body. But this concern is an unimportant one: as we shall see, the analysis of the body according to the four elements is that of a live body rather than a dead one, which, though leaving questions such as this unanswered, serves to emphasise the consistency of the Buddha's concern with human experience.

For the 'internal' element of motion the *Sutta* states:

> And what is the 'internal' element of motion? Whatever is internal to the individual and is movement [literally, 'wind'] or motion and the product of grasping; that is to say upward movements, downward movements, movement in the abdomen, movement in the belly, movements of any of the limbs, in-breathing and out-breathing, and whatever other thing is internal to the individual and is movement or motion [and which is] the product of grasping: this is called the 'internal' element of motion.[49]

I have translated the Pali word *vātā* as 'movements' in order to give this passage some meaning in English. Its literal meaning is 'wind', and this comprehensive description of wind passing all round the body, and along every limb, recalls the *Upaniṣadic* five *ānas*: *prāṇa* (the in-breath), *apāna* (the out-breath), *vyāna* (the circulatory or diffused breath), *udāna* (the up-breath) and *samāna* (the middle or equalising breath).[50] These were regarded as the vital faculties responsible for respiration, digestion and the distribution of food through the body.[51] Breath (*prāṇa*) was also considered to be the vitalising principle in the early *Upaniṣads*, frequently used as a synonym for Brahman.[52] The functions of the *Upaniṣadic prāṇas* do not correspond directly to those of the *vāyodhātu* according to the *Majjhima Nikāya*, since digestion, for example, is the province of the *tejodhātu*. Nor is there any understanding of *vāyu* as a vitalising principle in the Pali canon as there is in the case of heat: breathing is merely a bodily function. The Pali expression *aṅgamaṅgānusārino vātā* is not explained in the canon, but is understood by Buddhaghosa to refer to the winds (or forces) that produce flexing and extending and so on. This would be congruent with the abstract meaning of *vāyu*, motion.[53] There is evidence in the canon, however, (which is picked up in the commentarial literature) that wind acts as a 'humour':[54] normal wind conditions normal health, whereas winds which become strong (*vātā balīyanti*), or deranged winds (*ummāda vātā*), cause pains and/or uncontrolled movements of the body, eventually causing psychological derangement.[55] The similarity between the Pali description of *vāyu* and the *Upaniṣadic* description of the *prāṇas* is enough for it to be possible that the former was influenced by the latter.[56]

In two texts a description of the element 'space' (*ākāsa*) is also given:

> And what is the internal element of space? Whatever is internal to the individual, and is space or spacious, and the product of grasping; that is to say the nose and ear orifices, the mouth opening, the passages by which one swallows, retains and expels below what one has eaten, drunk, consumed or chewed, and whatever other thing is internal to the individual and is space or spacious [and which is] the product of grasping: this is called the 'internal' element of space.[57]

Though *ākāsa* is said to be both 'internal' and 'external', no description of 'external' *ākāsa* is given in either of the texts in which this description is found. *Ākāsa* does have an 'external' dimension in descriptions of the meditative states known as the *jhānas*. In such a context it is not, however, the equivalent of external spaces between things paralleling the description of the 'internal' space element as internal orifices and openings. It is, rather, a formless level where the apperception of visible shapes is transcended.[58]

Here we have a comprehensive analysis of the *rūpakkhandha* according to the *cattāro mahābhūtā*. The term *upādiṇṇaṃ* ('the product of grasping') indicates that all the factors included within the analysis of internal *rūpa* are *upādā*. We shall see in chapter IV, and again in chapter VII, that this is compatible with the way volitions, which correspond to grasping, condition every aspect of the arising of the individual in future lives.

The descriptions of each of the elements contain bodily parts or functions which might logically be expected to be found there: solid things are found in the analysis of the element of solidity, liquid things within the element of fluidity, and so on. In other words, the analysis is commonsensical. But the *tejo* and *vāyo dhātus*, and the *ākāsadhātu* when it appears, comprise parts and functions which we might not immediately describe as corporeal. Temperature, ageing and digestion, breathing and various bodily movements, and orifices or internal spaces, are defined as being part of the *rūpakkhandha*. Taken as a whole, this description of the *cattāro mahābhūtā* (plus *ākāsa*) gives us the human body as a whole in full working order. The analysis emphasises the characteristics and processes which enable the living body of a human being to function: this is not a description of a *dead* human body. It follows, then, that the term *rūpa* is not as strictly limited as one might in the first instance expect from the usual association of body with matter or from the common understanding that the word 'form' (the literal meaning of *rūpa*) means shape or appearance. From the comprehensive description we have here, *rūpa* does not refer to the physical body *qua* physical body; it is not concerned with what the body *is* but with its living characteristics understood in terms of the four elements.

We recall that the 'object' which corresponds to the sense (organ) eye (*cakkhu*) is form (*rūpa*), and that its main criterion is visibility. *Rūpa* as a *khandha* does not so clearly imply visibility. One might say that processes such as breathing, movement, and decay are visible, and if other processes such as digestion and temperature control were not operating one would be able to see that. This would correspond to the fact that in the 'external' dimension fire and wind are also visible (at least through their effects). But such suggestions do not seem to me to be in accord with the overall impression one gets from the description of the *rūpakkhandha*, and the internal organs are normally visible only potentially. Certainly visibility does not seem to be a primary characteristic of the *rūpakkhandha*.

The parts of the body referred to in the descriptions of the *paṭhavīdhātu* and the *āpodhātu* above are also found in the canonical material as a standard list of bodily parts to be used in a meditation exercise.[59] The standard list incorporates exactly the same parts as do the descriptions of the *dhātus* and is as follows: hair of the head, body hair, nails, teeth, skin, flesh, sinews, bones, bone-marrow, kidneys, heart, liver, membranes, spleen, lungs, intestines, mesentery, stomach, excrement, bile, phlegm, pus, blood, sweat, fat, tears, serum, saliva, mucus, synovic fluid and urine.[60] During meditation, a *bhikkhu* should realise that his body includes a collection of these physical items, none of which is to be identified as or with any sort of abiding self. Other bodily processes are referred to in these meditation exercises, such as breathing and movement, posture and decay.[61] None of these passages states that it is offering a description either of the *rūpakkhandha* as such or of the *cattāro mahābhūtā*. The meditation on the body in the *Satipaṭṭhāna Suttas*, however, is clearly intended to be comprehensive, including as it does a wide range of bodily activities, processes, postures and states of decay, in the sense that such meditations should bring the *bhikkhu* to realise that all such aspects of the body are similarly conditioned. It also includes a meditation on the fact that the body is composed of the four *dhātus* as follows:

> And again, *bhikkhus*, a *bhikkhu* contemplates this body as it is placed or disposed in respect of the elements, thinking 'There are in this body the elements of extension, fluidity, heat and motion'.[62]

No further analysis of the body according to *dhātu* is given, which again emphasises the lack of concern in the texts to understand the human body in terms of what its substance is.

The *rūpakkhandha*, then, is the living body of a human being. This is analysed according to the four (occasionally five) *dhātus*. 'Body' is an appropriate translation of *rūpa* when it refers to the *rūpakkhandha*, since even those phenomena included in this *khandha* which are not corporeal are nevertheless parts of or associated with the body. And *rūpa* which is external to the human body is not part of the *khandha* analysis as such. One might conclude this part of this chapter by suggesting that the emphasis on the characteristics of the human body which relate to how it functions, rather than what it is in terms of substance, is highlighted both by what is omitted from the descriptions discussed and by the style of the descriptions of what is included. It is in this respect that what appears to be merely an overview of this *khandha* is in fact singularly informative.

The Senses

According to the evidence in the *Sutta Piṭaka* the senses are central to the psychological/cognitive functioning of the human being. We shall see below that even consciousness, the *sine qua non* of human life, is classified according to the senses. And we shall also see in more detail in following chapters that all discursive thoughts, ideas and knowledge arise because of the simultaneous presence of a sense, its corresponding sense object and consciousness: from this threefold event, known as 'contact' (*phassa*), all cognitive activity, of whatever nature, arises; and, conversely, without such an event no cognitive activity takes place.[63] From this we see that the senses are not only the means by which the individual interacts with the 'external' world in which he or she exists, but are also the means by which cognitive experience subsequently leads either to progressing along the path to liberation or to remaining in bondage within *saṃsāra*. And yet in spite of their importance in the individual's psychological functioning, in the *Sutta Piṭaka* they are neither included in the analysis of the *rūpakkhandha*, as we have already seen, nor are they included in the analysis of any of the *arūpakkhandhas*. I have suggested above that though the *Abhidhamma* discusses the *āyatanas* at length, its understanding of them appears to be inconsistent. I have also explained that the terms commonly associated with the senses, *āyatana*, *indriya* and *dhātu*, need not immediately suggest that it is the physical sense organs that are being referred to in the terms *cakkhu*, *sota*, *ghāna* and so on. In looking at these points in more detail here, we shall, I think, indeed see that what is meant by the senses is not their physical organs but that they have a unique role which is as it were neither *rūpa* nor *arūpa*, and that this is why they are not included in the *khandha* analysis.

I have stated in the first part of this chapter that in common with other Indian religions, Buddhism recognises six senses. Be that as it may, casual reference to different passages in the Pali material can cause confusion concerning the number of senses there are. The standard canonical list of sense pleasures (*kāmaguṇā*) includes only five senses: eye (*cakkhu*), ear (*sota*), nose (*ghāna*), tongue (*jivhā*) and body (*kāya*).[64] We saw the same five, together with their corresponding objects (ten *āyatanas* in all), referred to in the *Dhammasaṅgaṇī* definition of *upādā rūpa* mentioned above.[65] But this and similar passages in the *Abhidhamma* are not suggesting that there are only five senses: the reason the *Dhammasaṅgaṇī* definition in question only includes five senses is because the author of this passage is defining *upādā rūpa*, in which he does not include *manas* and *dhammā*. Generally in Pali texts (including the *Abhidhamma*) the senses are sixfold. In the *paṭiccasamuppāda* formula, for example, when *nāmarūpa* is said to be the condition for the arising of the senses, the senses are stated to be sixfold.[66] The six senses are the five mentioned above as the *kāmaguṇā* plus *manas*. Their corresponding objects are (in Pali) *rūpa, sadda, gandha, rasa, phoṭṭhabba* and *dhammā*, usually translated (visible) form, sound, odour, taste, tangible things and mental objects. They are discussed repeatedly, though not in detail, both in the *Chachakkasutta*[67] and in the *Mahāsaḷāyatanikasutta*,[68] and an entire volume of the *Saṃyutta Nikāya* is entitled the *Saḷāyatana Vagga*.[69] The sensory events (*phassa*), which are discussed in chapter II, are sixfold according to the six senses.[70] We also read that in order to establish the moral basis from which a *bhikkhu* can proceed as an *ariyasāvaka*, all six senses have to be brought under control,[71] (a discipline which perhaps reflects one of the meanings of *āyatana*, which is 'exertion', 'effort', 'practice').

Where each of the *arūpakkhandhas* is described according to a sixfold sub-classification, the terms mentioned above which are often associated with the senses, *āyatana*, *indriya* and *dhātu*, are not used, just the names of the senses or sense objects themselves.[72] We read of *vedanā*, for example, that it is of six types. These arise from contact, and are classified according to the six senses.[73] Similarly the *viññāṇakkhandha* is of six types according to each of the six senses.[74] Both the *saññākhandha* and the *saṃkhārakkhandha* are again of six types, but these are classified not according to the six senses but to their objects.[75] The texts do not explain why two of the *arūpakkhandhas* are classified according to the senses and the other two according to the sense objects. The Pali word I have translated as 'types' is *kāyā* (literally 'bodies'). Though this is sometimes translated in this context as 'bases' or 'seats',[76] such translations act as red herrings, making it more difficult to understand why the classification differs. If one assumes, as has been done, that the senses refer to the physical sense organs, one might accept that an internal sense might be a 'seat' of a mental activity; but it is hard to see that an external object could be such a seat. If *kāyā* is translated as 'types', however, then neither the senses nor the objects need be considered as the actual 'bases' of the mental activities. Rather, the difference between *vedanā* and *viññāṇa* on the one hand and *saññā* and *saṃkhāra* on the other hand might be explained as follows: *saññā* and *saṃkhāra* are more developed and discursive levels of the cognitive process than are either *vedanā* or *viññāṇa* and as such they are externally focussed. So with regard to *saññā* one would apperceive a smell or a sound rather than the nose or ear. Likewise with *saṃkhāra*, one's volitions would be directed towards the smell or the sound and not the sense itself. Moreover, both are able to focus on a specific smell or sound rather than being limited to the general olfactory and auditory senses. Thus the six types of *saññā* and *saṃkhāra* are classified according to the external objects. Neither *vedanā* nor *viññāṇa* is so clearly defined, both functioning more generally in the cognitive process when the activity of the senses is more relevant. So with regard to *vedanā*, one has visual or auditory feeling rather than visible object or sound feeling. *Viññāṇa* too is visual or auditory. Both of them function at the general level of the visual or auditory sense, for the focussing on a specific external object is the function of the *saññā* or *saṃkhāra khandhas*.

The English words usually used in translations of the senses (eye, ear, nose, tongue, body and mind) suggest that in each case (with the exception of mind) it is the physical sense organ that is being referred to, which probably accounts for the tendency to describe them as 'seats' or 'bases', as mentioned above. And there is no doubt that (again with the exception of *manas*, which is discussed in the third part of this chapter), these are physical organs which are part of the human body. The terms most commonly associated with them, *āyatana*, *indriya* and *dhātu*, suggest, however, that they might also refer to something other than the physical organs themselves. Though all three of these terms have been translated as if they do refer to the physical organs, a consideration of their other meanings, together with some contexts in which the senses are referred to in the *Sutta Piṭaka*, suggests an interesting alternative.

In the *Saḷāyatana Vagga* of the *Saṃyutta Nikāya*, the six senses are defined as being *ajjhattaṃ*, personal or internal, and the six corresponding objects are defined as being *bāhiraṃ*, external, thus giving two 'sets' of six *āyatanas*. In the *Nidāna Saṃyutta*, however, which is concerned with explaining *paṭiccasamuppāda*, only the personal *āyatanas* are referred to by the term *saḷāyatana*.[77] This difference in usage in itself makes the term *āyatana* an ambiguous one, and it is unsurprising that the *Pali English Dictionary* does little to clarify the term when it states that *āyatana* means "sphere of perception or sense in general, object of thought, sense-organ and object".[78] The dictionary goes on to state "*āyatana* cannot be rendered by a single English word to cover both sense-organs ... and sense objects".[79] Other meanings of *āyatana* given in the *Pali-English Dictionary* are: "stretch, extent, reach, compass, region; sphere,[80] locus, place, spot; position, occasion ... relation, order."[81] It also means "exertion, doing, working, practice, performance", as mentioned above. If one considers *āyatana* in perhaps its most crucial context, that of the *paṭiccasamuppāda* formula, it is unlikely that it refers to the sense organs themselves. Though the definition of *saḷāyatana* in the *Nidāna Saṃyutta* is given in terms of *cakkhu, sota, ghāna, jivhā, kāya* and *manas*, it seems improbable that the physical sense organs would warrant their own stage in the description of the arising of an individual human being when no other physical organs are mentioned in the formula. *Nāmarūpa*, which precedes *saḷāyatana* in the common twelvefold version of the formula, is discussed in chapter VI. I suggest there that it does not mean 'mind and body' as commonly supposed, but that it means the 'name and form' of the individual in an abstract sense, according to which the psychological and eventually (at birth) the physical faculties of the individual develop. The *saḷāyatana* precede birth by several stages in the formula and thus represent part of the development of the psychological faculties of the individual: in this context it is virtually inconceivable that it is the physical sense organs in a literal sense that are being referred to. Rather, the context suggests that what is meant is the sphere or extent of vision, hearing, taste, and so on, the locus (in a non-physical sense) of the senses, which establishes the foundation (again in a non-physical sense) of the psychological life of the individual. Sphere, extent and locus are all meanings of *āyatana*. The 'external' *āyatanas* correspond to the 'internal' *āyatanas* because the interaction between the individual and the objective world is the 'occasion' when the spheres of vision, hearing, etc., are associated with their corresponding objects; it is the relation between, or the relating of, the internal and external aspects of the sensory event. Thus in the commentary to the *Dīgha Nikāya*, Buddhaghosa (to whom the commentary is attributed) defines *āyatana* as *samosaraṇa*, coming together or meeting.[82] The *Pali English Dictionary* definition of *āyatana*, when it refers to the senses and their objects, would do better to confine itself to "sphere of perception or sense in general" and omit "sense-organ and object", and there need be no concern with the lack of a single English word for both sense organs and sense objects.

The terms *indriya* and *dhātu* support such an interpretation of *āyatana*. *Indriya* means 'power' or 'faculty' in the sense of controlling principle or directive force.[83] In connection with the senses, it thus means the power or potential of the individual to have sensory experience: *cakkhindriya*, for example, means the personal potentiality for seeing.[84] Other *indriyas* mentioned in the *Sutta Piṭaka*, which in the *Abhidhamma* came to be systematised with many others,[85] include, for example, pleasure and pain, joy and grief, and equanimity,[86] none of which is physical but which refer respectively to the personal potentiality for pleasure and pain, joy, grief and equanimity. *Dhātu* literally means 'element', and is often associated with the four elements which define *rūpa*, the *mahābhūtā*. Another of its meanings is 'phenomenon' similar to the meaning of *dhamma* in some contexts.[87] We have seen above, however, that the four *mahābhūtā* can also have the abstract meanings of extension, fluidity, heat and motion. In the same way, the meaning of *dhātu* can be abstract. In the *Dhātu Saṃyutta,* where it is associated with the senses, we also find it used in connection with abstract characteristics such as radiance and beauty,[88] and ignorance.[89]

From all these meanings of *āyatana*, *indriya* and *dhātu*, as well as from the position of *āyatana* in the *paṭiccasamuppāda* formula, one might suggest that what is referred to by the terms *cakkhu*, *sota*, *ghāna* and so on is not primarily the sense organs eye, ear, nose, etc., but that the terms are to be interpreted figuratively as the faculties of vision, hearing, smell and so on. In English the word 'vision' has a quite different meaning from that of the word 'eye'. The latter only means the physical organ (unless it is being used as a verb, which would have a different context). The former involves the physical organ, but means more than that: it means the ability to see, or sight itself. Each sense faculty is a sphere or locus (in an abstract sense) for a potentiality: the potential to see or hear. What is particularly interesting about this interpretation of the senses is how it relates to their objects. Though the sense objects are not necessarily part of the human being, they too can be thought of as representing the potentiality for a sensory event. A sound is a sound whether anyone hears it or not, but it is also potentially part of an auditory experience for a human being. Thus the sense objects can also be referred to as *āyatana*, *indriya* and *dhātu.*

A figurative interpretation of the senses is also suggested by a metaphor associated with them in the *Sutta Piṭaka*, which is later picked up and used more frequently (and again systematically) by the *Abhidhamma* and commentarial traditions. In the *Sutta Piṭaka* we find several references to the senses as 'doors' or 'gates' (*dvāra*) which need to be guarded.[90] Such a metaphor suggests that they are both physical organs and openings at the same time. The description of the senses as 'guarded' or 'unguarded' gives the same metaphor a qualitative colouring, even where the word *dvāra* is not mentioned.[91] This metaphor is doubly appropriate to what we have been discussing here. On the one hand, it implies that there is an abstract meaning to the senses which goes beyond the physical sense organs. On the other hand, it indicates that the senses are a 'way in' or 'entrance', and in this sense they are of fundamental importance in the psychological processes of the human being. That they have to be guarded suggests that what one experiences through the senses can be interpreted or reacted to in a way which can be detrimental to one's progress on the path to liberation. This is explained in the *Sāmaññaphala Sutta*, where the Buddha tells King Ajātasattu how a *bhikkhu* guards the doors which correspond to his senses. When the *bhikkhu* sees a visible object with his visual faculty, the Buddha states, he is not entranced with views about its various characteristics. He is intent on restraining those things which give rise to unwholesomeness, evil, covetousness or dejection which flow over him for as long as he lives with his sense of sight unrestrained; he guards the visual sense, and attains restraint over it.[92]

The notion that the senses are doors which need guarding has to be understood in the context of the whole of the cognitive process or psychological life of the individual. It is significant that in the passage quoted in the last paragraph the *bhikkhu* is said not to be entranced with views about what he sees. It is not that the visual faculty itself has to see differently. As we shall see below in chapters II and IV, it is the involvement of the *saṃkhārakkhandha* in the cognitive process that gives rise to unwholesomeness, evil, covetousness or dejection. Though it is from the senses that feelings arise, and such feelings can in themselves be agreeable, disagreeable or neutral, the arising of any unwholesomeness (in its broadest sense, which means anything that is binding) is associated with volitions directed towards the feelings by the *saṃkhārakkhandha*. What has to be guarded is in fact one's reaction to what one experiences by means of the senses. It is precisely this that constitutes the struggle on the path to liberation: and just as it is not the fault of a door or an opening that an enemy enters and has to be fought inside the building, so it is not the fault of the senses themselves that one reacts unwholesomely to one's sensory experience. Both an *arahant* and a *puthujjana* might see exactly the same potentially desirable object; it is their reaction to that sight that is different. Illustrating its connection with the *saṃkhāras*, in the *Jātaka* the door imagery is associated with the ethical triad of thought, word, and deed (in the Pali this is *kāya, vacī, manas*).[93] Body, speech and mind are said to be the three doors which are to be guarded so that no evil is done in act, word or thought.[94]

Another metaphor associated with the senses in the *Sutta Piṭaka* confirms that it is not the senses themselves that give rise to binding volitions which have to be guarded against. This metaphor is of an empty village. We read in the *Saḷāyatana Saṃyutta* that 'empty village' is a name for the six personal, or internal, senses.[95] The emptiness of the village, that it is unoccupied, implies that it is not to be thought of in terms of an abiding self. It also implies that it is the locus of activity which is generated by something other than the physical infrastructure of the village itself. In the same passage we read that the corresponding external objects are referred to as 'village plunderers'.[96] This is because shapes, sounds, odours, tastes etc. are what we find entrancing. When the sphere of such an object comes into the sphere of the corresponding sense, our reaction might be to become entranced by it: to have 'views about its various characteristics' (to refer back to the *Sāmaññaphala Sutta*).

It is obvious that the physical sense organs themselves, being part of the body of the human being, are part of the *rūpakkhandha* whether they are singled out for mention in a classification or not. Indeed the major part of what is contained in the later texts about the senses concentrates on describing the physical sense organs in minute and extensive detail and classifies them clearly as *rūpa*.[97] But from the foregoing it also seems likely that in contexts where the senses are referred to in the *Sutta Piṭaka*, the terms *cakkhu*, *sota*, *ghāna* and so on are to be understood figuratively as the potential for vision, hearing, smelling and so on, rather than being *merely* the physical sense organs. This accords with contrasting references in later texts to the *āyatanas* being invisible, as mentioned above, thus implying the importance of their function and not their (visible) physicality.[98] So the question remains whether the senses as *āyatanas* should also be considered part of the *rūpakkhandha*. We have seen above that comprehensive descriptions of the *rūpakkhandha* are not restricted to physical organs. Indeed, we saw that the *khandha* includes processes such as breathing and movement.

In the *Aṭṭhasālinī*, however, one passage suggests why classifying the senses as *rūpa* may not be as straightforward as with some other processes. We read:

> The physical eye does not see because it is not conscious. Nor does consciousness see, because it is not an eye. But, when an object comes together with a sense door, one sees with one's consciousness together with the sense organ as the physical base.[99]

Though the descriptions of the *rūpakkhandha* refer to a live body, the relevant non-corporeal processes which life involves (such as breathing and temperature) do not specifically involve consciousness in the same way as a sensory experience does, according to the *Aṭṭhasālinī*: one does not have to be conscious *of* breathing or temperature regulation in order for them to function. Nor can consciousness be said to be part of the *rūpakkhandha*. What is suggested by the fact that in order to function there has to be the coming together of sense organ and consciousness, is that vision, hearing and so on are *potential* processes, bringing us back to the meaning we arrived at above in discussing the terms *āyatana*, *indriya* and *dhātu*. As such it would be inappropriate to attempt to classify them in terms of *rūpa* or *arūpa*: just as *phassa* (which is discussed in chapter II) is not classified in such terms, so the senses should remain unclassified, as they do in the *Sutta Piṭaka*.

Supporting this conclusion, and in striking contrast with the quantity of material on the physical characteristics of the sense organs, in the *Aṭṭhasālinī* there is also to be found one short paragraph which gives what I have referred to above as a 'theory of sense'. The theory is incomplete in that it does not make any mention of *manas* and *dhammā*. But this is probably because the theory is (oddly) included in the passage which discusses *upādā rūpa*, and *manas* and *dhammā* are not so defined. Maung Tin's translation of the passage states:

> For the eye has the characteristic of sentience for phenomena worthy of directly impinging on the object, or of sentience sprung from action caused

> by a desire to see the object. It has the function of drawing consciousness towards the objects; it has the localizing of visual cognition as its manifestation; it has the being produced by action caused by a desire to see as proximate cause. The ear has the characteristic of sentience for phenomena worthy of directly impinging on sounds, or of sentience sprung from action caused by a desire to hear sounds; it has the function of drawing consciousness towards sounds; it has the localizing of auditory cognition as its manifestation; and it has a proximate cause as above. The nose and the tongue (or smell and taste), and lastly the body or tactile sense may be analogously defined.[100]

There is a clear indication in this paragraph of *cakkhu* and *sota* (and so on) as potentialities. First is the use of the term *pasāda*, which Maung Tin translates as 'sentience'. Earlier in the same chapter, the *Aṭṭhasālinī* states that though the sense organs are corporeal (*maṃsa*), they comprise two aspects, *pasāda* and *sasambhāra*.[101] *Sasambhāra* means merely that it is a compound of physical parts. *Pasāda* literally means clearness or brightness, but in this context means something like 'sensitive surface'.[102] The introduction of the concept of *pasāda* clearly indicates that the eye is psychophysical. And we have an indication of *how* the physical sense organs (eyes) contribute to vision: they provide the physical sensitive surface on which objects might impinge. Second, desire to see is instrumental in as it were activating the sentience. Again the potentiality of vision is indicated: mere possession of a physical eye does not constitute seeing. Third, this passage confirms that vision is a conscious process.

An analogy to bring these things together and illustrate that sense is an epiphenomenon of all of them can be suggested in terms of music. The musical instrument represents the physical sense organ. On the one hand the instrument is comprised of minute physical parts, *sasambhāra*, and on the other hand it is also a sensitive surface, *pasāda*. The hands of a player represent the sense object. Neither of these (the instrument and the hands) constitutes music. Just as sense objects are *āyatanas* by virtue of representing the potential for an individual's seeing or hearing (and so on) but they are not limited to being part of such sensory processes, so the player's hands are not limited to being part of the creating of music. For there to be music, the musical instrument and the hands of a player have to be combined with conscious intention, or 'action caused by a desire to create music', to echo Maung Tin's translation above. On the one hand the musical instrument and the hands of the player are musical instrument *qua* musical instrument and hands *qua* hands respectively. On the other hand, they are potentialities for music. In the same way the physical sense organs and their corresponding objects are literally those things and also potentialities for the relevant senses, the *āyatanas*. Neither the musical instrument nor the hands of the player would be classified as music; and music would not be defined as physical merely because the instrument and the hands are physical. In the same way, neither the physical sense organs nor their corresponding objects are the senses, and the senses are not definable as physical.

In the text, *cakkhu*, the eye, is also referred to figuratively in that there is said to be an 'eye of wisdom' (*paññācakkhu*) which is of five kinds: the eye of awakening, the all-seeing eye, the eye of knowledge, the divine eye and the eye of *dhamma*.[103] This treatment of *cakkhu* is no doubt because of the role of insight in the path of liberation in Buddhism: such insight can be described in terms of seeing. But *paññācakkhu* refers to a qualitatively different kind of seeing which is more akin to cognition than to the level of the senses. *Paññā* is discussed in chapter v.

In sum, then, there is nothing in the *Sutta Piṭaka* to suggest that the *āyatanas* are classified as part of the *rūpakkhandha*, and no direct evidence of a theory of sense. Though the *Abhidhamma* and other later Pali material define *upādā rūpa* in terms of the *āyatanas*, it seems clear that if one considers the evidence as a whole, one can come to an understanding of the senses as neither *rūpa* nor *arūpa*. They are, rather, potentialities which determine the nature of each of the types of an individual's psychological processes. In order to be effected, the potentialities make use of a physical sense organ and also involve consciousness. So, one can metaphorically understand them as doors through which the individual subjectively interacts with the objective world.

Manas and *dhammā*: the sixth sense and its object

I have been arguing that the senses are not limited to the physical sense organs, and that even the external sense objects have a potentiality for sensory experience by a human being as well as their objectivity. In five cases out of six the corresponding physical location of the senses is nevertheless obvious to us, and such physical sense organs are part of the body of the human being, part of the *rūpakkhandha*. In five cases out of six it is also obvious to us what is meant by their corresponding external sense object. But the physical location of *manas*, the sixth sense, is never mentioned in the *Sutta Piṭaka* and neither the function of *manas* nor the identity of *dhammā* is clearly defined. I will first discuss the question of the physical location of *manas* in the light of the later Pali material. I will then go on to suggest that from references to *manas* in the *Sutta Piṭaka*, one can extract an understanding of its function, and the identity of *dhammā*. Again, reference to the way it is understood in the later material helps to clarify such an understanding.

According to Buddhist tradition, the physical basis of the mental faculties is the heart (*hadayavatthu*), and in Indian religion as a whole the Sanskrit word for 'heart' (*hṛdaya*) is often used to refer to cognitive acts, rather than just to an affective centre.[104] But in spite of the fact that its literal meaning is 'mind', nowhere in the Pali canon, not even in the *Abhidhamma Piṭaka*, do we read that the heart is the physical base of *manas*.[105] There is one oblique reference in the *Abhidhamma* to *hadaya* being synonymous with *manas* in a passage which is defining *citta*, but in the context it does not have the specific meaning of *hadayavatthu*.[106] One might in any case expect the *Abhidhamma* not to state that the heart (or anything else) is the physical location of *manas* since we have seen that *manas* is specifically defined in the *Abhidhamma* as *arūpa*. There is, however, an apparent inconsistency on this point, and in one passage there is the suggestion that *manas* does have a physical base.[107] The somewhat obscure Pali is translated by Aung as follows:

> That material thing on the basis of which apprehension and comprehension take place – that thing is related to both of them, as well as to their concomitants by way of the relation of Base.[108]

The grammatical structure *yaṃ rūpaṃ ... taṃ rūpaṃ* could not be less informative about the location of the physical base for *manas*. Not until the commentaries do we find the term *hadayavatthu* being used,[109] and it is identified as the location of *manas* by Buddhaghosa in his *Visuddhimagga*.[110] And Buddhaghosa accordingly includes *hadayavatthu* (amongst the other *āyatanas*) in his analysis of *upādā rūpa*.[111]

Aung suggests[112] that the omission of the term *hadayavatthu* from the canonical material is not accidental, proving simply that the compilers of the early material and founders of the *Abhidhamma* doctrine did not believe the heart to be the location of *manas*.[113] *Manas* is a sense, and as such it might not have been considered by the *Abhidhamma* tradition to have had sufficient cognitive function to be identified with the common pan-Indian understanding that *hadayavatthu* is the seat of the cognitive faculties. It is significant in this respect that in the *Sutta Piṭaka* it is *citta* and not *manas* that is associated with the heart, both explicitly and implicitly.[114]

Two writers within the (modern) Theravāda tradition assume the brain to be the physical location of *manas*. Ñānavīra Thera refers to a passage in the *Saḷāyatana Saṃyutta* which states that the senses are that by which, in the world, one is a perceiver and conceiver of the world.[115] Ñānavīra takes this passage as substantialistic (though it need not be taken in such a way) and states that just as the eye is a physical thing, so *manas* is the "mass of grey matter contained in my head".[116] Jayasuriya, writing about the psychology of the *Abhidhamma*, states that the "Heart or Mind-base element... [is] in the brain".[117] It is notable that in passages in the *Sutta Piṭaka* which refer to the sense organs in general, and *manas* in particular, the brain is never mentioned. And in only two occurrences of the standard list of parts of the body (discussed above) is the brain (*matthaluṅga*) mentioned. Both are in books in the *Khuddaka Nikāya*: the *Paṭisambhidāmagga*,[118] and the

Khuddakapāṭha.[119] The list is identical to the standard list of thirty-one parts found elsewhere in the *Sutta Piṭaka* save for the fact that it includes the brain (*matthaluṅga*) as the thirty-second part. The commentary does not acknowledge how unusual it is in including the brain, and no explanation for its inclusion here, or its exclusion elsewhere, is given.[120] The *Khuddaka Nikāya* is comprised of a variety of books, some of which are considered to be considerably later than other parts of the *Sutta Piṭaka.*[121] It is possible, therefore, that these two passages are late, and that *matthaluṅga* might have been added to the extant standard list as a part of the body which had become more widely known about. Alternatively, this list might have been one which circulated among different people from those who recorded the list which survives in other places in the *Sutta Piṭaka.*

The brain is also mentioned both in the *Vinaya*[122] and in the *Sutta Nipāta.*[123] The context in which it is found in the *Vinaya* is a discussion of a brain-destroying disease from which a householder is suffering. No other parts of the body are mentioned, and the passage does not offer an analysis of the body. The *Sutta Nipāta* passage, on the other hand, is more comprehensive:

> Joined together with bones and sinews, having a plastering of skin and flesh, covered with hide, the body is not seen as it really is – full of intestines, full of stomach, (full) of the lump of the liver, of bladder, of heart, of lungs, of kidneys and of spleen, of mucus, of saliva, of sweat, and of lymph, of blood, of synovial fluid, of bile, and of fat ... and its hollow head is filled with brain.[124]

Many of the parts mentioned are also included in the standard list. Probably because the *Sutta Nipāta* is in verse rather than prose, the order of those parts that are common to both is different; and several of the standard parts are omitted in the *Sutta Nipāta* passage.[125] It is acknowledged by scholars that much but not all of the *Sutta Nipāta* is very early. The inclusion of *matthaluṅga* here may be an indication that this particular passage is late. But it may only be that the brain was not an organ which was known to those early Buddhists who were concerned to give an analysis of the body, whether for classification or for meditational purposes. Certainly, there is no suggestion in the canonical material, early or late, that it is *manas* or the physical base of *manas.*

There are three possibilities concerning the location of *manas.* First, we have seen above that in the *Sutta Piṭaka* the senses are not explicitly stated to be *upādā rūpa.* I have suggested that this might be because they principally represent the potential processes of seeing, hearing and so on. Their corresponding physical organs might have been excluded from the classification partly because they are readily identified (in all but one case) and partly because the physical organs as such, though necessary, are of minor significance in the psychological implications of seeing. If the terms used to list the first five senses (*cakkhu*, *sota*, *ghāna*, *jivhā* and *kāya*) are actually intended to mean the psychological elements of vision, hearing, smell, taste and touch rather than the physical organs of eye, ear, nose, tongue and body, then in the *Sutta Piṭaka* those senses are not explicitly located: we know their locations because they are familiar to us. One is at a loss to locate *manas* only because its location is not obvious to us any more than it was obvious to the writers of the *Abhidhamma*.

Second, it is possible that though *manas* is part of the *rūpakkhandha*, it has no gross physical organ. We find in the *Dhātukathā*, another book in the *Abhidhamma Piṭaka*, a classification of *rūpa* which includes an analysis of it according to whether it is subtle or gross.[126] This would account for the non-corporeal aspects of the *rūpakkhandha* we have already discussed, and might explain the elusiveness of *manas* in being physically located. Third, from the evidence (or lack of it) in the *Sutta Piṭaka*, it remains a possibility that *manas* has no corresponding physical organ, whether gross or subtle. This might be another reason why the six senses as a whole are not classified within the *rūpakkhandha* in the *Sutta Piṭaka*. And it is clearly the implicit understanding in sections of the *Abhidhamma* where *manas* is omitted from descriptions of *upādā rūpa*.

There is insufficient evidence in the *Sutta Piṭaka*, or in the *Abhidhamma*, for us to know which of these three is correct. Nor do our general knowledge and observation help. We may know from observation, for example, that even if references to the senses in the texts are to be understood figuratively as referring to psychological processes rather than physical organs, a corpse will nevertheless still have the physical organs eye, ear, nose, tongue and body. But we do not know whether it also has a *manas*.

I turn now to the function of *manas* and the identity of its object, *dhammā*. *Manas* is one of the most ambiguous and confusing terms in Pali material. Western scholars and those working within the Theravāda Buddhist tradition usually translate it literally, as 'mind'. Given that *manas* is an *āyatana*, however, such a translation is perhaps questionable, since the word 'mind' tends to suggest that it undertakes processes that would be classified in one of the *arūpakkhandhas*. Though there have been some twentieth century Western philosophers (notably Wittgenstein and Ryle) for whom 'mental' processes such as thinking are *not* incorporeal processes, most Westerners are still very much influenced by the Cartesian dualism between mind and body, whereby thinking is a non-corporeal process. And in the Buddhist analysis of the person into *khandhas*, thinking is definitely not a process which is associated with any of the elements by which the body is characterised. The extent to which the Buddhist tradition's understanding of the sense *manas* attributes cognitive processes to it is no clearer than whether or not it has a physical location. The lack of clarity in this respect may well be because cognitive, thinking processes *are* clearly stated to be the function of certain mental faculties, as we shall see.[127] The ambiguity of the situation is exacerbated by the fact that the term *manas* is also frequently used in the *Nikāyas* in a generic sense (as opposed to the specific sense of *manas* as sense organ) in contexts where it *does* have a mental, cognitive meaning. And etymologically the word comes from the same root as the verb *maññati*, to think. Ascertaining in what sense *manas* is being used requires consideration of the contexts in which it is found, some of which are more ambiguous than others. In many passages it is contextually clear that it is as a generic term for the mind in its cognitive capacity that *manas* is being used. In a well-known passage, for example, it is used in sequence with *citta* and *viññāṇa*, which are definitely associated with cognitive activities.[128] Here the term *manas* clearly does not refer to the sense. Elsewhere, in contexts which one might loosely call 'formulaic', the formula appears sometimes with *manas* and sometimes with *citta* or *cetas*, which again are definitely mental or cognitive terms. Such contexts are discussed further in chapter v.

Ambiguity about the meaning of *manas* is compounded because the *Abhidhamma* tradition systematised the term, using various suffixes to give it different technical meanings in different contexts. Though these later technical usages of *manas* are occasionally mentioned in this chapter, their later technical meanings are far from obvious in the *Sutta Piṭaka*, the material with which I am primarily concerned. And the ambiguity is yet further exacerbated by the fact that *dhammā*, the object corresponding to *manas*, also has a multiplicity of meanings. When *manas* is translated as 'mind', *dhammā* tends to be translated accordingly as 'thoughts', 'ideas', 'mental images'.[129] Yet the term can refer to phenomena of any kind as well as to teachings and doctrines.[130]

In order to distinguish *manas* as sense from *manas* as 'mind' in general I will henceforth call the sense *manodhātu*. In the *Abhidhamma, manodhātu* has a technical meaning which distinguishes it from *manāyatana* and *manoviññāṇadhātu*. There, *manāyatana* is a collective term referring to the whole of consciousness, but it is not clear to me whether either *manodhātu* or *manoviññāṇadhātu* means *manas* as sense as discussed here.[131] My use of the term *manodhātu* in a completely non-technical way just to refer to the sense is similar to its use in the *Sutta Piṭaka* in contexts where all the senses are referred to as *dhātus*.[132]

As I have stated above, nowhere in the Pali material is the precise meaning or function of the sense *manodhātu* explicitly made clear. But from a consideration of the contexts in which it is found in the *Sutta Piṭaka* one can suggest that it is understood in two different ways, both of which have been adopted by the later *Abhidhamma* and commentarial traditions: as a unique quasi sense, and as an 'ordinary' sense.

The first meaning of *manodhātu* is suggested from passages in which it is referred to differently, as a unique sense rather than as the sixth in a series of senses each having a similar level of functioning. A passage in the *Khandha Saṃyutta* refers first to the first five senses and then to *manodhātu* separately. The passage does not explicitly offer an explanation of the meaning or function of *manodhātu*, and from the context one can only make a suggestion as to why it has been singled out, which I will do below.

The passage states that the first five senses (that is, not including *manodhātu*) manifest because of an erroneous belief in selfhood.[133] The next sentence makes most sense if translated: "there are [also], *bhikkhus*, *manas* and *dhammā*, which are the basis for knowledge/ignorance".[134] The *Sutta* goes on to state that it is through contact with ignorance that various (false) views regarding selfhood arise in ordinary people,[135] and a paraphrase of its conclusion, in order to draw out its meaning, might be:

> It is in the holding of such views that one persists as an individual in *saṃsāra*, that is, one who has the five senses. In the well-taught advanced disciple ignorance comes to an end and insight arises, there are no more (false) views concerning selfhood.[136]

A consideration of the main implication of this passage, though it is not precisely present in the Pali, serves to highlight the meaning of the passage itself. The implication is that for the advanced disciple who gains insight there will be no more persistence as an individual in *saṃsāra*; he or she will therefore no longer be reborn as someone with five senses, the manifestation of which is accompanied by the manifestation of a further so-called sense which is associated with the cognitive process. So the significance of the passage is that the arising of senses indicates that one is still ignorant and bound in the cycle of *saṃsāra*.

The use of *avijjā* (ignorance) in one reading of this passage can be explained because the cognitive process is that which takes place prior to liberating insight: it is *saṃsāric* cognition, which from the point of view of liberating insight is not *vijjā* but *avijjā*. Thus where *vijjā* means liberating insight, *manodhātu* is associated with ignorance rather than knowledge. Liberating insight is of a different nature, and according to this interpretation it does not involve *manodhātu*, even though the individual with the five senses is still manifest during the lifetime in which he or she achieves Enlightenment. On the other hand, the use of *vijjā* in connection with *manodhātu* can be explained because given that the eventual liberating insight is to a certain extent dependent on the *gradual* elimination of ignorance as the *bhikkhu* proceeds along the path, *manodhātu* might be associated with eventual knowledge: the *saṃsāric* perspective from which virtually everyone operates is that from which ignorance is gradually diminished and liberating knowledge is correspondingly built up, culminating in insight itself. And according to this interpretation, *manodhātu* may even be involved in such insight.

What this passage establishes, whichever variant one reads, is that *manodhātu* is different from the other senses. Since the context is concerned with ignorance or knowledge, this difference might be because according to Buddhist teachings liberation comes about by means of the cognitive faculties of which *manodhātu* is in some way the sense. As such it is directly involved in the process of liberation in a way the other senses are not.

The way in which *manodhātu* functions as the sense which is associated with the cognitive faculties is suggested elsewhere. We read that *manodhātu* functions as a 'collator' (*paṭisaraṇa*) for the five mutually distinct senses (*pañc' indriyāni*) and experiences or realises the scope of their activity.[137] *Paṭisaraṇa*, the word I have translated as 'collator', more literally means 'refuge', 'shelter' or 'help'.[138] I. B. Horner translates it as 'repository'.[139] In my opinion the context demands something more like 'collator', and, as we shall see when its function is explained in more detail, this is not incompatible with the more literal meanings: the other five senses are directed through it, as it were, and in acting as the collator of the data fed in by them it is both a repository for those data and also assists them in rendering those data comprehensible.

Mrs C. A. F. Rhys Davids discusses this passage in her *Buddhist Psychology*. She assigns to *manodhātu* the role of co-ordinator, and refers to it as the *sensus communis*, a description which has also been used by subsequent scholars.[140] Mrs Rhys Davids was no doubt drawing on the meaning given to the 'internal sense' referred to as *sensus communis* by Thomas Aquinas.[141] Accordingly, she suggests that *manodhātu* as *sensus communis* is the subjective correlative of *dhammā*, which it recognises as the objective *mundus sensibilis*.

What this seems to me to mean is that *manodhātu* serves as a special filtering and collating 'sense' which is the subjective side in our relation to the objective world, all of which is referred to collectively as *dhammā*. *Dhammā* as counterpart to *manodhātu* is a pluralistic representation of the world, which has a certain inherent rationality, and *manodhātu* is the receiver of these phenomena in general (without any initial specification as to sound, visible objects, odour, and so on): and it is able to act as their collator, rendering them cognisable for the cognitive faculties.[142] This is a necessary process since we receive data from different sensory objects simultaneously. The perception of a person, for example, might involve sight, hearing, smell and touch. The sense of sight, however, cannot itself distinguish colour from sound, odour and touch: we need something to synthesise all the sense impressions.[143] So, Mrs Rhys Davids writes, through *manodhātu* as *sensus communis*, "we get a simulated unity and simultaneity of impressions, which are really single and successive, if exceedingly and most delicately swift".[144] *Manodhātu* can also be considered a sense in that it 'senses' the 'sensibility' of phenomena (*dhammā*).[145] Rather than 'ideas', 'mental objects' and so on, *dhammā* according to this explanation of its meaning might therefore be translated as 'sensory phenomena', which covers the *saṃsāric* world in its entirety as experienced by us through our senses.[146]

In accord with understanding *dhammā* as all sensory phenomena, Geiger, in his *Pali Dhamma*, interprets *dhammā* as the "empirical world".[147] In the light of this, a point needs to be clarified about the *Khandha Saṃyutta* passage first cited above in which the existence of *manas* and *dhammā* were referred to after the arising of the five senses. Woodward's translation of this passage is that *manas* and *dhammā* are the *result* of the manifestation of the five senses.[148] In my opinion this is not what the passage means. It refers to *manas* and *dhammā* separately because they have a unique role in the cognitive process as data collator and raw data respectively. The raw data, *dhammā*, may be the empirical world as experienced through our senses, but that is not to say that the empirical world itself arises *because of* sensory activity.

It is not uncommon in the *Sutta Piṭaka* for the word *dhammā* to mean more than just sensory phenomena. In the *tilakkhaṇa* formula, for example (which is discussed in chapter IV), *dhammā* has the universal meaning of all phenomena of whatever nature. Such a meaning would obviously include more than Geiger's 'empirical world'. Another understanding of *dhammā* is that it refers to phenomena which are 'knowable', though as such one cannot either claim or deny their universality. Carter, for example, states that *dhammā* are phenomena that "can be grasped, known by the 'mind-organ' (*manas*) ... are themselves without substance but cooperate in a changing but orderly co-production in such a manner that they can be noted, thought out, and mastered, so to speak – internal psychic and external physical patterned processes, as 'knowables'."[149]

I agree with Carter's suggestion that *dhammā* as the object of *manodhātu* are knowable phenomena. But his statement needs, in my opinion, two qualifications. First, there is no evidence that the *manodhātu* has what we would call the mental faculties of grasping and knowing. In its capacity as *sensus communis*, it receives *dhammā* as incoming raw data at the preliminary stage of the cognitive process. Grasping and knowing both take place at subsequent stages of the cognitive process as functions of the various mental faculties. We saw above that in guarding the senses as doors, the *bhikkhu* must not be entranced. Though the Pali for this is *na nimittaggāhi*,[150] which more literally means that he must not seize upon (any sensory experience), I mentioned there that such entrancement or seizing comes not from the sense but from the *saṃkhārakkhandha*.[151] Even if one interprets Carter's use of the word 'grasps' metaphorically, as indicating something like 'pays attention to' or 'is conscious of', by stating that it 'knows' he would still be attributing more to *manodhātu* than we are able to confirm from the texts.

Second, Carter's description of *dhammā* as "internal psychic and external physical" phenomena is potentially ambiguous. The analysis of the *āyatanas* is into the subjective senses and the objective sense objects: the *āyatanas* as a whole represent the means whereby the individual as subject interacts with the objective world. As such the former are internal or subjective to the individual and the latter, including *dhammā*, are external or objective to the individual. I have deliberately stated 'external *or* objective' and not 'external' alone because knowables may not strictly be external, even if they are objective. *Dhammā* as knowables would include phenomena such as teachings, doctrines, concepts, and so on. It also includes thoughts and ideas insofar as these are objectified: someone else's thoughts and ideas, for example, or one's own previous thoughts and ideas which have become objectified through the lapse of time. The subjective mental processes which arise immediately subsequent to one's subjective interaction with the objective world, such as thinking and knowing, are not (yet) objectified and are thus not included in the term *dhammā* as the stream of incoming raw data: they are not the object but the *content* of the mind. So *dhammā* in the context of being the object of the *manodhātu* refers to all objective phenomena, and the sentence referred to above might have been clearer as 'objective psychic and physical' phenomena. Whether they are sensory or abstract, all such phenomena are filtered through or collated by the *manodhātu*, subsequent to which the cognitive processes function.

The fact that *manodhātu* also processes abstract or conceptual *dhammā*, as well as all other sensory *dhammā*, suggests its second role as that of an 'ordinary' sense: processing data which are specific to its nature, as it were. The abstract or conceptual *dhammā* are phenomena which are as specific to *manodhātu* as, say, sound is to the ear. So though all *dhammā* are processed by *manodhātu*, it also has this aspect to its function which one might consider to be a more 'normal' sensory function. I will return to this second understanding of *manodhātu* in the *Sutta Piṭaka* shortly.

The understanding of *dhammā* as objective phenomena in general rather than being limited to mere sensory phenomena is compatible with the use of *dhammā* in the *Satipaṭṭhāna Suttas*. In these *Suttas* the fourth *satipaṭṭhāna* is the contemplation of *dhammā*.[152] This exercise is to be undertaken considering in turn the *nīvaraṇas*, the *khandhas*, the *āyatanas*, the seven *bojjhaṅgas* and the four Noble Truths. The context suggests that it is the teachings on each of these things which are to be meditated upon; presumably why they were given, their significance, meaning, and so on. Here *dhammā* represents all phenomena which arise in the course of each meditation exercise, and the doctrinal concepts which form the objects of the meditation are as objective to the individual as are strictly external sensory phenomena.

Writing from within the Theravāda tradition, Nyāṇatiloka explains that the term *dhammā* refers to *nāmarūpa dhammā* "as presented to the investigating mind by mindfulness".[153] Though Nyāṇatiloka, following Buddhist tradition, interprets *nāmarūpa dhammā* as "bodily and mental phenomena", we shall see in chapter VI that this is not necessarily an appropriate interpretation of it: *nāma* is not the equivalent of *arūpa*, and therefore mental, *dhammā*. Rather, it is the equivalent of conceptual or abstract *dhammā*, which precisely fits with the conceptual or abstract (and objective) *dhammā* referred to in the last paragraph. *Rūpadhammā* refers to sensory phenomena. The nature and status of all *dhammā* later became the subject of extensive philosophical speculation within the Buddhist tradition as a whole, much of which is recorded in Vasubandhu's *Abhidharmakośa* and its *bhāṣya*. But there is no such speculation in the *Sutta Piṭaka*: there, even the term *nāmarūpa dhammā* is not used, let alone defined.

We find *manas* in one other context which appears to confirm its unique role as what one might call a quasi sense and that it functions as collator of a wide range of incoming data. This is in a reference to the level of awareness achieved in the fourth *jhāna*. "What can be understood through *manoviññāṇa*[154] when it is 'purified', that is when it is isolated from the five [other] senses?"[155] The reply is that one can know that space is unending (*ananto ākāso*), that consciousness is unending (*anantaṃ viññāṇam*) and one can know the sphere of no-thing (*ākiñcaññāyatana*). These three represent consecutive *jhāna* levels of meditation, none of which is knowable through the senses.

Here the role of *manodhātu* appears to be similar to that meant by *sensus communis* as described above, in that it collates the incoming data as the first stage of the cognitive process, but those data are what one might call supra-sensory rather than simply abstract or non-sensory. In another description of the *jhānas*, what one knows at the fourth level is described differently:

> ...through completely transcending all apperceptions based on appearance, through the cessation of apperceptions which are sensory in origin, through not paying attention to apperceptions of multiformity.[156]

Though in this passage the involvement of *manodhātu* is not explicitly stated, what one knows is clearly not from sensory data. Perhaps in line with this, the *Vibhaṅga* suggests that *manas* might function at even higher non-sensory levels when it states that both *manas* and *dhammā* are sometimes *lokiya* (worldly) and sometimes *lokuttara* (supramundane).[157]

I stated above that where *dhammā* refers to all phenomena whatsoever the term clearly referred to more than Geiger's 'empirical world'. We have now arrived at an understanding of *dhammā* when it is the object of *manodhātu* which includes sensory, non-sensory and supra-sensory phenomena. Whether or not this meaning of *dhammā* also represents more than Geiger's 'empirical world', on the grounds that it includes phenomena which are not actually empirical, is open to debate. The non-sensory and supra-sensory phenomena may not be empirical in the Western materialistic meaning of the word, but it may be a valid word to use in Buddhism. Even at supra-sensory *jhāna* levels phenomena are part of *saṃsāric* experience: in spite of terms such as 'the sphere of no-thing', such levels do not constitute liberating insight and are part of the *saṃsāric* cognitive process. They would not be psycho-cosmological 'spheres' if they were not.[158] On the other hand, if *dhammā* applies at *lokuttara* levels it might include within it the unconditioned as well as conditioned phenomena, as it does in the *tilakkhaṇa* formula (discussed in chapter IV). In view of the diversity of phenomena included within the term *dhammā*, it is perhaps unnecessarily ambiguous to define it as the empirical world when 'knowables' is more clearly an inclusive term.

An important implication of understanding *manodhātu* as *sensus communis* is that any and all sensory activity involves the activity of the *manodhātu*. If it is the coordinator and collator of *all* sensory input, then it is activated whenever any of the other five senses functions. In this respect it is unique among the senses; it functions, as already suggested, as a quasi sense. References in the canonical material to only five *kāmaguṇā* might be based on this assumption: though *manodhātu* would be involved in the process of the arising of visual, auditory, olfactory, gustatory and tactile pleasure it would not in itself be the basis for a specific type of pleasure in its own right.

But this assumption overlooks the 'normal sense' aspect of *manodhātu*, and it is this aspect alone which features in the second understanding of *manodhātu* that one can extract from the *Sutta Piṭaka*, to which I now return. Even if *manodhātu* functions as a quasi sense which processes all incoming raw data, another part of its function is as the sense which processes abstract phenomena, as we have seen above. As such, one might think that pleasure could be associated with these abstract thoughts or ideas. This possibility is referred to in some passages which are otherwise problematic in the light of the analysis of *manodhātu* as *sensus communis*. Such passages only treat *manodhātu* as an ordinary sense, that is the sixth in the series of senses, and assume that it functions in the same way as the other senses in relating to its corresponding object. Though such passages confirm one role of *manodhātu*, however, they indicate that for the authors of such passages it is not understood as comprehensively as has been described above.

An example of this is in the description of the arising of feelings in the *Madhupiṇḍikasutta*, which was quoted from above.[159] It gives exactly the same description for all six senses: visual, auditory, olfactory, gustatory, tactile and 'mental'. Thus the sentence construction for the description of 'mental feeling' is the same as it is for visual feeling.[160] No mention is made of the *manodhātu* being activated as collator for the other senses. Nor does the commentary on this passage suggest that *manodhātu* functions differently from the other senses: having described the arising of visual feeling, it states that the same process applies to auditory feeling and all the others.[161] Similar passages about the arising of feelings are found elsewhere in the canon.[162] Likewise, in many of the *Suttas* whose content is primarily concerned with the senses, the description given of *manodhātu* is in precisely the same formula as that given for the other five senses.[163]

Rahula, writing from within the Theravāda Buddhist tradition, also understands *manodhātu* in this way,[164] as does Ñānavīra Thera.[165] In such contexts *manodhātu* is translated as 'mind'. And as object corresponding to 'mind', *dhammā* is translated by words such as 'thoughts', 'ideas', 'mental images', 'mind states' or 'mental states'.[166] Such translations are justified because in these contexts there is no indication that the object corresponding to *manodhātu* is any less specific than are the objects corresponding to the other five senses. And if *manas* literally means 'mind' then it is understandable that a translator, and indeed the Theravāda tradition, might assume its object to be something like thoughts, ideas, mental images and so on. Such translations confirm that here the function of *manodhātu* is not considered to be that of receiving *all* incoming data whether sensory or abstract. Rather, in these contexts the understanding of *manodhātu* seems to be limited to its being the sense which processes the abstract phenomena discussed above, while sensory data (*rūpadhammā*) are the province of the other five senses.

In this understanding of *manodhātu*, then, only one aspect of it is recognised: that it is the sense which corresponds to abstract 'mental' objects. It is not seen as the collator of all the incoming data from the other senses. As such it functions in the same way as the other senses in that contact with abstract objects – the thoughts of another, a teaching, one's own previous thoughts – can give rise to 'mental' feelings and so on. This less comprehensive understanding of *manodhātu* might have a prosaic origin. It is possible that the mnemonic style of many of the passages found in the *Nikāyas* resulted in a sixfold analysis being included in a manner which made it impossible to convey the unique function of *manodhātu* in handling both the abstract phenomena which are said to be the object of it as a sense, and the other sensory data which it collates as *paṭisaraṇa*. It could simply have been that because of an oversight the passages in question were arranged mnemonically at the expense of comprehensiveness.

It might also simply be that we do not understand the meaning of *manas* as a sense and thus are unable to interpret the relevant passages correctly. And the Theravāda tradition perpetuates but does not co-ordinate the two meanings, showing that it is itself unclear as to the meaning of *manodhātu*. We have seen above that in the commentaries no distinction between *manodhātu* and the other five senses is introduced when commenting on canonical passages which refer to *manodhātu* as the sixth in a series of senses, and that writers within the Theravāda tradition accept *manodhātu* as a sixth sense in this way. But elsewhere in the commentaries and the Theravāda tradition, *manodhātu* is interpreted as a collator for all sensory data (that is as *sensus communis* as already defined). We read in the *Abhidhamma* commentarial literature, for example, that the apperception of a visible object arises at the door which is the visual sense and also at the door which is *manodhātu*. The same is the case with all the other senses.[167] Similarly, Karunadasa, writing about the Buddhist analysis of matter according to the *Abhidhamma* and Pali commentarial material, states: "...all the *rūpadhammas* become the objects of *manoviññāṇa*".[168] This does not mean that the objects of *manodhātu* are limited to *rūpadhammā*, but is confirming that the objects of the other five senses, collectively the *rūpadhammā*, are collated by *manodhātu*.

In spite of the unclear and/or conflicting evidence, one might suggest that the most satisfactory way of understanding *manodhātu* in the *Sutta Piṭaka* is that it has both a unique function as a collator of incoming data and also can be described in terms of the sixth in a series of senses in that it is the sense corresponding to 'mental' objects. The translation of *manas* and *dhammā* as 'mind' and 'mental objects', however, is potentially misleading, not least because of the ambiguity and insufficiency of such English words in this context: they are neither precise nor indicative of the complexities of the Pali terms. These translations might also imply too developed a cognitive role for these two *āyatanas*. Though we have seen the crucial role of *manodhātu* as collator of all incoming data (*dhammā*), which is the raw material for the cognitive process, the fact remains that they are included in classifications of the senses, and not in the analysis of the individual in terms of the *pañcakkhandhā* which gives such comprehensive attention to mental activities. And though it is this unique combination of being a sense and also functioning so crucially in all cognition that justifies calling it a quasi sense, this nevertheless does not make it (according to the analysis as given) part of the mental processes as such. What one can say is that just as the other five senses each act as the door between their particular kind of object and the subjective experience of the individual, so *manodhātu* (whether or not it has a corresponding physical organ, gross or subtle), as collator, acts as the door between the objective world in its entirety (whether it be *rūpa* or *arūpa*) and the cognitive experience of the individual. *Sensus communis* is a suitable name for it only insofar as such a name is not understood as limiting it to incoming *sensory* data. The English word 'sensitivity' has connotations which go beyond the *mere* senses: it implies an intuitive dimension which perhaps corresponds to the role of the *manodhātu* at trans-sensory levels of experience. Overall, however, *manodhātu* can perhaps not be translated by any current English term.

The figurative understanding of the senses as doors suggests not just that they link the individual and the objective world but that they are also the link between the *rūpakkhandha* and the four *arūpakkhandhas*: not strictly the former nor the latter themselves, they nevertheless have their *rūpa* aspect (with the possible exception of *manodhātu*) and yet function as that by which all the activities of the *arūpakkhandhas* are sub-divided. That they are explicitly classified (if confusingly) in the *Abhidhamma* is perhaps unsurprising since the *Abhidhamma* is primarily concerned with classifying. The analysis of the human being into *khandhas* in the *Sutta Piṭaka*, on the other hand, is not intended to be a comprehensive classification. It describes the *rūpa* and *arūpa* aspects of the way an individual manifests which, when understood, illustrates the inappropriateness of thinking in terms of separate selfhood: not only is this clearly the didactic context in which they are frequently referred to in the texts, but we have seen from our examination of just one of the *khandhas* a manifest absence of any attempt to be descriptively comprehensive. The senses themselves are not included in *this* analysis because what is relevant about them is neither *rūpa* nor *arūpa*. But their necessary role in the functioning of the human being is perhaps why they are included in the *paṭiccasamuppāda* formula.

Notes

1. SN, Vol III.
2. SN.III.86: *Kiñca bhikkhave rūpaṃ vadetha? Ruppatīti kho bhikkhave tasmā rūpan ti vuccati. Kena ruppati, sītena pi ruppati uṇhena pi ruppati jighacchāya pi ruppati pipāsāya pi ruppati ḍaṃsa-makasa-vātātapa-siriṃsapa-samphassena pi ruppati. Ruppatīti kho bhikkhave tasmā rūpan ti vuccāti.*
3. Wayman (1984, p.619) discusses the use of the pun on *nāma* by Vasubandhu, Saṃghabhadra and Asaṅga. *Namana* literally means 'bending', and the point is that the four *arūpakkhandhas* (collectively taken to mean *nāma*, though this assumption is discussed in chapter VI) "go towards objects (*artha*) as though naming them, thus 'bending' toward them ... [and] because when the body disintegrates, these aggregates, so to say, bend toward another existence".
4. For example, MA.I.221; Vism p.528.
5. KS.III.73, n.1.
6. cf. Monier Williams' *Sanskrit English Dictionary*, p.884 and p.904.
7. KS.III.73, n.1. Karunadasa (1967, p.9f) discusses the use of *ruppati*.
8. For example, SN.III.59: *Katamañca bhikkhave rūpaṃ? Cattāro ca mahābhūtā catunnaṃ ca mahābhūtānam upādāya rūpaṃ idaṃ vuccati bhikkhave rūpaṃ.*
9. For example, MN.I.423, III.241. In the *Abhidhamma*, *ākāsadhātu* is considered to be part of the category of *upādā* ('secondary ' or 'derived') *rūpa* (for example, Dhs 638). As we shall see, *upādā rūpa* is systematised and classified in the *Abhidhamma* in a way which is completely absent from the four main *Nikāyas* of the *Sutta Piṭaka*.
10. MN.I.185ff, 421ff, III.240ff: *Paṭhavīdhātu* [*āpo-*, *tejo-*, *vāyu-*] *siyā ajjhattikā siyā bāhirā*. I mentioned in the Introduction the convention where *ajjhattaṃ* and *bahiddhā* are used to make a distinction between oneself and others. Here, this convention is not being used (save in the sense that what is external to oneself includes other people). In the *Paṭisambhidāmagga* of the *Khuddaka Nikāya*, there is a classification of what is 'internal' (*ajjhatta*) and 'external' (*bahiddhā*). Among other characteristics, they are defined as being 'produced by craving' (*taṇhāsambhūta*), suggesting they are *upādā* (see the discussion below). The senses and sense objects are the factors classified, but they are not specifically stated to be *rūpa* (Paṭis I.76–78).
11. cf. Harvey, 1991, p.3.
12. *Udāna* VIII.i: *Atthi bhikkhave tad āyatanaṃ, yattha n'eva paṭhavī na āpo na tejo na vāyo* ... . Pande (1983, p. 71f) discusses the lateness of the prose sections of the *Udāna* as, in effect, commenting on the earlier verses it contains. Our quotation is part of a prose section, maybe indicating that the question of the conditioned nature of the *cattāro mahābhūtā* needed to be clarified. The passage need not (and, in my opinion, should not) be interpreted ontologically: the four elements are a feature of *saṃsāric* perception, not of 'seeing things as they really are' (Nirvana). Nor does the term *āyatana*, often translated as 'sphere', necessarily have spacial implications: we shall see in the next section of this chapter that when used in connection with the senses it has no spacial meaning. In the context quoted here, 'condition' is meant in the sense of 'state', with no causative connotations.

13. cf. Dhs 877–80, where it states that some *no-upādā rūpa* does not result from karma. In chapter IV, we shall see that it is intention that conditions all five of the *khandhas* in future lives, including the body.
14. Asl p.305: *Tattha upādīyatī ti upādā. Mahābhūtāni gahetvā amuñcitvā tāni nissāya pavattantī ti attho.*
15. SA.III.276.
16. Dhs 594: *Cakkhāyatanaṃ, sotāyatanaṃ, ghāṇāyatanaṃ, jivhāyatanaṃ, kāyāyatanaṃ; rūpāyatanaṃ, saddāyatanaṃ, gandhāyatanaṃ, rasāyatanaṃ, phoṭṭhabbāyatanaṃ.*
17. *Vibhaṅga* p.70ff: *Catunnaṃ mahābhūtānaṃ upādāya.*
18. *Expositor*, Vol.II, chapter III, a translation of Asl p.305ff.
19. Dhs 596. cf. also Nyāṇatiloka, 1957, p.23. Karunadasa (1967, p.31) states that derived *rūpa* is not defined until the commentaries, overlooking the extensive *Abhidhamma* explanations.
20. Vism p.444. Buddhaghosa makes one exception from the *āyatanas*, tangible data (*phoṭṭhabbāyatana*). Ñāṇamoli, in his translation of the *Visuddhimagga* (1964, p.489, n.13), points out that in the *Paramattha-mañjūsā*, the *Visuddhimagga* Commentary, it is explained that the exception is because tangibles are included in primary *rūpa*.
21. cf., for example, Rahula, 1985, p.20f, and Ñānavīra Thera, 1987, p.98ff.
22. For example in the *paṭiccasamuppāda* formula, the *Chachakkasutta*, MN.III.280ff; the *Mahāsaḷāyatanikasutta* (MN.III.287ff) and the *Saḷāyatana Vagga* (SN, Vol. IV).
23. SN.II.3, *et freq.*
24. For example, the *Chachakkasutta* and the *Saḷāyatana Vagga*.
25. For example, *Vibhaṅga* 70ff.
26. Dhs 586: *Yan taṃ rūpaṃ ajjhattikaṃ, taṃ upādā, yan taṃ rūpaṃ bāhiraṃ, taṃ atthi upādā, atthi nopādā.*
27. Dhs 743 (I take it that this is referring back to Dhs 596).
28. Dhs 1045. cf. also Dhs 1208, 1418.
29. Dhs 744.
30. The use of the term *anidassa* with regard to the *āyatanas* at *Vibhaṅga* 70ff does not mean that the physical sense organs are not indicated, but that one cannot, in seeing the sense organs, actually see any more than their material constituents: it is their function as senses that is not visible. cf. Dhs 1087–90.
31. For example, SN.III.46, V.205; MN.I.180. Sometimes (for example at SN.III.46, V.205) these are fivefold, excluding *manas*, but at MN.I.180 *manas* is referred to as *manindriyaṃ*.
32. For example, in the *Dhātu Saṃyutta*, SN.II.140ff. The *Abhidhamma* systematises the *āyatanas*, *indriyas* and *dhātus*, and the senses are included in all three classifications. cf. Nyāṇatiloka, 1957, pp.27ff. These terms are discussed further in part 2 of this chapter.
33. Sn 170: *Katamaṃ taṃ upādānaṃ yattha loko vihaññati ... pañca kāmaguṇā loke manochaṭṭhā paveditā.*
34. For example, at SN.III.58f.
35. SN.III.47.
36. Ñānavīra, 1987, p.26. cf also Gethin's discussion of the term *upādānakkhandha* (1986, p.37ff).
37. MN.I.185f, 421f, III.240f.
38. MN.I.189.
39. MN.I.185: *Katamā c'āvuso ajjhattikā paṭhavīdhātu? Yaṃ ajjhattaṃ paccattaṃ kakkhaḷaṃ kharigataṃ upādiṇṇaṃ; seyyathīdaṃ kesā lomā nakhā dantā taco maṃsaṃ nahāru aṭṭhī aṭṭhimiñjā vakkaṃ hadayaṃ yakanaṃ kilomakaṃ pihakaṃ papphāsaṃ antaṃ antaguṇaṃ udariyaṃ karīsaṃ, yaṃ vā pan'aññam pi kiñci ajjhattaṃ paccattaṃ kakkhaḷaṃ kharigataṃ upādiṇṇaṃ, ayaṃ vuccat'āvuso ajjhattikā paṭhavīdhātu.*
40. *Katamā c'āvuso ajjhattikā āpodhātu? Yaṃ ajjhattaṃ paccattaṃ āpo āpogataṃ upādiṇṇaṃ; seyyathīdaṃ pittaṃ semhaṃ pubbo lohitaṃ sedo medo assu vasā kheḷo siṅghāṇikā lasikā muttaṃ, yaṃ vā pan' aññam pi kiñci ajjhattaṃ paccattaṃ āpo āpogataṃ upādiṇṇaṃ, ayaṃ vuccat' āvuso ajjhattikā āpodhātu.*
41. *Katamā ca ajjhattikā tejodhātu? Yaṃ ajjhattaṃ paccattaṃ tejo tejogataṃ upādiṇṇaṃ seyyathīdaṃ yena ca santappati yena ca jiriyati yena ca pariḍayhati yena ca asitapītakhāyitasāyitaṃ sammā pariṇāmaṃ gacchati, yaṃ vā pan' aññam pi kiñci ajjhattaṃ paccattaṃ tejo tejogataṃ upādiṇṇaṃ, ayaṃ vuccati ajjhattikā tejodhātu.*
42. I. B. Horner (trans.), MLS.I.4, n.9.
43. MN.I.296: *Yadā kho āvuso imaṃ kāyaṃ tayo dhammā jahanti: āyu usmā ca viññāṇaṃ, athāyaṃ kāyo ujjhito avakkhitto seti yathā kaṭṭhaṃ acetanan ti.* cf also SN.III.143; DN.II.335.
44. MN.I.295.
45. MN.I.296.
46. *Āyusaṃkhārā*: the context implies that all three factors are included in the plural (MN.I.295).

47. See chapter IV. cf also Reat, 1991, p.299f.
48. MN.I.188.
49. *Katamā ca ajjhattikā vāyodhātu? Yaṃ ajjhattaṃ paccattaṃ vāyo vāyogataṃ upādiṇṇaṃ; seyyathīdaṃ uddhaṅgamā vātā adhogamā vātā kucchisayā vātā koṭṭhasayā vātā aṅgamaṅgānusārino vātā assāso passāso, yaṃ vā pan' aññam pi kiñci ajjhattaṃ paccattaṃ vāyo vāyogataṃ upādiṇṇaṃ: ayaṃ vuccati ajjhattikā vāyodhātu.*
50. Bṛ. Up. 1.5.3, 3.9.26; Ch. Up. 3.13, 5.19–23. Ten breaths are mentioned but not listed at Bṛ. Up. 3.9.4. cf. also Reat, 1991, p.213ff.
51. The later Mt. Up. 2.6 describes the respective function of each breath in detail.
52. cf, for example, Bṛ. Up. 3.9.9, 4.1.3, 5.13.2, 6.1.1; Ch. Up. 3.15.4, 5.1.1.
53. Vism 350.
54. SN.IV.230; AN.II.87, III.131, V.110.
55. Pv. II.6 and PvA. 94. cf. also *Vibhaṅga* 84.
56. Reat (1991, p.214ff) traces and discusses the fifteen vital, perceptual and volitional faculties (each of the three consists of five faculties) in the *Upaniṣads*.
57. MN.I.423; III.241: *Katamā ca ajjhattikā ākāsadhātu? Yaṃ ajjhattaṃ paccattaṃ ākāsaṃ ākāsagataṃ upādiṇṇaṃ, seyyathīdaṃ: kaṇṇacchiddam nāsacchiddam mukhadvāraṃ, yena ca asitapītakhāyitasāyitaṃ ajjhoharati, yattha ca asitapītakhāyitasāyitaṃ santiṭṭhati, yena ca asitapītakhāyitasāyitaṃ adhobhāgā nikkhamati; yaṃ vā pan' aññam pi kiñci ajjhattaṃ paccattaṃ ākāsaṃ ākāsagataṃ upādiṇṇaṃ: ayaṃ vuccati bhikkhu ajjhattikā ākāsadhātu.*
58. For example, MN.I.352: *rūpasaññānaṃ samatikkama.*
59. MN.I.57; AN.III.323, V.109; DN.II.293; SN.V.278.
60. For example at MN.I.57: *Atthi imasmiṃ kāye kesā lomā nakhā dantā taco maṃsaṃ nahāru aṭṭhī aṭṭhimiñjā vakkaṃ hadayaṃ yakanaṃ kilomakaṃ pihakaṃ papphāsaṃ antaṃ antaguṇaṃ udariyaṃ karīsaṃ pittaṃ semhaṃ pubbo lohitaṃ sedo medo assu vasā kheḷo siṅghāṇikā lasikā muttan ti.*
61. The processes included vary, the *Satipaṭṭhāna Suttas* (MN.I.57; DN.II.293) being the most comprehensive.
62. *Puna ca paraṃ bhikkhave bhikkhu imam eva kāyaṃ yathāṭhitaṃ yathāpaṇihitaṃ dhātuso paccavekkhati: atthi imasmiṃ kāye paṭhavīdhātu āpodhātu tejodhātu vāyodhātūti.*
63. We shall see in chapter IV that there are exceptions to this. But such exceptions take place at such an advanced stage on the meditative/soteriological path that they do not compromise the importance of the senses in the cognitive process.
64. e.g. DN.I.245; MN.I.266; AN.III.411; SN.IV.225: at these references the *kāmaguṇā* are listed. There are other references to the term *pañca kāmaguṇā* which do not explicitly state what they are, for example AN.III.411; DN.II.271, III.131, 234. cf. Reat, 1990, p.227ff on the five classical sense faculties in the *Upaniṣads*.
65. Dhs 594ff.
66. *Nāmarūpa-paccayā saḷāyatanaṃ.*
67. MN.III.280ff.
68. MN.III.287ff.
69. SN, Vol. IV.
70. MN.III.239.
71. MN.I.180f, 266, 346.
72. SN.III.59ff.
73. *Chayime vedanākāyā: cakkhusamphassajā vedanā, sotasamphassajā vedanā, ghānasamphassajā vedanā, jivhāsamphassajā vedanā, kāyasamphassajā vedanā, manosamphassajā vedanā.*
74. *Chayime viññāṇakāyā: cakkhuviññāṇaṃ, sotaviññāṇaṃ, ghānaviññāṇaṃ, jivhāviññāṇaṃ, kāyaviññāṇaṃ manoviññāṇaṃ.*
75. So for the *saññākhandha* we read: *chayime saññākāyā: rūpasaññā, saddasaññā, gandhasaññā, rasasaññā, phoṭṭhabbasaññā, dhammasaññā*, and the *saṃkhārakkhandha* is described in the same way except that *cetanā* is substituted for *saññā* in the Pali.
76. For example, KS.III.52f.
77. For example, SN.II.3: *Katamañca bhikkhave saḷāyatanaṃ? Cakkhāyatanaṃ sotāyatanaṃ ghānāyatanaṃ jivhāyatanaṃ kāyāyatanaṃ manāyatanaṃ.*
78. PED, p.105.
79. Ibid., quoting from Aung, 1963.
80. When it is found in contexts where the *jhānas* are being described it is usually translated 'sphere'.

81. PED, p.105.
82. DA.I.124f.
83. PED, p.121.
84. PED makes this suggestion.
85. Gethin (1992, chapter 4) discusses in detail the complete list of twenty-two *indriyas*, first explicitly mentioned together in the *Vibhaṅga* but also found unsystematically scattered throughout the *Indriya Saṃyutta* (SN.V.13ff). The *Saṅgīti Suttanta* (DN.III.207ff) refers to eighteen *indriyas* at DN.III.219, 239.
86. SN.V.207: *Sukhindriyaṃ dukkhindriyaṃ somanassindriyaṃ domanassindriyaṃ upekhindriyaṃ.*
87. *Dhammā* as the object(s) corresponding to *manas* is discussed below.
88. SN.II.150: *ābhādhātu, subhadhātu.* Though such terms may have meditative levels as their primary reference, this does not invalidate the point I am making.
89. SN.II.153: *avijjādhātu.*
90. For example, DN.I.63, 70, 250; SN.II.218, IV.103, 117, 194. In the *Chāndogya Upaniṣad* (III.13), the heart is said to have five 'openings of the gods' (*deva-suṣaya*), corresponding to the five senses. They are the 'doorkeepers' of the 'world of heaven' (*svargasya lokasya dvāra-pā*). cf. Radhakrishnan, 1953, p.390. cf. also Cousins, 1981, which discusses the way a 'sense-door process' is developed in the *Abhidhamma.*
91. MN.I.180, 221; AN.II.16.
92. DN.I.70: *Kathaṃ bhikkhu indriyesu guttadvāro hoti ... idha bhikkhu cakkhunā rūpaṃ disvā na nimittaggāhī hoti nānuvyañjanaggāhī. Yatvādhikaraṇam enaṃ cakkhundriyaṃ asaṃvutaṃ viharantaṃ abhijjā-domanassā pāpakā akusalā dhammā anvāssaveyyuṃ tassa saṃvarāya paṭipajjati, rakkhati cakkhundriyam, cakkhundriye saṃvaraṃ āpajjati.*
93. Again, this triad is discussed in chapter IV.
94. J.I.276: *Kāyadvāraṃ vacīdvāraṃ manodvāran ti tīṇi dvārāni rakkha, mā kāyena pāpakammaṃ kari mā vācāya mā manasā.*
95. SN.IV.174: *Suñño gāmo ti kho bhikkhave channam ajjhattikānam adhivacanaṃ.* The term *āyatana* is not mentioned here, though from its presence in the next sentence quoted above one can infer it. In her translation of the *Dhammasaṅgaṇī* (in which this metaphor is referred to) Mrs Rhys Davids suggests that *āyatanānam* be included in this sentence (*A Buddhist Manual of Psychological Ethics*, p.160, n.2).
96. SN.IV.175: *Corā gāmaghātakā ti kho bhikkhave channaṃ bāhirānam āyatanānam adhivacanaṃ.*
97. Asl p.305ff.
98. *Vibhaṅga*, p.70ff: with the exception of *rūpa* as visible object.
99. Asl p.399f: *Cakkhu rūpaṃ na passati, acittakattā; cittaṃ na passati, acakkhukattā. Dvārārammaṇa-saṃghaṭṭanena pasādavatthukena cittena passati. Citta* seems to be used in a general sense of 'mind' or 'consciousness' here. This term is discussed in chapter V. In the *Abhidhamma* tradition the eye is sometimes referred to as *pasāda*. This is discussed below.
100. *The Expositor*, Vol II, p.408f, translating Asl p.312: *Etesu hi rūpābhighātārahabhūtappasādalakkhaṇaṃ daṭṭhukāma-tānidānakammasamuṭṭhānabhūtappasādalakkhaṇaṃ vā cakkhu rūpesu āviñjanarasaṃ cakkhuviññāṇassa ādhārabhāvapaccupaṭṭhānaṃ daṭṭhukāmatā-nidānakammajabhūtapadaṭṭhānaṃ. Saddābhighātārahabhūtappasādalakkhaṇaṃ sotukāmatānidānakammasamuṭṭhānabhūtappasādalakkhaṇaṃ vā sotaṃ saddesu āviñjanarasaṃ sotaviññāṇassa ādhārabhāvapaccupaṭṭhānaṃ sotukāmatānidāna-kammajabhūtapadaṭṭhānaṃ* (and the form is the same for the other three senses). Maung Tin's translation of *bhūtappasāda* as "sentience for phenomena" is questionable. It has been suggested to me by Mr. Lance Cousins that *bhūta* here is likely to mean *mahābhūta* and that *pasāda* has the technical meaning of a sensitive point of subtle *rūpa* within the eye itself. So this might read: "the eye has the characteristic of (having) a sensitive point and of (being comprised of) the four elements" (my translation).
101. Asl p.306. So of *cakkhu* it states: *Maṃsacakkhu pi sasambhāracakkhu pasādacakkhū ti duvidhaṃ hoti.*
102. In some contexts in the *Sutta Piṭaka*, *pasāda* also means mental composure or serenity. Gethin (1992, p.112ff) discusses the close relationship, in such contexts, between *pasāda* and *saddhā*, faith, in a psychology of 'confidence'.
103. Asl p.306: *Tesu buddhacakkhu samantacakkhu ñāṇacakkhu dibbacakkhu dhammacakkhū ti pañcavidhaṃ paññācakkhu.*
104. cf. Collins, 1987a, p.357.
105. This fact was first pointed out by Shwe Zan Aung in his *Compendium of Philosophy* (Aung, 1963, p.277ff.); cf. Nyāṇatiloka, 1980, p.73, and C. A. F. Rhys Davids, 1974, p.LXXXVIff and

1914, p.71, n. 1. Karunadasa, 1967, p.62–3 also discusses the fact that the identification of *hadayavatthu* with *manas* is a post-canonical development.

106. Dhs 6.
107. *Tikapaṭṭhāna*, Part I, p.4: *Yaṃ rūpaṃ nissāya manodhātu ca manoviññāṇadhātu ca vattanti, taṃ rūpaṃ manodhātuyā ca manoviññāṇadhātuyā ca taṃ sampayuttakānañ ca dhammānaṃ nissayapaccayena paccayo.*
108. Aung, 1963, p.278.
109. *Aṭṭhasālinī*, p.264: *Lakkhaṇādito pan' esā duvidhā pi manoviññāṇadhātu … hadayavatthupadaṭṭhānā ti veditabbā.*
110. Vism 447: *Manodhātu-manoviññāṇadhātūnaṃ nissayalakkhaṇaṃ hadayavatthu.* An important proviso has to be added here. Because of the addition of the suffixes *dhātu* and *viññāṇadhātu* in the commentarial tradition as a whole, precise comparisons between such terms and the *manas* of the *Sutta Piṭaka* are necessarily handicapped. Others have made detailed studies of the development of the terminologies (cf. for example, Cousins, 1981). My aim here is to draw out an overview in order to suggest a coherent general picture.
111. Vism 444.
112. Aung, 1963, p.278.
113. cf Karunadasa, 1967, p.62f: possible reasons for the failure to identify the physical location of the *manodhātu* are discussed.
114. PED gives extensive examples of both explicit and implicit associations of *citta* with the heart: pp.266ff. *Citta* is discussed further in chapter v.
115. SN.IV.95: *Yena lokasmiṃ lokasaññī hoti lokamānī.*
116. Ñānavīra, 1987, p.96.
117. Jayasuriya,1963, p.51.
118. Paṭis. I.6.
119. KhP p.2.
120. *Paramatthajotikā* I, p.60.
121. Ñāṇamoli (trans.), *Minor Readings*, introduction.
122. Vin.I.274.
123. Sn 199.
124. *Aṭṭhīnahārusaññutto tacamaṃsāvalepano chaviyā kāyo paṭicchanno yathābhūtaṃ na dissati, antapūro udarapūro yakapeḷassa vatthino hadayassa papphāsassa vakkassa pihakassa ca siṃghāṇikāya khelassa sedassa medassa ca lohitassa lasikāya pittassa ca vasāya ca … ath' assa susiraṃ sīsaṃ matthaluṅgassa pūritaṃ …* I have used Norman's translation (1992, p.21f).
125. Zysk (1991, p.143, n.54) is mistaken in giving this *Sutta Nipāta* reference for the standard list of parts of the body.
126. Nārada, in his translation of the *Dhātukathā* for the Pali Text Society (the *Discourse on Elements*), helpfully clarifies this in his tabulations of the complex contents of the *Dhātukathā*. Existence at levels of subtle *rūpa* is discussed below in the chapter on *manomaya*.
127. One passage suggests that *manas* as a sense and the mental processes as a whole were considered to be linked through the fact that the power of the mind at every level conditions our future lives. This is discussed in chapter vii, when the subject will be clearer to us.
128. SN.II.95: *Cittam iti pi mano iti pi viññāṇam iti pi.* This passage has been taken to mean that *citta, mano* and *viññāṇa* are being used synonymously. This need not be the case, and these terms will be discussed in further detail below.
129. cf., for example, Rahula, 1985, p.21; KS.III.52.
130. Carter discusses the term *dhamma* as religious teaching in his book *Dhamma: A Study of a Religious Concept* (1978).
131. cf. Nyāṇatiloka, 1980, p.115, and 1957, p.28.
132. SN.II.140ff.
133. SN.III.46: *Asmīti kho pana bhikkhave adhigate atha pañcannaṃ indriyānaṃ avakkanti hoti: cakkhundriyassa sotindriyassa ghānindriyassa jivhindriyassa kāyindriyassa. Avakkanti* literally means that the five senses 'descend', but the meaning here is figurative, and best conveyed by 'manifest'. Elsewhere *avakkanti* is used in the sense of 'descending into the mother's womb'. This is discussed in chapter v.
134. *Atthi bhikkhave mano atthi dhammā avijjādhātu.* The editor of this passage notes that *avijjādhātu* is only found in one manuscript, and that others read: *atthi bhikkhave mano atthi dhammā atthi vijjādhātu* (hence my inclusion of both ignorance and knowledge in the translation). The

translator for the PTS, F.L. Woodward, considers the reading *avijjādhātu* more appropriate to the context and translates accordingly (KS.III.41, n.2).

135. *Avijjāsamphassajena bhikkhave vedayitena phuṭṭhassa assutavato puthujjanassa asmīti pi'ssa hoti, ayam aham asmīti pi'ssa hoti, bhavissanti pi'ssa hoti, na bhavissanti pi'ssa hoti, rūpī bhavissanti pi'ssa hoti, arūpī bhavissanti pi'ssa hoti, saññī bhavissanti pi'ssa hoti, asaññī bhavissanti pi'ssa hoti, nevasaññī nāsaññī bhavissanti pi'ssa hoti.*
136. *Tiṭṭhanti kho pana bhikkhave tatth'eva pañcindriyāni. Ath'ettha sutavato ariyasāvakassa avijjā pahīyati vijjā uppajjati. Tassa avijjāvirāgā vijjuppādā asmīti pi'ssa na hoti, ayam aham asmīti pi'ssa na hoti, bhavissanti, na bhavissanti, rūpī, arūpī, saññī, asaññī, neva saññī nāsaññī bhavissanti pi'ssa na hotīti.*
137. MN.I.295; SN.V.218: *Pañc' imāni indriyāni nānāvisayāni nānāgocarāni … kim paṭisaraṇam, ko ca nesaṃ gocaravisayaṃ paccanubhoti?… Mano paṭisaraṇaṃ, mano ca nesaṃ gocaravisayaṃ paccanubhoti.*
138. It is used in this more literal sense at, for example, MN.III.9 and MN.I.310.
139. MLS.I.355. Mrs Rhys Davids discusses the translation in the introduction to her translation of the *Dhammasaṅgaṇī* (1974, p.LXXXVII).
140. C.A.F. Rhys Davids, 1914, p.68ff. cf also Reat, 1990, p.225f and p.243ff.
141. cf. Copleston, 1955, p.173f.
142. cf. also PED, p.520.
143. Aquinas gives the 'internal sense' the further function of being that by which we know that we *see* a visible object rather than hear it; that we *hear* a sound rather than feel it, and so on. Reat (1990, p.225f and p.243ff) discusses the meaning of *manas* in the *Upaniṣads*, where it has many meanings ranging from *sensus communis* right up to "the supreme faculty of the soul, capable of apprehending ultimate truth". Reat also discusses the role of *manas* in the pre-*Upaniṣadic Vedas* (p.107ff), where it is most commonly stated to be the locus of emotions or the repository of the individual's character traits. One such epithet is *nṛmanas*: 'herominded'. Zaehner (1969, p.156) compares the Buddhist understanding of *manas* as *sensus communis* with *manas* in the *Bhagavad Gītā*, where it sometimes is the controller of the senses (3.7; 6.24) and sometimes has to be controlled (2.60, 67). In the well-known parable of the chariot in the *Kaṭhopaniṣad*, *buddhi* is the charioteer, *manas* is the reins and the senses are the horses: so there *manas* is perhaps neither controller nor controlled but an implement of control.
144. C. A. F. Rhys Davids, 1914, p.70.
145. PED, p.520.
146. In the chapter which describes the evolutes of *prakṛti*, the *Sāṃkhya Sūtras* state that *manas* is the principal (*pradhāna*) evolute "because it is the receptacle of all *saṃskāras*": *Tathā 'śeṣasaṃskārādhāratvāt* (*Sāṃkhya Sūtras*, II.42).
147. Geiger, 1920, p. 80–2.
148. KS.III.41.
149. Carter, 1978, p.2. cf also p.61f.
150. DN.I.70.
151. In the *Chāndogya Upaniṣad* (III.2) nose, speech, tongue, eye, ear, mind, hands, and skin are said to be the eight 'graspers' (*grahāḥ*: lit. 'graspings') (Radhakrishnan translates this as 'perceivers' – 1953, p.215). But it is their objects (*atigrahā*) which do the grasping: *jihvā* (for example) *vai grahaḥ, sa rasenātigrāheṇa gṛhīta*… The notion of grasper and grasped might be a figurative indication that the functioning of the senses requires the coming together of sense and object; or it might more generally be a metaphor for the relationship between subjective experience and the objective world. This notion was developed in later Buddhist systematic philosophy.
152. MN.I.60; DN.II.301: *Puna ca paraṃ bhikkhave bhikkhu dhammesu dhammānupassī viharati.*
153. Nyāṇatiloka,1980, p.42.
154. In common with the other senses, in order to function *manodhātu* is 'activated' by *viññāṇa*, hence *manoviññāṇa*.
155. MN.I.293: *Nissaṭṭhena h'āvuso pañcahi indriyehi parisuddhena manoviññāṇena kiṃ neyyan ti?*
156. MN.I.352: … *sabbaso rūpasaññānaṃ samatikkamā paṭighasaññānaṃ atthagamā nānattasaññānaṃ amanasikārā.* (In translating, I have paraphrased slightly in order to draw out the meaning.)
157. *Vibhaṅga* p.76: *Dasāyatanā lokiyā; dvāyatanā siyā lokiyā siyā lokuttarā.* This comes in a chapter where *manas* and *dhammā* are always referred to as the eleventh and twelfth of the *āyatanas*.
158. The psycho-cosmological spheres are discussed in chapter VII.
159. MN.I.111f.

160. *Manañ c'āvuso paṭicca dhamme ca uppajjati manoviññāṇaṃ, tiṇṇaṃ saṅgati phasso, phassapaccayā vedanā, yaṃ vedeti taṃ sañjānāti... Cakkhuñ c'āvuso paṭicca rūpe ca uppajjati cakkhuviññāṇaṃ, tiṇṇaṃ saṅgati phasso, phassapaccayā vedanā, yaṃ vedeti taṃ sañjānāti...*
161. MA.II.77: *Sotañc'āvuso ti ādisu pi es' eva nayo.*
162. For example at MN.III.280ff, 287ff.
163. The *Mahāsaḷāyatanikasutta* (MN.III.287ff); the *Chachakkasutta* (MN.III.280ff); and much of the *Saḷāyatana Saṃyutta* (SN, Vol. IV).
164. Rahula, 1985, p.23.
165. Ñānavīra Thera, 1987, p.94ff.
166. cf, for example, Rahula, 1985, p.23; KS.IV.56 and *passim; Further Dialogues*, Vol II, p.315ff.
167. Asl 74: *Rūpārammaṇaṃ hi javanaṃ cakkhudvāre pi uppajjati manodvāre pi; saddādiārammaṇesu pi es'eva nayo.* Elsewhere in the same book (Asl 264) we read the following: *Lakkhaṇādito ... manoviññāṇadhātu ... haḷārammaṇavijānana-lakkhaṇā-santīraṇādirasā...* From the context and meaning of this passage it appears possible that *manoviññāṇadhātu* is the equivalent of *manodhātu* in the *Sutta Piṭaka.* Here the characteristics of *manoviññāṇadhātu* are said to be knowing the six sense objects and having the property of investigating them. cf. Cousins, 1981, where the development and meaning of the technical *Abhidhamma* and commentarial terminologies are discussed.
168. Karunadasa, 1967, p.63. Similarly, Karunadasa's use of the term *manoviññāṇa* appears to refer to the same thing.

CHAPTER II

The Vedanākhandha

Introduction to the *arūpakkhandhas*

THE FOUR *KHANDHAS* OTHER THAN the *rūpakkhandha* are collectively called *arūpa* in the Pali texts. They are sometimes referred to in scholarly works and translations as the 'mental' *khandhas*, in the sense of being opposed to the corporeal (*rūpa*) *khandha*. We have seen in the discussion of the *rūpakkhandha*, however, that the term *rūpa* is not limited to corporeality. Defining the *arūpakkhandhas* as 'mental' in this polar sense should therefore be done with caution. And just as the composition of the *rūpakkhandha* was not described in terms of substance, so one should not anticipate that the *arūpakkhandhas* comprise some sort of mental entity. In describing the four elements which comprise *rūpa*, I stated that they represented the occurrence of certain states or processes which are characterised by solidity (or extension), fluidity, heat and motion. The *arūpakkhandhas* might be similarly interpreted as the occurrence of certain states or processes that are not characterised according to the four elements. In Buddhism this distinction does not imply the ontological dualism posited by Descartes' well-known polarisation of consciousness (which is unextended) and matter (whose primary property is extension). Rather, one might suggest that it implies that the states or processes occur at different levels on a spectrum of density. Those which are designated by the term *rūpa* occur at levels on the spectrum which are characterised by the four great elements. Though the most dense of these is solid, that they include heat and motion illustrates that their range is considerable. Those states or processes which are designated by the term *arūpa* occur at levels on the spectrum which do not have any of the characteristics associated with *rūpa*. The significance of this spectrum is discussed in chapter VII. The four *arūpakkhandhas* are *vedanā, saññā, saṃkhāra* and *viññāṇa*.

The Vedanākhandha

Vedanā is usually translated as feeling or sensation. We read in the *Khandha Saṃyutta* that there are six kinds of feeling.[1] Literally, the Pali states that they are feeling which arises through contact of eye, feeling which arises through contact of ear, through contact of nose, through contact of tongue, through contact of body, through contact of mind (*manas*). I have already suggested in chapter I that in such contexts the terms used to refer to the senses, *cakkhu*, *sota*, *ghāna* and so on, mean the faculties of vision, hearing, taste, etc. rather than the physical organs of eye, ear and tongue. This passage, therefore, is better translated as stating that the different types of feeling arise from visual contact, auditory contact, gustatory contact, olfactory contact, tactile contact and 'mental' contact.

In the *Madhupiṇḍikasutta* of the *Majjhima Nikāya*, the arising of feeling is stated to be dependent on the presence of several factors: consciousness, at least one of the organs of sense, and contact between the organ and its corresponding external object of sense. The feeling is subsequently apperceived (or identified).[2] The *Sutta* describes the arising of feelings according to each of the senses, the process being the same in each case. So of visual feeling, for example, we read as follows:

> Visual awareness arises because of eye and [visible] forms; contact [is the] combination of the three; feelings are caused by the contact; that which one feels, one apperceives (or identifies)...[3]

This passage makes more sense of the sixfold definition of feeling referred to above as we now see that (visual) contact is defined as the combination of consciousness, eye and visible form. Thus contact is more than the *mere* contact of eye and visible form: it is the *conscious* coming together of sense organ and corresponding object. In other words, it is a conscious sensory event. This passage also makes clear that visual awareness (also often called 'eye consciousness') (*cakkhuviññāṇa*) is a prerequisite for the whole process of the arising of the feeling: if there can be no visual contact without the presence, or activation, of *cakkhuviññāṇa*, then without it there can be no feeling.

There are many different descriptions of the types of *vedanā*. By far the most commonly referred to are the three types covered by the term *tisso vedanā*: agreeable, disagreeable and neutral.[4] It is this analysis which stands first in the *Vedanā Saṃyutta*.[5] It is also stated that *vedanā* which is agreeable, disagreeable and neutral is experienced (*vedayitaṃ*) either bodily or mentally,[6] making six types of feeling in all.[7] And in the *Satipaṭṭhāna Sutta* it states that agreeable, disagreeable and neutral feelings can be experienced with regard to material (*sāmisa*) or non-material (*nirāmisa*) things.[8] These last two sentences have been interpreted as meaning that feelings have both a physical and a mental aspect.[9] In my view, however, it seems more likely that the first refers to the fact that feelings that have a tactile origin are experienced bodily (*kāya* is the object corresponding to the sense of touch) and feelings that have a non-tactile origin are experienced mentally: so, for example, the agreeable feelings we experience as a result of hearing or seeing something nice are not in this sense 'bodily' feelings. In the *Dīgha Nikāya* it states that bodily pain is produced through bodily contact; grief is an example of mental pain, which arises through mental contact (*manosamphassajaṃ*).[10] As *manas* appears to be understood in this context as meaning the 'mental' sense, and grief does not obviously arise from eye, ear, nose or tongue, this passage does not explicitly support my suggestion that the bodily/mental analysis differentiates between *kāya* as the tactile sense object and all other sense objects. But it does support the point I am making, which is that this analysis refers to different types of feeling and does not mean that all feelings have both physical and mental aspects. With regard to the second sentence, *sāmisa* and *nirāmisa* are used to make a distinction between the experience of feelings which arise from the *rūpakkhandha*, which means from sensory contact, and the experience of feelings which arise from levels of meditation. This is explained in the *Vedanā Saṃyutta*, where feelings are stated to be of three kinds, delightful (*pīti*) agreeable (*sukha*) and neutral (*upekhā*). *Sāmisa* refers to the five *kāmaguṇā*.[11] *Nirāmisā(aṃ) pīti/sukhaṃ/upekhā*, however, is experienced in levels of meditation (*jhāna*).[12] Elsewhere *āmisa* is put in opposition to *dhamma*, with a similar contrast in meaning.[13] We are told that a feeling is pleasant or unpleasant depending on whether pleasure or pain is the dominant feature of the feeling.[14]

Many different classifications of feelings are given in the *Vedanā Saṃyutta*. It starts by stating that feelings are of two kinds (bodily and mental), or three kinds (agreeable, disagreeable and neutral). It continues with five, six, eighteen, thirty-six and one hundred and eight kinds. The five kinds are the moods (*indriya*) of pleasure, pain, joy, grief and indifference.[15] The six kinds are those which arise from contact with each of the six senses. The eighteen kinds are the six ways (presumably according to the senses) of paying attention to (*upavicāra*) joy, grief and indifference respectively.[16] The thirty-six feelings comprise a more complex analysis of feeling in that it relates the six forms of joy, grief and indifference (that is, each of them experienced according to the six senses) with the worldly life and with the renunciatory life in turn.[17] According to the analysis into one hundred and eight feelings, the thirty-six feelings can be classified as past, present or future.[18]

The analysis that pleasant, unpleasant and neutral feelings can be experienced as worldly (*gehasita*) or as renunciatory (*nekkhammasita*) is also given in the *Majjhima Nikāya*.[19] The distinctions 'worldly' and 'renunciatory' apply to the manner in which the feelings arise: whether they arise from the perception of material things, or whether they arise from the discernment of the transitory nature of things seen. This reflects the distinction made throughout the Pali canon between the ordinary (ignorant) man, the *puthujjana*, and the advanced disciple of the Buddha's teaching, the *ariyasāvaka*. The well-taught *ariyasāvaka* knows, for example, that there is a refuge from disagreeable feeling other than happiness through sense pleasures.[20] He or she would, presumably, experience feelings as renunciatory. This is also described as having feelings but being detached from them.[21]

In one text a lay person, Pañcakaṅga, expresses his doubts about neutral feeling and insists that there are only two kinds of feeling, agreeable and disagreeable. He repeatedly refuses to accept the venerable Udāyi's teaching that there are three kinds of feeling, including neutral. Eventually the Buddha pronounces that different people explain *vedanā* in different ways, and that they are all correct. According to some explanations there are only two, but it is also correct to say that there are three, five, six, eighteen, thirty-six and one hundred and eight kinds of feeling.[22] The Buddha goes on to make the point that inevitably some people will quarrel about how many kinds of feelings there are, but that such quarrelsomeness is futile and harmful. It is far better to accept that people can understand the matter differently and to dwell in harmony with the different opinion.

Vedanā is sometimes translated as 'sensation' rather than 'feeling', and it could be argued that 'sensation' is a word which is more readily associated with neutrality than is 'feeling', which is more often associated in our minds with pleasure or pain. The word 'sensation' also implies a connection with the senses, which might be said to be more appropriate to *vedanā*, which requires the coming together of a sense organ and its corresponding sense object in order to arise. But 'feeling' *can* be used neutrally: it is not uncommon to say 'I feel indifferent about that'. And not only is it commonly accepted that feelings require sensory activity, even if this is not obviously implicit in the word itself, but in the Buddha's analysis of the *khandhas* this does not only apply to the *vedanākhandha* but to all four of the *arūpakkhandhas*. The main reason I prefer the use of the word 'feeling' rather than 'sensation' in translating *vedanā* is, however, because I suggest that *vedanā* has a cognitive dimension which is conveyed by the word 'feeling' but not by 'sensation'. The word *vedanā* comes from √*vid*, which has a twofold meaning involving both knowledge and (mere) feelings: intellectually it means to know and experientially it means to feel. In *vedanā* both of these meanings are relevant. Though itself referring only to potential cognitive processes, the wording of the twelvefold *paṭiccasamuppāda* formula suggests that the purely sensory event takes place when 'contact' occurs. The Pali word for this contact is *phassa*, and it is from *phassa* that *vedanā* then arises, which in turn subsequently gives rise to craving (*taṇhā*). From this we see that *vedanā* is more than the (mere) sensory event: it is one stage further on in the process. We have also seen above that feelings are intrinsically pleasant, unpleasant or neutral. This also implies that at the level of the feeling itself there is a degree of discrimination or cognition sufficient for its classification in one of these three ways. A further point arises from the description given above of the arising of feeling, which is that it illustrates that it is part of a process involving both *saññā* and *viññāṇa*. We shall see below in the chapters on these two *khandhas* that both of these are part of the cognitive process. But the *saṃkhārakkhandha* is not involved. Again as we shall see below (in chapter IV), this is where the emotions Westerners associate with feelings come from.[23]

The cognitive role of *vedanā* is unsubtle: one might say that it is affective rather than intellectual cognition. It is nevertheless significant enough to be an important factor in understanding the role of the *vedanākhandha* correctly. From a psychological point of view, it is not too difficult for us to understand that *vedanā* is part of the cognitive process. We know, for example, that feelings can be expressed cognitively: if we say we are feeling sad, we also mean that we *know* that we are experiencing sadness. We also commonly refer to feelings as a vague level of knowledge in expressions such as 'I have the feeling that this is correct', or 'I feel there is something wrong here'. Thus *vedanā* plays a part, however nebulous, in the cognitive process of an individual. It is perhaps significant that *vedayita*, the (irregular) past passive participle of the verb *vedeti*, from which *vedanā* comes, is often interpreted as meaning 'experienced' rather than 'felt'. And 'experience' might be a better translation of *vedanā* when it is found in the context of the cognitive process as a whole: in English to state that cognition necessarily involves experience is more readily acceptable than stating that it necessarily involves feelings. I will return to the question of the cognitive role of *vedanā* in the chapter on the *viññāṇakkhandha*, when we will have more information available to us.

What the discussion here has shown is that though different types of feelings are referred to, descriptions of what feelings are emphasise the way they arise. The concern is not with understanding what a feeling is *per se*, but in seeing that feelings arise as part of a process.

I have pointed out above that according to the twelvefold version of the *paṭiccasamuppāda* formula, feeling (*vedanā*) has contact (*phassa*) as its condition and that feeling itself is therefore more than *mere* sensory event. And in the description of the arising of feeling to which I have referred it is also from *phassa* that feeling is stated to arise. Indeed, in the *Phassamūlaka Sutta* in the *Vedanā Saṃyutta* the dependence of *vedanā* on *phassa* is stressed: the three feelings (agreeable, disagreeable and neutral) are born of contact, rooted in contact, caused by contact, conditioned by contact.[24] Before going on to discuss the *saññākhandha*, therefore, it would seem appropriate to investigate the role of *phassa* in more detail.

Phassa

In the *Majjhima Nikāya* passage which describes the arising of, say, visual feeling (and the form of the Pali is the same for all six senses), *phassa* is said to be the combination of three things: eye, (visible) object and consciousness.[25] This is what I have suggested should be understood as the conscious (visual) sensory event. And it is from this conscious sensory event that feeling arises.[26] Elsewhere the way in which *phassa* gives rise to agreeable, disagreeable or neutral feeling is described by means of analogy. So of agreeable feeling we read that just as when two sticks come into contact together (i.e. when there is friction between them), warmth and heat are produced, but when the two sticks are separated and kept apart, the warmth and heat dissipate and are no longer produced, in just this way agreeable feelings arise because of the appropriate *phassa* and do not arise when the appropriate *phassa* ceases.[27] There is no suggestion in the text that this description refers exclusively to bodily (tactile) feelings, and the reference to contact as tactile has to be understood as meaning the coming together of any of the senses and a corresponding object. This point is stressed by the commentator on the *Brahmajāla Sutta* who states that sense and object are not to be thought of as literally touching one another: rather, *phassa* is what occurs when there is the appropriate coming together of the two (and *viññāṇa*).[28] A further point about the analogy of the sticks is that it raises the possibility that *phassa* itself is agreeable, disagreeable or indifferent. That appropriate feelings arise from appropriate contact suggests that, say, the agreeableness of the feeling is determined at the *phassa* stage of the process of the arising of the feeling.

As we shall see in chapter III, the passage from which I have quoted a description of the arising of feeling states that as the process continues apperception and identification of the experience in question take place. I have also suggested, partly in the light of this passage but also in the light of others (which are discussed fully in chapter V) that *vedanā* is not to be understood as *mere* feeling but that it is part of the cognitive process as a whole. It follows from this suggestion that *phassa* is also a *sine qua non* of the cognitive process as a whole. That this is the case is explicitly supported by some canonical passages in which *phassa* is found. In the *Brahmajāla Sutta*, in which the Buddha systematically refutes a wide variety of views held by Brahmans and ascetics, *phassa* is stated to be involved in each and every one of the views referred to.[29] Without *phassa*, the *Sutta* states, none of those views would be held.[30] All of the views arise because of continual contact in the six spheres of contact.[31] And in the *Saṃyutta Nikāya* we read that (visual) contact is defined as the meeting, coincidence, coming together of eye, visible object and consciousness.[32] Later the passage states: "Contacted one feels, contacted one thinks, and contacted one apperceives".[33] In a description of the five *khandhas* in the *Khandha Saṃyutta* of the *Saṃyutta Nikāya* we read that it is from the arising of *phassa* that *vedanā*, *saññā* and *saṃkhāra* arise, and from its cessation that they cease.[34] In the same passage, *rūpa* is said to arise and cease according to the arising and cessation of food (*āhāra*), and *viññāṇa* arises and ceases according to the arising and cessation of *nāmarūpa*. These differences are unsurprising if one remembers that the classification into *khandhas* is an analysis rather than a prescription for the arising of the human being. What is meant, therefore, is that the body is dependent for its functioning on food; and *vedanā*, *saññā* and *saṃkhārā* are dependent for their functioning on *phassa* (which the passage has defined as the conscious sensory event). *Viññāṇa* is not dependent on *phassa* since *phassa* involves *viññāṇa*. It is, rather, dependent on *nāmarūpa*. *Nāmarūpa* is discussed in chapter VI, when it will become clearer in what sense *viññāṇa* might be said to be dependent on it.

It appears from what we have seen thus far that it is reasonable to describe *phassa*, which is defined as the contact which takes place when *viññāṇa*, sense organ and sense object come together, as a conscious sensory event, as I have suggested. But in the *Cūḷavedalla Sutta*, we find *phassa* used in a context where this definition and understanding of *phassa* do not seem quite appropriate.[35] The nun Dhammadinnā is asked by Visākha how many contacts impinge (*phusanti*: literally 'contact' or 'touch') on a *bhikkhu* when he has emerged from the meditation which involves the stopping of apperception and feeling.[36] Dhammadinnā replies that when a *bhikkhu* emerges from the attainment of the cessation of apperception and feeling three contacts impinge on him: the contact as void, the contact that is signless (i.e. without any object), and the contact that is undirected (i.e. free from all longings).[37] Here *phassa* seems to mean something like 'impression': when a *bhikkhu* emerges from the (highest) meditative level, *saññāvedayitanirodhasamāpatti*, he is conscious of the impression of voidness, signlessness and freedom from longing. These have not arisen as a result of the coming together of *viññāṇa*, sense organ and sense object because the *bhikkhu's* meditative state was one which transcended such activity.[38] But when he emerges from this state and sensory experience returns, he has an impression of his non-sensory experience. One might say that the impression occurs when his non-sensory experience comes in contact with sensory experience. Such impressions are distinct from, perhaps less 'defined' than, the conceptions which are associated with the *saññākhandha*, discussed in chapter III. The contrast appears to be between conscious discursive thought, from which conceptions arise, and meditative experience (which is non-discursive), from which impressions arise.

In an unusual passage in the *Mahāniddesa*, a book of the *Khuddaka Nikāya*, the significance of the impressions of voidness, signlessness and freedom from longing (*suññato phasso*, *animitto phasso*, and *appaṇihito phasso*) becomes clear. The passage gives a commentary on the term 'a seer of discrimination in respect of contacts' (*vivekadassī phassesu*). First, a comprehensive list of different types of *phassa* is given which is not found elsewhere. This first of all includes contact relating to the six senses, then goes on to include verbal and sensory contact, contact from agreeable, disagreeable and indifferent feeling; good, bad and indifferent contact; contact of the sensory, form and formless realms; void, signless and desireless contact; mundane and supramundane contact; past, future and present contact.[39] The passage goes on to state that the *vivekadassī* regards all such contacts except for *suññato phasso, animitto phasso*, and *appaṇihito phasso* as free from self, from what belongs to a self, from what is permanent, stable, unchanging.[40] *Suññato phasso, appaṇihito phasso* and *lokuttaro phasso* are not explicitly referred to, but the passage then states that whatever contacts are noble, rid of the *āsavas*, supramundane, connected with the void, are seen as free from passion, ill-will, ignorance and so on.[41] Because *suññato, appaṇihito* and *lokuttaro phasso* are not stated to be free from a self, Pérez-Remón draws on this passage to support his thesis that early Buddhism posits a non-empirical Self.[42] In fact all this passage seems to be stating is that there are some kinds of *phassa* which are associated with those things which are commonly mistaken for a permanent self, but which the *vivekadassī* comes to realise are not associated with such a self, and other kinds of *phassa* which are conducive to liberating insight, where such a sense of self is not relevant.

Elsewhere, two of the types of contact listed in the *Mahāniddesa* referred to in the last paragraph, are referred to in a way which suggests that they represent an understanding that *phassa* is of two distinct kinds, not including the meditative impressions mentioned above. These are *adhivacanasamphassa* and *paṭighasamphassa*. In the *Mahānidāna Suttanta* of the *Dīgha Nikāya*, for example, these terms are used to describe the way in which *nāmarūpa* gives rise to *phassa* in a ninefold version of the *paṭiccasamuppāda* formula which excludes the *saḷāyatanā* link.[43] *Nāmarūpa* is discussed more fully in chapter VI. In the *Vibhaṅga* (of the *Abhidhamma Piṭaka*), *paṭighasamphassa* and *adhivacanasamphassa* refer to *saññā*,[44] and this context will also be referred to below in chapter III. In both of these two contexts, however, *paṭighasamphassa* refers to *phassa* in the sense of sensory contact, and *adhivacanasamphassa* refers to *phassa* which is verbal or conceptual, that is abstract. Neither of these two contexts refers to the non-sensory *jhānas*: it follows from what we have seen in the *Mahāniddesa* passage that the *lokuttara* types of *phassa* transcend conceptualisation. They indicate that the range of 'ordinary' (i.e. non-*lokuttara*) *phassa* includes two kinds: sensory contact in the *literal* sense (*paṭigha* means 'striking against' and refers to the 'meeting' of sense organ and sense object) or sensory contact in the abstract sense (a good translation of *adhivacanasamphassa* would be 'metaphorical contact'). This distinction probably corresponds in the first instance to the contrast between the first five senses and the *manodhātu* as the 'standard' sixth sense: the latter functioning abstractly by comparison with the others; and also to the two aspects of the *saññākhandha* discussed fully in chapter III. There, on the one hand, the literal sense of sensory contact corresponds to apperception, and, on the other hand, its abstract sense to conception.

It also seems clear that *phassa* is a conscious event, whether sensory or metaphorical contact, or meditative impression. It is defined as the coincidence of *viññāṇa*, sense and sense object. And as abstract impression on emerging from *jhāna*, it is experienced when consciousness is once again 'normal'. It is thus clear that the English word 'contact', which tends to have a tactile or spacial connotation, is insufficient on its own to convey the full meaning of *phassa*. Rather, the meanings of *phassa* which we have discussed suggest that it refers to the moment of contact between the subjective world of the individual and the objective world with which he or she interacts. This explains why consciousness is included in the definition of *phassa*, for the individual is not interacting with the world if he or she is not conscious, and why the consciousness of the event is of more significance than the (mere) contact. In the Buddha's teaching it is what happens subjectively that matters.

Writing as a modern Theravāda *bhikkhu*, Ñānavīra suggests that if one understands that *phassa* is primarily contact between subject and object, rather than contact between eye, forms and eye consciousness, then it is possible to see that such contact implies the presence of the illusion of 'I' and 'mine'. Thus for an *arahant*, when there is cessation of such illusion, there is also *phassanirodha*.[45] He refers to a verse in the *Udāna*, which states: "Contacts impinge dependent on ground; how should contacts impinge on a groundless one?".[46] His point is that eye as sense organ is a sense organ in *puthujjana* and *arahant* alike, and is a mere physiological aspect of the human being. Eye consciousness as a subjective aspect of the human being, on the other hand, is part of that human being's psychological constitution and is affected by his or her degree of insight on the path to liberation. *Phassa* as a practical function continues for an *arahant*, when cognitive faculties still function on the basis of eye, visible forms and eye consciousness. But it must no longer be regarded as contact with *me*, or with *him*, or with *some*body, Ñānavīra states. He refers to the *Saḷāyatana Sutta*, where it states that the Blessed One possesses an eye (and all the other sense organs), he sees visible forms with the eye; but he has no desire and lust, and his *citta* is wholly freed.[47] Having no desire and lust is a concomitant of no longer having false notions of 'I' and 'mine' according to Buddhist teachings. According to Ñānavīra, then, the subjective aspect of *phassa* implies the involvement of some illusory sense of 'I' in relation to the objective world. This is borne out by the role of *phassa* in the continued *saṃsāric* existence of an individual, the continuity of which will cease after *arahant*ship is attained.

A final point is that the verb from which *phassa* comes, *phusati*, is also used in contexts where its meaning is perhaps an extension of the meanings contact and impinge. The expression *ceto-samādhiṃ phusati*, for example, means "[the *bhikkhu*] attains a state of concentration of the mind".[48] *Nirodhaṃ phusati* means "he attains cessation".[49]

Phassa, then, is of two kinds and is found in two corresponding contexts. Most commonly it refers to the conscious sensory or metaphorical contact which is a *sine qua non* for the arising of feelings and for the cognitive process as a whole. It also refers to an abstract impression which is also conscious but which does not originate from the coming together of a sense and its corresponding sense object.

Notes

1. SN.III.59f: *Katamā ca bhikkhave vedanā? Chayime bhikkhave vedanākāyā ... cakkhusamphassajā vedanā, sotasamphassajā vedanā, ghānasamphassajā, jivhāsamphassajā, kāyasamphassajā, manosamphassajā vedanā.*
2. MN.I.111. Apperception is the function of the *saññākhandha*, the subject of chapter III.
3. *Cakkhuñ-c'āvuso paṭicca rūpe ca uppajjati cakkhuviññāṇaṃ, tiṇṇaṃ saṅgati phasso, phassapaccayā vedanā, yaṃ vedeti taṃ sañjānāti...* .
4. e.g. DN.III.275; SN.II.53, 82, IV.204, 207, etc; AN.III.400: *Sukhā vedanā dukkhā vedanā adukkhamasukhā vedanā.*
5. SN.IV.204.
6. *Kāyikaṃ vā cetasikaṃ vā.*
7. MN.I.302; SN.IV.208, etc. However, the *Abhidhamma* classifications note only five types of feeling: bodily agreeable and disagreeable, mentally agreeable and disagreeable and neutral. cf., for example, *Vibhaṅga* 72 and Dhs 133.
8. MN.I.59.
9. This is suggested by Reat, 1987, p.23.
10. DN.II.306: *Kāyikaṃ dukkhaṃ ... kāyasamphassajaṃ ... domanassaṃ ... cetasikaṃ dukkhaṃ ... manosamphassajaṃ.*
11. SN.IV.236: *Katamañca bhikkhave sāmisā(aṃ) pīti/sukhaṃ/upekhā? Pañc'ime bhikkhave kāmaguṇā.*
12. The *Sutta* states: *Idha bhikkhave bhikkhu ... pathamaṃ jhānam ... dutiyaṃ jhānam ... tatiyaṃ jhānaṃ upasampajja viharati; idaṃ vuccati bhikkhave nirāmisaṃ sukhaṃ.*
13. cf., for example, MN.I.12.
14. MN.I.303: *Sukhā kho āvuso vedanā ṭhitisukhā vipariṇāmadukkhā, dukkhā vedanā ṭhitidukkhā vipariṇāmasukhā.*
15. SN.IV.232: *Katamā ca bhikkhave pañca vedanā? Sukhindriyaṃ dukkhindriyaṃ somanassindriyaṃ domanassindriyam upekkhindriyaṃ imā vuccanti bhikkhave pañca vedanā.*
16. *Cha somanassupavicārā cha domanassupavicārā cha upekkhupavicārā; imā vuccanti bhikkhave aṭṭhārasa vedanā.*
17. *Cha gehasitāni somanassāni/domanassāni/upekkhā cha nekkhammasitāni somanassāni/domanassāni/upekkhā.*
18. *Atītā chattiṃsa vedanā, anāgatā chattiṃsa vedanā, paccuppannā chattiṃsa vedanā; imā vuccanti bhikkhave aṭṭhasata vedanā.*
19. MN.III.216ff.
20. SN.IV.209: *Pajānāti bhikkhave sutavā ariyasāvako aññatra kāmasukhā dukkhāya vedanāya nissaraṇaṃ.*
21. SN.IV.213: *So sukhaṃ/dukkhaṃ/adukkhamasukhaṃ ce vedanaṃ vediyati visaññutto naṃ vediyati.*
22. SN.IV.223f.
23. In a description of the *vedanākhandha*, Pio (1988, p.9f) gives a long account of different emotions. In my opinion, she has fallen into the trap of projecting a Western interpretation of feelings onto the *vedanākhandha.*
24. SN.IV.215: *Tisso imā bhikkhave vedanā phassajā phassamūlakā phassanidānā phassapaccayā.*
25. MN.I.111: *Cakkhuñ c'āvuso paṭicca rūpe ca uppajjati cakkhuviññāṇaṃ, tiṇṇaṃ saṅgati phasso.*
26. *Phassapaccayā vedanā.*

27. MN.III.242f; SN.IV.215: *Seyyathāpi, bhikkhu, dvinnaṃ katthānaṃ samphassasamodhānā usmā jāyati tejo abhinibbattati, tesaṃ yeva dvinnaṃ katthānaṃ nānābhāvā vinikkhepā yā tajjā usmā sā nirujjhati sā vūpasammati; evam eva kho, bhikkhu, sukhavedanīyaṃ phassaṃ paṭicca uppajjati sukhā vedanā … tass' eva sukhavedanīyassa phassassa nirodhā yaṃ tajjaṃ vedayitaṃ sukhavedanīyaṃ phassaṃ paṭicca uppannā sukhā vedanā sā nirujjhati sā vūpasammatīti.*
28. DA.I.125: *Ettha ca kiñcāpi āyatanānaṃ phusana-kiccaṃ viya vuttaṃ, tathā pi na tesaṃ phusana-kiccatā veditabbā. Na hi āyatanāni phusanti, phasso va taṃ taṃ ārammaṇaṃ phusati. Āyatanāni pana phasso upanikkhipitvā dassitāni.*
29. DN.I.42: *Tatra, bhikkhave, ye te samaṇa-brāhmaṇā sassatavādā sassataṃ attānañ ca lokañ ca paññāpenti catuhi vatthūhi* [and so on with all the different views], *tad api phassa-paccayā.*
30. DN.I.43: *Tatra, bhikkhave, ye te samaṇa-brāhmaṇā sassatavādā sassataṃ attānañ ca lokañ ca paññāpenti catuhi vatthūhi* [etc], *te vata aññatra phassā paṭisaṃvedissantīti n'etaṃ ṭhānaṃ vijjati.*
31. DN.I.45: *Sabbe te chahi phassāyatanehi phussa phussa paṭisaṃvedenti.*
32. SN.IV.68: *Cakkhuñca paṭicca rūpe ca uppajjati cakkhuviññāṇaṃ … Yā kho bhikkhave imesaṃ tiṇṇaṃ dhammānaṃ saṅgati sannipāto samavāyo, ayaṃ vuccati bhikkhave cakkhusamphasso.*
33. SN.IV.69: *Phuṭṭho bhikkhave vedeti, phuṭṭho ceteti, phuṭṭho sañjānāti.*
34. SN.III.60: *Phassasamudayā vedanāsamudayo, phassanirodhā vedanānirodho … phassasamudayā saññāsamudayo phassanirodhā saññānirodho … phassasamudayā saṃkhārasamudayo, phassanirodhā saṃkhāranirodho.*
35. MN.I.302.
36. *Saññāvedayitanirodhasamāpattiyā vuṭṭhitaṃ pan' ayye bhikkhuṃ kati phassā phusantīti?*
37. *Saññāvedayitanirodhasamāpattiyā vuṭṭhitaṃ kho āvuso Visākha bhikkhuṃ tayo phassā phusanti: suññato phasso, animitto phasso, appaṇihito phasso ti.* The predicative form *suññato* does not seem to affect the meaning or parallelism between the three types of *phassa*.
38. This state is referred to again in chapter v.
39. *Mahāniddesa*, Vol I, p.222. cf. also pp.52–3: *Phasso ti cakkhusamphasso sotasamphasso ghānasamphasso jivhāsamphasso kāyasamphasso manosamphasso adhivacanasamphasso paṭighasamphasso sukhavedanīyo samphasso dukkhavedanīyo samphasso adukkhamasukhavedanīyo samphasso kusalo phasso akusalo phasso avyākato phasso kāmāvacaro phasso rūpāvacaro phasso arūpāvacaro phasso suññato phasso animitto phasso appaṇihito phasso lokiyo phasso lokuttaro phasso atīto phasso anāgato phasso paccuppanno phasso … ayaṃ vuccati phasso.*
40. *Vivekadassī phassesu ti cakkhusamphassaṃ* [and so on] *vivittaṃ passati attena vā attaniyena vā niccena vā dhuvena vā sassatena vā avipariṇāmadhammena vā.*
41. *Athavā ye te phassā ariyā anāsavā lokuttarā suññatapaṭisaṃyuttā, te phasse vivitte passati rāgena dosena mohena*, etc.
42. Pérez-Remón, 1980, p.176
43. DN.II.62.
44. *Vibhaṅga* 6.
45. Ñānavīra, 1987, p.91.
46. *Udāna* 2.4: *Phusanti phassā upadhiṃ paṭicca, nirūpadhiṃ kena phuseyyuṃ phassā?*
47. SN.IV.164. *Saṃvijjati kho āvuso Bhagavato cakkhu* [and so on], *passati Bhagavā cakkhunā rūpaṃ, chandarāgo Bhagavato n'atthi, suvimuttacitto Bhagavā.* The meaning of *citta* is discussed further in chapter v.
48. DN.I.13, III.30,108, etc.
49. DN.I.184; *Abhidhammatthasangaha* IV.11.

CHAPTER III

The Saññākhandha

THERE ARE SIX TYPES OF *saññā* and, like feelings, they arise through contact of the six subjective senses with their corresponding 'external' objects.[1] The precise function of the *saññākhandha* has been considered difficult to assess since the term *saññā* is used in different ways in the canonical material. Mrs Rhys Davids, for example, wrote of it: "The apparently capricious way in which the intension of the term *saññā* is varied in the *Piṭakas* makes it difficult to assign any one adequate English rendering".[2] It is true that most canonical references to it do not give an explanation of what it means or what it does. There are, however, exceptions, and from a consideration of such explanations, together with careful analysis of the context in which the term is found, one can ascertain that there appear to be two different ways in which *saññā* is understood. On the one hand, it is found in contexts where it is said to have a discriminatory or identificatory role. Though sometimes such a role is indicated in what appears to be a merely token definition of *saññā*, there being no clear understanding on the part of the author as to its precise role, elsewhere the discriminatory role is more clearly defined. On the other hand, it is also clear that conceptual processes of various kinds (ideas, imagination, abstract conceptions, and so on) are part of its role.[3]

Saññā as Apperception

An example of what appears to be a token definition of *saññā* is found in the *Khandha Saṃyutta*.[4] The context is one of many where the Buddha is recorded as explaining that one should understand oneself in terms of the five *khandhas*. In this particular passage he is explaining why each of the *khandhas* is referred to as it is.

The precise meaning of the description of *saññā* is unclear. The Pali could be translated as follows:

> What, O monks, do you call *saññā*? One perceives, O monks; that is why the word *saññā* is used. Perceives what? Perceives blue, yellow, red and white. One perceives, O monks; that is why the word *saññā* is used.[5]

The rendering of *sañjānāti* simply as 'one perceives' here, is, perhaps, somewhat unsatisfactory, because perception as such might be considered to be a sensory function – of the eye. Even allowing for the fact that the word 'perception' has an elasticity of meaning which can extend it beyond a simple sensory function, it is nevertheless inadequate, and certainly too ambiguous, to express accurately the meaning of *sañjānāti* (or *saññā*). An alternative translation would be 'one identifies', giving *sañjānāti* a more discriminatory meaning, and the *saññākhandha* a discriminatory function: "Identifies what? Identifies [that a colour is] blue, yellow, red or white [rather than green, orange, or brown, etc.]". In the passage describing the arising of feeling, to which I have already referred,[6] it is clear from the Pali that *sañjānāti* does not mean 'one perceives', since it is directed towards something that has not only already been seen, but about which a feeling has also already arisen. Perception is neither required nor meaningful at this stage. The context demands that it be translated in a way which conveys that it is discriminatory, and/or that it acts in some way as a comprehender or processor of what has already taken place.

So, on the face of it, 'one recognises' is a preferable translation to 'one perceives' in the *Khandha Saṃyutta* passage. But the situation is complicated by the fact that in the same *Khandha Saṃyutta* passage recognition or identification seems to be the function of the *viññāṇakkhandha*. The Pali description of *viññāṇa* corresponds structurally to the description of *saññā*; *sañjānāti* being replaced by *vijānāti* and various gustatory qualities, such sourness, sweetness, saltiness, replacing the colours.[7] In the context of this passage it is difficult to translate *vijānāti* in a way which does not incorporate discriminatory knowledge: *viññāṇa* distinguishes that something is sour, sweet, salty, and so on.[8] The solution may be that even if *saññā* and *viññāṇa* are both to be understood as discriminatory faculties, they differ in the degree, or level, of discrimination for which they are responsible. So, for example, it may be that *viññāṇa* identifies that something has colour and *saññā* identifies that it is yellow; or that *viññāṇa* identifies that something is sour and *saññā* identifies it as lemon.[9] Unfortunately, the *Khandha Saṃyutta* passages on *saññā* and *viññāṇa* respectively are not directly comparable in this respect, so we cannot from this material alone ascertain the precise function of *saññā* (or of *viññāṇa*). The colours and flavours referred to in the passage are standard lists, so it may be the case that the author of this passage did not know the difference between *saññā* and *viññāṇa* and merely gave two different standard lists as a way of avoiding giving a proper definition of each of them. If the author understood *viññāṇa* as the faculty of discrimination, it may even be that as far as he was concerned *saññā* had no readily identifiable function, but he felt obliged to offer some token description of it as one of the *khandhas* (or *vice versa*).

The *Mahāvedallasutta* also gives what appear to be token definitions of both *saññā* and *viññāṇa*.[10] Here too the definitions imply that both are discriminatory: *viññāṇa* is said to discriminate (*vijānāti*) pleasure, pain and the absence of pleasure or pain and the standard list of colours is again the example given for what *saññā* discriminates. The discrimination between feelings according to pleasure, pain and their absence is also mentioned in the *Satipaṭṭhāna Suttas*,[11] but there it is mentioned as part of the process of attaining insight rather than as a brief definition of the function of *viññāṇa*: the cognitive verb used is *pajānāti* rather than *vijānāti*. The *Mahāvedallasutta*, which is discussed in chapter v, gives a comprehensive description of the cognitive process. As we shall see, the function of *viññāṇa* is to provide 'consciousness of' all cognition rather than to discriminate. But the brief definitions given in this *Sutta* for these two terms do little to clarify their roles. What we seem to have here is another example of the author of the passage having difficulty in defining the terms he is using: he is able to describe the cognitive process using the relevant terminology, but when it comes to defining the *khandhas* involved in the cognitive process he resorts to standard formulas in place of adequate definitions. Alternatively, both of these passages may reflect the practical difficulties associated with an oral tradition: the ease with which teachings that are standardised for mnemonic purposes can end up in contexts that are not quite suitable.

Centuries later, Buddhaghosa gives more comprehensive definitions of both *saññā* and *viññāṇa* as cognitive faculties (*jānanabhāva*) (along with *paññā*), and he uses colours as examples for both of them, thus making a proper comparison possible. The difference between *saññā* and *viññāṇa*, he explains in his *Visuddhimagga*, is that the former identifies an object as blue or yellow but cannot bring about the penetration of its characteristics as impermanent, unsatisfactory and impersonal.[12] The latter identifies an object as blue or yellow, penetrates its characteristics, but cannot bring about, even through endeavour, the manifestation of the supramundane path.[13] It is *paññā* that does all these things.[14] Thus Buddhaghosa understands all three as discriminatory faculties. He goes on to give the analogy of the understanding of a child, an adult and an expert respectively. While there may be the germ of such a threefold division of cognitive functions in the *Sutta Piṭaka*, it is far from being as tidy and consistent as Buddhaghosa presents it. And we shall see in chapter v that though it is integral to the cognitive process, *viññāṇa* is not specifically discriminative.

If we return to the passage in the *Sutta Piṭaka* describing the arising of feeling, we have a context which gives us a much clearer description of *saññā* as a faculty which discriminates or identifies. It is significant that *viññāṇa* in this context has no discriminatory function, but is stated to arise when eye (for example) and visible object are mutually present.[15] Here *viññāṇa* has the meaning of the 'awareness' which underlies or 'attends' all human (i.e. conscious) experience.[16] We then saw that the feeling subsequently gives rise to *saññā*.[17] The Pali continues: *yaṃ sañjānāti taṃ vitakketi, yaṃ vitakketi taṃ papañceti*. To make sense of this, it is relevant that in classical Sanskrit one of the meanings of *saṃjñā* (Pali *saññā*) is 'name'.[18] In Buddhism, the *saṃsāric* cognitive process is based on not seeing things as they really are: and this misperception is what constitutes the ignorance which generates continued *saṃsāric* existence. Misperception involves 'naming': the process by which what we see or experience is identified by us according to our understanding of it. It is also relevant that though the Pali *papañceti* is usually understood to mean 'to be obsessed' (so the phrase above is translated "what one reasons about obsesses one"[19]), in Sanskrit *prapañca* means manifoldness. It is the term used by the great Mahāyāna Buddhist Nāgārjuna in his *Madhyamakakārikā* to indicate that which needs to cease in order for liberation to take place:[20] manifoldness implies our mistaken imposition of separateness upon things that are in reality dependently originated. The *Pali English Dictionary* states that it is unclear whether *papañca* means the same in Pali as it does in Sanskrit. In my opinion, the context in which we find it here demands a similar interpretation of it. While such manifoldness could be understood in terms of obsession, in the sense that it is our misperception of the way things are that brings about the various desires which represent bondage (or 'obsess' us), the meaning of the passage is more readily understood if we translate *papañceti* as 'one causes to become manifold'. *Papañca* is associated with *saññā* throughout this *Sutta* in a manner which suggests that manifoldness is a concomitant of identification. And the significance of such manifoldness here, as for Nāgārjuna, is that it implies that in perceiving manifoldly one is attributing separate independent existence to everything one perceives. That this is the meaning of *papañca* is confirmed by other passages in the *Sutta Piṭaka* in which it is found. In the *Saḷāyatana Saṃyutta*, for example, we read:

> Men who have conceptions of manifoldness of some kind go on separating things when apperceiving; but [eventually] he [a *bhikkhu*] drives out everything that is [thus] constructed by the mind and to do with the mundane life and proceeds to a life of renunciation.[21]

In this passage there is a clear indication that the attribution of manifoldness, in the sense of separateness, where there is (according to the Buddha's teaching) no such separateness, is part of *saṃsāric* perception: the term *manomaya*, constructed by the mind (literally, 'mind-made'[22]) indicates that *papañca* is not perception of 'things as they are' (*yathābhūtaṃ*) but that the *bhikkhu* has to proceed from such mundane ('constructed') *saṃsāric* perception. Similarly, in the *Aṅguttara Nikāya* we read that whoever is given to manifoldness will not reach Nirvana.[23] In two other passages in the *Aṅguttara Nikāya*, we read that the classical 'unanswered questions' (referred to in the Introduction) are *papañcitaṃ*,[24] and that other such views are the result of "making manifold what is not (really) manifold".[25]

Johansson points out that such examples "bind the concept of *papañca* to the psychological area of associative and analytical thought",[26] and

Ñāṇananda has suggested the translation 'conceptual proliferation'.[27] Both Johansson and Ñāṇananda discuss *papañca* in considerably more detail than is necessary to understand it in the context we are discussing in this chapter. Neither of them, however, appears to have understood the profound implication of *papañceti* as making manifold. Johansson, for example, sums up his chapter as follows: "*Papañca* is, then, a word for a vaguely defined prolific tendency, in the fields of imagination, thought and action. It is the tendency to produce associations, wishful dreams and analytic thought."[28] But this surely misses the much more profound point that in seeing things as manifold one is attributing independent existence to them, and to oneself as perceiver. Nāgārjuna's *Madhyamakakārikā* are above all concerned to refute independent existence and to teach dependent origination, and in singling out the term *papañca* he is giving us an indication of the underlying meaning of it. This meaning is also indicated in the *Sutta Nipāta* where it states: "The wise man should put a stop to the thought 'I am', which is the root of all naming in terms of manifoldness".[29] Of this passage, Johansson states: "It [*papañca*] is an ego-related activity, which gives satisfaction to human vanity and pride ... To get rid of *papañca* is therefore one of the problems of the Buddhist disciple".[30] In Buddhism, ego-related activity is more than just satisfying to human vanity and pride: it is *the* fundamental ignorance which has to be eradicated. And the use of *asmi* in the above sentence is surely both literal and figurative; that is, it means both the erroneous sense of 'I am' on the part of the individual *bhikkhu*, *and* the erroneous attribution of independent existence to that which he sees as manifold. Furthermore, as the fundamental ignorance which has to be eradicated, it is *the* problem for the Buddhist disciple, as Nāgārjuna states, not merely one of them.

To return to our discussion of *saññā*, from the *Majjhima Nikāya* passage we are discussing here, we see that *saññā* has a discriminatory or identificatory function which is in effect one of 'naming'. This in turn leads on to the various thought processes (*vitakka*) of *saṃsāric* existence, and a separated or manifold way of interpreting our experiences. This sequence is confirmed in the *Sutta Nipāta*, where we read:

> One who is conscious of neither a conception nor a false conception, and who is neither unconscious nor conscious of a conception that has disappeared: for one who has attained such a state, form disappears, for naming in terms of manifoldness arises subsequent to conceptions.[31]

As Johansson points out, the first part of this probably refers to the higher *jhāna* levels in which there are no conceptions of form.[32] The second part clearly confirms that *papañca* follows *saññā*.

From this perhaps the most satisfactory translation of *saññā* would be 'apperception', which implies both that its function is discriminatory, and also that it incorporates a function of assimilation or comprehension of what has been perceived so that identification can take place. Such apperception (which one might also call the way we name things) and the resulting thoughts and application of manifoldness, would be 'accurate' in ultimate terms according to one's degree of insight as to the way things really are. This differs from the assimilatory function of *manodhātu* in that *manodhātu* collates sense impressions in order to impose some sort of pattern or order, whereas the *saññākhandha* assimilates data at a more 'refined' or 'classified' level. *Manodhātu* renders sensory data comprehensible, whereas the *saññākhandha* does the comprehending: the former is a preparatory stage for the latter, cognitive process. This is perhaps to be expected from the etymology of the word *saññā*: the prefix *saṃ* functions similarly to the Greek *syn* (synthesis) and the Latin *con* or *co* (comprehension, cognition): *saññā* synthesises the raw data presented to it by the *manodhātu*.[33] This distinction is formally recognised in the *Abhidhamma*, where it is explicitly stated that *saññā* operates on information from the *manodhātu*:

> What, then, is *saññā*? *Saññā* is the apperception, the apperceiving, the state of having apperceived which arises because of contact with *manodhātu*; this, then, is *saññā*.[34]

One might think from the foregoing that the *saññākhandha* is associated, at least to some extent, with discursive thought. The discrimination, assimilation and/or comprehension, and 'naming' of what might loosely be called incoming data all involve at least some degree of thinking *about* the data. And in the *Jātaka*, the expression *saññā karosi* is clearly used in the sense of 'you think'.[35] But though both *vitakka* and *papañca*, which are described as taking place subsequent to the activity of *saññā*, are more obviously discursive processes, whether or not *saññā* itself is discursive remains unclear.[36]

The use of the standard list of colours in definitions of *saññā*, and the fact that the example given of the arising of feeling is referring to visual feeling, does not mean that *saññā* functions only in connection with visual perception. Feelings based on the other senses arise in the same way and subsequently go through the same identificatory and interpretative process:[37] the *Khandha Saṃyutta* states that *saññā* is sixfold according to the six senses,[38] and in the *Mahāsatipaṭṭhāna Suttanta saññā* is explicitly linked with all the senses.[39]

Saññā as Conception

The fact that *saññā* functions as the 'naming' faculty means that it can also be thought of as the faculty of conception, or what Johansson calls 'ideation'.[40] Johansson makes his suggestion not because *saññā* is the 'naming' faculty but on the grounds that the colours referred to in the definitions of *saññā* can be both visually apperceived and also imagined. In the context of *saññā* as naming faculty, this might be further explained as follows: *saññā* identifies our experience, and for as long as one is unenlightened it as it were superimposes *saṃsāric* criteria onto reality 'as it really is', or apperceives reality through *saṃsāric* spectacles. In so doing, concepts (Johansson would call them 'ideas') are generated as well as 'things' being named; and such concepts or ideas may be of a much less specific nature than, say, the interpretation of a single visual perception. In this respect *saññā* functions in the sense of 'conception' (which I prefer to 'ideation') rather than 'apperception'. Put differently, the functioning of *saññā* is not dependent on the co-temporal input of sensory data. When such sensory data *is* co-temporal, *saññā* apperceives (identifies) them; when they are *not* co-temporal, *saññā* functions conceptually. The latter might either be in the sense specifically suggested by Johansson, of imagining a (previous) apperception (one might describe this as the bringing to mind of an image of an earlier identification). Or it might be in the less specific and more asbtract sense of imagining or conceiving of something that has not actually been apperceived as it is (presently) being imagined or conceived of. As mentioned in the discussion of *phassa*, in the *Abhidhamma* the twofold role of *saññā* as apperception and conception is referred to as *paṭighasamphassajā* and *adhivacanasamphassajā* respectively:[41] apperceptions arise from sensory experience and are described as 'gross' (*oḷārikā*), conceptions are abstract and are described as 'subtle' (*sukhumā*).

We read elsewhere that at the meditative levels known as the *arūpajjhānas*, which are beyond sensory experience and (therefore) apperception,[42] a meditator can have abstract conceptions even though he or she does not 'sense' that sphere.[43] The abstract conceptions are that 'space is infinite' (*ananto ākāso ti*), 'consciousness is infinite' (*anantaṃ viññāṇaṃ ti*), 'there is no-thing' (*natthi kiñcī ti*), which correspond to the first three *arūpajjhānas*. The fourth *arūpajjhāna* is non-conceptual as well as being beyond apperception: *nevasaññānāsaññāyatana*.

The distinction between apperception and conception is illustrated in a passsage in the *Majjhima Nikāya* where we read that gods with *rūpa* are the product of *manas*[44] and *arūpa* gods are the product of *saññā*.[45] From the context, it is not clear whether there are such gods or whether they are being referred to hypothetically.[46] What is obviously being referred to is the difference between gods which have form, which can be apperceived, and gods without form, which can only be conceived of.[47]

The role of *saññā* as the faculty of conception is referred to in the *Aṅguttara Nikāya* where the Buddha mentions four types of distorted conception (*visaññā*) as having ideas of permanence in what is impermanent, of satisfactoriness in unsatisfactoriness, of the concept of self in impersonality, and the idea of beauty in what is not beautiful.[48] The Buddha's use of the term *visaññā* to refer to these four types of erroneous conception has the concomitant implication that *saññā* can be correct: if the term *saññā* on its own meant erroneous conception, there would be no need of the prefix *vi*. So though certain conceptions may be incompatible with 'seeing things as they are', other conceptions may also be correct: the term *saññā* does not in itself mean *false* conceptions. This is illustrated in a description of deep meditation given by Sāriputta. On the one hand, he states that deep meditation is a state "in the world but without any concept of the world".[49] This suggests that ideas or concepts are of an ongoing nature, part of our general *saṃsāric* experiential baggage, and that in our normal waking state what we experience as the 'world' involves 'naming' by us according to our level of insight. On the other hand, in such meditation Sāriputta is nevertheless able to have a specific idea,[50] in this instance that Nirvana is the end of rebirth,[51] which is clearly not false according to Buddhist teaching.

There is no suggestion that the world is *merely* conceptual, only that it is *saññā* that interprets it according to our level of insight. We find *saññā* described as 'like a mirage',[52] but the passage is one in which each of the *khandhas* is being described in a manner which conveys its impermanence: the context does not imply that *saññā* is being singled out as unreal. In this context, it is relevant that the meditative levels of the *rūpajjhānas* and the first three *arūpajjhānas* (or spheres – *āyatana*) are all referred to as *saññā*.[53] These three *arūpajjhānas* have already been referred to above. The fourth *arūpajjhāna* is called the realm of neither-conception-nor-non-conception[54] (which is why it did not feature in the *Aṅguttara Nikāya* passage which gave the abstract conceptions of the meditator in the *arūpajjhānas*). The fourth *arūpajjhāna* does not, however, represent the attaining of insight any more than the preceding *jhānas* do: it is a state free from conceptions of whatever nature, and is conducive to the attainment of Nirvana since it is thus free from any notion of 'I',[55] but liberating insight has still to be achieved. There is controversy about whether the subsequent and highest meditative level of the cessation of conception and feeling (*saññāvedayitanirodha*) represents liberation or not.[56] If it does, then it cannot be just because of the cessation of conceptions. Not only does the fourth *arūpajjhāna*, which, as I have said, does not represent liberation, also appear free from conceptions, but it is also stated elsewhere that the destruction of the *āsavas* (which does represent liberation) can take place in one who has conceptions. Indeed, the experience is described as being the highest activity of *saññā*.[57] It would appear from this that *saññā* not only apperceives and conceives all our *saṃsāric* experiences, sensory and abstract, but is also instrumental in identifying the liberating experience. And though it precedes *papañca* when *papañca* occurs, it would appear that *papañca* is not automatically a result of *saññā*, as might be inferred from the description of the arising of feeling.[58] Supporting the points made in this and the last paragraphs, it is stated in the *Abhidhamma* that *saññā* can be bad, good and neither-good-nor-bad.[59]

We also read of the conceptual activity of *saññā* as conception being deliberately used, in the sense of a visualisation process or mindfulness exercise, to give names to things or concepts in a way which conduces to subsequent 'right thinking', rather than only to a continuation of *saṃsāric* perception, so aiding the *bhikkhu*'s progress towards liberation. This function of *saññā* might be called the 'constructive imagination', since it represents a process of good/positive (constructive) conditioning of one's faculty of apperception by means of deliberate conceptualising (constructing). The most simple example of this is the three 'conceptions of a *bhikkhu*', found in the *Samaṇasaññā Vagga* in the *Aṅguttara Nikāya*. The three conceptions are: "I have come to a state of being without caste; my livelihood is dependent on others; I must dress [or behave] myself differently".[60] A sick *bhikkhu*, Girimānanda, is also taught ten conceptions (*dasa saññā*) in order to allay his illness.[61] The ten are: impermanence, selflessness, unpleasantness, wretchedness, abandoning, dispassion, cessation, discontentedness with all the world, the impermanence of all *saṃsāric* phenomena, and mindfulness of inbreathing and outbreathing.[62] Each of these is subsequently elaborated in an explanation of what it represents. Elsewhere in the *Aṅguttara Nikāya* there is another list of ten conceptions given for the purpose of attaining the deathless, Nirvana (*amatogadhā amatapariyosānā*): conceptions of what is unpleasant, of death, of the repulsiveness of food, of distaste for all the world, of impermanence, of unsatisfactoriness in impermanence, of selflessness in unsatisfactoriness, of abandoning, of dispassion, of cessation;[63] and another for the purpose of preventing any evil unprofitable states overpowering one's state of mind.[64] In the *Saṃyutta Nikāya* we find similar conceptions, but with the addition of the four *brahma vihāras*.[65] The 'conception of impermanence' (*aniccasaññā*), if practised and developed, is specifically stated to cause all sensual lust, all desire for form, all desire for continued existence, all ignorance and all notion of 'I' to come to an end.[66] Conversely from certain appropriate insights the corresponding conceptions of impermanence (*aniccasaññā*), unsatisfactoriness (*dukkhasaññā*) and selflessness (*anattasaññā*) arise.[67]

The foregoing suggests that this deliberate use of *saññā* in the sense of constructively imagining certain conceptions acts psychosomatically: the imagining of a mental state that is being aspired to contributing in some way to the achieving of the aspiration. This role of *saññā* is further supported in the *Dīgha Nikāya* where we read that if a *bhikkhu* turns his attention to the idea of light, and sustains the idea of day [i.e. light] both during the day and the night, both during night and day, then with his thoughts open (or unveiled) and uncovered he develops a luminous mind.[68] This is one of the four developments of concentration, *samādhi bhāvanā*. Similarly, we read that if a *bhikkhu* enters and abides in the idea of happiness and lightness, then his body is lighter, softer, more plastic and more luminous, and he is able to levitate easily.[69] This is part of how psychic power (*iddhi*) is established.[70]

From all of the foregoing, it seems likely that the *saññākhandha* represents the processes of apperceiving and conceptualising, where apperceiving refers to the identificatory process that takes place on receiving incoming sensory data and conceptualising refers to the process of bringing to mind any abstract images, conceptions, ideas and so on which are not co-temporal with incoming sensory data. Those passages where this is only referred to by means of the standard list of colours are those where *viññāṇa* seems to be understood as the faculty of discrimination and the difference between the two faculties is not clearly defined. There is clear evidence elsewhere, however, that *saññā* has an identificatory function. As conception (in the sense of constructive imagination) it can also be used as a meditational tool with which to develop insight.

Another passage which refers to *saññā* is particularly interesting, although it is not a passage in which the physical and mental faculties are being analysed or explained. In the *Poṭṭhapāda Sutta*[71] the Blessed One is asked by Poṭṭhapāda how the mental state of *abhisaññānirodha* (?the cessation of consciousness – discussed below) comes about. During the conversation between Poṭṭhapāda and the Blessed One, we come across *saññī hoti* (he becomes conscious) in apposition with *asaññī hoti* (he becomes unconscious). Throughout the *Sutta* the word *saññā* is used in the sense of 'consciousness' as a blanket term for mental awareness in general, or the sum of the mental faculties. But it is also used in the sense of the arising or cessation of particular 'conceptions', or states of consciousness (such as joy or desire), which is achieved through training the mind,[72] and *saññaggam* (highest consciousness) is referred to as something which is to be achieved, a meditational goal, as it were.[73] At a point where the Blessed One is describing various meditational states,[74] we also read: "there arises in him a consciousness, subtle but yet actual, of everything being within the sphere of the infinity of cognition".[75] So in this *Sutta* as a whole, *saññā* appears to cover an extraordinarily wide range of meanings and functions. An explanation for this might be that the Buddha's interlocutor, Poṭṭhapāda, is not a Buddhist (in the *Sutta*, he is described simply as a *paribbājako*, a wandering mendicant). It is possible that the Buddha conducted the conversation using terms in a way which was meaningful to Poṭṭhapāda even if this was not how he would have used them himself in a different circumstance. The *Sutta* is unusual in being the only one in which the term *abhisaññānirodha* is found. Rhys Davids, in his translation of this *Sutta*, remarks that it is the earliest reference to the term in Indian literature.[76] It has usually been interpreted to mean the cessation of consciousness in the sense of 'trance', the *Pali English Dictionary*, for example, stating that the prefix *abhi* qualifies the whole compound, giving it the meaning 'trance'.[77] Its actual meaning, however, remains unclear, and though this passage is an interesting one, its uniqueness does not in any way detract from the consensus derivable from other passages about the meaning of *saññā*.

Notes

1. SN.III.60.
2. C.A.F. Rhys Davids (trans.) *Buddhist Psychological Ethics*, p.6, n.4.
3. In using words such as 'ideas', 'imagination', 'conceptions', and so on, I assume their everyday common sense meaning and intend no association with technical usages by psychologists or philosophers.
4. SN.III.87.
5. *Kiñca bhikkhave saññaṃ vadetha? Sañjānātīti kho bhikkhave tasmā saññā ti vuccati. Kiñca sañjānāti? Nīlam pi sañjānāti pītakam pi sañjānāti lohitakam pi sañjānāti odātam pi sañjānāti. Sañjānātīti kho bhikkhave tasmā saññā ti vuccati.*
6. MN.I.111.
7. *Kiñca bhikkhave viññāṇaṃ vadetha? Vijānātīti kho bhikkhave tasmā viññāṇan ti vuccati. Kiñca vijānāti? Ambilam pi vijānāti tittakam pi vijānāti kaṭukam pi vijānāti madhukam pi vijānāti khārikam pi vijānāti. Akhārikam pi vijānāti loṇakam pi vijānāti aloṇakam pi vijānāti. Vijānātīti kho bhikkhave tasmā viññāṇam ti vuccati.*
8. An alternative interpretation of *vijānāti* is given in chapter v.
9. cf. Williams (1992): in (Tibetan) Mahāyāna Buddhism, the precise classificatory role of *saṃjñā* (the Sanskrit form of *saññā*), as suggested here, has become clarified.
10. MN.I.292ff.
11. MN.I.59; DN.II.298.
12. Vism 437: *Saññā nīlaṃ pītakan ti ārammaṇasañjānanamattam eva hoti; aniccaṃ dukkham anattā ti lakkhaṇapaṭivedhaṃ pāpetuṃ na sakkoti.*
13. *Viññāṇaṃ nīlaṃ pītakan ti ārammaṇañca jānāti lakkhaṇapaṭivedhañ ca pāpeti. Ussakkitvā pana maggapātubhāvaṃ pāpetuṃ na sakkoti.*
14. *Paññā vuttanayavasena ārammaṇañ ca jānāti, lakkhaṇapaṭivedhañ ca pāpeti, ussakkitvā maggapātubhāvañ ca pāpeti. Paññā* is discussed in chapter v.
15. MN.I.111: *Cakkhuñ-c'āvuso paṭicca rūpe ca uppajjati cakkhuviññāṇaṃ.*
16. I will return to this function of *viññāṇa* below under point (2) in chapter v.
17. *Yaṃ vedeti, taṃ sañjānāti.*
18. Monier-Williams' *Sanskrit-English Dictionary*, p.1133.
19. I. B. Horner (trans.) MLS.I.145.
20. MK 1.1, in Williams, 1977, p.72.
21. SN.IV.71: *Papañcasaññā itarītarā narā papañcayantā upayanti saññino; manomayam gehasitañca sabbaṃ panujja nekkhammasitam irīyati.* I have translated *saññā* as 'conceptions' in this and some of the following sentences. The notion that conceptual processes are part of its role is discussed below.
22. *Manomaya* is considered in greater detail in chapter vii.
23. AN.III.294: *Yo papañcaṃ anuyutto … virādhayi so nibbānaṃ.*
24. AN.IV.68f.
25. AN.II.161: *Appapañcaṃ papañceti.*
26. Johansson, 1978, p.191.
27. Ñāṇananda, 1986, p.4.
28. Johansson, 1978, p.195.
29. Sn 916. cf. also, AN.IV.229: *Mūlaṃ papañcasaṃkhāyā … mantā 'asmī ti' sabbam uparundhe.*
30. Johansson, 1878, p.195.
31. Sn 874: *Na saññasaññī na visaññasaññī no pi asaññī na vibhūtasaññī, evaṃ sametassa vibhoti rūpaṃ, saññānidānā hi papañcasaṃkhā.*
32. Johansson, 1978, p.193.
33. cf. Verdu, 1979, p.41.
34. Dhs 4: *Katamā tasmiṃ samaye saññā hoti? Yā tasmiṃ samaye tajjā manoviññāṇadhātusaṃphassajā saññā sañjānanā sañjānitattaṃ; ayaṃ tasmiṃ samaye saññā hoti.* And in the *Abhidharmakośabhāṣya*, Vasubandhu states that *saññā* means "identifying what is indicated by sense objects", an interpretation very similar to that which we have arrived at here: Abh K B II.24: *viṣayanimittodgrahaṇa.* (Verdu (1979, p.41f) mistakenly attributes this to the *Kośa* itself.) The technical translation of *viṣayanimittodgrahaṇa*, given to me by Paul Williams in a personal communication, is "apprehending of the *nimittas* – the signs of class-inclusion – with

reference to an object". This specifically refers to the discriminatory (i.e. classificatory) aspect of *saññā* as more formally understood in later Buddhist schools of thought. cf. also Williams 1992.

35. J.II.71.
36. The *Abhidhamma* defines *vitakka* as 'thinking of' something and *vicāra* as 'thinking about' the same thing. Both are terms used in a technical sense in meditation. This is explained in Cousins 1992.
37. MN.I.112.
38. SN.III.60.
39. DN.II.309.
40. Johansson, 1979, p.92.
41. *Vibhaṅga* 6.
42. AN.IV.427: *Rūpasaññānaṃ samatikkamā paṭigha-saññānaṃ atthaṅgamā.*
43. *Evaṃ saññī ... tad āyatanaṃ no paṭisaṃvedeti.*
44. MN.I.410: *Devā rūpino manomayā.*
45. *Devā arūpino saññāmayā.*
46. The commentary states (MA.III.122) that both are the product of meditative states, in the *rūpa* and *arūpa jhānas* respectively: *jhānacittamayā ... arūpa jhānasaññāya saññāmayā.*
47. In a personal communication, Lance Cousins informs me that the Theravāda tradition would probably understand this passage to mean that the minds of the formless gods can be known. I will discuss the term *manomaya*, which has arisen twice in this chapter, more fully in chapter VII.
48. AN.II.52: *Anicce niccasaññino dukkhe ca sukhasaññino anattani ca attā ti asubhe subhasaññino ...*
49. AN.ff.9: *Na idhaloke idhalokasaññī ahosiṃ.*
50. *Saññī ca pana ahosin ti.*
51. *Bhavanirodho nibbānaṃ ... saññā uppajjati.*
52. SN.III.142: *Marīcikūpamā saññā.*
53. For example, SN.IV.217: *Rūpasaññā, ākāsānañcāyatanasaññā, viññāṇañcāyatanasaññā* and *ākiñcaññāyatanasaññā.*
54. *Nevasaññānāsaññāyatanaṃ.*
55. SN.IV.294f.
56. *Saññāvedayitanirodhaṃ samāpannassa saññā ca vedanā ca niruddhā honti:* "both conception and feeling have ceased when one has attained the cessation of conception and feeling".
57. AN.III.202: *Yathā saññissa anantarā āsavānaṃ khayo hoti, idaṃ saññānaṃ aggaṃ.*
58. MN.I.111: *Yaṃ sañjānāti taṃ vitakketi, yaṃ vitakketi taṃ papañceti.*
59. *Vibhaṅga* 6: *kusalā, akusalā, avyākatā.*
60. AN.V.210: *Vevaṇṇiyamhi ajjhūpagato, parapaṭibaddhā me jīvikā, añño me ākappo karaṇīyo ti.*
61. AN.V.108f: *Yaṃ bhikkhuno Girimānandassa dasa saññā sutvā so ābādho ṭhānaso paṭippassambheyya.*
62. *Aniccasaññā, anattasaññā, asubhasaññā, ādīnavasaññā, pahānasaññā, virāgasaññā, nirodhasaññā, sabbaloke anabhiratasaññā, sabbasaṃkhāresu aniccasaññā, ānāpānasati.*
63. AN.V.105: *Asubhasaññā, maraṇasaññā, āhāre patikkūlasaññā, sabbaloke anabhiratasaññā, aniccasaññā, anicce dukkhasaññā, dukkhe anattasaññā, pahānasaññā, virāgasaññā, nirodhasaññā.*
64. AN.V.107: *No cittaṃ bhavissati na c'uppannā pāpakā akusalā dhammā cittaṃ pariyādāya ṭhassanti.* cf. also DN.III.289.
65. SN.V.130ff.
66. SN.III.155: *Aniccasaññā bhikkhave bhāvitā bahulīkatā sabbaṃ kāmarāgaṃ pariyādiyati sabbaṃ rūparāgaṃ pariyādiyati sabbaṃ bhavarāgaṃ pariyādiyati sabbaṃ avijjaṃ pariyādiyati sabbam asmimānaṃ pariyādiyati samūhanti.*
67. AN.III.443f.
68. DN.III.223: *Idh' āvuso bhikkhu ālokasaññaṃ manasikaroti, divā saññaṃ adhiṭṭhāti yathā divā tathā rattiṃ, yathā rattiṃ tathā divā, iti vivaṭena cetasā apariyonaddhena sappabhāsaṃ cittaṃ bhāveti.*
69. SN.V.283: *Sukhasaññañca lahusaññañca kāye okkamitvā viharati, tasmiṃ samaye tathāgatassa kāyo lahutaro ceva hoti mudutaro ca kammaniyataro ca pabhassarataro ca ... appakasiren'eva paṭhaviyā vehāsam abbhuggacchati.*
70. This ability to use meditative states to effect a change in the state of one's body is discussed further in chapter VII.
71. DN.I.178ff.
72. DN.I.182: *Evam pi sikkhā ekā saññā uppajjanti, sikkhā ekā saññā nirujjhanti.*

73. DN.I.184.
74. The *jhānas* and *vimokkhas*.
75. DN.I.184: *Viññāṇañcāyatanasukhumasaccasaññā tasmiṃ samaye hoti.* I have used T. W. Rhys Davids' translation (*Dialogues*, p.250).
76. *Dialogues*, p.251.
77. PED, p.70. cf. also CPD s.v. *abhisaññānirodha*, which gives the same rendering.

CHAPTER IV

The Saṃkhārakkhandha

SAṂKHĀRA HAS BEEN VARIOUSLY AND often confusingly translated by terms such as mental formations, habitual tendencies or dispositions, conditional aggregates, and former impressions, terms which have little precise meaning for us in English. The term *saṃkhāra* occurs in many different contexts in the *Nikāyas*, and has been notoriously difficult to explain and understand. We can, however, substantially clarify its meaning by looking at it in three distinct contexts: in the *tilakkhaṇa* formula, as the second link in the *paṭiccasamuppāda* formula, and the *saṃkhārakkhandha*. We shall see that the second and third of these contexts are closely linked through the cyclic nature of karma and through the Buddha's ethicising of the law of karma, and how this largely functions through the ethical life of the individual. Though in both the second and third of these contexts one can initially come to a relatively clear understanding of the meaning of *saṃkhāra*, we shall see that in fact the boundaries between the two contexts are blurred and extended through their mutual involvement in the overall causal nexus which provides the 'fuel' by which the individual persists in *saṃsāra*.

Saṃkhāra in the *Tilakkhaṇa* Formula

First, and fundamentally, the term appears in the *tilakkhaṇa* formula. I put this first, and say that it is fundamental, because the *tilakkhaṇa* formula describes the nature of *saṃsāric* existence as a whole, insight into which is liberating knowledge according to the Buddha's teachings. Clarifying what it means in this formula also shows how different the meanings of *saṃkhāra* can be, since in this context its meaning is significantly different from the two which follow. In the passage in the *Aṅguttara Nikāya* where this formula is found,[1] it is stated that the formula refers to 'the fact that things are a certain way' (*dhammaṭṭhitatā*), and 'the fact that there is a regularity of things' (*dhammaniyāmatā*) which applies whether or not a *tathāgata* (an epithet of the Buddha) appears in the world.[2] The formula is: "all conditioned phenomena (*saṃkhārā*) are unsatisfactory, all conditioned phenomena (*saṃkhārā*) are impermanent, all phenomena (*dhammā*) are selfless".[3] In fact all the phenomena of *saṃsāric* experience, of whatever kind, are conditioned: this is precisely why they are impermanent and unsatisfactory. So all *saṃsāric* phenomena are *saṃkhāras* (or *saṃkhata* – conditioned; the two words are virtually interchangeable). The construction of the word *saṃkhāra* itself gives us insight as to its precise meaning: the verb *kar* (Sanskrit: *kṛ*) basically means 'make' or 'do'; but the addition of the prefix *saṃs* gives 'make' the more specific meaning of 'put together', 'compose', 'form' or 'condition'. As nothing to do with *saṃsāric* experience is *asaṃkhata*, what this clearly means is that nothing exists as an ultimate element or simple: all *saṃsāric* phenomena are 'formed' or 'conditioned'. This is re-stating that all *saṃsāric* phenomena are dependently originated.

The characteristic referred to in the third line of the formula, selflessness (*anattā*), is implicit in the meaning of *saṃkhāra*: being conditioned does not allow for the independence that selfhood presupposes. But in this third line, *saṃkhārā* is juxtaposed with the word *dhammā*. *Dhammā* refers here to all phenomena, whether conditioned (*saṃkhata*) or otherwise: in other words the last line of the formula, all things are selfless (*sabbe dhammā anattā*), includes the *saṃkhata* phenomena of *saṃsāric* experience referred to in the first two parts of the formula, but it goes further than they do in that it includes the unconditioned (*asaṃkhata*), which in the Buddha's teachings refers specifically to the experience of Nirvana. Impermanence and unsatisfactoriness are not attributed to the unconditioned, but it is important to establish that for it too, along with conditioned phenomena, any attribution of independent selfhood is erroneous.

First, then, the term *saṃkhāra* refers to all the phenomena of *saṃsāric* existence: there exists nothing in *saṃsāra* which is not *saṃkhata*. Everything being discussed here in connection with the five *khandhas*, for example, is, as well as any other meaning or significance it may have, a *saṃkhāra*. This is what is meant when the nun Vajirā describes a 'being' (*satta*) as a "mere heap of *saṃkhāras*".[4] In this context, the term means, therefore, conditioned, dependent, formed (rather than spontaneous or independent) phenomena: it means *saṃsāric* phenomena.

Saṃkhāra in the *Paṭiccasamuppāda* Formula

Second, *saṃkhāra* is the second link in the formula of *paṭiccasamuppāda*.[5] In order to ascertain the meaning of *saṃkhāra* in this context, it is important to understand the purpose of the formula. It has usually been understood to have been intended as a metaphysical formula explaining the nature of *saṃsāra* as such. Indeed the doctrine of *paṭiccasamuppāda* above all states that all *saṃsāric* phenomena are causally originated, conditioned. At the beginning of a canonical passage in which the formula is given, the Buddha states that he is teaching dependent origination and about things which have arisen dependently.[6] He also states that he is referring to the way things are (*dhammaṭṭhitatā*), the fact that there is a regularity of things (*dhammaniyāmatā*), and that things are causally related (*idappaccayatā*).[7] We saw the first two of these phrases used in introducing the *tilakkhaṇa* formula above. The third, *idappaccayatā*, is used elsewhere in the canon in a context which indicates clearly that it is a term which refers to the metaphysical nature of *saṃsāra*.[8] Such phrases support the usual understanding of *paṭiccasamuppāda*, that it describes the conditioned nature of *saṃsāra*.

I suggest, however, that the term *paṭiccasamuppāda* – dependent origination – applies to a general doctrine, and that the actual *formula* given by the Buddha is intended to have a more specific purpose. This is to explain the 'how' of *human* existence in *saṃsāra*, to give a synthetical formula which explains the mechanics of how a human being *is* a human being. The dilemma in response to which it might have been given could have gone something like this: 'If the whole of *saṃsāric* experience is *paṭiccasamuppanna* (i.e. it consists only of conditioned, dependently originated, phenomena), if all that can be said about conditioned phenomena is that they are impermanent and unsatisfactory, and if absolutely all phenomena are selfless, how does what we experience as an individual life actually function? How does it hang together as a seemingly coherent whole? One might be able to accept that inanimate things are unsatisfactory, impermanent and selfless, but the case of human beings is more complex and requires further elucidation.'

My suggestion that the formula has this purpose is well supported in the texts. Most significantly, this purpose is implied by the fact that the formula itself refers specifically to a human being. Terms such as ignorance, consciousness, senses, feelings, birth, old age and death, are clearly referring to a human being.[9] In the *Mahānidāna Suttanta* in the *Dīgha Nikāya*, which is one of the most important passages dealing with *paṭiccasamuppāda*, each stage of the formula is further elaborated in terms of human characteristics such as holding opinions, quarrelling, slander and lies, and so on.[10] Elsewhere, the formula is given in order to explain *dukkha*, the term the Buddha used to describe the *saṃsāric* experience of human beings, as stated in the first Noble Truth.[11] It is precisely because *saṃsāric* experience is *dukkha* that the Buddha gave his teaching to lead people away from it: it was the human condition he was concerned about. The formula is used in other contexts to describe the Middle Way: the lack of independent existence of anything at all is conceived of as the 'middle way' between existence and non-existence.[12] But the fact that it is so obviously associated with the human being surely reflects both the Buddha's express statement that he was solely concerned with helping people to gain Enlightenment and so escape from the cycle of *saṃsāra*, and also that he was not concerned to give ontological explanations. The achieving of Nirvana involves 'seeing things as they really are' (*yathābhūtaṃ*), but exactly what things really are is never described by the Buddha: only the way to achieve such insight oneself is described. This suggestion is also supported in the texts by the fact that understanding the teaching is stated to mean that one will no longer ask questions about individual existence in *saṃsāra*, past, future, or present, such as "Am I, or am I not? What am I? How am I? This 'being' that is 'I', where has it come from, where will it go?".[13]

Paṭiccasamuppāda as a generally applicable doctrine which demonstrates that all things are causally originated is unquestionably fundamental to the Buddha's teaching. In some contexts where the formula is also given, and in one context where the formula is not given, the general doctrine is stated as follows: "When this is, that is; when this arises, that arises; if this is not, that is not; when this ceases, that ceases".[14] The modern way of putting this is "When A is, B is; A arising, B arises; when A is not, B is not; A ceasing, B ceases".[15] In my opinion, however, it is only through understanding that the purpose of the twelvefold formula itself is specifically to explain how human beings exist in *saṃsāra* that one understands it accurately.[16] This is certainly the case when it comes to understanding what *saṃkhāra* means in this context: the term applies to the way in which a human being arises, not to the way in which *saṃsāra* in the wider sense of the objective world in general arises, and confusing the two can be very misleading. My point is that the formula is *not* explaining that the 'stuff' of *saṃsāra* (the objective world) is the *saṃkhāras*, *viññāṇa* and so on, conditioned by ignorance. I will return to this point below.

The formula varies as to the number of 'links' it contains. The common twelvefold version (given in the Introduction) starts with ignorance, and states that ignorance is the condition for the arising of the *saṃkhāras*, which in turn are the condition for the arising of *viññāṇa*, *nāmarūpa*, the *saḷāyatanas*, and so on. It explains the whole cycle of human existence, how individuals are reborn again and again. As existence is thought to be cyclical in Buddhism, it seems most likely that the formula is intended to be understood as circular rather than linear; but given that liberation from the *saṃsāric* cycle is brought about by insight, it is perhaps not surprising that the formula as given should begin with ignorance. 'Ignorance' simply means 'lack of insight'. This can vary in degree, but always means that liberating insight has not taken place. This, indeed, is why there *is* continued *saṃsāric* existence as an individual. Ignorance represents the prime condition for the human condition as a whole. And because of such ignorance or lack of insight, certain volitional and formative activities, called *saṃkhāras*, take place, which in turn are the specific conditions of a particular human being. I say 'specific' and 'particular' because in this case *saṃkhāra* is not merely a generic term covering all conditioned phenomena. Here, *saṃkhāras* arise according to the nature of the ignorance of each individual: no two people's ignorance is precisely the same (it is dependent on where someone is on the path to liberation) and so no two people's *saṃkhāras* are the same. To understand in what way they are volitional, it helps if one bears in mind that according to the Buddha's teaching, karma (action) is *cetanā* (volition), and that the words karma and *saṃkhāra* come from the same verbal root, *kar* (Sanskrit: *kṛ*). How one acts or intends, therefore, is conditioned by one's level of ignorance (or knowledge), and so long as they are conditioned by ignorance, such actions or intentions continue to have their place as a condition for the arising of a particular individual. We read in the canon that only an ignorant person (*purisapuggalo*) will have good or bad intentions; when ignorance has ceased, he or she will have neither good nor bad intentions.[17] The term *saṃkhāra* has sometimes been translated or interpreted as 'formation'.[18] When it refers to *saṃkhāra* as the second link in the *paṭiccasamuppāda* formula, this is a particularly apt translation because it has more of an actively *formative* meaning than mere 'volition' has. That the *saṃkhāras* are formative is also implied from their position as the condition for the subsequent arising of an individual. In an abstract sense they are the *creative* principle in a human being.

The second meaning of the word *saṃkhāra*, then, is the active and formative principle which, conditioned by ignorance, in turn conditions (or forms) the arising of a particular individual. One might say that it is the individualising faculty, in the sense of being the formative principle which distinguishes individual A from individual B. We shall see in chapter v how, by way of association with the faculty of consciousness (*viññāṇa*), this subsequently gives rise to the 'name and form' of the individual concerned. 'Formative activities' would perhaps be an appropriate translation of the term *saṃkhāra* in this context.

Saṃkhāra as a *Khandha*

The third relevant context in which the term *saṃkhāra* is found is the *saṃkhārakkhandha*. I have put this third because understanding what it means here is facilitated by having already looked at the preceding two contexts. As we shall see, the meaning of *saṃkhāra* here is closely related to that in the *paṭiccasamuppāda* formula, with one distinction. Once again, we need to bear in mind the reason for the analysis of the person into *khandhas* in order to grasp its proper meaning. We have already seen that the *tilakkhaṇa* formula explains the fundamental nature of *saṃsāric* existence in general, and that the *paṭiccasamuppāda* formula is a synthetical explanation of the 'how' of individual human existence. As we know, the *khandhas* also apply to human existence, but analytically rather than synthetically: they show that while it is possible to show *how* an individual human being arises, as the *paṭiccasamuppāda* formula does, that individual should be understood not in terms of separate selfhood but in terms of how each *khandha* can be seen to 'contribute' certain key characteristics of the human being as a whole. The analysis is entirely impersonal (in the psychological rather than the metaphysical sense of impersonal), and is not at all intended to explain a particular or specific human being in the way the *paṭiccasamuppāda* formula can.

In the *Khandha Saṃyutta*, the *saṃkhārakkhandha* is defined as the six groups of volitional activity.[19] Once again the sixfold classification is according to the connection of the six senses with their corresponding six objects. Significantly, this definition of the *saṃkhārakkhandha* clearly separates what in the West would probably be called 'will' from other mental states.[20] In Buddhism, the teaching that karma is intention makes it particularly important that this be clearly defined: the nature, presence or absence of volitional states determines the way in which, and extent to which, one is 'bound'.

This is established in another definition of *saṃkhāra* given in the *Khandha Saṃyutta*. From the Pali one can see that there is a complex play on verbal and nominal forms of words associated with *saṃ* √*kar*: *Saṃkhataṃ abhisaṃkharontīti bhikkhave tasmā saṃkhārā ti vuccanti*.[21] What it means is: "The *khandha* of volitional activities is so called because they volitionally construct (*abhisaṃkharonti*) conditioned phenomena (*saṃkhataṃ*)". The passage goes on:

> What conditioned phenomena do they volitionally construct? They volitionally construct the conditioned phenomenon that is the body as body; they volitionally construct the conditioned phenomenon which is [the *khandha* of] feeling as feeling; they volitionally construct the conditioned phenomenon which is [the *khandha* of] apperception as apperception; they volitionally construct the conditioned phenomenon which is [the *khandha* of] the volitional activities as volitional activities; and they volitionally construct the conditioned phenomenon which is [the *khandha* of] consciousness as consciousness.[22]

What this passage clearly indicates is the way in which the individual's will determines his or her future *saṃsāric* existence: one's volitions are the instrumental factor in the coming-to-be of the entire human being.[23] The key role played by volitional activities in the cyclic *saṃsāric* existence of an individual human being is further discussed below.

The *saṃkhārakkhandha* is unique among the *khandhas* in that it need not, and indeed ultimately should not, be 'activated' in the functioning of a human being. We have already seen above, in our discussion of the *paṭiccasamuppāda* formula, that ignorance is the condition for the arising of the formative activities (*saṃkhāras*). Ultimately, a *bhikkhu* is aiming to substitute knowledge for ignorance, in which case the condition for the arising of these formative activities will cease. Indeed the *paṭiccasamuppāda* formula is given in reverse in the *Nikāyas* to illustrate how it is possible for human existence in the cycle of *saṃsāra* to cease. Similarly, the analysis into *khandhas* shows that a human being can function without the involvement of the *saṃkhārakkhandha*, without volitions in the sense that is intended here. The description of the arising of visual feeling, for example, to which we have already referred, shows clearly that it is quite possible for the feeling to arise without any involvement at all of the *saṃkhārakkhandha*:

> Visual awareness arises because of eye and [visible] forms; contact [occurs] when there is a combination of the three; feelings are caused by contact; that which one feels, one apperceives...[24]

From this we can see that the sensory activity, including both the organ and object of sense, involves the *rūpakkhandha*; awareness is the function of the *viññāṇakkhandha*;[25] apperception takes place in the *saññākhandha*: and these three *khandhas* are involved in the activating and recognising of what is experienced in a fourth – the *vedanākhandha*. The feeling can be agreeable, disagreeable or neutral, but the *saṃkhārakkhandha* is only involved if there is a concomitant volition concerning the feeling: if it is an agreeable feeling, a concomitant volition might be to desire it; if it is a disagreeable feeling, one might be revolted by it. In practice, the feelings of an unenlightened individual usually are accompanied by volitions, and this is illustrated by the fact that in the *paṭiccasamuppāda* formula feelings are said to be the condition for the arising of craving (*taṇhā*). But one can, and ultimately should, experience feelings *without* any concomitant volitions: an *arahant* is able to experience pleasant and unpleasant feelings while remaining entirely detached from them. This is stated in the *Vedanā Saṃyutta*, where we read that the well-taught Ariyan disciple has no repugnance for painful feeling, or delight in sensual pleasure.[26] The process of analysing the person into *khandhas* shows how this is a constitutional possibility. An interesting passage in the *Majjhima Nikāya*, which is discussed in detail in chapter v, states that it is impossible to separate *vedanā*, *saññā* and *viññāṇa*, but does not say that *saṃkhāra* is similarly inseparable.[27]

The *saṃkhārakkhandha*, then, is the *khandha* of the will, and it might be translated as the 'volitional constituent' of the human being.

The Cyclic Causal Nexus

As we have seen, both the *saṃkhārakkhandha* and the *paṭiccasamuppāda* formula are specifically connected with the *saṃsāric* experience of the human being. It is perhaps not surprising, then, that the meaning of *saṃkhāra* in each of these two contexts should be closely linked, as we shall now see.

First, however, I return to the point made above that there is one difference between the meaning of *saṃkhāra* as a *khandha*, that is as the volitional constituent of a human being, and its meaning as the second link in the chain of the *paṭiccasamuppāda* formula, the formative activities. This is that the volitional constituent does not function as that which conditions or forms the constitution of the individual for this life (as can be inferred from the fact that its inactivity does not affect the composition of an individual). Rather, the volitions of the *saṃkhārakkhandha* are concerned with how the individual operates: his or her day to day volitions during this life. This difference is compatible with the fact that the *paṭiccasamuppāda* formula is a synthetical explanation of how a human being functions, while the *khandha* formula is analytical: the former is creative and the latter is not. It is also compatible with the fact that there are two distinct aspects to the way karma works. In the first instance, *saṃkhāra* as formative activities, the second link in the *paṭiccasamuppāda* formula, forms the human being *for* this life: it is the creative aspect of karma. In the second instance, the *saṃkhārakkhandha*, which is the volitional constituent of that human being *in* this life, functions according to the way he or she has been formed: it is what we might call the operative aspect of karma. Being cyclical, of course, the operative karma of this life will (unless it is neutral) become the creative karma of a future life: one's present volitions eventually condition the ignorance on which future formative activities are based. This is explicitly evidenced in the passage above which defines the *saṃkhārakkhandha* as volitionally constructing the human being.

The difference between the meanings of *saṃkhāra* in these two contexts is by way of their representing two aspects of karma, which is itself the linking factor between them. It is in this sense of the cyclical nature of karma that Frauwallner, who translates *saṃkhāra* as *Gestaltung*, 'formation', states that it "signifies that something is put in a condition of readiness which further influences and operates", and compares this with its meaning in the classical Sāṃkhya system, where the term *saṃkhāra* denotes "the condition of the wheel which is moving in rotation and continues to move of itself".[28] Interestingly, the word *(abhi)saṃkhāra* is used in the *Aṅguttara Nikāya* in a passage in which a wheelright is discussing how long a wheel will continue to roll: a wheel will keep rolling for as long as 'the impulse that set it rolling' lasts.[29] This is clearly an apt analogy for the 'wheel of *saṃsāra*', which is a popular way of expressing the cyclical nature of the two different aspects of *saṃkhāra* being discussed here, and which together might be said to be the 'fuel' of the individual in *saṃsāra*. Frauwallner is attempting to give a single translation for these two meanings of *saṃkhāra*, which I have called 'formative activities' and 'volitional constituent' respectively. While this is a perfectly legitimate aim, there is nevertheless an ambiguity which results from using one translation rather than analysing the differences between the contexts in which the term is found. In fact, from the discussion above of the two aspects of karma represented by the two meanings of *saṃkhāra* which I have suggested, we are in a better position to see that where such a single translation is required, Frauwallner's 'formation' *can* have the connotation of both the creative and the operative aspects of the term in these two contexts. But it does not immediately convey the cyclic nature of the two kinds of volition, and without first offering an analysis of the two meanings this twin connotation might easily be missed. Confusion may also arise because 'formations' has been used extensively by I. B. Horner in her numerous translations to refer solely to *saṃkhāra* when it is part of the *paṭiccasamuppāda* formula: its creative aspect.[30] She uses 'habitual tendencies' when translating *saṃkhāra* as the fourth of the five *khandhas*. The best single translation is 'inherited forces', since here there is a much clearer implication in the word 'inherited' of an operative aspect and in the word 'forces' of a creative aspect.[31] That volitions are 'inherited' does not necessarily mean that they are entirely pre-determined (without at least a degree of free will the Buddha's ethicising of the law of karma would be pointless), but they are nevertheless as conditioned as any other aspect of the individual by one's overall moral state in one's previous life or lives.

A frequently used formula brings together the two meanings of *saṃkhāra* as aspects of the ethical life of the individual which functions cyclically in his or her continuing rebirth process through the law of karma. This is the triad 'thought, word and deed' by which all the actions of an individual are carried out. Highlighting both the ethical nature of this triad, and the way the *saṃkhāras* condition the individual's life in every way, we read in *Kukkuravatikasutta*: "One volitionally acts through body, speech and thought".[32] It is according to whether such actions are harmful (*sabyābajjhaṃ*) or harmless (*abyābajjhaṃ*) that one is subsequently reborn, the *Sutta* states. Elsewhere this triad is described in terms of karma, with karma being used as a synonym for *saṃkhāra*.[33] Taking the two passages together, we see the Buddha's ethicising of karma clearly tied in with the function of the *saṃkhārakkhandha* as the *khandha* of volitions. E. J. Thomas, in his *History of Buddhist Thought*,[34] suggests that the division of *saṃkhāra* into *kāya*, *vacī* and *citta* (or *manas*) is the earliest classification of the *saṃkhārakkhandha*. He is referring to the fact that the later *Abhidhamma* classifies the *saṃkhārakkhandha* according to fifty different mental activities, only one of which is volition.[35]

There is another early classification in the *Saṅgīti Suttanta*, not mentioned by Thomas, which ties in the ethical teaching by using a different triad. This is into good (*puñña*), bad (*apuñña*), and (literally) imperturbable or stationary (*āneñja*).[36] The literal translation of *āneñja* might suggest that this classification includes karmically neutral volitions. According to the commentary, however, *āneñjābhisaṃkhāro* here refers to the will for rebirth in the *arūpa loka*, and this meaning of the term is also found in the *Abhidhamma*.[37] The context of the *Dīgha Nikāya* passage does not help us in determining the way in which it is being used, because the *Saṅgīti Suttanta* gives lists for recitation purposes without any explanations: it is generally agreed to be a kind of proto-*Abhidhamma*, an early work of scholastic classification, no doubt for mnemonic purposes. But the view of the commentator that *āneñjābhisaṃkhāro* is not referring to neutral volition is supported by the other context in which the same triad is found.[38] Here the three types of *saṃkhāra* of the triad are stated to be the volitions of an ordinary ignorant man (*avijjāgato purisapuggalo*), and the passage goes on to state that when ignorance has been replaced by wisdom the *bhikkhu* will not have volitions of these three types.[39] Rebirth in the *arūpa loka* (or the result of any other volition which is not neutral) is ultimately undesirable since it does not represent liberation. So a *bhikkhu* in whom ignorance had been replaced by wisdom would not have such volitions. We have here, then, two early triadic classifications which might be applied to the activity of the *saṃkhārakkhandha*, both of which are ethical in nature.

We also find the former of these triads, that into *kāya*, *vacī* and *citta*, in a passage where it is clear from the context that the classification is referring to *saṃkhāra* as the second link in the *paṭiccasamuppāda* formula rather than to the *saṃkhārakkhandha*. This is located in the *Nidāna Saṃyutta*, the section of the *Sutta Piṭaka* which discusses the doctrine of *paṭiccasamuppāda*, and the passage is describing the links of the *paṭiccasamuppāda* formula in turn. *Saṃkhāra* is defined in terms of body, speech and mind.[40] In a passage in the *Abhidhamma*, we find the two triads linked in a description of *saṃkhāra* as the second link in the *paṭiccasamuppāda* formula. So formative activities (*saṃkhāras*) which are good, bad or desirous of the *arūpaloka*, are bodily, verbal and mental.[41] The application of these triadic ethical classifications of *saṃkhāra* to both of these two contexts, the *saṃkhārakkhandha* and *saṃkhāra* as the second link in the *paṭiccasamuppāda* formula, clearly emphasises the interconnectedness of these two kinds of *saṃkhāra* in the cyclic continuum of the individual in *saṃsāra* as well as their significance in the ethical process.

A word needs to be said at this point about the role of *saṃkhāra* in conditioning future rebirth. I have said that the *saṃkhārakkhandha* as the operative aspect of karma becomes the creative aspect of karma in determining a subsequent individual life, and this was evidenced in the *Khandha Saṃyutta* passage where the constituents of the human being were all said to have been volitionally constructed. In the *Saṃkhāruppattisutta* in the *Majjhima Nikāya* the Buddha explains the arising of *saṃkhāras* in a different context.[42] The *Sutta* states that a *bhikkhu* who possesses faith (*saddhā*), moral standing (*sīla*), learning (*suta*), detachment (*cāga*) and wisdom (*paññā*) can set his mind to being reborn in a particular favourable circumstance, such as a wealthy noble (*khattiyamahāsāla*), brahmin or householder, a god, or in one of the many *brahma* realms. Together with the five qualities, a *bhikkhu*'s mind must have 'constant inclinations' (*bhāvitā bahulīkatā*) towards the rebirth he desires. The *Sutta* is somewhat simplistic in style, and it is therefore tempting to interpret it equally simplistically, and assume that it is intending to explain how a *bhikkhu* is able to will himself into a nice rebirth if he so wishes. This indeed it does, and illustrates the way in which his inclinations or intentions in one life condition his subsequent life. One might in any case expect to find a passage on this subject included in the canonical material since it is a pan-Indian belief that one can to a greater or lesser extent choose or influence one's next life by one's particular aspirations at the time of death.[43] And the Buddha's teaching that karma is volition gives considerably more credence to this notion. But the message the *Sutta* contains is far more powerful if considered in the light of its final paragraph. This states that a *bhikkhu* who has reached the advanced stage implied by possession of the five qualities of faith, moral standing, learning, detachment and wisdom, need not have inclinations towards a specific favourable rebirth such as those already mentioned. He also has the choice of liberation, which is achieved through the extinction of the *āsavas*. Since one of the *āsavas* is the desire for continued becoming, we can see that it is the extinction of this altogether, rather than desiring to continue to become in a favourable circumstance, that is necessary in order to bring about the liberating factor of no subsequent arising (rebirth) at all.[44] So while this *Sutta* does serve to illustrate that specific mental inclinations can produce specific results, the message of the *Sutta* is, rather, a warning of the binding power of volitions.

Having discussed *saṃkhāra* in the contexts of the *paṭiccasamuppāda* formula and the *saṃkhārakkhandha* and established a relatively clear understanding of how each contributes in its own way to the cyclic ethical activities of the individual, I turn now to illustrating that, in practice, the complex of volitional factors of which an individual is comprised is far from being so clearly defined. Volitions do not come to fruition according to a set temporal pattern. They can therefore lie dormant, as it were, and for long periods of time condition the constitution of the individual through the cyclic way the formative activities and the volitions condition each other. The term used in Pali to indicate this is *anusaya*, which means: "bent, bias, proclivity, the persistence of a dormant or latent disposition, predisposition, tendency. Always in a bad sense".[45] 'Bad' of course means binding, not bad in the legal sense of criminal or even in the simple sense of unpleasant. The English term 'bias' is perhaps a good word to convey the connotations associated with *anusaya*. That *anusaya* implies 'bad' tendencies is suggested in passages which equate their absence with the absence of other fundamentally binding factors. In the *Sutta Nipāta* we read of "the *bhikkhu* in whom there are no latent tendencies, in whom the unwholesome roots are destroyed".[46] The venerable Khemaka, who has managed to eradicate overt identification with each of the five *khandhas*, still has not "eradicated the tendency to think 'I am'".[47] The subtle nature of this tendency is likened in the text to a soiled cloth which has been washed clean but which still has about it the vague smell of salt or cow-dung. It has to be returned to the washerman to leave it for some time in a sweet-scented coffer (analogous to further meditation on selflessness). The vague smell will then be completely removed.

Though this passage illustrates that Khemaka's persisting notion of 'I am' is subtle, it also suggests that the *anusayas* function at a very deep level. They are almost what one would describe as 'part of human nature'. In the *Mahāmāluṅkyasutta*, the Buddha states that even in a baby there are the latent tendencies to the view of (identifying with) its own body, to doubt, to clinging to customs and rituals, to sense pleasure, and to ill-will towards other beings.[48] The *Saṅgīti Suttanta* lists seven *anusayas*: sense pleasures, anger, views, doubt, conceit, the desire for continued existence and ignorance,[49] and each of these is found in many places throughout the *Sutta Piṭaka*. Elsewhere a triplet is given: obstinacy, prejudice and bias.[50] The profundity of the *anusayas* is perhaps most strongly suggested by the fact that four of them mentioned here, sensual desire, the desire for continued existence, views and ignorance, are together referred to as the *āsavas*. These are the last binding factors to be eradicated by the disciple on the path, and their eradication is accompanied by Enlightenment.

The association of the *anusayas* with the *āsavas* reinforces the suggestion made above that they are almost what one would describe as 'part of human nature'. Cyclically reinforced over many lives, they have become deeply embedded in an individual's psychological make-up. They are the origin of unwitting, *asampaja*, actions.[51] We also see the threefold classification of volitions according to bodily actions, speech and thoughts identified with breathing, discursive thought, and apperception and feeling respectively, all of which are normal processes in every human being.[52] This is perhaps why the term 'roots', *mūlā*, is so often associated with binding defilements in Pali material: they have to be rooted out. Paradoxically, however, it is volition which is applied in the rooting out process. In the light of the deeply embedded nature of the *anusayas* (or *āsavas*), which fuel one's continued *saṃsāric* existence, this process is so difficult that it is referred to as going 'against the current', *patisotagāmi*.

We have seen that *saṃkhāra* and karma are classified according to good and bad. Though in popular teaching good volitions or actions are usually said to lead to a favourable rebirth, they can also be used intentionally to direct one's will towards the following of the Eightfold Path and eradicating the roots of defilement. In the *Sabbāsavasutta*, for example, it states that the *āsavas* can be eradicated by wisely paying attention (*yoniso manasikāra*) to their control (*saṃvara*), to endurance (*adhivāsanā*) and so on.[53] All of these are deliberately or volitionally applied. We also find the terms *patthanā* and *paṇidhi*, respectively meaning aspiration and mental resolve, in association with *cetanā*, volition, in contexts where all three can be used towards the continuing of *dukkha* or can be directed towards activities which conduce to *sukha*, its direct opposite (and as such sometimes used as a synonym for Nirvana).[54] A *bhikkhu* has to keep his thoughts under control by a deliberate act of will (*saṃkhāra*) involving habitual restraint.[55]

The way the *saṃkhāras* act as a 'fuel' for the individual's continuing *saṃsāric* existence is not difficult to understand from all of the foregoing. We can see the way volitions in one life condition a subsequent life and how this process is reinforced through its cyclic nature. We have also seen how fundamentally this is embedded in the psychological nature of the human being, in the desire for continued existence, for example. This probably explains why the term *saṃkhāra* is also used together with *āyu* or *jīvita* to mean the 'life-force'. In the *Mahāparinibbāna Sutta*, we read that the Buddha can either deliberately hold on to this life force[56] or give it up and die.[57] Elsewhere it is used as one of the defining characteristics of a live person: without it there is only a dead body.[58]

In view of the complexity of the causal process, it seems reasonable to suggest that the goal of volitional inactivity mentioned above applies only to those volitions that are potentially karmically binding:[59] volitions such as hate, desire, anger have to be distinguished from those karmically neutral volitions which are continually involved in the practical functioning of an individual, such as deciding to sleep, eat, sit down, and so on. The former are to be eradicated, the latter continue and are insignificant to one's progress on the Path. What this means is that karmically neutral actions are not *technically* volitions. This is relevant to understanding the meaning of *saṃkhāra* both in the *paṭiccasamuppāda* formula and in the *saṃkhārakkhandha*. In the case of the *paṭiccasamuppāda* formula, in spite of the fact that *saṃkhāras*, the volitional formative activities which condition an individual, are dependent on ignorance, it is possible for a human being to continue to function even after all ignorance has been eradicated. One only has to recall that the Buddha continued to live for forty-five years after his Enlightenment to realise that this is the case. This need not be problematic if one considers the formula in the spirit in which it was intended rather than pedantically applying logic to it. As already stated, the formula is intended to show how a human being's continued rebirth is primarily dependent on ignorance, and once ignorance is eradicated there will be no more rebirth; the life of an Enlightened individual may continue until death takes place in due course but that death will not be the condition for rebirth. It is at the death of an Enlightened individual that the entire causal nexus, including karmically neutral activites, ceases. In the case of the *saṃkhārakkhandha*, it would seem that this *khandha* is only activated when volitions in the technical sense take place: karmically neutral, or non-technical, activities do not involve the *saṃkhārakkhandha*. Once again, no problems arise if one bears in mind the purpose of giving the analysis: the Buddha's overriding concern was to offer a path to liberation rather than a complete classification of every process that occurs, and, since karmically neutral activities are not a soteriologically significant factor within human existence, they do not have to be part of an analysis of the human being which is given for the sole purpose of leading to liberating insight. The technical status of *saṃkhāras* is suggested in passages which state that Nirvana, the cessation of ignorance, is the stilling (or cessation) of *saṃkhāras*.[60] At this point one's state of mind is without volitional activity.[61] But at this point that part of the causal nexus which fuels one's basic functioning as a human being nevertheless continues.

A final point concerning *saṃkhāra* brings me back to the suggestion that it is important to understand that the *paṭiccasamuppāda* formula applies to the way a human being arises and not to the way *saṃsāra* in the general sense of the objective world arises. We can see that the meaning of *saṃkhāra* in the *tilakkhaṇa* formula differs from its meaning as the second link in the *paṭiccasamuppāda* formula and in the *saṃkhārakkhandha* in that the first has a passive meaning, 'conditioned phenomena', and the last two have an active meaning, 'formative activities' and 'volitional constituent'. We saw above that all the phenomena of *saṃsāric* experience are *saṃkhāras*, and in this sense all the *khandhas* and parts thereof are *saṃkhāras* regardless of any other more specific function they may have. Given also that the *paṭiccasamuppāda* formula describes a process wherein the *saṃkhāras* are the active and formative principle of individual *saṃsāric* continuity, one might say, as Franke does, that the term *saṃkhāra* refers both to process and product. In making this point, however, it is crucial to understand (as Franke does not) both that this can be said only with reference to human *saṃsāric* continuity, and also that both process *and* product are concerned with method and not with substance (that is, with how it works rather than with what it is). Franke claims[62] that *saṃkhāra* is both process and product of an entirely mental creative activity; that the process, being based on ignorance, is psychological, and the product imaginary. He makes this claim for the world as a whole. Franke has failed to understand that the *paṭiccasamuppāda* formula is intended to explain the 'how' of *human saṃsāric* existence, not the 'what' of the world as a whole. He erroneously states on the one hand that because the *saṃkhāras* are conditioned by ignorance and give rise to the subsequent parts of the chain, the entire process is mental, and mistakenly claims on the other hand an idealistic ontological status for the product.[63] In my opinion, it cannot be claimed that the *saṃkhāras* are both process and product of the objective world (*saṃsāra*) as a whole, because we have no evidence to support the supposition that the world is volitionally formed, only that it is conditioned (*saṃkhata*).

Notes

1. AN.I.286. The formula itself is also found at *Dhammapada* 5-7; 277-279. cf. also MN.I.336; DN.II.157.
2. F.L. Woodward translates *dhammaṭṭhitatā* as 'causal law of nature' and *dhammaniyāmatā* as 'orderly fixing of things' (GS.I.264f). His translation of the formula itself is misleadingly incorrect because he gives 'phenomena' for both *saṃkhārā* and for *dhammā*.
3. *Sabbe saṃkhārā dukkhā, sabbe saṃkhārā aniccā, sabbe dhammā anattā.*

4. SN.I.135: *Satto ... suddhasaṃkhārapuñjo.*
5. For example, at SN.II.25 and throughout the *Nidāna Saṃyutta.*
6. SN.II.25: *Paṭiccasamuppādañca vo bhikkhave desissāmi paṭiccasamuppanne ca dhamme.*
7. Ibid.
8. For example, SN.I.136: ... *duddasaṃ idaṃ ṭhānam: yad idam idappaccayatā paṭiccasamuppādo*: "This is something hard to perceive: that this is conditioned by that, it is dependently originated."
9. The formula may also refer to other beings on the *saṃsāric* cycle of rebirth: animals, *devas* and so on. But the path to liberating insight is primarily given in terms of the human condition and it is this with which this book is concerned.
10. DN.II.55ff: *Diṭṭhūpādāna ... tuvaṃtuva-pesuñña-musāvādā.*
11. For example, AN.I.177; SN.II.2 etc.; MN.I.190.
12. *Anupagamma majjhena tathāgato dhammaṃ deseti.* There are many examples of such contexts in the *Nidāna Saṃyutta*; for example, SN.II.17. cf. Mrs C. A. F. Rhys Davids' comment in *Dialogues* Vol II, p.42f.
13. SN.II.27: ... *ahaṃ nu kho smi, na nu kho smi; kiṃ nu kho smi; kathaṃ nu kho smi; ahaṃ nu kho satto kuto āgato so kuhiṃgāmī bhavissatī ti.*
14. MN.II.32 (without the formula); SN.II.28,95; MN.III.63. Not at DN.II.55f or AN.I.176f. *Imasmiṃ sati, idaṃ hoti; imass' uppādā idaṃ uppajjati; imasmiṃ asati, idaṃ na hoti; imassa nirodhā idaṃ nirujjhati.*
15. cf. Rahula, 1978, p.53.
16. I will henceforth make this distinction: the term *paṭiccasamuppāda* means the doctrine of dependent origination, whereas the *paṭiccasamuppāda* 'formula' refers to the chain itself.
17. SN.II.82.
18. For example, I. B .Horner in her translations for the Pali Text Society. See her note at MLS, Vol.I, p.xxiv.
19. SN.III.60: *Katamā ca bhikkhave saṃkhārā? Chayime bhikkhave cetanākāyā.*
20. I am using 'will' in a general commonsense way and do not imply any technical meaning which may be associated with specific philosophies.
21. SN.III.87.
22. *Kiñca saṃkhatam abhisaṃkharonti? Rūpaṃ rūpattāya saṃkhatam abhisaṃkharonti, vedanaṃ vedanattāya saṃkhatam abhisaṃkharonti, saññaṃ saññattāya saṃkhatam abhisaṃkharonti, saṃkhāre saṃkhārattāya saṃkhatam abhisaṃkharonti, viññāṇaṃ viññāṇatthāya saṃkhatam abhisaṃkharonti.*
23. Collins (1982, p.202) translates *saṃkhataṃ abhisaṃkharontīti tasmā saṃkhāra* as "(people) form a construction, thus they are 'formations'". Though this translation may be philosophically correct, it makes no mention either of the *khandha* the passage is defining or of the role of volitions in the constructing of an individual.
24. MN.I.111: *Cakkhuñ c'āvuso paṭicca rūpe ca uppajjati cakkhuviññāṇaṃ, tiṇṇaṃ saṅgati phasso, phassapaccayā vedanā, yaṃ vedeti taṃ sañjānāti... .*
25. The *viññāṇakkhandha* is discussed in chapter v.
26. MN.IV.209: *Tassā yeva kho pana dukkhāya vedanāya paṭighavā na hoti ... kāmasukhaṃ nābhinandato.*
27. MN.I.293: *Yā c'āvuso vedanā yā ca saññā yañ ca viññāṇaṃ ime dhammā saṃsaṭṭhā no visaṃsaṭṭhā, na ca labbhā imesaṃ dhammānaṃ vinibbhujitvā vinibbhujitvā nānākaraṇaṃ paññāpetuṃ.*
28. Frauwallner, 1973, p.159.
29. AN.I.112: *Yāvatikā abhisaṃkhārassa gati.*
30. cf. Horner's note, MLS, Vol.I, p.xxiv.
31. Gombrich, 1971, p.346.
32. MN.I.389: *Kāyasaṃkhāraṃ abhisaṃkharoti ... vacīsaṃkhāraṃ abhisaṃkharoti ... manosaṃkhāraṃ abhisaṃkharoti.*
33. MN.I.415ff: *Kāyakammaṃ ... vācīyakammaṃ* and *manokammaṃ*. The interchangeability of *citta* and *manas* in this context is discussed in chapter v.
34. Thomas, 1933, p.61, n.2.
35. For example, Dhs 62.
36. DN.III.217: *Tayo saṃkhārā: puññābhisaṃkhāro, apuññābhisaṃkhāro, āneñjābhisaṃkhāro.*
37. DA.III.998 and *Vibhaṅga* 135: *...atamo āneñjābhisaṃkhāro? Kusalā cetanā arūpāvacarā, ayaṃ vuccati āneñjābhisaṃkhāro ti.*
38. SN.II.82.
39. *Ato kho bhikkhave bhikkhuno avijjā pahīnā hoti vijjā uppannā, so avijjāvirāgā vijjuppādā n'eva puññābhisaṃkhāram abhisaṃkharoti, na apuññābhisaṃkhāram abhisaṃkharoti, na āneñjābhisaṃkhāram abhisaṃkharoti.*

40. SN.II.4: *Katame ca bhikkhave saṃkhārā? Tayo 'me bhikkhave saṃkhārā kāyasaṃkhāro vacīsaṃkhāro cittasaṃkhāro: ime vuccanti bhikkhave saṃkhārā.*
41. *Vibhaṅga* 135: *Tattha* [in the *paṭiccasamuppāda* formula] *katame avijjāpaccayā saṃkhāra? Puññābhisaṃkhāro apuññābhisaṃkhāro āneñjābhisaṃkhāro kāyasaṃkhāro vacīsaṃkhāro cittasaṃkhāro. Vibhaṅga* 340 only mentions the first triad.
42. MN.III.99: *Saṃkhāruppattiṃ vo, bhikkhave, desissāmi.*
43. Gombrich (1971, chapter 5) discusses how this is understood by Buddhists in a village setting in Sri Lanka.
44. MN.III.103: *Ayaṃ, bhikkhave, bhikkhu na katthaci uppajjati na kuhiñci uppajjatīti.*
45. PED, p.44.
46. Sn 14: *Yassānusayā na santi keci mūlā akusalā samūhatāse.* cf. also Sn 369.
47. SN.III.130: *Asmīti anusayo asamūhato.*
48. MN.I.433: *Sakkāyadiṭṭhānusayo, vicikicchānusayo, sīlabbataparāmāsānusayo, kāmarāgānusayo, sattesu byāpādānusayo.*
49. DN.III.254: *Kāmarāgānusayo, paṭighānusayo, diṭṭhānusayo, vicikicchānusayo, mānānusayo* (this is usually associated with 'I am'), *bhāvarāgānusayo, avijjānusayo.*
50. *Adhiṭṭhānābhinivesānusayā.* For example at MN.I.136, III.31, 240; SN.II.17, III.10, 135, 161; AN.V.111.
51. AN.II.158, SN.II.40. cf. also AN.I.171.
52. MN.I.301.
53. MN.I.7.
54. For example, AN.I.32, V.212.
55. AN.I.254: *Sasaṃkhāra-niggayhavāritavato.*
56. DN.II.99.
57. DN.II.106.
58. MN.I.296. This passage, where *āyusaṃkhāra* is combined with heat, *usmā*, and consciousness, *viññāṇa*, was referred to in chapter I and is also discussed in chapter V. cf. also DN.II.335.
59. I use the word 'karmically' here in the (possibly Westernised) general meaning of that which binds an individual to the cycle of rebirth.
60. SN.I.136; AN.I.133: *Sabbasaṃkārasamatho... nibbānaṃ.*
61. *Dhammapada* 154: *Visaṃkhāragataṃ cittaṃ.*
62. Franke, 1913, pp.307–18. I am indebted to Birte Plutat for assistance in translating from the German.
63. Reat (1987 *passim*, and 1990, chapter VI, especially pp. 317ff) makes the same mistake. Reat bases his idealistic interpretation of the *paṭiccasamuppāda* formula on his understanding of *nāmarūpa*, which will be discussed in chapter VI.

CHAPTER V

The Viññāṇakkhandha

THE FOURTH AND LAST OF the *arūpakkhandhas* is the *viññāṇakkhandha*. Unlike the terms used to denote the other three *arūpakkhandhas* (*vedanā, saññā* and *saṃkhāra*), *viññāṇa* is often used in the Pali texts as a generic term to denote 'mind' in general. This generic use means that it is found in many different contexts in which there is no clear indication of its precise meaning or function as a *khandha*. The lack of clarity is compounded by the fact that other terms are also used in a generic sense to denote 'mind' in general; and they too have their own specific meanings in other contexts. By the time the *Abhidhamma* was compiled, numerous different terms had been introduced to denote general mental activity,[1] the meanings of which were elaborated in the commentaries.[2] In the *Sutta Piṭaka*, however, the most common terms used, often seemingly interchangeably with *viññāṇa*, are *citta* and *manas*.[3] All three are used far from systematically: on the one hand, the same term means different things in different places; on the other hand, the meanings of the terms overlap and they sometimes appear to be being used synonymously.

The term *viññāṇa* is usually translated as 'consciousness' or 'awareness'. Because one of the most fundamental characteristics of human beings is that they are conscious, this makes it a particularly important term in the analysis of the human being. But because there is such a widely diverse use of the term in the *Sutta Piṭaka*, it is not immediately obvious that the authors or compilers of the material had a clear understanding of what the *viññāṇakkhandha* is or does. We have already had some indication that defining *viññāṇa* is not likely to be a simple matter. In the discussion on the *saññākhandha* we saw that in a brief description of each of the five *khandhas* in the *Khandha Saṃyutta*, both *saññā* and *viññāṇa* were defined as discriminative faculties, with standard formulas being used in each case. The difficulty in understanding the term is not helped by the fact that to this day philosophers, psychologists, doctors and theologians, not to mention physicists, of both East and West continue to speculate about what consciousness is: there is no consensus as to its meaning or function.

In attempting to define *viññāṇa* here, many of the numerous contexts in which it occurs are necessarily omitted: a thorough analysis of them all would constitute a book in itself. My concern has been to draw on those contexts which I consider both to be important and to offer some clarification of the term. I will first attempt to establish how one might understand the meaning and function of *viññāṇa* as a *khandha*. An overview of the mass of unsystematic contexts in which it is found has suggested five headings under which it is most helpful to do this, though some of the points made under each heading will overlap: (1) *Viññāṇa* as impermanent, (2) *Viññāṇa* as 'consciousness of', (3) *Viññāṇa* as a factor in cognition, (4) *Viññāṇa* as providing continuity, and (5) *Viññāṇa* as evolving. In imposing such headings on unsystematic material there is of course the danger that one is projecting onto it a greater degree of coherence than exists in the texts. Indeed, such is the lack of any systematic approach in the texts that to a certain extent this is unavoidable if one is to attempt to come to any meaningful understanding of the function of *viññāṇa*. But so far as I am aware none of what I will discuss under these headings is significantly compromised by anything I have omitted. Similarly, though some of the contexts on which I have drawn do not explicitly identify *viññāṇa* as a *khandha*, in my opinion these contexts are nevertheless relevant in an attempt to understand how the *khandha* functions. In the second part of this chapter, I will discuss the common association of *viññāṇa* with *kāya*, body, and will suggest that even if this is understood as an alternative analysis of the human being it is nevertheless compatible with the *khandha* analysis. And in the third part I shall also briefly discuss the terms *citta* and *manas* in both their generic and their more specific meanings.

Viññāṇa as a *Khandha*

1. *Viññāṇa* as impermanent

In the introduction to the *arūpakkhandhas* at the beginning of chapter II, I suggested that they might be described as the occurrence of certain states or processes which do not involve the four *mahābhūtā*. In considering *vedanā*, *saññā* and *saṃkhāra*, this suggestion does not present any conceptual problems. We do not tend to think of feelings, apperceptions or conceptions, and volitions or will, as permanent; our experience of them is that they constantly change, and they can all readily be understood as processes which operate given the appropriate conditions. *Viññāṇa*, however, has connotations which are both substantive and permanent. Such connotations derive partly from the association in the *Upaniṣads* of the Sanskrit term *vijñāna* with Brahman. In the *Bṛhadāraṇyaka Upaniṣad*, for example, Brahman is defined as consciousness and bliss.[4] It is cardinal to *Upaniṣadic* teaching both that Brahman is permanent and also that it is 'being', *sat*.

Because it is also cardinal to *Upaniṣadic* teaching that there is a macrocosmic/microcosmic correspondence between Brahman and *ātman*, it follows that the consciousness, *vijñāna*, of the individual is also permanent and is 'being': it is the essential *stuff*, both of the individual and the cosmos.[5] The connotations associated with *viññāṇa* also derive from the common translation of *viññāṇa* as 'consciousness'. In English, this nominal form is open to interpretation as a substantive noun, suggesting that consciousness is some sort of permanent entity. Such a translation allows ontological significance to be projected onto the term *viññāṇa* and tends to suggest that it is not ordinarily conditioned. Finally, our subjective experience is that our consciousness is in some sense the common denominator of all our experiences. It seems to us to have some degree of constancy.

I shall discuss further the way in which *viññāṇa* functions as a process under point (2). And I shall discuss its apparent constancy under point (4). Here our concern is to establish that any interpretation of *viññāṇa* as permanent is erroneous. The most fundamental point to make here is that any suggestion of permanence does not accord with the key doctrinal teachings of the Buddha. The doctrine of *paṭiccasamuppāda* and the *tilakkhaṇa* formula, for example, underline that everything that is connected with *saṃsāric* experience is conditioned, dependently originated, and therefore impermanent. With regard to the constitution of the individual, we also see in the standard twelvefold version of the *paṭiccasamuppāda* formula that *viññāṇa* arises conditioned by ignorance and the formative activities. In an alternative version which appears in the *Mahānidāna Suttanta*, the formula begins with *viññāṇa*, but it is stated that *viññāṇa* and *nāmarūpa*, given as the second link in the chain, are mutually conditioning.[6] Similarly, the *khandha* analysis with which we are concerned was given by the Buddha in order to illustrate his teaching that no part of the individual should be thought of as having independent existence (self-hood). So of *viññāṇa*, for example (and the form of the Pali is the same for each of the *khandhas*), we read that the well-taught *ariyasāvaka* "does not view *viññāṇa* as self, nor self as possessing *viññāṇa*, nor *viññāṇa* in self, nor self in *viññāṇa*".[7] None of these doctrinal teachings is compatible with attributing permanence to *viññāṇa*.

One passage on the *paṭiccasamuppāda* formula which might be considered to indicate that *viññāṇa* is some sort of enduring transmigrating entity is in the *Mahānidāna Suttanta*, where the ninefold version of the *paṭiccasamuppāda* formula is given. Though I cited this *Sutta* above as stating that *viññāṇa* and *nāmarūpa* are mutually conditioning, we read further on in the *Sutta* that *viññāṇa* 'descends' or 'enters' into a mother's womb.[8] Literally the Pali means: "If *viññāṇa* did not descend into a mother's womb, would *nāmarūpa* take shape therein?" The context of the passage is an explanation of what is meant by the various stages of the chain in the *paṭiccasamuppāda* formula, where *viññāṇa* is followed by *nāmarūpa*. The meaning of *nāmarūpa* will be discussed in chapter VI and need not concern us here. This passage has been construed to mean that *viññāṇa* is the reincarnating factor which 'descends' into a woman's womb when conception takes place, and without which the embryonic individual would not take shape.[9] But an alternative interpretation of this passage is as follows: a human being will not develop if all the relevant constituents are not present; and the development of the individual, indicated by the term *nāmarūpa*, requires the faculty of *viññāṇa*. These two interpretations imply very different roles for *viññāṇa*.

The key word in this passage is *okkamissatha*, from a verb which literally means 'descend' or 'enter'. But it also has a figurative meaning, perhaps indicated in English by 'arise' or 'manifest'. In glossing *okkamissatha*, the commentary on this passage states that it means 'entering', but, importantly, it adds 'as it were'.[10] We also find the same verb used figuratively elsewhere in the Pali material. The expression *sukhasaññaṃ okkamitvā*,[11] for example, does not imply that the sense of happiness literally 'descends'; and likewise *okkante middhe*[12] does not mean that sluggishness literally 'descends'. I mentioned in chapter 1 that where we find *avakkanti* associated with the senses, the meaning is best conveyed by 'manifest'.[13] Two consecutive *Suttas* in the *Nidāna Saṃyutta*, which form part of a series of *Suttas* illustrating the dependently arising links of the *paṭiccasamuppāda* formula, use the verb *avakkanti*, also literally 'descending' or 'entering', in connection with *nāmarūpa* and *viññāṇa* respectively.[14] In both contexts the meaning is clearly intended to be figurative: that *nāmarūpa* and *viññāṇa* arise dependently. In view of this figurative use of the verb *avakkanti* elsewhere, together with the fact that the *Mahānidāna Suttanta* also states that *viññāṇa* and *nāmarūpa* are mutually conditioning, it seems unlikely that this passage should be interpreted to mean that *viññāṇa* is an enduring transmigrating entity. Moreover, the *Mahānidāna Suttanta* passage on the *paṭiccasamuppāda* formula ends by reiterating the interdependency of *viññāṇa* and *nāmarūpa* and by stating that the cycle of rebirth, ageing, death and rebirth is experienced by *nāmarūpa* together with *viññāṇa* (*nāmarūpaṃ saha viññāṇena*): at no stage in the process is *viññāṇa* independent.[15] Nor can one deduce that *nāmarūpa* and *viññāṇa* together form some sort of enduring reincarnating entity: we are told elsewhere[16] that there is no coming or going, decease or rebirth, persistence, growth or increase of *viññāṇa* without *all* the other *khandhas*, and the *rūpakkhandha* manifestly is not permanent. The point of these passages is to establish that *viññāṇa* is conditioned.

Though we shall see under point (4) that *viññāṇa* functions as the provider of a sense of continuity, the evidence does not suggest that it should be understood to be an enduring reincarnating entity. The use of verbs which mean 'descend' or 'enter' are a linguistic convention which indicate that *viññāṇa* is a vital factor in the arising of an individual and in the *saṃsāric* experience.

The fact that *viññāṇa* is not permanent or unconditioned is more specifically confirmed, explicitly and implicitly, in many passages in the *Sutta*

Piṭaka. It is recorded in the canon that adherents to an abiding soul theory, also referred to as 'eternalists', tended to assume that this was the role of *viññāṇa*. This view is emphatically and comprehensively refuted by the Buddha when, for example, it is propounded by a *bhikkhu* named Sāti. Sāti repeatedly states: "Insofar as I understand the *dhamma* taught by the Lord, it is that this *viññāṇa*, not another, transmigrates and continues from life to life".[17] The Buddha replies:

> Foolish man, have I not said in many ways that *viññāṇa* is dependently originated; that without conditions there is no arising of *viññāṇa*? Foolish man, you slander me through your misunderstanding, and you also destroy yourself and produce much demerit. Foolish man, this will be harmful and painful for you for a long time.[18]

A passage in the *Nidāna Saṃyutta* emphasises even more the transient nature of *viññāṇa*. Though here *viññāṇa* is being used generically, together with *manas* and *citta*, the analogy given in the passage would by extension apply to *viññāṇa* as a *khandha*: if the 'mind' as a whole is impermanent, then any constituent of it could not be permanent. The Buddha states that what we call *viññāṇa* (and *citta* and *manas*):

> ... arises as one thing and ceases as another, by day and by night. Just as a monkey moving through the forest or the woods holds on to a branch, lets it go and holds on to another; in the same way what we call *viññāṇa* (and *citta* and *manas*) arises as one thing and ceases as another, by day and by night.[19]

This idea was developed by the *Abhidhamma* and commentarial traditions, and by many later Buddhist sects, into a theory of 'momentariness' (*khaṇikavāda*, Sanskrit: *kṣaṇikavāda*).[20] But in the *Sutta Piṭaka*, the purpose of this passage is simply to illustrate that one's mental processes are impermanent. And its concern is not to establish that the object(s) of one's mental processes are constantly changing (though of course they are) but that this is how one's mind operates subjectively: the context of the *Sutta* indicates that it is to one's subjective experience that the Buddha is referring.

The impermanence of *viññāṇa* is implicit in passages which state that it is dependent on the other four *khandhas*. In the *Khandha Saṃyutta*, for example, we read: "By means of body (the form of the Pali is the same for the other *khandhas*), *bhikkhus*, *viññāṇa*, having a foothold, will persist".[21] In the *Sāmaññaphala Sutta*, one of the fruits of the life of a *religieux* who has attained the meditative state of the fourth *jhāna* is said to be that he has so purified himself that he is able to turn his thoughts (*citta*[22]) to gaining insight into the relationship between his body and *viññāṇa*: he realises that his body has form, is made up of the four elements, it arises from father and mother and is nourished by boiled rice, and is subject to impermanence, decay, abrasion, dissolution and disintegration.[23] He also understands that his *viññāṇa* is bound up with his body and tied to it.[24] The passage goes on to give an analogy to explain that the relationship between *viññāṇa* and *kāya* is like that between gem and thread in a necklace. This analogy suggests that just as both gem and thread have to be present in order for there to be a necklace at all, so it is with the human being: body and *viññāṇa* are interrelated and interdependent. Indeed, the passage implies that far from being an independent entity, *viññāṇa* is bound up with and *dependent on* the body: *viññāṇaṃ ettha sitaṃ ettha paṭibaddhaṃ* means 'here [to this body] is *viññāṇa* bound and tied'. The analogy of the gem on a thread further suggests that occurrences of consciousness are held together, as it were, by their common physical locus, a particular body. The way in which *viññāṇa* represents continuity of experience is discussed further under point (4). Of importance to the point we are discussing here is that in the meditative state of the fourth *jhāna*, a *bhikkhu* gains the insight that as an 'individual' he comprises both body and *viññāṇa,* integrally bound up with and dependent on each other: without either of them there is no 'individual' at all.

One further example will suffice to illustrate that *viññāṇa* is conditioned and impermanent. A passage in the *Nidāna Saṃyutta* states:

> If we neither will, nor determine, nor are occupied with anything, there is no arising of an object for the persistence of consciousness. There being no object, there is no foothold for consciousness.[25]

This indicates that *viññāṇa* only functions when there are other concomitant mental states which are primarily of a volitional nature. We saw in chapter IV that volitions form the causal nexus which ties us to the wheel of rebirth. Thus our *saṃsāric* existence is both kept going and characterised by volitions of various different sorts. In order to function, *viññāṇa* is dependent on this 'fuel' of *saṃsāric* existence; it does not function independently. This point is also made in the twelvefold version of the *paṭiccasamuppāda* formula, where *viññāṇa* arises conditioned by *saṃkhārā*.[26] And conversely, it is when volitions cease that *viññāṇa* ceases.[27]

From all of these references, both to general doctrinal teachings and to contexts in which *viññāṇa* is specifically discussed, it is clear that *viññāṇa* is impermanent. Doctrinally, it is, as part of the *saṃsāric* existence of a human being, subject to dependent origination. More specifically, we have seen that it does not function independently of a body, and it is dependent for its occurrence and persistence on there being other concomitant mental states.[28]

2. *Viññāṇa* as 'consciousness of'

I mentioned above that one of the reasons why *viññāṇa* tends to have connotations which are substantive and permanent is because it is usually translated as 'consciousness'. Here, I will draw on canonical references which indicate that *viññāṇa* functions as a process which is better conveyed by the translation 'consciousness *of*'.[29]

One of the *Khandha Saṃyutta* passages to which I have already referred in introducing each of the preceding *khandhas* puts the question "And what, *bhikkhus*, is *viññāṇa*?".[30] The reply is: "There are these six types of *viññāṇa*: visual, auditory, olfactory, gustatory, tactile and mental. When name and form arise, *viññāṇa* arises; when name and form cease, *viññāṇa* ceases".[31]

Of this reply, I will discuss here only the six types of *viññāṇa*. In order to interpret the second part of this statement we need to consider the meaning of the term *nāmarūpa*. This is a substantial subject and will be discussed at length in chapter VI. The usual translation of the Pali terms referring to the six types of *viññāṇa*, *cakkhuviññāṇa*, *sotaviññāṇa*, etc., is 'eye consciousness', 'ear consciousness', and so on, which has little or no precise meaning for us in English. By using a little licence, however, in interpreting the terms in the light of what we now know about the senses, much more sense can be made of the Pali terms. If we translate the words *cakkhu*, *sota*, *ghāna*, *jivhā*, *kāya* and *mano* not as the organs of sense themselves but as representing the functions of those organs of sense, that is sight or seeing, hearing, smelling, and so on, and if we specifically word the translation of each term as a genitive *tappurisa* compound, then we have the following: *cakkhuviññāṇa*, for example, would mean awareness of sight or seeing; *sotaviññāṇa* would be awareness of sound or hearing; *ghānaviññāṇa* awareness of taste, and so on. The same meaning is perhaps achieved more elegantly by translating as 'visual awareness', 'auditory awareness', and so on, but by using the overtly genitive wording in the first instance we gain a clearer understanding of the *viññāṇakkhandha* as providing 'consciousness (or awareness) *of*'.

We can gain some idea of how this occurs from the passage we have already discussed in previous chapters which shows that *viññāṇa* is a key factor in the arising of feelings and apperception. This passage, in the *Madhupiṇḍikasutta*, states: "Visual consciousness arises because of eye and visible form ... auditory consciousness arises because of ear and sound (and so on through all six senses)".[32] The presence of the three, the *Sutta* states, is called 'contact', *phassa*. If we consider this together with the analogy which states that the activity of *viññāṇa* can be likened to the way a monkey travels through a forest grasping and letting go of branches, we see both how *viññāṇa* works as a process and also that it provides awareness *of* each stage of the process. In arising as it were sequentially from one or other of the senses coming into contact with its corresponding 'external' stimuli (and we have seen that *manodhātu* collates this mass of incoming data), *viññāṇa* is a process which provides seemingly continuous awareness. And in arising dependent on specific senses, it provides us with awareness *of* sight, hearing, taste, and so on. In our subjective experience of awareness, we *know* that at certain times we see, hear, taste, and so on. This point is highlighted when we consider that if we have not been aware of a sound then we have not heard it: awareness of the sound *is* hearing it, and visual awareness *is* sight. Of course that does not necessarily mean that if we have not been aware of a sound then it has not happened, but for an individual to be able to say 'I heard a sound' he or she has to have been aware, or conscious, *of* it.

A passage about the arising of consciousness elsewhere in the *Majjhima Nikāya* emphasises that one has to be conscious *of* by stating that *samannāhāra*, 'attention', is a part of the process. It states:

> If the individual's eye[33] is intact and external (visible) forms come within its range, but there is no appropriate attention, then there is no arising of the appropriate type of consciousness. But when the individual's eye is intact, external (visible) forms come within its range, and there is appropriate attention, then there is the arising of the appropriate type of consciousness.[34]

Reat suggests that from these two passages about the arising of consciousness:

> ... two equations emerge: (1) faculty + object + *viññāṇa* = *phassa/samannāhāra*, and (2) faculty + object + *phassa/samannāhāra* = *viññāṇa*. Sensory contact, accompanied by appropriate attention, is as necessary for consciousness as consciousness is for sensory contact and appropriate attention.[35]

The term *samannāhāra* also means 'coming together', so it is possible that the terms *phassa* and *samannāhāra* are broadly interchangeable in these contexts as Reat suggests. The 'attention' referred to here does not appear to refer to *deliberately* paying attention, but, rather, to the fact that a conscious event provides one with awareness of its object; without awareness of its object it is not a conscious event.

Elsewhere we read that *viññāṇa* is categorised according to sense only because a particular sense is the origin of its arising, not because there are different kinds of consciousness. The passage states:

> Consciousness is known by this or that name [i.e. visual, auditory, olfactory (and so on)] because an appropriate condition arises. If consciousness arises because of eye and visual form, it is known as visual consciousness (and so on).[36]

In the same way, the *Sutta* goes on by way of analogy, a fire is defined according to what is burning. If it is burning sticks, twigs, and so on, it is known as a stick or twig fire.[37] The analogy implies that just as fire is fire whatever is burning and whatever name is given to it, so *viññāṇa* is *viññāṇa* whatever sense originated the cognition and whatever name is given to it as a result: it is not fire or *viññāṇa* itself that is of different types. This analogy accords well with understanding *viññāṇa* as 'consciousness of'. As fire can be described as the process of burning which only occurs given appropriate conditions, so consciousness can be described as a process of being aware which occurs given appropriate conditions. Though those conditions are infinitely variable, in the case of the former the relevant characteristic of fire is burning, and in the case of the latter the relevant characteristic of the *viññāṇakkhandha* is providing consciousness *of* them.

The association of consciousness of with attention referred to above, however minimal that attention might be, raises the question of how 'involuntary' reactions are accounted for. I have suggested that if one is not conscious of a sound then one has not heard it. We can, however, sometimes react 'involuntarily' to a sound *without* being conscious of it: in sleep, for example, a loud sound can cause one to make a movement even if there is absolutely no consciousness of the sound at all. We also experience peripheral awareness which we do not seem to be conscious *of*. We regularly avoid obstacles in our path while our attention is wholly elsewhere, for example. Though such experiences of peripheral awareness might indicate the minimal level to which consciousness of, or awareness, operates, this question is not explicitly dealt with in the *Sutta Piṭaka*. Nor is the experience of involuntary reactions explained. This is a significant omission because involuntary reactions such as wet dreams became the subject of controversy in the early Buddhist *saṅgha*: if they are unconscious, do they constitute a volition with moral implications?[38]

One passage in the *Sutta Piṭaka* is problematic when it comes to translating *viññāṇa* as 'consciousness of'. This is in the *Mahāvedallasutta*, where *viññāṇa* appears to be identified as a 'life principle' (*āyusaṃkhāra*). The context (referred to in earlier chapters) is one in which Sāriputta states that the five senses (*pañc'indriyāni*) are dependent on vitality (*āyu*), vitality is dependent on heat (*usmā*), and likewise heat is dependent on vitality.[39] Sāriputta then introduces the term *āyusaṃkhārā*, and goes on to state: "When three things leave this body, life, heat and *viññāṇa*, then this body lies down abandoned, cast off, like a senseless log of wood".[40] The suggestion is that life, heat and *viññāṇa* collectively represent some sort of basic life principle, and there is little room here for *viññāṇa* to mean 'consciousness of'. But there are only two contexts in which *viññāṇa* is used in this way.[41] In other contexts where the term *āyusaṃkhāra* is used it either appears in the singular,[42] or is not explicitly associated with *viññāṇa*.[43] It is possible that the notion of *viññāṇa* as a life principle contributed to the development in later Buddhist traditions of more elaborate theories of consciousness. In the *Sutta Piṭaka*, however, it does not significantly compromise the many other contexts in which *viññāṇa* seems to mean 'consciousness of'.[44]

Several times in this chapter I mention that being conscious is a fundamental characteristic of a human being and this might be why it is associated with the life-principle in the *Mahāvedallasutta*. But in Buddhism there is a further reason for suggesting that it is consciousness of that is of greater importance. This is the Buddha's teaching that karma is volition. The purpose of this teaching is precisely that one should be conscious of the process of cyclic rebirth that is fuelled by one's volitions: the qualitative causal dimension implicit in the Buddha's definition of karma requires consciousness *of* what one is willing. This association between consciousness of and spiritual progress might also explain why there is no discussion of peripheral awareness or involuntary reactions: they are not spiritually relevant.

So having established that *viññāṇa* is impermanent, we see here that descriptions of *viññāṇa* in the *Sutta Piṭaka* also suggest that it functions as a process of being aware, and that a good translation of it is 'consciousness of'. Another way of putting this point would be to say that while in the *Upaniṣads* consciousness is the very stuff of existence, in Buddhism consciousness is not explained in terms of a metaphysical entity. The Buddha's teaching is more concerned with how the human being operates than with what he or she consists of, and *viññāṇa* refers to the process which provides consciousness *of*.[45]

3. *Viññāṇa* as a factor in cognition

As one might expect, *viññāṇa*, awareness, is a key factor in the cognitive process. This is indicated in the passage in the *Majjhima Nikāya*, to which I have referred several times, which begins "Visual consciousness arises because of eye and visible form".[46] We discussed the passage in full in the chapter on the *saññākhandha*. I need not repeat the Pali here, but in English it continues:

> Contact [occurs] when there is a combination of the three; feelings are caused by contact; that which one feels, one apperceives; that which one apperceives, one reasons about; that which one reasons about, one causes to become manifold.

This passage represents our normal *saṃsāric* experience and the way in which we interpret it; it describes the *saṃsāric* cognitive process, in which *viññāṇa* is here seen to be a key factor. It appears at the beginning of the sentence because it is a prerequisite to every stage in the cognitive process. The sensory event, *phassa*, which gives rise to feeling, does not occur simply because of the proximity, or, to give *phassa* its literal meaning, because of the contact of eye and visible form: *viññāṇa* has to be present at the preliminary stage of the process. When *phassa*, the sensory event, subsequently gives rise to feeling, this is then identified by *saññā*. This is then followed by discursive thought (reasoning, *vitakka*) and the process of seeing things as manifold, as discussed above. It is the function of *viññāṇa* to enable us to be aware of each of these aspects of the cognitive process.

In chapter III, I referred to a passage in the *Saṃyutta Nikāya* which appeared to suggest that there is a discriminative function to *viññāṇa*, and that this can be applied to each of its six types. The passage was translated there as follows: "And what *bhikkhus*, do you call *viññāṇa*? It is called *viññāṇa* because it discriminates".[47] *Viññāṇa* appears to discriminate whether something is sour or bitter, acid or sweet, alkaline or non-alkaline, saline or non-saline. The tentative suggestion was made in chapter III that the difference between the discriminatory functions of *saññā* and *viññāṇa* might be one of degree: *viññāṇa* discerns that a taste is sweet or sour, but it is *saññā* that discriminates or identifies it more precisely as, for example, sugar or lemon. But we also noted that the author(s) both of this passage and the similar passage in the *Mahāvedallasutta* seem to have difficulty describing the difference between *saññā* and *viññāṇa*, using standard formulas about colours and tastes. The verbs used in both these passages to define *viññāṇa* and *saññā* are *vijānāti* and *sañjānāti* respectively.[48] These verbs are associated with cognition, but neither of them has a precise meaning and their use further indicates that the author(s) had difficulty in attempting to define *viññāṇa* and *saññā*. The description of the cognitive process can assist us here, in that it contains no suggestion that *viññāṇa* acts in a discriminatory capacity. If one bears this in mind, together with the understanding of *viññāṇa* as consciousness of, one can make more sense of the apparent confusion created by the author(s) of the *Saṃyutta Nikāya* passage and the *Mahāvedallasutta*. Kalupahana makes the helpful suggestion that the phrase *vijānāti … tasmā viññāṇan ti vuccati* might be interpreted "*viññāṇa* stands for the function of 'being conscious'".[49] This accords with *viññāṇa* as consciousness of, and as such it functions in providing awareness when something is discriminated, regardless of whether the discrimination is general or precise. Perhaps this is the point that the author of these passages has failed to understand. I have stated that we have to know that we hear something. We also have to know when we discriminate something. *Viññāṇa* does not specifically do the discriminating, but, rather, is the awareness by which we experience every stage of the cognitive process, including the process of discriminating.

In this sense, *viññāṇa* is comparable to *prajñā* as described in the *Kauṣītakī Upaniṣad* (which is almost certainly later than the time when the Buddha was teaching). There we read:

> Verily, without *prajñā*, speech does not make known any name at all. One thinks 'My mind was elsewhere; I was not aware of this name'. Without *prajñā*, breath does not make known any smell at all. One thinks 'My mind was elsewhere; I was not aware of any smell' (and so on through all the senses).[50]

The passage concludes:

> Without *prajñā*, no thought whatever would happen. One would not be aware of what one should be aware of.[51]

The *Mahāvedallasutta* gives us an account of the way in which the three *arūpakkhandhas* of *vedanā*, *saññā* and *viññāṇa* function together in the cognitive process, and the centrality of the cognitive process to making progress on the path to liberating insight is also illustrated, using the cognitive term *paññā*. The different cognitive terms are not clearly explained and their different meanings have to be drawn out. It appears from the *Sutta* that *paññā* refers to a specific type, or attainment, of cognition. Sāriputta is being questioned by one Koṭṭhita the Great. Koṭṭhita wants to know in what respect one is described as either *duppañña* or *pañña*.[52] Sāriputta explains:

> One is said to be *duppañña* if one does not comprehend 'this is *dukkha*', 'this is the arising of *dukkha*', 'this is the cessation of *dukkha*' and 'this is the course leading to the cessation of *dukkha*'.[53]

Conversely, one is said to be *pañña* if one does comprehend these things. The verb I have translated as 'comprehend' is *pa√ñā* which is within the range of cognitive verbs such as *saṃ√ñā* and *vi√ñā* to which I have already referred, none of which has a precise meaning. The prefix *pa*, however, suggests an intensification of *ñā*, to know, giving us a meaning such as 'to know completely', or 'to know qualitatively better'. This meaning is also suggested by the context in which we find it used in the *Mahāvedallasutta*. Completely knowing or comprehending the Four Noble Truths is indispensable for liberating insight, and thus it is qualitatively different from other kinds of knowledge. This qualitatively different knowledge can perhaps be translated as 'wisdom'. *Paññā*, therefore, seems to refer not just to the cognitive process that all human beings experience but to the cognition of someone who has advanced in understanding the teachings of the Buddha; one who is well on the way to 'seeing things as they really are'.

In chapter III I mentioned that Buddhaghosa understood *paññā* to contribute to insight in a way which neither *saññā* nor *viññāṇa* does, and suggested there that Buddhaghosa's interpretation is more systematic than that found in the *Sutta Piṭaka*. Many contexts in the *Sutta Piṭaka* nevertheless indicate that *paññā* is of a qualitatively different nature from other knowledge. It is implicit in the fact that the term is used in the traditional threefold division of the Eightfold Path into *paññā*, *sīla*, and *samādhi*. Here a distinction is made between cognitive wisdom (*paññā*) and the meditative experience (*samādhi*). Though both are to be practised or cultivated, in the Buddhist teaching it is the penetrating insight which is achieved through wisdom, rather than meditative levels *per se*, which constitute liberation. As a division of the Eightfold Path, *paññā* covers 'right view' (*sammā diṭṭhi*) and 'right thought' (*sammā saṅkappa*). We read in the *Majjhima Nikāya* that 'right view' is of two kinds, mundane and supramundane.[54] It is supramundane 'right view', which is of the Path (leading to liberation), that is associated with *paññā*.[55] The importance of developing *paññā* is highlighted in other canonical passages. We read, for example, that it is through wisdom that the advanced *bhikkhu* comes to see dependent origination and conditioned phenomena as they really are.[56] The development of *paññā* results in the eradication of ignorance.[57] Even the destruction of the *āsavas* can be realised through the development of *paññā*.[58] Elsewhere the Buddha describes Sāriputta as having *paññā* that is great (*mahā*), broad (*puthu*), joyful (*hāsa*), alert (*javana*), clever (*tikkha*) and penetrating (*nibbedhika*). Here *paññā* clearly means Sāriputta's wisdom, since the Buddha goes on to state that he, Sāriputta, is able to teach *dhamma* even as well as the Buddha.[59] Finally, it is only through wisdom (*paññā*) that things are properly understood, intellectual and discursive knowledge is insufficient.[60]

The *Mahāvedallasutta* continues with definitions of the terms *vedanā*, *saññā* and *viññāṇa* (and the absence of clear definitions has been discussed above). Koṭṭhita goes on to ask Sāriputta whether *vedanā*, *saññā* and *viññāṇa* are associated or whether they are dissociated; is it possible, he wants to know, that they will be seen to be separate from each other after repeatedly analysing them.[61] Sāriputta replies as follows:

> *Vedanā*, *saññā* and *viññāṇa* are associated, not dissociated, and even after repeatedly analysing them one does not see them as separate from each other: that which one feels, one apperceives; that which one apperceives, one is aware of. Therefore they are associated, not dissociated, and even after repeatedly analysing them one does not see them as separate from each other.[62]

Koṭṭhita also asks whether *viññāṇa* and *paññā* are associated or dissociated, and whether one can see them as separate from each other after repeatedly analysing them. The reply to this too is that they are associated, and that whatever one comprehends, that one is aware of; and whatever one is aware of, that one comprehends.[63] Then Koṭṭhita asks: if they are so associated, what is the difference between *paññā* and *viññāṇa*? Sāriputta tells him that *paññā* is to be developed (*bhāvetabbhā*) and *viññāṇa* is for everything that is to be known (*pariññeyyaṃ*).[64] My translation of *pariññeyyaṃ* as 'for everything that is to be known' is clumsy, but what I want to convey is that the difference between *paññā* and *viññāṇa* is that *viññāṇa* functions as the faculty which provides awareness of everything (indicated by the prefix *pari*) that is to be known (*jñeyyaṃ*), and this contributes to the development of wisdom, which is developed (*bhāvita*) and eventually culminates in liberating insight. In this passage *viññāṇa* is singled out from the cognitive faculties to be discussed alongside *paññā* because it is, as we have seen, the fundamental factor without which no process takes place: it as it were 'activates' the cognitive process because without awareness there is no cognition or experience of any kind. Its inextricable association with *vedanā* and *saññā* in the cognitive process is unequivocally stated by Sāriputta, and we have already seen an example of how all three work together in the arising of a feeling. Its inseparability from *paññā* implies that wisdom has to be conscious: you have to know what you know. This is compatible with the fact that the term *saññā* was used to refer to liberating insight: we saw above that insight has to be identified. Here we see that it has to be known.

I suggest that this passage is giving us a picture of the way the cognitive process works and the contribution it makes to, and its involvement with, the development of the wisdom that is an indispensable prerequisite for proceeding to liberating insight. We have the three mental *khandhas* of *vedanā*, *saññā* and *viññāṇa* working together, each contributing to the process: *vedanā* as affective cognition, *saññā* as discriminatory or identificatory cognition, and *viññāṇa* as consciousness of each and every part of the process as a whole. The absence of the *saṃkhārakkhandha* here will not surprise us since we have seen that it is the source of volitions, which are to be neutralised completely if wisdom is to be attained. *Viññāṇa*, the *khandha* which provides awareness, represents the very basis of all knowledge, and while the highest levels that constitute liberating insight may be qualitatively and inconceivably different knowledge from mundane cognitions, one is nevertheless conscious of it in some way: this much is evident from the Buddha's accounts of his own experience of Enlightenment.[65]

4. *Viññāṇa* as providing continuity

I have suggested that one of the reasons why *viññāṇa* tends to have connotations of permanence is because our subjective experience of being conscious is that it is constant. When awake we do not experience discontinuity between different moments of awareness: the process appears to us to be a continuous one. I referred to the analogy of the monkey moving through the forest, constantly changing his grasp from branch to branch. Though this illustrates the impermanence of *viññāṇa*, it also suggests how it represents continuity. For the monkey, the experience is of travelling. In the same way, our experience is that our consciousness has continuity. Even when we wake after being asleep, our consciousness seems to us to continue as it did before we slept. The same is true after other periods of being 'unconscious', such as having an operation or even being in a coma. It even appears to function at times when one is not 'normally' conscious. People relate that while asleep they are aware of dreams, or that they have had awareness while in a coma, and even severely mentally ill people have some sort of awareness of their surroundings. With respect to continued *saṃsāric* existence as a whole, I have already stated that it is volition of various different kinds which provide the 'fuel' for this, as also discussed fully in chapter IV. This 'fuel' is a complex of factors which causes our continued existence even in states of total unconsciousness. With respect to the continuity of consciousness while in deep (i.e. dreamless) sleep, the *Abhidhamma* and commentarial tradition developed the theory of *bhavaṅga*.[66] This theory is not present in the *Sutta Piṭaka*, but it is interesting that the term *bhavaṅga* appears in the *Aṅguttara Nikāya* as follows: "There are, monks, four constituents (*aṅgāni*). What four? *Rūpa*, *vedanā*, *saññā* and *bhava*".[67] Here the close association between *saṃkhāra* and *viññāṇa* is indicated by the fact that they are both represented by the term *bhava*, becoming. It is the operation of consciousness, propelled by volitions, that quintessentially constitutes continued *saṃsāric* existence.

But the continuity I am referring to here is that which we associate specifically with being conscious. Because we are conscious of *all* our experiences, *viññāṇa* as the process of being conscious in this way provides us with a *sense of* continuity.[68] It is a sense of continuity of a subjective nature: we are each conscious of our *own* experiences. This does not imply a spacial limitation to what we are conscious of. We shall see below under point (5) that in Buddhist meditation the individual's awareness (*viññāṇa*) of experiences is said to be 'unlimited'. But it is the individual meditator who is conscious of his or her own experiences, whatever they may be. We discussed above a passage in the *Sāmaññaphala Sutta* which stated that the relationship between *viññāṇa* and the body was analogous to a gem on a thread.[69] I suggested there that this analogy not only confirms the impermanence of *viññāṇa* because it is dependent on a body, but also that it further suggests that occurrences of consciousness are held together, as it were, by their common physical locus, a particular body. Similarly just as the *paṭiccasamuppāda* formula can explain the arising of a particular individual, so this synthetical formula also suggests that each individual's *viññāṇa* is subjective to themselves: it functions conditioned by the individual's ignorance and *saṃkhārā*.

The subjective sense of continuity is not merely historical. It also gives us an expectation of continuity in the future. It is perhaps because of this that *viññāṇa* is classified as one of the four 'foods' (*āhārā*) which contribute to continued existence.[70] In the *Āhāravagga* in the *Nidāna Saṃyutta*, *viññāṇa* is singled out. To the question "Of what is consciousness the food?", the reply is: "The food which is consciousness is the cause of renewed becoming, of rebirth in the future".[71] From this, it seems that the sense of continuity provided by being aware of our existence becomes in itself a factor which contributes to our continued becoming. One might infer from this that it is consciousness that acquires some sort of 'momentum'. But it is more likely that the expectation of continuity of awareness functions as some sort of volition.[72] In one passage on the four foods, we read that they themselves are dependent on volitions such as passion, delight and craving, and without such volitions *viññāṇa* will not be 'stationed'.[73] As *saṃsāric* existence continues, however, so one subjectively continues to associate it with continuity of awareness, and that sense of continuity becomes inseparable from a desire for continued existence: consciousness becomes propelled by volitions. And, as already mentioned, desire for continued existence is so fundamental a part of our experience that it is one of the three *āsavas* that is rooted out only immediately prior to liberation.

This sense of continuity provided by *viññāṇa* is also emphasised when it is described as a 'stream'.[74] In the *Sampasādanīya Suttanta* in the *Dīgha Nikāya*, for example, one "insight meditation" (*dassana samāpatti*) is described as follows: "He understands a man's stream of consciousness, unbroken in both cases, which is stationed both in this world and in the next world".[75] Two points arise from this passage. The first is the notion that *viññāṇa* is 'stationed'. This is a common metaphor which is discussed further under point (5). Of relevance to us here is that the term translated as 'station' is always *ṭhiti*, or some variation of it (here *patiṭṭhitaṃ*). This term itself implies continuity: being 'stationed' implies that it 'persists'. As the *Pali English Dictionary* points out, were the term intended to have spacial significance, it is more likely *ṭhāna* would have been used.[76] The second point that arises from this passage is that the process of being aware is to be discerned in meditation, and it is likened to a stream. The implication is that just as the flow of a stream appears to be continuous, so *viññāṇa* continues to function from life to life. This does not imply that *viññāṇa* is a permanent entity which transmigrates: there is no part of a stream which can be said to be permanent; it is changing all the time. It means that the individual's *viññāṇakkhandha* functions as the process of being aware as seemingly continuously as a stream flows. And as the flowing of a stream depends on a supply of water, so the continuity of *viññāṇa* is dependent on the volitions which fuel the cycle of lives in *saṃsāra*. Conversely, as we saw under point (1), when that volitional fuel comes to an end, there will no longer be any need for *viññāṇa* to function.[77] Similarly, in the *Māra Saṃyutta* we read that the *bhikkhu* Godhika's *viññāṇa* is not 'stationed' (*appatiṭṭhitena*) again (does not persist) at his death because he has destroyed craving and the root of craving (*samūlaṃ taṇhaṃ*).[78] The 'unbroken stream' is compatible with the general Indian belief that rebirth follows immediately after death.

5. *Viññāṇa* as evolving

The cycle of *saṃsāric* existence which consists of a series of rebirths is occasionally referred to in the *Sutta Piṭaka* as the 'evolving' of beings.[79] By good deeds one 'evolves' to heaven,[80] and by bad deeds one 'evolves' to rebirth as a hungry ghost.[81] Given the fundamental role of consciousness in the life of the human being that we have seen, it is unsurprising that in one place it is *viññāṇa* that is said to 'evolve'.[82] This expression is not used systematically and does not always appear to suggest that beings evolve in the sense of making progress along the path to liberation; it is used, as we have just seen, to indicate a bad rebirth, for example, more in the sense of a metaphor for rebirth. But the point of the Buddhist teachings is that individuals should make progress along the spiritual path, and that progress can be understood in terms of the evolving of *viññāṇa*.

I have discussed under point (4) the way in which *viññāṇa* is the provider of a sense of continuity because it functions throughout the cycle of lives in *saṃsāra*. And I have also referred to a passage which stated that *viññāṇa* is 'stationed' in successive lives,[83] to Godhika's *viññāṇa* no longer being 'stationed',[84] and also to the fact that the body provides a 'platform' for *viññāṇa* where it is 'stationed'.[85] It is this expression (usually *ṭhiti* or some variation of it), which can be translated as 'station' or 'platform' and which has the connotation of persistence, which is more frequently used in association with *viññāṇa* to indicate the different types of *saṃsāric* existence experienced by individuals. Each 'station' (or life) is sometimes simply referred to as 'a consciousness', and "every consciousness whatever" is described as: "past, future or present, one's own or someone else's, gross or subtle, low or high, far or near".[86] A *tathāgata* is said to know "all the stations of consciousness".[87] As the disciple makes progress on the path to liberation, so *viññāṇa* is 'stationed' in more favourable rebirths, culminating in rebirth in one or more of the *rūpa* or *arūpa lokas*.[88] These *lokas* are also attained at certain levels of meditation, and so in meditation too *viññāṇa* can be 'stationed' at different levels.

We have seen that in the process of rebirth *viññāṇa* provides a sense of continuity without being a permanent transmigrating entity. Likewise, we can interpret the 'stationing' of *viññāṇa* metaphorically, so it refers simply to the existence of an individual in a particular life or at a particular level during which the *viññāṇakkhandha* fulfils the function of providing awareness: the centrality of consciousness to the human condition allows *viññāṇa* to function as a metaphor for the entire life of the individual.

But this metaphor notwithstanding, during each life *viññāṇa* functions as the provider of awareness and the sense of continuity, and we also read that when stationed, it "seeks enjoyment, persists, grows and increases".[89] This can be interpreted as the enjoyment (in the sense of experience) of a particular life, the persistence of the functioning of *viññāṇa* throughout the life, and its participation in the growth and development of the human being as he or she matures. One might think this sense is more likely because this expression also occurs in association with *nāmarūpa*: we read that if *viññāṇa* is cut off in a young person there would be no "persistence, growth or increase" of *nāmarūpa*.[90] But I suggest that the expression 'growth and increase' might also relate to the way *viññāṇa* can be understood to evolve, and that this can be explained as follows.

The Buddhist path to liberation is a progression from ignorance to insight. 'Normal' *saṃsāric* cognition represents ignorance,[91] and the path leads the disciple through progressively subtle, and eventually formless, levels of meditation, culminating in the attainment of insight. Both normal *saṃsāric* existence and the various meditative levels correspond to cosmological levels, in which one can be reborn as well as experiencing them in meditation. This can be summed up by saying that the metaphor of the spiritual path underlies Buddhist cosmology.[92] At every stage of one's progress along the path to liberation one's experience, which is one's 'consciousness of' one's life, is conditioned by one's level of ignorance. That ignorance is characterised by volitions of various kinds and degrees, which are summarised in Buddhist teachings by the expression 'greed, hatred and delusion', and it is a pan-Indian phenomenon to state that the consciousness of an ignorant person is 'defiled', 'veiled', 'tainted', and so on. As progress along the path is made, ignorance is reduced and one's experience is characterised by increasing insight. Decreasing ignorance is therefore accompanied by (or leads to) the experience of subtle and formless levels of meditation and/or rebirth. At every one of these levels *viññāṇa* provides awareness and a sense of continuity. As the individual progresses, the consciousness provided by *viññāṇa* becomes qualitatively different: it is increasingly less conditioned (or 'restricted') by 'normal' *saṃsāric* ignorance. The four formless levels (the *arūpajjhānas*), for example, are described as 'the plane of infinite space' (*ākāsānañcāyatana*), 'the plane of infinite consciousness' (*viññāṇañcāyatana*), 'the plane of nothingness' (*ākiñcaññāyatana*) and 'the plane of neither apperception (or conception) nor non-apperception' (*nevasaññānāsaññāyatana*).[93] Though from a perspective of 'normal' awareness we cannot know precisely what is meant by these descriptions of the *arūpajjhānas*, it is clear that they represent experience which is quite different from that of *saṃsāric* existence which is in the cosmological level known as the *kāmadhātu*. 'Infinite space' and 'infinite consciousness' might mean the intensification of awareness as one withdraws from the limiting objectivity of *saṃsāric* perception, or one might describe it as the 'expansion' of awareness which accompanies the breaking of the boundaries of *saṃsāric* cognition; 'the plane of nothingness (no-thing-ness)' and 'the plane of neither apperception nor non-apperception' are likely to refer to levels at which one ceases to 'make manifold'. Whatever their meaning, at all of these levels *viññāṇa* continues to provide consciousness of: the individual continues to be aware. Even the practice of *saññāvedayitanirodha*, which one can attain subsequent to experiencing the fourth *arūpajjhāna*, and which involves the suspension of all conceptual activity *as we know it* does not mean a cessation of consciousness *as such*.[94] In describing the goal of the path as insight into how things really are (*yathābhūtaṃ*), the Buddha indicated that consciousness functions at the final level: we have already seen above that one has to *know* what one knows (*paññā* is accompanied by *viññāṇa*). This is the case even though the final insight transcends any familiar cognitive experience. Because *viññāṇa* provides awareness at all these levels, it is *viññāṇa* that can be described as becoming less 'defiled' by ignorance. And as the awareness it provides is progressively less limited according to one's degree of ignorance, so it can be said to 'grow and increase'.

According to the Buddha's teaching, insight is also called purity: the path to insight is a path of purification, the removing of the 'defilements' referred to above. This correspondence between insight and purity explains why *viññāṇa* can also be described as 'purified' in the sentence "that by which one knows, when it is purified and cleansed".[95] The *Abhidhamma* and commentarial traditions, and many later Buddhist schools, developed the idea that *viññāṇa* in its 'natural' state is pure. In the Theravāda tradition, this idea is contained in its theory of the *bhavaṅga* mind.[96] But in the *Sutta Piṭaka* the implication is not that *viññāṇa* returns to its natural state, but that as the individual progresses on the spiritual path, so *viññāṇa* gradually functions in a way that can be described in terms of purity. Once again, this accords with the Buddha's concern only to explain how insight can be achieved. And just as he remains silent on the subject of possible existence after liberation, so he also comments on the "inconceivability of the beginning".[97]

The *viññāṇa* of an *arahant* is also said to be 'radiant'. If it is not restricted by the objectivity of ignorance, an analogy for the 'unlimited' or 'unbounded' (by ignorance) awareness it provides is that it 'radiates'.[98] And when ignorance is eradicated entirely, *viññāṇa* can be said to be 'free' or 'liberated'. Radiance is most often attributed to *citta*, and this will be discussed later in this chapter. But in the *Kevaḍḍha Sutta* in the *Dīgha Nikāya* we find the following sentence describing the *viññāṇa* of an *arahant*: *Viññāṇaṃ anidassanaṃ anantaṃ sabbato pahaṃ*.[99] A variant reading for *pahaṃ* here is *pabhaṃ*, and from the context it seems most likely to me that this variant makes most sense.[100] With *pabhaṃ*, the sentence reads: "[His] *viññāṇa* is formless [literally, 'invisible'], unlimited, and radiates all round". This reading is compatible with the statement that of all things that radiate, a Buddha is said to be the best, his radiance is beyond compare.[101] The correspondence between insight and purity referred to above also explains why beings are said to 'evolve to the radiant levels'.[102] The subtle or formless (again 'unbounded') levels which are attained on the path to purity are described in terms which correspond to the state of the individual.

Another way of understanding the association of *viññāṇa* with terms such as 'purity' and 'radiance' is to interpret its role as the provider of awareness on the path to insight as being analogous to the providing of light for one who needs to see. As one cannot see without light, so one cannot be aware without *viññāṇa*. According to this metaphor, then, as one progresses along the path to insight, so the 'light' that is shed by the *viññāṇakkhandha* (in the sense of the awareness it provides) becomes purer and more radiant. The metaphor is one of progressing from darkness to light, or of becoming en-light-ened.[103] Again, it is not that *viññāṇa* is an entity which either becomes or is revealed to be purer or more radiant, but that the key role played by *viññāṇa* in the path to insight lends itself to its being identified metaphorically in this way.

So *viññāṇa* can be said to evolve because it operates as the provider of awareness as the individual progresses along the path to liberating insight. As insight replaces ignorance, so *viññāṇa* provides awareness of the individual's changing experience. And as that changing experience involves the breaking of the boundaries (separateness) which arise because of ignorance, so *viññāṇa* 'expands' or 'evolves' and is eventually 'free'.[104]

Summary

To sum up the way *viññāṇa* operates as a *khandha*, we have seen first that it has no more permanence than anything else in *saṃsāra*. The tendency to attribute permanence to it is emphatically refuted in the *Sutta Piṭaka* and is incompatible with the fundamental doctrinal teachings of the Buddha. *Viññāṇa* is, rather, the process of being conscious. As such, it is integral to the cognitive process, providing subjective awareness at all stages. Similarly, because the *viññāṇakkhandha* functions throughout the series of lives of an individual in the *saṃsāric* cycle, it provides a sense of continuity both within a single life and also from life to life, such continuity being likened to a stream. Being conscious is so fundamental to human experience, that an individual life is sometimes described as a 'station' of *viññāṇa*. And it is because the functioning of *viññāṇa* is fundamental to human experience that as the individual progresses from ignorance to insight, *viññāṇa* can be said to 'evolve': *viññāṇa* provides awareness of the changing experiences and insights which accompany spiritual progress.

Viññāṇa with *Kāya*

In the discussion of *viññāṇa* as a *khandha*, I have several times mentioned that it is fundamental or integral to life as a human being. Indeed, this is our subjective experience of consciousness, and the reason why the term has attracted so much interest and speculation in all ages and cultures. It is perhaps for this reason that the term *viññāṇa* is used in so many contexts in the *Sutta Piṭaka* with so many different meanings: it is used to signify virtually any and every mental state, sometimes being used in the same *Sutta* with more than one meaning. Here, I will discuss the common association of *viññāṇa* with *kāya*, body. I have mentioned that the individual life is sometimes expressed by stating that *viññāṇa* is 'stationed': the centrality of consciousness allows it to be used as a general metaphor for an entire life. In association with *kāya*, *viññāṇa* is often used as a metaphor for 'mind' in general: all the individual's mental faculties without further analysis. Thus *viññāṇa* and *kāya*, mind and body, together represent the individual human being as a whole.

We have seen that each of the *khandhas* is more properly understood as a process rather than as offering an analysis which polarises physical and mental entities. It is perhaps surprising, therefore, to find the human being so often described in the *Sutta Piṭaka* in terms of mind and body. But though the analysis of the human being into *khandhas* might give a greater degree of insight into the fact that we consist of various processes, our normal subjective experience nevertheless *is* one of being conscious and having a physical body. At a practical level, this is a simple and acceptable way of understanding ourselves, and the terms *viññāṇa* and *kāya* are used to designate the former and the latter respectively.

Though the following of the Buddhist path, in particular the meditation exercises, gives understanding that the individual is more complex than at first appears, the simpler analysis is a useful convention for others who do not have that insight. This is illustrated in the *Mahāvaggo Sattamo*, which is one context in which *viññāṇa* is used both generically, in the general sense of 'mind', and in the more specific sense of a *khandha*. In the section where it is used generically it appears in opposition to 'body' (*kāya*), and this is clearly stated to be the way 'ordinary people' (*puthujjana*) understand themselves.[105] In the section of the *Sutta* where it is used to refer to the *khandha*, it is stated that the *ariyasāvaka* understands that the individual he appears to be is made up of five *khandhas*.[106] In other words, while the ordinary person thinks about the human being conventionally, it is part of the *ariyasāvaka*'s agenda to make a more refined analysis than simply 'mind and body'. Here the generic meaning appears to be a popular convention and the specific meaning is used for a more sophisticated group. But the convention is also used by the Buddha and his close associates, as we shall see below, illustrating its usefulness at all levels.

In contexts in which *viññāṇa* is used generically in opposition to 'body', the expression most frequently used is *saviññāṇaka kāya*, 'the body with mind'.[107] In the *Aṅguttara Nikāya*, for example, Ānanda questions the Buddha as follows:

> Is it possible that a *bhikkhu* can attain such formless meditation that in this body and mind, or in anything external to it, he has no notion of 'I' or 'mine'?[108]

The Buddha replies that it is indeed possible, and briefly tells Ānanda how to bring this about. In the following *Sutta*, Sāriputta exclaims to the Buddha that he is ready to teach the *dhamma*. The Buddha replies: "Then, Sāriputta, you must train yourself as follows. In this mind and body, or in anything external to it, there is no notion of 'I' or 'mine'".[109] In a third similar example,[110] the Buddha tells some *bhikkhus* that it is advantageous not to think in terms of self, to have no idea of 'I' and 'mine', in the body with mind, or in anything outside it.[111] In none of these examples is any other analysis of the individual given, only *saviññāṇa kāya*. So *saviññāṇa kāya* is a general expression which serves well in a situation where one wants to convey the meaning of the whole human being's bodily and mental faculties. In contexts where it appears together with *bahiddhā sabbanimittesu*, the implication is that one should not think in terms of 'I' or 'mine' (that is, separate individuality) in anything at all, whether it be subjectively or objectively. So in such contexts *saviññāṇa kāya bahiddhā ca* also serves well to convey everything within *saṃsāric* existence as a whole.

Two further points need to be considered concerning passages in which those with considerably advanced insight are stated to understand the human being in terms of body and consciousness. We have discussed some such passages here when the Buddha is talking with his close disciples Sāriputta and Ānanda, and under point (1) I referred to a passage where the relationship between the body and *viññāṇa* (which was described in terms of a gem on a thread) was discerned at the meditative state of the fourth *jhāna*. I suggested that these passages show that such an analysis was a useful convention at all levels. But they can also be construed to mean that *viññāṇa* was considered so central to the life of a human being that it is singled out as the faculty whose relationship with the body needs to be fully understood. The complexity of *viññāṇa*, which is apparent from the variety of headings under which it has been discussed in this chapter, and its association with permanence, might mean that insight into its relationship with the body comes at an advanced stage of meditation.

It might also be the case that the analysis of the human being in terms of *kāya* and *viññāṇa* is earlier than that into *khandhas*. The *Pali English Dictionary*, for example, suggests that the generic meaning of *viññāṇa* is its "simpler unecclesiastical, unscholastic popular meaning" and that its classification as a *khandha* is part of "ecclesiastical scholastic dogmatic".[112] This implies that the latter is considerably later than the former. While in my opinion this division is too formal, and there are many contexts in which both analyses appear together, it may nevertheless be the case that some passages which only mention the simple analysis are early. The *Dīgha Nikāya* passage containing the analogy of the gem and the thread might be a case in point. The passage also refers to the fact that liberating insight is attained from the fourth *rūpajjhāna*. Elsewhere, insight follows from the *arūpajjānas*, which are attained subsequent to all the *rūpajjhānas*, and it might be that the fourfold analysis is earlier than the eightfold one.[113]

The possible lateness of the *khandha* analysis has also been brought up by (among others) Mrs C. A. F. Rhys Davids in a paper entitled *Towards a History of the Skandha-Doctrine*.[114] In this paper Mrs Rhys Davids contends that the analysis of the human being into *khandhas* was a late "editorial increment", interpolated into texts which originally stated that man was simply body (*kāya*) and consciousness (*viññāṇa*).[115] Though she states that her research is not comprehensive, she contends that the interpolations are suggested by the presence of material about the *khandhas* in some contexts where they appear to be an ill-fitting gloss or insertion, and also by the absence of any mention of them in some contexts where one might expect them to be included, notably the section on 'fives' in the *Aṅguttara Nikāya*.

Mrs Rhys Davids' main concern is that the *khandha* analysis is reductionist, and the implication of institutional systematisation in PED's description of it as "ecclesiastical scholastic dogmatic" also perhaps has reductionist connotations. The earlier analysis into *kāya* and *viññāṇa* is understood by Mrs Rhys Davids to have meant that the intelligent, persistent, 'indwelling' man (*viññāṇa*) enjoyed and used his group (*kāya*) of faculties. In the *khandha* analysis *kāya* is replaced by *rūpa* and *viññāṇa* becomes a mere *aspect* of mind.[116]

Though textual analysis of this kind is not the specific concern of this book, I would make two brief comments on the matter of a possible interpolation. The first is to express my surprise that such a comprehensive exercise, if such it was, neither more efficiently excised the earlier view if it was incompatible with it, nor was included in obvious contexts such as the 'fives' section of the *Aṅguttara Nikāya*. Second, Manné and others whose work is specificaly in the area of textual analysis have shown that different kinds of *Suttas* were written and compiled for a different (usually didactic) purpose.[117] This might explain why certain teachings are more prominent in some texts than in others. And it also might explain why in some places teachings are put differently and over time come to be mixed together. Aside from these two points, my concern here, rather, is to suggest that the *khandha* analysis is not incompatible with the simple analysis of the human being as *saviññāṇakāya*, and, more importantly, that if it *was* late then it was not reductionist in the manner Mrs Rhys Davids suggests.

First, the use of the term *rūpa* in the *khandha* analysis rather than the more specific term *kāya* seems to me merely to indicate that the body is comprised of elements that are similar in structure or characteristics to those of *rūpa* when it occurs anywhere else. This is not incompatible with understanding the human body as a 'group' (*kāya*). On the contrary, it stresses that the body is comprised of a group of processes which are classified according to four kinds of characteristics, and I have suggested that these characteristics are best understood in terms of solidity, fluidity, heat and motion. The more complex term *rūpa* allows the reader to gain more understanding of how the body is constituted in a way the designation *kāya* does not.

Second, if the use of *viññāṇa* as a generic term in association with *kāya* (notably in the expression *saviññāṇakāya*) was early as well as being a simple and/or popular convention, it emphatically does not follow that the earlier meaning of the term was the 'intelligent, persisting, indwelling man'. We have seen, for example, that when Sāriputta states that he is ready to teach the *dhamma*, the Buddha replies:

> Then, Sāriputta, you must train yourself as follows: in this mind and body, or in anything external to it, there is no notion of 'I' or 'mine'.[118]

Likewise, in our discussion of the passage in the *Sāmaññāphala Sutta* which stated that the relationship between *viññāṇa* and the body was analogous to a gem on a thread,[119] we saw that there was no suggestion that *viññāṇa* is a persisting 'essence' of man. Rather, in emphasising its dependence on a body the passage illustrates the impermanence of *viññāṇa*. And its impermanence has been discussed and illustrated in many other ways.

There remains an important point, however. Though in my opinion there is no suggestion in the *Sutta Piṭaka* that *viññāṇa* was ever as exalted as Mrs Rhys Davids would like, there is no suggestion either that it was ever as reduced to nothing as Mrs Rhys Davids fears. This point has two aspects. First, we have established at some length the complexity of its functions. We have seen that it is the *sine qua non* of all awareness and cognition, that it is the provider of continuity and can be said to evolve. It is so central to human existence that it is used as a metaphor for an individual life. By including it in an analysis of the human being into *khandhas*, none of these functions is diminished. What the *khandha* analysis does do is to give more detailed information about how the human being is constituted in a way which is intended to assist in attaining liberation by preventing identification with any component of the empirical individual.

Second, and more important, is that to identify *viññāṇa* in any context with an abiding essence of man is to fall into the trap of projecting onto material which is concerned with how things operate an interpretation in terms of what they are. So if comprehensive textual analysis were to support the suggestion that the *khandha* analysis was interpolated into the texts, it cannot in my opinion be considered fundamentally to alter or compromise any earlier teaching. Though the analysis of the human being which it gives may be more comprehensive than others, it is nevertheless compatible with the central doctrinal tenets of the Buddha's teachings.

The term *viññāṇa*, then, is used specifically to indicate that constituent of the human being which provides certain functions as we have discussed above. It is also used generically to indicate both an individual life and, more commonly, the mental processes as a whole. When used in the latter sense, it is frequently found in conjunction with the term *kāya*.

Manas and *Citta*

The two terms most closely associated with *viññāṇa* in the *Sutta Piṭaka* are, as I have already indicated, *manas* and *citta*, and the three terms are sometimes used in sequence to refer to one's mental activities as a whole.[120] Like *viññāṇa*, *manas* and *citta* are sometimes used in the generic and non-technical sense of 'mind' in general.[121] And like *viññāṇa*, they are used in many contexts, often with different meanings even in one sentence.[122] Sometimes a passage contains both *manas* and *citta* in the sense of 'mind', each associated with a different adjective,[123] and sometimes *citta* is used in association with *kāya* to indicate 'body and mind'.[124] Of the numerous contexts in which both *manas* and *citta* are found, I can only select here what I consider to be the most important for an understanding of their main meanings. I will first discuss *manas* in contexts where it is used to mean 'thinking', and will suggest that in such contexts *manas* is in effect being used in the non-technical sense of 'mind', and that by extension this is regarded in general terms as that with which one thinks. We shall also see that sometimes thinking is not so much the general activity of the mind but is a deliberate activity which might also be described as volitions. We shall see that *citta* is also used to mean thoughts, and that several of its cognate forms are used actively in the sense of thinking or willing. I will go on to suggest, however, that the primary meaning of *citta* itself is not active, but that it represents one's 'state of mind'.

Because several terms which are grammatically closely associated with *citta* will be mentioned in the following discussion, we need first to consider the relationship between them before looking at *manas* and *citta* separately. The cognate forms are *cintā*, *cetas*, *cinteti*, *ceteti* and *cetanā*. We know that all these terms come from the same two closely associated verbal roots, *cit* and *cint*.[125] In Sanskrit, the two verbs have slightly different meanings: *cint* means to think, whereas *cit* has a more abstract or cognitive meaning of to perceive, know or appear. The two roots are conflated in Pali and are generally understood to mean to think. In Sanskrit, *citta* is the past participle of the root *cit*, but the *Pali English Dictionary* less specifically states it is the past participle of *cinteti*.[126] So in Pali *citta* literally means 'thought' and by extension also has the non-technical meaning of 'mind'. We shall see that it has a further specific meaning (which I suggest is its primary meaning) which reflects its passive form. *Cintā*, which in Pali means 'the act of thinking', is an abstract noun from the root *cint* according to Whitney,[127] or from the root *cit* according to PED[128] (in which case it has been nasalised). *Cetas* is a noun from the root *cit* which in Pali is only found in the instrumental, *cetasā*, or in a compound *ceto-*. When the term *cetasā* is used, *cetas* has almost exactly the same meaning as does *citta* when *citta* is used in the general sense of 'mind'. Thus *cetasā* is what one does 'with the mind': thinking. A frequent use of *cetas* in a compound is *cetovimutta*, 'liberated through *cetas*'. In Pali this is a technical term used to describe a certain sort of liberation with which we are not concerned here.[129] In the *Abhidhamma* tradition *cetas* was developed into another technical term, *cetasika*, and applied to an analysis of all possible mental states, but this is not found in the *Sutta Piṭaka*. Finally, *cetanā* is an action noun formed from the root *cit*. In Pali this term means more than just 'thinking'. Emphasising its active form, it has the technical meaning of volition, and actively separates deliberate willing from the general activity of thinking. Where the verb *cinteti* is not used, we shall see that one thinks 'with the mind': *manosaṃkhāra/kamma* or *cittasaṃkhāra/kamma, manasā* or *cetasā*. Willing, however, is more specifically indicated by *cetanā*: it is the term the Buddha uses to define karma.[130]

With regard to the term *manas*, this has already been discussed when it has the specific meaning of a sense, which I have called the *manodhātu*, and another specific use is discussed below in the chapter on *manomaya*. I will discuss here the way it is used as 'thoughts' (or thinking), and occasionally as 'volitions'. That the term *manas* is used in the sense of 'thoughts' is unsurprising since it comes from the same verbal root as *maññati*, to think, and is etymologically connected to the English words 'mind' and 'mental'. We have seen above the problems this presents for understanding the meaning of *manas* as a sense. There its role could be associated with mental processes through its function as the collator of incoming data which it then presents, as it were, to the *saññākhandha* for further processing. The *manodhātu* itself, however, does not function as a mental faculty. The use of the term *manas* in the sense of thinking appears to be an extension of its use in a generic and non-technical sense as 'mind' in general. In a non-technical sense one might simply define thinking as mental activity and so state that one thinks 'with the mind', *manasā*. And the fact that in some passages the emphasis is more overtly on what appears to be volitional activity might also be because volitions are in effect deliberate thoughts: the distinction between thinking and willing becomes blurred. Technically, however, we are reminded in some contexts that in defining karma as volition the Buddha separates the will from thinking. And one can see how this can be so: one can, for example, make a conscious act of will not to think negative thoughts.

Manas appears as the general thinking faculty in numerous contexts. For example, in the *Sutta Nipāta* we read: "thinking over views with the mind",[131] which implies that *manas* is that which thinks. And elsewhere in the same text we read: "If he is a buddha, one who sees without obstructions, he will verbally answer the questions asked in [your] mind".[132] This is a reference to the ability of one who has gained insight to 'read' other people's minds. But it also implies that *manas* is the faculty which thinks, or 'asks questions'. A similar passage is found in the *Dīgha Nikāya*: "Ask me whatever question you wish that is in your mind".[133] Elsewhere we read that *manas* as a thinking faculty has to be purified: "Our mental activity (i.e. thoughts) will be completely purified".[134] In this, the Buddha states, the *bhikkhus* are to train themselves.[135] Finally, *manas* is often used together with the verbal root *kar* in the sense of 'paying attention'. The term *manasikāra* is often used to express this,[136] and we also frequently find the following passage: "Listen and pay attention well and I will speak".[137] One has to direct one's attention to the right things: liberation, for example, is described in terms of not paying attention to any outward sign, and paying attention to the signless realm.[138] The commentary glosses *sabbanimittānañ ca amanasikāro* as Nirvana.[139] Though to 'pay attention' is the appropriate English idiom, *manasikāra* in fact simply means 'applying the mind', and this term suggests how the distinction between willing and thinking becomes blurred in practice: deliberate thinking is in effect indistinguishable from willing. This is apparent in a passage that might be translated either as: "Just as this man's volitions are directed, so after this state of mind he will reflect that reflection", or as: "Just as this man's thinking is directed ...".[140] The point is that the thinking is intentional.

Some contexts attribute a volitional aspect to *manas* in a different way. For example, the eighteen 'investigations of the mind' (*aṭṭhādasa manopavicārā*) consist in investigating whether something has given rise to joy, grief or equanimity (*somanassa, domanassa* or *upekhā*).[141] *Manas* is also said to be 'pleased', to be 'delighted', to be 'angry', and to be 'irritated'.[142]

A frequent synonymous use of the terms *manas* and *citta* is found in the common ethical triad of *kāya, vācā* and *manas/citta* which was mentioned in chapter IV. In simple terms, this means 'body, speech and mind', and it refers to the categories more usually expressed in English as 'thought, word and deed'. The English expression better conveys the meaning of the Pali formula than does the simple translation. This triad represents three ways of practising *sīla*, the morality which *bhikkhus* have to develop alongside their training in meditation and insight. That *manas* and *citta* in such contexts mean thoughts in the general sense that thinking is the function of the 'mind' is more readily apparent in contexts where the three terms of the formula appear as compounds with *saṃkhāra* and with *kamma*.[143] Their association with the terms *saṃkhāra* and *kamma*, both of which have the general meaning of activity, makes the compound mean 'activity of the mind', or 'thinking'. This is clear from one context which states:

> A bodily action is to be done [only] after much attention, a verbal deed is to be done [only] after much attention, a mental action is to be done [only] after much attention.[144]

This context clearly implies that *manasā kammaṃ* is the thinking which mentally (as opposed to bodily or verbally) puts into action previous deliberations (more usually specifically called volitions). The same is the meaning of the expression *manosaṃkhāraṃ abhisaṃkharoti*.[145] Such usages were discussed in chapter IV.

This point is also more readily apparent in contexts where the triad is found in the instrumental, *kāyena, vācāya, manasā/cetasā*. I have mentioned that when used in the instrumental case the noun *cetas* has the same meaning as does *citta* when it is used to represent the mind in a non-technical sense. The most well-known context in which this formula is found is in the definition of karma: "I say, *bhikkhus*, that karma is volition. Having willed, one acts through body, speech and mind".[146] At first sight the second sentence here appears to have the rather odd meaning of 'having willed (mental activity), one acts through the mind (more undifferentiated mental activity)'. But this is a context in which the will is clearly distinguished from thoughts, and so the definition of karma means: "*Bhikkhus*, I say that action is the will. It is according to one's will that what are referred to as bodily actions, speech and thoughts take place". So while the term *cetanā* means 'will', these passages suggest that the use of *manas* and *citta* in these contexts, whether alone or together with *saṃkhāra* or *kamma*, are intended to indicate thinking as mental activity. And the instrumental terms *manasā* and *cetasā* have the same meaning.[147]

If we recall the discussion in chapter IV on *anusaya*, latent tendencies, we see that the process of thinking following volition can happen unwittingly. The latent tendencies themselves are expressed in thought (and word and deed).[148] Here again the close association between volitions and thoughts is illustrated. Even those thoughts which arise unwittingly have the causal nexus of volitions as their origin. And once again we can see the cyclic nature of how this operates if we consider two other contexts in which the threefold formula of thought, word and deed is found. The first is in the *Saṃyutta Nikāya*, where it is suggested that one owns one's actions of thought, word and deed, and carries them forward to the next life as a threefold 'karmic baggage', as it were.[149] More explicitly, we read in the next *Sutta* that bad bodily actions, speech and thoughts lead to an unfavourable rebirth and good bodily actions, speech and thoughts lead to a favourable rebirth.[150] Not only do volitions condition our thoughts, but by putting those volitions into action thoughts contribute to the cyclic volitional process in a way which in practice blurs the distinction between volitions and thoughts even if doctrinally the will is distinguished from other mental activity.

To sum up, we have seen that the term *manas* is frequently used in contexts which suggest that it means thinking, and that this is often expressed in the general sense that *manas* is 'that which thinks' or in the sense that thinking is what one does 'with the mind'. Thinking is closely associated with volitions, because mental activity is one of the three ways that volitions are stated to manifest themselves: having willed, one acts through body, speech and thoughts. And volitions are also described in terms of deliberate thinking. The close association between thinking and willing might account for some contexts in which *manas* is described in terms which suggest that it actually *has* volitions. One further point arises in connection with the close association between volitions and thinking as a general activity of *manas*. It is significant because in the description of the cognitive process in the *Sutta Piṭaka*, the term *manas* is not used (except for the preliminary role of *manodhātu* as discussed). The discursive activities in cognition itself are the function of *saññā*, together with reasoning (or reflection) (*vitakketi*) and making manifold (*papañceti*).[151] This suggests that the 'thinking' that *manas* does is more closely linked to volition than to the discursive processes which are associated with apperception: it is the mental activity which follows from having willed, whenever that willing took place.

Thinking as the general activity of the mind also applies to contexts where *citta* means thoughts. We have seen in these examples the use of *cetas* as a synonym for *cittasaṃkhāra* or *cittakamma*, meaning general activity of the mind, or thoughts, and that in such contexts these terms are synonymous with *manas/manasā*. I also mentioned above that *citta* is etymologically cognate with the verb *cinteti*, to think. This verb appears so many times in the *Sutta Piṭaka* that it is unnecessary for me to cite examples here. *Citta* is also, though not often, used in nominal form to mean thought, and, as I have stated above, in Pali this is its literal meaning. In a short section of the *Saṃyutta Nikāya* entitled *Cintā*, 'the act of thinking', we read "*Bhikkhus*, do not think an evil and unwholesome thought".[152] The *Sutta* goes on to state that one should think the four Noble Truths. The importance of thoughts is summed up in the following passage: "The world, *bhikkhu*, is led by thoughts, it is carried along by thoughts, it proceeds under the control of thoughts which have arisen".[153] In the Introduction I discussed the use of the term *loka* to mean the life or experience of the individual human being. Here we see that it is thoughts which dominate and shape that life. As one's willing conditions one's thoughts (*cetayitvā* … *kammaṃ karoti manasā*), so it is those thoughts which condition one's future. We saw in chapter IV the way different types of *saṃkhāra* in fact act cyclically. What we have here is the same process expressed in different terms. And those terms also suggest why thoughts are sometimes described in terms that one might more readily associate with willing. In a non-technical sense the mental activity we have been discussing here includes both willing and thinking, not just the general cognitive process.

In these two passages in which *citta* means 'thought' we can see two factors which are significant to what in my opinion is its alternative, central meaning. The first is that as 'thought' it always appears in the singular. Though this might indicate that it functions as a collective noun, in my opinion it is because its central meaning is expressed in the singular case, and 'thought' is in fact a secondary meaning extended from this. The second point is that the nominal term *citta* has a passive meaning, corresponding to its grammatical form as a passive past participle: 'a thought', not 'thinking'; the activities associated with *citta* as 'mind' in general are expressed by the active terms *cinteti* or *cetasā*. The central meaning of *citta* I would like to suggest is also passive in meaning. This is that it represents one's 'state of mind'. By this I mean that *citta* is the term used to refer to the qualitative picture, as it were, of the way all one's mental processes are functioning at any given moment. This is very different from any of the different mental processes of which the whole 'mind' is comprised: *citta* is neither an entity nor a process (which probably accounts for its not being classified as a *khandha*, nor mentioned in the *paṭiccasamuppāda* formula), but is a term which abstractly indicates one's progress on the path, or, even more generally, one's mental condition.[154] One might suggest that it corresponds to one of the possible meanings of the term *citta* as the past participle of the root *cit* in Sanskrit: the 'appearance' of the mind at any given time. I noted that in the passage cited above which states that the world is led by thoughts, the term *citta* is in the singular and suggested that the singular form reflects the more central meaning of *citta*. The passage could in fact also be interpreted according to this meaning, so that what it is stating is that as *citta* is a qualitative indication of the state of one's mind, so it also qualitatively indicates the way in which one conditions one's existence in *saṃsāra*.

Understanding *citta* to mean 'state of mind' clarifies otherwise confusing passages, such as the following examples: "Without understanding the thoughts of his mind, one is reborn in life after life (literally, 'runs from existence to existence') with a restless state of mind".[155] Likewise: "My state of mind is not of such nature that it will return to *kāmabhava* levels of existence;[156] knowing this, one's state of mind is well acquainted with wisdom".[157] Johansson suggests these (and other similar) passages imply that *citta* "seems to signify a surviving entity".[158] But what they are indicating is that one's state of mind reflects one's progress, or lack of it, on the path to insight.

In the *Satipaṭṭhāna Suttas* we read that *citta* is to be 'meditated upon': "How does a *bhikkhu* proceed to meditate on [his] state of mind *qua* [his] state of mind?".[159] By doing this he will see whether he is passionate or detached (*sarāgaṃ cittaṃ vītarāgaṃ vā*; literally, 'a state of mind with passion or without passion'), whether or not he has hatred (*sadosaṃ cittaṃ vītadosaṃ vā*), whether or not he is deluded (*samohaṃ cittaṃ vītamohaṃ vā*), and so on. This meditation on the state of his mind also tells the *bhikkhu* what types of meditation he has practised: if it has 'become great' (*mahaggataṃ cittaṃ*) this indicates that he has attained certain meditative levels (*jhāna*). This was referred to under point (5) above, where I suggested that as one progresses on the path to insight so one's awareness is progressively less restricted and can be said to 'grow' or 'increase'. Here we see that that attainment alters one's state of mind, and, further, that an examination of one's state of mind correspondingly indicates the meditative attainment. This is implicit in a simile we are given elsewhere where the state of mind of one who is ignorant is likened to a "dirty, stirred up and muddied pool of water", and that of one who is enlightened is "transparent, clear and not stirred up".[160] The meditation exercises described in the *Satipaṭṭhāna Suttas* are for the purpose of detached observation, as we shall discuss in chapter VIII. But we read in the *Cetokhilasutta* that the purpose of knowing that one's states of mind are unwholesome is so that one can direct one's attention towards getting rid of such unwholesomeness and thus make progress in the *dhamma*.[161] Thus a passage in the *Majjhima Nikāya* states: "A *bhikkhu* has power over his state of mind; he is not the slave of his state of mind".[162]

We also read in the *Majjhima Nikāya* that it is in *citta* that one's "wholesome moral habits" (*kusalasīlā*) and "unwholesome moral habits" (*akusalasīlā*) originate (*cittasamuṭṭhānā*).[163] I stated earlier in this chapter that the association in the *Upaniṣads* and the Vedānta traditions of *cit* with Brahman might be one reason why *citta* is sometimes understood in terms of an entity. Passages such as this in the *Majjhima Nikāya* which state that it is the source of volitions, also probably account both for substantialistic interpretations of *citta*[164] and for definitions of it solely in terms of thinking,[165] in both cases overlooking the central meaning I have suggested here of 'state of mind'. But such passages do not refer to an entity nor to *citta* as that which wills. If they did, one might ask why it is not included either in the analysis of the human being into *khandhas*, or in the *paṭiccasamuppāda* formula. What is meant here is that as it is the complex causal nexus of volitions which one experiences (discussed in chapter IV) that continuously conditions one's actions, thoughts and so on, and as one's state of mind at any given moment as it were reflects that complex causal nexus, so the causal origin of one's actions, thoughts and so on can become associated with one's state of mind. But this is a manner of speaking. Though *citta* from moment to moment as it were reflects one's causal nexus, this does not mean that it actually *is* that causal nexus: it is perhaps better understood as an abstract reflection. We see here an important similarity between *viññāṇa* and *citta*: they are both associated with the qualitative condition of a human being. *Viññāṇa* functions as the provider of awareness and continuity by which one knows one's moral condition (in its broadest sense), and *citta* is an abstract representation of that moral condition. This reflects the fact that ethical concerns (also in their broadest sense) are paramount in Buddhism. In attempting to understand the close association of *citta* and volitions indicated by the manner of speaking referred to in this paragraph, one can perhaps understand better the fact that *citta* comes from the same verbal root as the active terms *cetanā, cetas* and *cinteti*.

It is important to remember here that an indication of meditative attainment also represents progress on the path to insight in a cognitive sense. The removal of unwholesome states does not correspond to becoming 'nicer' in some sentimental sense. Though the defilements which represent ignorance are described in moral terms, and though the development of morality (*sīla*) is fundamental to the Buddhist teachings, the removal of defilements implies the development of wisdom, which is part of the cognitive process. In giving us an abstract picture of our state of mind, *citta* reflects one's cognitive as well as one's more strictly moral progress. In this sense it has a broader meaning than when the term *citta* is used in the sense of mind in general or thinking.

The *bhikkhu* having power over his *citta*, we also frequently read that it is to be 'tamed' (*dantaṃ*), controlled (*guttaṃ*) and 'guarded' (*rakkhitaṃ*).[166] The guarding and taming of *citta* is the subject of the *Cittavaggo* chapter in the *Dhammapada*.[167] Such injunctions are meant metaphorically: because the state of one's mind is an indicator of one's spiritual progress, one should ensure that it does not indicate unwholesome states. In effect, the 'guarding' is done by the process referred to above: one consciously wills to concentrate on the *dhamma*.

In similar vein, we read that a *bhikkhu* 'purifies' his *citta* (*cittaṃ parisodheti*),[168] and that it becomes 'radiant' (*sappabhāsaṃ cittaṃ bhāveti*).[169] The radiance (*pabhassara*) of *citta* is likened to the radiance of pure gold, and, like gold, it can be defiled.[170] We saw the term *pabhassara* used to describe *viññāṇa*, and I there suggested that it meant that as one progresses from ignorance to insight, so one's awareness is progressively less restricted by the objectivity of *saṃsāric* perception and can be said to 'radiate'. It functions as it were as the 'light' of knowing. As those stages are reached, so one's state of mind will reflect the fact that one's volitional activity is ceasing. Eventually, this is a state of *visaṅkhāragataṃ cittaṃ*,[171] and corresponds to the transparent and radiant state of the unmuddied pool of water.[172] In the *Aṅguttara Nikāya* we read: "This state of mind is luminous, but it is defiled by defilements from outside".[173] Though this passage might be construed as suggesting that *citta* has 'original' purity, in the context of the Buddha's teachings as a whole it is no more likely that this passage about *citta* is intended to suggest *original* purity than that *viññāṇa* should be thought of in such a way, as discussed earlier in this chapter. But because one's state of mind is in fact an abstraction, there is an abstract sense in which *citta* might in principle be thought of as pure: just as a pool of water might be thought in principle to have a calm surface which reflects all ripples and muddiness, so one's state of mind might be thought in principle to be luminous but to reflect all mental activity.

The attaining of a 'purified' *citta* corresponds to the attaining of liberating insight. And just as *viññāṇa* is described as being 'free', so *citta* is also described as being 'completely liberated'.[174] At liberation, it is *citta* which is stated to be 'free' of all the *āsavas*.[175] By extension from this, one who has attained liberating insight is frequently referred to as *cetovimutta*. This has a technical meaning with which we need not be concerned here.[176] What it indicates in general terms, however, is that at liberation one's state of mind reflects no defilements, no ignorance. And as defilements and ignorance represent bondage, so their absence is described in terms of being free.

It is perhaps because *citta* is a general qualitative indicator that the *Abhidhamma* and commentarial traditions developed its association with the heart as a psycho-affective centre. A reference to this in the *Pali English Dictionary*, for example, describes *citta* as:

> The heart (psychologically). i.e. the centre and focus of man's emotional nature [more properly, volitions] as well as that intellectual element which inheres in and accompanies its manifestations, i.e. thought.[177]

The association with the heart does not imply, as it might in the West, that *citta* is thought of in the sentimental terms referred to above. In pan-Indian thought the heart is associated with one's mental faculties.

To sum up, then, our discussion here of the terms *citta* and *manas* has shown that both are frequently used in a generic non-technical sense of 'mind' in general. Both are also associated in general terms with the activity of the mind, and this is primarily the thinking which originates in volitions. *Manas* is particularly used to refer to such mental activity. We have seen that though the verbal root *cit*, from which we get the term *citta*, also gives us the active terms *cetanā*, *cetas* and *cinteti*, all of which are specifically associated with volitions or thinking, the nominal term *citta* itself primarily has the passive meaning of one's 'state of mind'. This is neither an entity nor a process, but, rather, is an abstract qualitative indication of the moral and cognitive condition of a human being at any given time.

Notes

1. cf. Dhs p.10 and *Vibhaṅga* p.144, where the following list is given: *Cittaṃ … mano mānasaṃ hadayaṃ paṇḍaraṃ mano* [sic] *manāyatanaṃ manindriyaṃ viññāṇaṃ viññāṇakkhandho tajjā manoviññāṇadhātu.*
2. e.g. Asl p.274ff.
3. Pieris (1980) discusses the different terms found in the *Abhidhamma* and commentaries. Not even then, he states (p. 213), are the three terms *viññāṇa*, *citta* and *manas* formally differentiated.
4. Bṛ. Up. III.9.28: *Vijñānam ānandam brahma.* The more frequent use of *cit* in similar contexts in the *Upaniṣads* and the Vedānta traditions has corresponding consequences for scholarly understanding of *citta* in Buddhism.
5. cf Reat, 1990, p.295. Reat refers to Bṛ. Up. 2.1.17, and discusses the *Upaniṣadic* suggestion that consciousness in some way emanates less essential levels of consciousness.
6. DN.II.56: *Iti kho Ānanda nāmarūpa-paccayā viññāṇaṃ, viññāṇa-paccayā nāmarūpaṃ.*
7. For example, at MN.III.18. cf also SN.III. 56f, 68, 86ff, 103: *Sutavā ariyasāvako … na viññāṇaṃ attato samanupassati, na viññāṇavantaṃ vā attānaṃ, nāttani vā viññāṇaṃ, na viññāṇasmiṃ vā attānaṃ.* A similar passage is found at Vin.I.12–3.
8. DN.II.63: *Viññāṇaṃ va hi Ānanda mātu kucchiṃ na okkamissatha, api nu kho nāmarūpaṃ mātu kucchismiṃ samucchissatha?* PED (p.687) states that the derivation and meaning of *samucchati* is uncertain. The context suggests that it is highly likely to be from *saṃ* √*murch*, to become solid, and should thus read *saṃmucchissatha*.
9. For example, Johansson, 1979, p.57.
10. DA.II.502: *Na okkamissathā ti pavisitvā pavattamānaṃ viya paṭisandhivasena na ppavattissatha.*
11. SN.V.283.
12. Miln. p.299: the lateness of this text does not matter here; what it illustrates is an example of a linguistic convention.
13. SN.III.46.

14. SN.II.90ff: *Nāmarūpassa avakkanti hoti* and *viññāṇassa avakkanti hoti. Nāmarūpassa avakkanti hoti* is also found at SN.II.66.
15. DN.II.63ff. The same ninefold *paṭiccasamuppāda* formula is given at DN.II.31ff, with explicit statements that *viññāṇa* and *nāmarūpa* are mutually dependent (pp.32, 34 and 35).
16. SN.III.53ff.
17. MN.I.256f: *Tathā 'haṃ bhagavatā dhammaṃ desitaṃ ājānāmi yathā tad ev' idaṃ viññāṇaṃ sandhāvati saṃsarati, anaññān ti.*
18. MN.I.258: *Nanu mayā moghapurisa anekapariyāyena paṭiccasamuppannaṃ viññāṇaṃ vuttaṃ; aññatra paccayā natthi viññāṇassa sambhavo ti. Atha ca pana tvaṃ moghapurisa attanā duggahītena amhe c' eva abbhācikkhasi attānañ-ca khaṇasi bahuñ-ca apuññāṃ pasavasi. Taṃ hi te moghapurisa bhavissati dīgharattaṃ ahitāya dukkhāyāti.* How a *bhikkhu* should acquire such a fundamentally erroneous view of the Buddha's teaching is explained in the commentary on this passage (MA.II.305). Here it states that Sāti was not learned, but was a repeater of *Jātakas* (in other words, he was essentially a story teller) who mistakenly thought that, alone of all the *khandhas*, *viññāṇa* was unconditioned.
19. SN.II.95: *Yaṃ ca kho etaṃ bhikkhave vuccati cittam iti pi mano iti pi viññāṇam iti pi taṃ rattiyā ca divasassa ca aññad eva uppajjati aññaṃ nirujjhati. Seyyathāpi bhikkhave makkaṭo araññe pavane caramāno sākhaṃ gaṇhati, taṃ muñcitvā aññaṃ gaṇhati; evam eva kho bhikkhave yad idam vuccati cittam iti pi mano iti pi viññāṇaṃ iti pi taṃ rattiyā ca divasassa ca aññad eva uppajjati aññaṃ nirujjhati.* cf. also MN.I.60.
20. The development of the theory of momentariness, and its imagery in Theravāda Buddhist sources, is discussed in detail by Collins (1982, p.237ff).
21. SN.III.53: *Rūpupāyaṃ bhikkhave viññāṇaṃ tiṭṭhamānaṃ tiṭṭheyya.* The CPD (s.v. *upaya*) reads *upaya* for *upāya* in the title of this *Sutta*, which is given in the PTS edition as *upāyavaggo pathamo.* The CPD reading suggests the above quotation would be amended so that a translation would read: "by attaching to body ...". This does not seem significantly to alter the point being illustrated here.
22. *Citta* is discussed separately in the third part of this chapter.
23. DN.I.76: *So evaṃ pajānāti: Ayaṃ kho me kāyo rūpī cātum-mahā-bhūtiko mātāpettikasambhavo odana-kummāsupacayo anicc-ucchādana-parimaddana-bhedana-viddhaṃsana-dhammo.* cf. also MN.III.17.
24. *Idañ ca pana me viññāṇaṃ ettha sitaṃ ettha paṭibaddhan ti.*
25. SN.II.65f: *Yato ca kho bhikkhave no ceva ceteti no ca pakappeti no ca anuseti ārammaṇam etaṃ na hoti viññāṇassa ṭhitiyā. Ārammaṇe asati patiṭṭhā viññāṇassa na hoti.*
26. cf. also SN.II.101: the four 'foods' (*āhārā*), which include *viññāṇa*, are themselves each dependent on passion (*rāga*), delight (*nanda*) and craving (*taṇhā*).
27. For example, MN.I.53: *saṃkhāranirodhā viññāṇanirodho.* cf. also SN.II.82: *viññāṇaṃ ... anabhisaṃkhārañca vimuttaṃ.* In what sense *viññāṇa* is 'released' is discussed under point (5).
28. None of the discussion under this point precludes the possibility that *viññāṇa* might be associated with a 'subtle body', a possibility which is illustrated in chapter VII.
29. I intend no connection with any technical philosophical usage of 'consciousness of'. I am using this expression simply to note the difference between a substantive entity (suggested by the single word 'consciousness') and the process of being conscious ('consciousness of').
30. SN.III.61.
31. *Chayime bhikkhave viññāṇakāyā: cakkhuviññāṇaṃ sotaviññāṇaṃ ghānaviññāṇaṃ jivhāviññāṇaṃ kāyaviññāṇaṃ manoviññāṇaṃ. idaṃ vuccati bhikkhave viññāṇam. Nāmarūpasamudayā viññāṇasamudayo; nāmarūpanirodhā viññāṇanirodho.*
32. MN.I.111f: *Cakkhuñ-c'āvuso paṭicca rūpe ca uppajjati cakkhuviññāṇaṃ ... sotañ-c'āvuso paṭicca sadde ca uppajjati sotaviññāṇaṃ ... .*
33. *Ajjhattikaṃ cakkhuṃ*: I have translated this as 'the individual's eye' because 'personal eye' is not an English expression, and the context suggests it is referring to the physical eye and not some abstract 'internal' faculty.
34. MN.I.190: *Ajjhattikañ-ce āvuso cakkhuṃ aparibhinnaṃ hoti bāhirā ca rūpā āpāthaṃ āgacchanti no ca tajjo samannāhāro hoti, n' eva tāva tajjassa viññāṇabhāgassa pātubhāvo hoti. Yato ca kho āvuso ajjhattikañ-c'eva cakkhuṃ aparibhinnaṃ hoti bāhirā ca rūpā āpāthaṃ āgacchanti tajjo ca samannāhāro hoti, evaṃ tajjassa viññāṇabhāgassa pātubhāvo hoti.*
35. Reat, 1987, p.19.
36. MN.I.259: *Yañ - ñad - eva bhikkhave paccayaṃ paṭicca uppajjati viññāṇaṃ tena ten' eva saṅkhaṃ gacchati: cakkhuñ-ca paṭicca rūpe ca uppajjati viññāṇaṃ, cakkhuviññāṇan t' eva saṅkhaṃ gacchati ... .*

37. *Seyyathā pi bhikkhave yañ - yad - eva paccayaṃ paṭicca aggi jalati tena ten' eva saṅkhaṃ gacchati. Kaṭṭhañ (sakalikañ* and so on) *- ca paṭicca aggi jalati, kaṭṭhaggi t'eva saṅkhaṃ gacchati.*
38. The controversy is discussed in Cousins (1991).
39. MN.I.295.
40. MN.I.296: *Yadā kho āvuso imaṃ kāyaṃ tayo dhammā jahanti, āyu usmā ca viññāṇaṃ, athāyaṃ kāyo ujjhito avakkhitto seti yathā kaṭṭhaṃ acetanan-ti.*
41. MN.I.296; DN.II.335.
42. For example, DN.II.106; AN.IV.311; *Udāna* 64.
43. At SN.II.266 the plural is used but not defined.
44. Reat (1990, p.301) cross-references the *Mahāvedallasutta* use of *viññāṇa* with contexts in which it is used with *kāya* to mean the individual as a whole, which I discuss in the second part of this chapter. In my opinion the two contexts are not comparable: in the former, *viññāṇa* is explicitly associated with the life principle; in latter contexts, it has a generic meaning of 'mind' in a general and non-technical sense.
45. Reat (1990, p.296) also makes this distinction.
46. MN.I.111f.
47. SN.III.87: *Kiñca bhikkhave viññāṇaṃ vadetha? Vijānātīti kho bhikkhave tasmā viññāṇan ti vuccati. Kiñca vijānāti? Ambilam pi vijānāti tittakam pi vijānāti, kaṭukam pi vijānāti madhukam pi vijānāti, khārikam pi vijānāti akhārikam pi vijānāti, loṇakam pi vijānāti aloṇakam pi vijānāti, vijānātīti kho bhikkhave tasmā viññāṇan ti vuccati.*
48. And we shall see below that *pajānāti* is used in defining *paññā.*
49. Kalupahana, 1979, p.234.
50. K. Up.III.7: *Na hi prajñāpetā vāṅ nāma kiñcana prajñāpayet, anyatra me mano'bhūd ity āha nāham etan nāma prājñāsiṣam iti, na hi prajñāpetaḥ prāṇo gandhaṃ kañcana prajñāpayet, anyatra me mano'bhūd ity āha nāham etaṃ gandhaṃ prājñāsiṣam iti* ... . The term *prajñā* is not systematically used in the *Upaniṣads*, and it does not directly correspond to *viññāṇa* in all contexts in which it is found. And the senses in the *Upaniṣads* do not exactly correspond to the six senses in the Pali canon. But the function of *prajñā* in the cognitive process as described in this passage in the *Kauṣītakī Upaniṣad* is nevertheless very similar to that of *viññāṇa.*
51. *Na hi prajñāpetā dhīḥ kācana sidhyen na prajñātavyaṃ prajñāyeta.*
52. MN.I.292: *Kittāvatā nu kho āvuso duppañño/pañño ti vuccatīti?*
53. *Na-ppajānāti na-ppajānāti kho āvuso, tasmā duppañño ti vuccati. Kiṃ na-ppajānāti? Idaṃ dukkhan ti na-ppajānāti, ayaṃ dukkhasamudayo ti na-ppajānāti, ayaṃ dukkhanirodho ti na-ppajānāti, ayaṃ dukkhanirodhagāminī paṭipadā ti na-ppajānāti.*
54. MN.III.72: *Lokuttarā sammā diṭṭhi.*
55. *Katamā ca, bhikkhave, sammādiṭṭhi ariyā anāsavā lokuttarā maggaṅgā? Yā kho, bhikkhave ... paññā paññindriyaṃ paññābalaṃ dhammavicayasambojjhaṅgo sammādiṭṭhi maggaṅgā.* Masefield (1986) discusses the lokuttara meaning of 'right view'.
56. SN.II.27: *Tathā hi bhikkhave ariyasāvakassa ayañca paṭiccasamuppādo ime ca samuppannā dhammā yathābhūtaṃ sammāpaññāya sudiṭṭhāti.*
57. AN.I.61: *Paññā bhāvitā kam atthaṃ anubhoti? Yā avijjā sā pahīyati.*
58. DN.III.230: *Āsavānaṃ khayo paññāya sacchikaraṇīyo.* In this passage *paññā* is one of four *sacchikaraṇīyā dhammā.*
59. SN.I.191: *Evaṃ eva kho tvaṃ Sāriputta mayā anuttaraṃ dhammacakkaṃ pavattitaṃ sammadeva anupavattesī ti.*
60. MN.I.133: *...ekacce moghapurisā dhammaṃ pariyāpuṇanti ...; te taṃ dhammaṃ pariyāpuṇitvā tesaṃ dhammānaṃ paññāya atthaṃ na upaparikkhanti, tesaṃ te dhammā paññāya atthaṃ anuparikkhataṃ na nijjhānaṃ khamanti.* The Pali contrasts wisdom with learning by rote, which I have interpreted as figuratively representing intellectual activity. cf. also Johansson, 1979, p.197ff for a discussion of *paññā*, which he translates as 'understanding'.
61. *Yā c'āvuso vedanā yā ca saññā yañ ca viññāṇaṃ ime dhammā saṃsaṭṭhā udāhu visaṃsaṭṭhā; labbhā ca pan' imesaṃ dhammānaṃ vinibbhujitvā vinibbhujitvā nānākaraṇaṃ paññāpetun ti.*
62. *Yā c'āvuso vedanā yā ca saññā yañ ca viññāṇaṃ ime dhammā saṃsaṭṭhā no visaṃsaṭṭhā, na ca labbhā imesaṃ dhammānaṃ vinibbhujitvā vinibbhujitvā nānākaraṇaṃ paññāpetuṃ. Yaṃ h'āvuso vedeti taṃ sañjānāti, yaṃ sañjānāti taṃ vijānāti, tasmā ime dhammā saṃsaṭṭhā no visaṃsaṭṭhā, na ca labbhā imesaṃ dhammānaṃ vinibbhujitvā vinibbhujitvā nānākaraṇaṃ paññāpetun ti.*
63. *Yaṃ h' āvuso pajānāti taṃ vijānāti, yaṃ vijānāti taṃ pajānāti.*
64. *Paññā bhāvetabbā viññāṇaṃ pariññeyyaṃ, idaṃ nesaṃ nānākaraṇan ti.*

65. cf. Williams (1992, p.194f) for a discussion of the conceptual and linguistic problems associated with describing a trans-conceptual insight.
66. Its role in deep sleep is discussed by Collins (1982, p.240ff). cf. also Aung, 1963, p.10ff.
67. AN.II.79: *Cattār' imāni bhikkhave aṅgāni. Katamāni cattāri? Rūpaṅgaṃ vedanaṅgaṃ saññaṅgaṃ bhavaṅgam.* As far as I am aware this is the only time *bhavaṅga* appears in the *Sutta Piṭaka*. cf. also Jayatilleke, 1949, p.216. The reading of *bhavaṅga* here is, however, disputed. Cousins (1981, p.2 and n.4) suggests that it first appears in the *Paṭṭhāna*, and that the term in the *Aṅguttara Nikāya* should read *bhavaggaṃ*.
68. Though what I am discussing here only relates to well people, the importance of a sense of continuity to the human condition is indicated by the modern tendency to refer to those who are irreversibly comatose, or otherwise permanently unconscious, as 'vegetables'.
69. DN.I.76.
70. For example, MN.I.261; DN.III.228, 276; SN.II.11ff, 101. The others are solid food (*kabaḷinkārāhāra*), contact (*phassa*), and volitions (*manosañcetanā*).
71. SN.II.13: *Kissa nu kho bhante viññāṇāhāro ti? Viññāṇāhāro āyatiṃ punabbhavābhinibbatiyā paccayo.*
72. The commentarial tradition introduced the expression *abhisaṃkhāra-viññāṇa* (SA.II.259; SnA.1.39), but this is not found in the *Sutta Piṭaka*. cf. also Collins, 1982, p.205ff. We also saw above that in one context *viññāṇa* is associated with the term *āyusaṃkhāra*.
73. SN.II.101: *Viññāṇe ce bhikkhave āhāre atthi rāgo atthi nandi atthi taṇhā patiṭṭhitaṃ tattha viññāṇaṃ.* The common translation of *patiṭṭhitaṃ* as 'stationed' is discussed below, and under point (5).
74. The metaphor of the stream is a common one in the canon, perhaps because the term *saṃsāra* is derived from √*sṛ*, which means, amongst other things, to flow. At SN.I.15 we find the expression *bhavasota*, 'stream of becoming', used to refer to the series of lives in *saṃsāra*. It is also used to denote the Noble Eightfold Path at SN.V.347: *ariyo aṭṭhaṅgiko maggo soto.* Those who gain the necessary spiritual status to follow the path and not fall away (this is described in several different ways) are called 'stream-winners', *sotāpannā* (cf., for example, SN.II.68f, V.346f, 357, 376; *et freq*: cf. PED, p.725). Collins (1982, p.249ff) usefully divides the stream metaphor into negative and positive contexts: the stream of *saṃsāra*, which one wants to reverse or 'go against', and the stream to liberation, which one wants to follow or 'go with' (to oversimplify).
75. DN.III.105: *Purisassa ca viññāṇa-sotaṃ pajānāti ubhayato abbocchinnaṃ idhaloke patiṭṭhitañ ca paraloke patiṭṭhitañ ca*; cf. also DN.III.134.
76. PED, p.619.
77. For example, MN.I.53: *Saṃkhāranirodhā viññāṇanirodho.*
78. SN.I.121f.
79. DN.I.17: *Saṃvaṭṭanikā sattā*; cf. also SN.V.49.
80. For example, AN.II.54, III.46; DN.I.51, III.66: *Sagga-saṃvattanika.*
81. AN.IV.247: *Pittivisaya-saṃvattanika.* cf. also Collins, 1982, p.297, n.8.
82. MN.II.262: *Saṃvattanikaṃ viññāṇaṃ.*
83. DN.III.105.
84. SN.I.121f. cf. also SN.II.65, III.124.
85. SN.III.53: *Viññāṇaṃ tiṭṭhamānaṃ tiṭṭheyya.* cf. also DN.III.228.
86. SN.III.68: *Yaṃ kiñci viññāṇaṃ atītānāgatapaccuppannaṃ ajjhattaṃ vā bahiddhā vā oḷārikaṃ vā sukhumaṃ vā hīnaṃ vā panītaṃ vā yaṃ dūre santike vā, sabbaṃ viññāṇaṃ.*
87. Sn 1114: *Viññāṇaṭṭhitiyo sabbā.*
88. The possible different 'stations' for *viññāṇa* are summed up in nine categories at DN.II.68: *Satta kho imā viññāṇaṭṭhitiyo dve ca āyatanāni.*
89. SN.III.53: *Rūpapatiṭṭhaṃ nandupasevanaṃ virūlhiṃ vuddhiṃ vepullam āpajjeyya.* cf. also MN.I.101; SN.V.47: by following the Noble Eightfold Path one attains growth, increase and maturity in the *dhamma.*
90. DN.II.63: *Viññāṇaṃ daharass'eva sato vocchijjissatha … api nu kho nāmarūpaṃ vuddhim virūlhiṃ vepullaṃ āpajjissathāti? No h' etaṃ.* In chapter VI, I suggest that the term refers to the conceptual and formational 'blueprint' of the individual for any given life. As the individual progresses on the spiritual path, it is possible that as that blueprint changes for each life it can also be thought to 'evolve'. But it does not appear to have that meaning in the *Dīgha Nikāya* passage cited here.
91. The 'lesser' beings which inhabit various hells are also part of the cycle of *saṃsāra*, and their level of cognition might be lower than that of humans. But it is the human condition

with which I am concerned here, and I cannot go into other possibilities. In any event, they do not affect the point I am making.

92. The psycho-cosmological levels are tabulated by Collins (1982, p.217). This correspondence is also discussed in chapter VII.
93. DN.I.35, *et freq* (cf. PED, p.286).
94. This term was discussed briefly in chapter III. Griffiths discusses in detail the state of *saññāvedayitanirodha* in his paper "Pure Consciousness and Indian Buddhism" (1990). cf. also Griffiths, 1986 and Williams, 1992.
95. MN.III.242: *Viññāṇaṃ … parisuddhaṃ pariyodātaṃ, tena viññāṇena kiñci jānāti.* There is some ambiguity in this passage about how *viññāṇa* comes to be purified and cleansed, but the implication is that it comes through the following of the Buddhist teachings.
96. In section (4) I referred to a different interpretation of the term *bhavaṅga* in the *Aṅguttara Nikāya*. But in view of the fact that this reading is disputed, one cannot suggest that there is a later divergence from an original meaning. The *bhavaṅga* mind as naturally pure is discussed by Collins (1982, p.246).
97. SN.II.178f, 187, III.149, 151, V.226, 441: *anamataggāyaṃ*. cf. also Kalupahana, 1979, p.235.
98. In the Brahmanical tradition insight (which is the realisation that *ātman* is Brahman) is also associated with light, and this theme is also developed in later schools of Buddhism.
99. DN.I.223.
100. There is considerable scholarly discussion on this word. cf, for example, Lamotte, 1980, p.2079, n.2; Norman, 1987, pp.23–31; Ruegg, 1969, p.412, n.2; and there is a discussion of the different ways scholars have interpreted this word in *Dialogues* I, p.283, n.2.
101. SN.I.15: *Tattha tattha pabhāsati sambuddho tapataṃ seṭṭho, esā ābhā anuttarā ti.*
102. DN.I.17: *Ābhassara-saṃvattanikā sattā*; cf. also SN.I.95.
103. In a personal communication, Lance Cousins has suggested to me that radiance here has an experiential content rather than being a metaphor. And (though Mr. Cousins did not suggest this) this might correspond to the subjective experience of illumination that accompanies insight: from the subjective point of view the progress from darkness to light might well seem more literal than metaphorical.
104. In my paper "*Anattā*: A Different Approach" (1995), I have included the metaphorical interpretations described here to illustrate a particular hermeneutic approach to the Buddha's teachings.
105. SN.II.94.
106. SN.II.95.
107. In a mnemonic passage, the *Saṅgīti Suttanta* (DN.III.216), we find the term *sakkāya* used to refer to the human being as a whole. It is also used in this sense at MN.III.284.
108. AN.I.132: *Siyā nu kho bhante bhikkhuno tathārūpo samādhipaṭilābho yathā imasmiñ ca saviññāṇake kāye ahaṃkāra-mamaṃkāra-mānānusayā nāssu, bahiddhā ca sabbanimittesu ahaṃkāra-mamaṃkāra-mānānusayā nāssu?*
109. AN.I.133: *Tasmāt iha Sāriputta evaṃ sikkhitabbaṃ: imasmiñ ca saviññāṇake kāye ahaṃkāra-mamaṃkāra-mānānusayā na bhavissanti, bahiddhā ca sabbanimittesu ahaṃkāra-mamaṃkāra-mānānusayā na bhavissanti.*
110. AN.IV.53. cf. also SN.II.252, 253; SN.III.79f, 80f, 169, 170.
111. In the PTS translation of this passage, E. M. Hare translates *saviññāṇakāya* as 'discriminative body' (GS.IV.30). This is, as Mrs Rhys Davids points out in her introduction (p.VI), misleading: the body is not itself discriminative. Harvey (1981) also states that *kāya* (in the sense of corporeal body) can "be seen to have a mental component". Harvey states (p.92) that the presence of the terms *nāmakāya* and *rūpakāya* in the canon (for example, at DN.II.62) implies that both *nāma* (the mental faculties) and *rūpa* (the physical body) are faculties or characteristics of *kāya* (the physical body). I disagree with this interpretation, and take *kāya* here to have its abstract meaning as 'aggregate', not 'physical body'. And in concluding that such passages show that the term *saviññāṇakāya* represents all five *khandhas* (p.90f), Harvey goes on to argue that *kāya* refers to the first four, giving *viññāṇa* a uniquely significant role. Again, I do not agree with this analysis.
112. PED, p.618.
113. This is suggested in PED, p.286.
114. C. A. F. Rhys Davids, 1937.
115. Ibid., p.405.

116. Ibid., p.409f.
117. Manné, 1990.
118. AN.I.133: *Tasmāt iha Sāriputta evaṃ sikkhitabbaṃ: imasmiñ ca saviññāṇake kāye ahaṃkāra-mamaṃkāra-mānānusayā na bhavissanti, bahiddhā ca sabbanimittesu ahaṃkāra-mamaṃkāra-manānusayā na bhavissanti.*
119. DN.I.76; cf also MN.III.17.
120. For example, SN.II.94.
121. For example, *manas*: Sn 1144; DN.I.213, III.103; AN.I.170; SN.III.93, V.74; *Dhammapada* 390; Sn 967. *Citta*: SN.I.194, 207, V.263; DN.III.223; AN.I.170, IV.86.
122. DN.I.20, III.32.
123. For example, SN.III.93, V.74.
124. For example, DN.I.20, III.32; SN.III.2ff, V.66; AN.II.137. The term *sacittakāya* is not found.
125. PED's mention of the two stems, *cit* and *cet*, is unhelpfully confusing (p.266).
126. PED, p.266.
127. Whitney, 1885, p.47.
128. PED, p.268.
129. cf. Gombrich, 1994, seminar 3.
130. *Cetanā'haṃ kammaṃ vadāmi.* cf. also Böhtlingk and Roth, 1858, s.v. 4.*cit, cint, cintā, cetas.*
131. Sn 834: *Manasā diṭṭhigatāni cintayanto.*
132. Sn 1005: *Anāvaraṇadassāvī yadi buddho bhavissati, manasā pucchite pañhe vācāya vissajjessati.*
133. DN.II.275: *Puccha ... maṃ pañhaṃ yaṃ kiñci manas' icchasi.*
134. MN.I.272: *Parisuddho no manosamācāro bhavissati.* cf. also *Dhammapada* 96 and 233.
135. *Evaṃ hi vo bhikkhave sikkhitabbaṃ.*
136. DN.III.104, 108f, 112, 227, 273; MN.I.296, *et freq.*
137. For example, SN.II.24: *Suṇātha sādhukam manasi karotha bhāsissāmi.* Manné (1990, p.34f) cites formulas used to open discourses of various types which include this sentence.
138. MN.I.296: *Sabbanimittānañ ca amanasikāro, animittāya ca dhātuyā manasikāro.*
139. MA.II.352.
140. DN.III.104: *Yathā imassa bhoto manosaṃkhārā paṇihitā, tathā imassa cittassa anantarā amuṃ nāma vitakkaṃ vitakkessatīti.*
141. MN.III.216f.
142. Respectively: SN.I.133: *Me nirato mano*; Sn 424: *Me rañjatī mano* (cf. also *Dhammapada* 116); MN.I.377, Sn 659: *manopadosa*; *Dhammapada* 233: *manopakopa*. Johansson (1965, p.186f) states that such contexts suggest *manas* functions as an affective centre. But the feelings and emotions here referred to are more properly understood as volitions, as I have discussed in chapter II.
143. MN.I.389, 373, 415ff; SN.II.4; DN.III.191: *kāyasaṃkhāra, vācīsaṃkhāra, mano* (or *citta*) *saṃkhāra* (and similarly with *kamma*). The generality of the meaning of the term *citta* in such contexts is indicated at MN.I.301 where *cittasaṃkhāra* is stated to comprise both *saññā* and *vedanā*. Though some scholars (for example Reat, 1990, p.313) have attempted to give a complex analysis of this passage, in my opinion it suggests that *citta* comprises general mental activity, or 'mind' in a non-technical sense.
144. MN.I.415: *Paccavekkhitvā paccavekkhitvā kāyena kammaṃ kattabbaṃ, paccavekkhitvā paccavekkhitvā vācāya kammaṃ kattabbaṃ, paccavekkhitvā paccavekkhitvā manasā kammaṃ kattabbaṃ.*
145. MN.I.389.
146. AN.III.415: *Cetanā 'haṃ bhikkhave kammaṃ vadāmi. Cetayitvā kammaṃ karoti kāyena vācāya manasā.* cf. also DN.III.104.
147. The term *manosañcetanā*, which is stated to be one of the four *āhāras* (DN.III.228), probably has a similar meaning that volitions become mental activity.
148. AN.II.158; SN.II.40: *Asampajāno... manosaṃkhāraṃ abhisaṃkharoti.*
149. SN.I.93: *Yañ ca karoti kāyena vācāya uda cetasā, taṃ hi tassa sakaṃ hoti, tañca ādāya gacchati.*
150. SN.I.94: *So kāyena duccaritaṃ carati vācāya duccaritaṃ carati manasā duccaritaṃ carati; so kāyena duccaritaṃ caritvā vācāya duccaritaṃ caritvā manasā duccaritaṃ caritvā, kāyassa bhedā paraṃ maraṇā apāyaṃ duggatiṃ vinipātaṃ uppajjati ... So kāyena sucaritaṃ carati vācāya sucaritaṃ carati manasā sucaritaṃ carati; so kāyena sucaritaṃ caritvā vācāya sucaritaṃ caritvā manasā sucaritaṃ caritvā kāyassa bhedā param maraṇā sugatiṃ saggaṃ lokam uppajjati.* cf. also SN.I.102; AN.I.63; Sn 232; DN.III.96.
151. MN.I.111.

152. SN.V.418: *Mā bhikkhave pāpakam akusalaṃ cittaṃ cinteyyātha.*
153. AN.II.177: *Cittena kho bhikkhu loko niyyati, cittena parikissati cittassa uppannassa vasaṃ gacchatīti.*
154. Johansson (1965, p.166ff) states that it is "conceived predominantly as an entity ... on the other hand [it] may be used for the produced processes themselves [i.e. thoughts]". In his lengthy paper he nowhere suggests that *citta* means 'state of mind', and assumes that its passive form implies the existence of an entity.
155. *Udāna* p.37: *Avidvā manaso vitakke hurāhuraṃ dhāvati bhantacitto.*
156. The different levels of existence are discussed further in chapter VII.
157. AN.IV.402: *Anāvattidhammaṃ me cittaṃ kāmabhavāyā ti paññāya cittaṃ suparicitaṃ hoti.*
158. Johansson, 1979, p.157.
159. MN.I.59; DN.II.299: *Kathañ-ca bhikkhave bhikkhu citte cittānupassī viharati?*
160. AN.I.9: *Udakarahado āvilo lulito kalalībhūto ... udakarahado accho vippasanno anāvilo.*
161. MN.I.101ff.
162. MN.I.214: *Bhikkhu cittaṃ vasaṃ vatteti, no ca bhikkhu cittassa vasena vattati.*
163. MN.II.27. cf. also MN.I.36; DN.I.71, II.81, III.270.
164. For example, Johansson, 1965, p.168 and 1990, p.157. Though elsewhere Johansson places the emphasis on *citta* as the thinking faculty (1990, p.161).
165. For example, Kalupahana, 1979, p.235; Reat, 1990, p.296.
166. AN.I.7, 261, III.435; SN.I.48.
167. *Dhammapada* 33ff.
168. DN.I.71, 77. cf. also SN.V.69.
169. DN.III.223; SN.V.278; AN.I.8 (*pasannacittaṃ*), 10.
170. SN.V.92.
171. *Dhammapada* 154.
172. The term *acittaka*, which Paul Griffiths translates as 'mindless' (1986 and 1990 *passim*) when it relates to the condition of *saññāvedayitanirodha*, suggests either that at that point one's state of mind cannot be discerned: it is 'blanked out', as it were; or in this context the term *citta* means 'thought' or mental activity, and this state is one in which such activity is absent.
173. AN.I.10: *Pabhassaram idaṃ bhikkhave cittaṃ tañ ca kho āgantukehi upakkilesehi upakkiliṭṭhaṃ.*
174. For example, SN.III.13, 45: *Cittaṃ suvimuttaṃ.*
175. DN.II.81: *Cittaṃ sammad eva āsavehi vimuccati.*
176. cf. Gombrich, 1994, *op.cit.*
177. PED, p.266.

CHAPTER VI

Nāmarūpa

THE EXPRESSION *NĀMARŪPA* IS AN important one in ancient Indian psychology. The term *nāma* (name) on its own is first found in the *Ṛg Veda* where the *ṛṣis* gave names to things.[1] The expression used for this is *nāmadheya* – 'conferring a name'. Later, in the *Bṛhadāraṇyaka Upaniṣad*, when Yājñavalkya is asked what it is that does not forsake a man when he dies, his answer is 'name'.[2] Name-conferring must, then, have been an important enough process for Yājñavalkya on this occasion to state that the name is eternal, a characteristic one might expect to be attributed to *ātman* rather than *nāma*.[3] Yet in the giving of a name, some sort of abstract or notional identity is established which is independent of the empirical thing or individual. We need only consider that when someone we know dies, their name and all that is associated with it does not die, but conceptually represents that person to us in our memories. Likewise with, say, a book: its name persists even if the book itself is destroyed.

The earliest instance of the pairing of *nāma* with *rūpa* is probably in the *Śatapatha Brāhmaṇa*, and it continues to be found in *Āraṇyaka* literature and is not uncommon in the *Upaniṣads*. Scholars of Buddhism have commonly interpreted *nāmarūpa* as a metaphor for 'mind (*nāma*) and body (*rūpa*)', but the original meaning in the *Brāhmaṇas* and *Upaniṣads* is nearer to its literal meaning: 'name (*nāma*) and (visible) form (*rūpa*)'. The two examples given above clearly indicate that this is how *nāma* on its own is understood. And we shall see from the following examples that this is also the case with the compound *nāmarūpa*.

In the earliest reference in the *Śatapatha Brāhmaṇa* we read that when the universe consisted just of undifferentiated Brahman (neuter), it differentiated itself by means of *nāmarūpa*: whatever has a name, that is *nāma*; whatever one knows by its form (even if it has no name), that is *rūpa*.[4] *Nāma* and *rūpa* are Brahman's two means of manifestation or representation, described as the two great forces (or monsters) of Brahman, and the two great tempting appearances of Brahman.[5] Similarly, we read in the *Bṛhadāraṇyaka Upaniṣad* (which is the last part of the *Śatapatha Brāhmaṇa*) that the unmanifest or undifferentiated (*avyākṛta*) world became differentiated (*vyākṛta*) by means of *nāma* and *rūpa* (*nāmarūpābhyām*); even today, it states, the world is differentiated in the same way, by saying of someone (or something) 'he [or it] is called so-and-so; he looks like such-and-such'.[6]

Also in the *Bṛhadāraṇyaka Upaniṣad*, the universe is said to be triadic in nature: name and form together with action (karma).[7] This is also the triadic nature of *ātman*, though karma in this instance is said to arise from *ātman*.[8] This part of the triad need not concern us further here. *Nāma* and *rūpa* together are said to be the real.[9] Everything that is *nāma* arises from speech (*vāc*); and everything that is *rūpa* arises from the eye.[10] *Vāc* was an important term in the Brahmanical religion prior to the time of the Buddha as it was one of the subjects of speculation about the nature of the self and the universe in the late *Vedic* and early *Upaniṣadic* period. Here, however, apart from connotations associated with such speculation, the association of *nāma* with *vāc* suggests the conceptual nature of *nāma*: that it is the conferral of differentiation by verbal means, i.e. the practice of naming referred to above.

There is no cosmic significance associated with eye (*cakṣus*), but the association of *rūpa* with eye is interesting for different reasons. On the one hand, in Pali canonical descriptions of the *āyatanas*, *rūpa* appears as 'visible object', corresponding to the sense 'eye'. In the Pali context, *rūpa* does not have eye as its *source*, as in the *Upaniṣad*, but it is nevertheless defined as that which is visible. The other point of interest is the etymological link between *rūpa*, *varpas* and *varṇa*, through the root *vṛ*.[11] According to Louis Renou *varpas* signifies change or metamorphosis of form, including deceptive appearances, practically equivalent in usage to *vivarta* (though *vivarta* is from √*vṛt*, not √*vṛ*).[12] This suggests that though *rūpa* is what the eye sees, such visual perception is not necessarily what really is, a teaching which was to become systematised by the proponents of Vedānta. Renou suggests that the term *varṇa*, the classical word for 'colour', seems to intend a 'category of recognition' in terms such as *dāsa-* or *ārya-varṇa*, rather than difference merely of colour.[13] Such a meaning is considerably more conceptual than visible, and moves a long way from the meaning of *rūpa* as the sense object corresponding to the eye, and also from any suggestion that the main criterion of *rūpa* is visibility. The etymological link between *rūpa* and *varṇa* is interesting partly because sometimes such links can throw a different light on a word and help in understanding its meaning, and partly because in Pali *Abhidhamma* literature, *rūpa* is again associated with 'colour' (as well as shape).[14] The term used for 'colour' is *vaṇṇanibhā*, 'coloured appearance', which suggests that *rūpa* is form which is apparent by means of colour. Shwe Zan Aung, the translator of a late Pali text, the *Abhidhammattha Saṅgaha*, states in his notes to that translation that the most appropriate understanding of *rūpa* is as colour plus extension (*vaṇṇa* and *paṭhavī*).[15] Likewise, in his *Abhidharmakośabhāṣya*, Vasubandhu indicates that *varṇa* alone is too narrow a definition of *rūpa* when he explains that *rūpa* is of two kinds, shape (*saṃsthāna*) and colour (*varṇa*).[16] Wayman has suggested that in the *Abhidhamma* context *rūpa* can best be understood as the verbal noun 'colouring', meaning 'touching up', 'filling out', 'giving body to'.[17] And it may be that Vasubandhu's inclusion of *saṃsthāna* in his definition of *rūpa* results in a similar meaning to that proposed by Wayman. Wayman's suggestion brings the meaning of *rūpa/varṇa* nearer to the more general criterion of visibility, which is the main characteristic of *rūpa* where it is the object of the sense 'eye', and also of *rūpa* as part of the cosmic triad in the *Bṛhadāraṇyaka Upaniṣad* passage we have been discussing here. While *nāma*, the conferral of a name, is a conceptual differentiation by verbal means, *rūpa* is differentiation by means of (visible) appearance or form: as the earlier passage of the *Upaniṣad* puts it, 'he [or it] is called so-and-so, and looks like such-and-such'. The *Upaniṣadic* understanding of *nāmarūpa*, then, is, as stated above, close to the literal meaning of the term. One might put this differently and suggest that name and form together confer individuality, and that in this figurative sense, therefore, *nāmarūpa* does have a psychophysiological meaning. Reat suggests that in the *Upaniṣads nāmarūpa* is used to denote the "conceptual and apparitional aspects of a given object".[18] This fits well with the notion of individuality, since both concept (which represents name) and appearance are peculiar to the individual. And in spite of Yājñavalkya's statement about *nāma* being eternal, which is perhaps characteristically profound, *nāmarūpa*, as both conceptual and apparitional aspects, is associated with the temporal existence of a thing as much as with the duration of an individual's lifetime. Thus the *Muṇḍakopaniṣad* states that just as flowing rivers cast off name and form when they flow into the ocean, so one who knows is freed from name and form and attains the divine person, higher than the high.[19]

Just as scholars of Buddhism have often understood the term *nāmarūpa* to refer to 'mind and body' rather than its more literal meaning of 'name and form',[20] so the later Theravāda tradition has understood *nāmarūpa*. Such an understanding, however, is scarcely compatible with the main context in which *nāmarūpa* is found in the Pali canon, which is as the fourth link in the usual twelvefold version of the chain of dependent origination, the *paṭiccasamuppāda* formula. In another version of the formula, *nāmarūpa* appears as the second link in the chain, but is still preceded by *viññāṇa*. If mind and body arise at this stage, how can one make sense of the subsequent arising of what seem to be mental faculties, and why do we find *jāti*, birth, so much further along the chain? Several suggestions have been made to explain this, both within the Theravāda tradition and outside it,[21] most of which have been in terms of spreading the chain over the previous, present and next lives of the individual. In the following discussion of *nāmarūpa* we will see that some of the contexts in which the term is found in the *Sutta Piṭaka* do suggest that it means 'mind and body'. I will also suggest that in contexts where such an interpretation is problematic, primarily the *paṭiccasamuppāda* formula, an alternative interpretation makes considerably more sense of *nāmarūpa*. And the alternative interpretation of *nāmarūpa* also makes more sense of the formula itself.

Nāmarūpa is a relatively common term in the *Sutta Piṭaka*, and *nāma* and *rūpa* are formally paired together in the canonical 'lists of twos'.[22] In a post-canonical text, the *Milindapañha*, the two are said to be inseparable.[23] The term has been interpreted by scholars as meaning 'mind and body' for two reasons. First, there are a few passages in the Pali material where such a meaning might be implied. For example, there are passages in the *Sutta Piṭaka* where it is used to indicate the individual as a whole, in much the same way *saviññāṇakāya* is. We find such a usage in the *Saṃyutta Nikāya*, where one of the metaphors describing an *arahant*'s freedom from rebirth is the total cessation of mind and body.[24] A similar use of *nāmarūpa* occurs in the *Sutta Nipāta*.[25] The second reason is because later Theravāda Buddhist exegetes have also understood *nāmarūpa* to mean 'mind and body' and have said so in some influential and widely read texts. In some passages, *nāmarūpa* is defined as representing the individual as a whole. In his *Visuddhimagga*, for example, Buddhaghosa states that in meditation a *bhikkhu* defines *nāmarūpa* in terms of the five *khandhas*, with *nāma* representing the four *arūpakkhandhas* and *rūpa* the *rūpakkhandha*.[26] In the chapter in the *Visuddhimagga* entitled 'Description of the Purification of View' (*Diṭṭhivisuddhiniddeso*), Buddhaghosa discusses definitions of *nāmarūpa* at some length. Quoting several canonical passages which illustrate the selflessness of the human being in terms of the *khandhas*, the body, and *dukkha*, he goes on to state that all such passages are in fact saying that the human being is only *nāmarūpa*, and that no self is found therein because in the ultimate sense there *is* only *nāmarūpa*.[27] This clearly equates *nāmarūpa* with the five *khandhas* as representing the individual as a whole, analysed according to body and mind. In two other non-canonical Pali texts, the *Netti Pakaraṇa* and the *Abhidhammattha Saṅgaha*,[28] and in the commentary on the *Dhammapada*, we find the same definition.[29]

Nāmarūpa is most frequently found in the *Sutta Piṭaka* associated with *viññāṇa*, usually as consecutive links in the *paṭiccasamuppāda* formula, and the two together have been understood by later exegetes to represent the individual. In the version of the *paṭiccasamuppāda* formula found in the *Dīgha Nikāya*, for example, we read that *viññāṇa* and *nāmarūpa* are mutually dependent,[30] and that the experience of the cycle of *saṃsāra* is by means of *nāmarūpa* together with *viññāṇa*.[31] Neither *nāmarūpa* nor *viññāṇa* on its own is sufficient cause for the subsequent development of an individual.[32] Elsewhere *viññāṇa* is said to be dependent on *nāmarūpa*, the other way round from the *paṭiccasamuppāda* formula.[33] Though, as we have seen, Buddhaghosa defined *nāma* as representing all four of the *arūpakkhandhas*, he also discusses *nāmarūpa* together with *viññāṇa* in the chapter of his *Visuddhimagga* where he deals with each part of the *paṭiccasamuppāda* formula in turn. He interprets the two of them according to the analysis of the person into *khandhas*. Thus *rūpa* and *viññāṇa* correspond to their respective *khandhas*, leaving *nāma* to represent the remaining three mental *khandhas* of *vedanā*, *saññā* and *saṃkhāra*. As well as stating that *nāma* is three *arūpakkhandhas*, he defines *rūpa* in terms of the four elements.[34] The *Dīgha Nikāya* passage where *nāmarūpa* and *viññāṇa* are said to be mutually conditioning, which has also been referred to in chapter v, is one in which the *paṭiccasamuppāda* formula begins with *viññāṇa* as the condition for the arising of *nāmarūpa*, omitting *avijjā* and *saṃkhāra*.[35] It may well be that *viññāṇa* and *nāmarūpa* are stated to be mutually conditioning so that independent existence cannot be projected onto *viññāṇa* as the first link in the chain. But to a reader of this text, or of any other which states their mutual dependency, who is aware that elsewhere *nāmarūpa* is explained as the four *khandhas* other than *viññāṇa*, the passage suggests that the mutually conditioned pair represent the individual as a whole, particularly since it also states that together they experience *saṃsāra*.

The only definition given of *nāmarūpa* in the *Sutta Piṭaka* does not explicitly refer to the *khandhas*, but it is given in a way which has been interpreted as implying that translating *nāma* as 'mind' is appropriate. *Rūpa* is again defined as the four elements (and their derivitives) and *nāma* is said to consist of feeling, apperception, volition, sensory contact and attention.[36] *Vedanā*, *saññā*, *cetanā*, *phassa* and *manasikāra* might all be said to be 'mental' rather than 'physical'. In the *Papañcasūdanī*, the commentary on the *Majjhima Nikāya*, an analysis according to the *khandhas* is projected onto this definition, so *saññā* is said to stand for the *saññākhandha*, *vedanā* for the *vedanākhandha*, and *cetanā*, *phassa* and *manasikāra* collectively represent the *saṃkhārakkhandha*.[37] The canonical passages where this definition of *nāma* is found are dealing with the *paṭiccasamuppāda* formula. As *viññāṇa* is the condition for the arising of *nāmarūpa*, the definition of *nāma* given in the commentary ensures that all five *khandhas* are explicitly included in this passage, thus encompassing the mental and bodily faculties of the individual as a whole.

From all of the foregoing it is perhaps unsurprising that scholars have translated *nāmarūpa* as 'mind and body'. It is significant, however, that nowhere in the *Sutta Piṭaka* is *nāma* explicitly defined in terms of the *arūpakkhandhas*, or in terms of *khandhas* at all. Only one definition of *nāma* is given, that it is *vedanā*, *saññā*, *cetanā*, *phassa* and *manasikāra*, as mentioned in the last paragraph. *Rūpa* is consistently defined in terms of the four *mahābhūtā* and their derivatives, but only in those contexts which are explaining the human being in terms of the five *khandhas* is it specifically referred to as the *rūpakkhandha*. In the discussion above on the *rūpakkhandha* we saw that parts of the *khandha* are either not visible or their visibility is unknown, unlike *rūpa* as visible object of the sense 'eye'. And because as a *khandha* it is associated specifically with the human body, we concluded '*khandha* of the body' to be an appropriate definition. With regard to the term *rūpa* as part of the compound *nāmarūpa*, there is no suggestion in canonical material that it is limited by a criterion of visibility. But the compound is almost exclusively found either in the context of representing a human being as a whole, or in the context of the *paṭiccasamuppāda* formula. In chapter IV I suggested that the *paṭiccasamuppāda* formula should be understood as referring specifically to the 'how' of human existence within *saṃsāra*. It follows, therefore, that the term *rūpa* in the compound *nāmarūpa* also refers to the human being. In this respect I disagree with Reat, who suggests that *nāmarūpa* has a wider application because the human body is more usually referred to as *kāya*.[38] The human body is indeed often referred to as *kāya*. It is also referred to as *sarīra*. But in every analysis of the human being according to the five *khandhas* the term used to refer to the body is *rūpa*. We have already seen that the same term also refers to that which is external to the human body; but we have also seen descriptions of the *rūpakkhandha* in which *rūpa* unequivocally refers to the human body. Perhaps Reat overlooks the fact that in connection with the human body *rūpa* has a wider meaning than that which is visible; it includes processes and functions which are definitely not physical, for example. It may well be the case, as I will suggest below, that in principle *nāmarūpa* might apply to that which is external to the human being. But when it is found in the context of the *paṭiccasamuppāda* formula it applies to the human being; and thus *rūpa* refers to the human body in the same way *rūpakkhandha* does. In making this statement I am not, however, suggesting that *nāma* corresponds to the four *arūpakkhandhas*. On the contrary.

I mentioned above that in the *Milindapañha*, a post-canonical text, *nāma* and *rūpa* are stated to be inseparable. In the *Mahānidāna Suttanta* of the *Dīgha Nikāya*,[39] which is the *Sutta* in which *nāmarūpa* and *viññāṇa* are stated to be mutually conditioning, we find another passage referring to the inseparability of *nāma* and *rūpa*. The passage also gives us insight into a meaning of *nāmarūpa* which does not present logical problems when attempting to understand the *paṭiccasamuppāda* formula. Here the Buddha is explaining the *paṭiccasamuppāda* formula to Ānanda. He points out that he has stated that *nāmarūpa* is the condition for the arising of sensory contact (*phassa*). He explains by asking Ānanda whether, if those various characteristics by which *nāma* is conceived of were absent, there would be any corresponding discernment of verbal impression with regard to *rūpa*. Ānanda correctly replies that there would not.[40] Similarly, he asks if those various characteristics by which *rūpa* is conceived of were absent, would there be any corresponding discernment of sensory impression with regard to *nāma*, and again Ānanda replies that there would not.[41] Next the Buddha establishes the inseparability of *nāma* and *rūpa* by asking if the various characteristics of both kinds were absent, would there be any discernment of either verbal or sensory impression, and the answer is that there would not.[42] And finally, he establishes that without the various characteristics by which *nāmarūpa* is identified there would be no discernment of sensory contact.[43]

This passage tells us two things about *nāmarūpa*. First, it confirms the mutual dependency of *nāma* and *rūpa*: without one, there would not be the other. Second, and more significantly for our attempt to suggest an alternative meaning for *nāmarūpa*, we learn that *nāma* is described as giving rise to a verbal or conceptual, that is abstract, impression on *rūpa*, and *rūpa* is described as giving rise to a sensory impression on *nāma*, and that there are thus these two aspects to the compound as a whole. The Pali words which are used for what I have called verbal or conceptual and sensory impression are *adhivacanasamphassa* and *paṭighasamphassa* respectively. And the significance of this is more readily apparent if we remember that we met with both these terms in the discussions on *phassa* and the *saññākhandha*. The two types of *phassa* were abstract impression and sensory contact; and the two terms represented *saññā* as conception and apperception respectively. I suggest that this is relevant to understanding the role of *nāmarūpa* and that *nāmarūpa* represents a stage which one might call the 'blueprint' of the individual in terms of concept and conceived. It should go without saying that in Buddhism this 'blueprint' has no independent identity as early Greek notions of 'form' have. It is, rather, dependent on the *saṃkhāras*, which, as we have seen, are the creative aspect of the individual, in themselves conditioned by ignorance. Rather than representing 'mind', *nāma* provides an abstract identity for the individual. And we arrive at a meaning which is also the literal meaning of the word *nāma*: the individual's 'name'. This is not *mere* name, but, rather, 'name' as the entire conceptual identity of the individual. *Rūpa* provides 'form' or recognisability to the individual in the sense of giving shape to that abstract identity which, eventually, is apperceivable by means of sensory impression. At that stage, the form, *rūpa*, acquires solidity or extension, *paṭhavī*, and the characteristics of the other *mahābhūtā*. *Nāmarūpa* is thus name and named, and neither has any meaning or significance without the other: they are mutually necessary. And what this passage in the *Mahānidāna Sutta* is stating is how they relate, how they are said to give rise to 'contact'. It states that according to the various characteristics of each, they impinge on or have contact with each other abstractly, or conceptually, in the case of *nāma* on *rūpa*; and by means of being that which is conceived, that which will be apperceivable, in the case of *rūpa* on *nāma*. The meaning of *nāmarūpa* in the *paṭiccasamuppāda* formula is, then, name and form, in a way which is remarkably close to the *Upaniṣadic* understanding of *nāmarūpa* discussed at the beginning of this chapter.[44]

That *nāma* means conceptual identity is illustrated in a slightly different way in a passage in the *Aṅguttara Nikāya* which discusses the perception of an *arahant*. I have already referred to this passage in chapter III in order to illustrate the abstract conceptual function of *saññā*. The passage states that the perception of an *arahant* is similar to that attained in the *arūpajjhānas*, which is beyond form perception and where apperception has ceased:[45] there is just that which is *called* 'vision', but no sensing of objects or the *sense* of sight; that which is *called* 'hearing', but no sensing of sound or the *sense* of hearing; that which is *called* 'smelling', but no sensing of odour or the *sense* of smell; and so on through all the senses.[46] Here the senses only have abstract identity.

Nāma is also defined, in the *Mahāniddesa,* as distinguishing mark or identity; it is the giving of names to things in our everyday experience in order to distinguish one thing from another.[47]

Neither of these passages is suggesting that *nāma* and *rūpa* as they appear as a link in the *paṭiccasamuppāda* formula are separable because neither of them is directly discussing *nāmarūpa* in that context. I quote them merely to illustrate that conceptual identity is a recognised definition of the term *nāma* in the *Sutta Piṭaka.*

I have already mentioned that many explanations of the *paṭiccasamuppāda* formula have been in terms of spreading the twelvefold sequence over more than one life, and this is how several Buddhist schools, including the Theravāda tradition, have attempted to make sense of it.[48] The most common division is that the first two links in the chain, *avijjā* and *saṃkhāra,* represent the past life; the next eight links, *viññāṇa* to *bhava* inclusive, represent the present life; and the last two links, *jāti* and *jarāmaraṇa* represent the future life. While such a division avoids the anomaly of appearing to have two births for one life, it nevertheless leaves the present life somewhat incomplete: that this life might end with 'becoming' (*bhava*) is somewhat unconvincing.

Another of the explanations offered for the position of *nāmarūpa* near the beginning of the *paṭiccasamuppāda* formula, with the subsequent development of mental faculties and *jāti* further along the chain, is that *nāmarūpa* represents physiological conception.[49] Collins associates this suggestion with contexts in which both *nāmarūpa* and *viññāṇa* are referred to in terms of 'descent' (into the womb).[50] He states that the 'descent' of *viññāṇa* is the first 'moment' of consciousness when *viññāṇa* is about to join with the material causes of an embryo. In the Theravāda tradition (as well as in other schools of Buddhism), this 'moment' of consciousness is also referred to as the *gandhabba.* The 'descent' of *nāmarūpa* is the moment when the *gandhabba* and the material, or psycho-physical, causes of an embryo are conjoined. Though such an explanation also avoids the problem of two 'births' in the *paṭiccasamuppāda* formula, it seems unlikely that the Buddha intended the formula to be understood physiologically: there is no mention in it of the development of the body, and the tone of the formula is much more psychological than physiological.

In my opinion, a better explanation is provided by the suggestion that *nāmarūpa* is the conceptual and formational blueprint of the individual. In the terms of the formula, on-going ignorance is the condition for the arising of the individual's *saṃkhāras.* These condition consciousness, which is a prerequisite for human life since human life is conscious. This consciousness in turn is the condition for the arising of *nāmarūpa,* and on the basis of this conceptual and formational blueprint the individual has psychological faculties peculiar to him or her, is born (giving 'substance' to the form), ages, and dies, and the process may continue in a similar way in future lives. I have suggested above that the mutual dependence of *nāmarūpa* and *viññāṇa*, which is stated in versions of the *paṭiccasamuppāda* formula which begin with *viññāṇa*, is established in order to prevent independent existence being ascribed to *viññāṇa*. But given the alternative interpretation of *nāmarūpa* which I have suggested, it is not difficult to see that their mutual dependence could also be because these two represent the most fundamental aspects of the human being in his or her present life. *Avijjā* and *saṃkhārā* are 'inherited' from the previous life or lives. *Viññāṇa* and *nāmarūpa* are what actualise the individual in *this* life: and they are mutually necessary to the subsequent development of the individual. This would explain the *Saṃyutta Nikāya* passage referred to in chapter v where *viññāṇa* is said to be dependent on *nāmarūpa*.[51] It may be convenient to regard the 'conception' (in the physiological sense) model and the 'blueprint' model as literal and metaphorical aspects of the same process. But since there is no mention in the formula of the physical development of the embryo it does not bear too literal a biological interpretation.

Elsewhere the relationship between *nāmarūpa* and conception is explicitly referred to, but unfortunately it is not clear whether the passage is intended to equate or to separate the two. The passage is found in the *Aṅguttara Nikāya*,[52] and is concerned to refute the erroneous views of other teachers, such as that there is a creator God (*issaranimmāna*), that all things are uncaused and unconditioned (*sabbaṃ taṃ ahetu-appaccayā*). In it we find a version of the *paṭiccasamuppāda* formula which is not found anywhere else in the *Sutta Piṭaka*, or, to my knowledge, in the Pali material as a whole. This gives an account of conception. The formula states that the six *dhātus* are the condition for the descent of the embryo, there being such descent there is *nāmarūpa*, *nāmarūpa* is the condition for the arising of the six senses, which subsequently give rise in turn to contact and feeling. This, the Buddha states, is *dukkha*.[53] From this we see that the description of the relationship between the descent and *nāmarūpa* does not use the usual terms of causation, *upādāya* or *paccayā*, as does the rest of the formula. It states, rather, that 'there being descent, there is *nāmarūpa*'. It is thus not clear whether the descent is the condition for the arising of *nāmarūpa*, or whether the two are coincidental: the same thing. This structure is not normally found in the various *paṭiccasamuppāda* formulas, so it may be that the passage is stating that they are coincidental, especially since *upādāya* and *paccayā* are used for the rest of the formula. But the structure *is* found in the general causal formula of the *paṭiccasamuppāda* doctrine: this being, that arises ... (*imasmiṃ sati, idaṃ hoti* ...).[54] This doctrinal statement is not intended to indicate coincidence, but, rather, the law of dependent origination. What makes this 'conception' version of the formula particularly unusual and difficult to interpret is that it is not given as an alternative to the usual version of the *paṭiccasamuppāda* formula: the common twelvefold version immediately follows it in the text. It is also not clear how the six *dhātus* are the condition for conception. The *dhātus* are defined earlier in the passage as the four *mahābhūtā*, *viññāṇa* and *ākāsa*. The relationship between these and conception is nowhere explained. Even if one were to understand the *mahābhūtā* and *viññāṇa* to represent the bodily and mental aspects of the individual, this would not explain why *ākāsa* is separate; and it is difficult to see how these could *give rise* to conception. In view of its uniqueness and since it is immediately followed by the twelvefold version of the *paṭiccasamuppāda* formula, it may be that the 'conception' formula was interpolated into the text here. Or alternatively it may be that the 'conception' formula was considered incomprehensible and the twelvefold formula was interpolated. In any event, the formula does not help us in ascertaining the relationship, if any, between conception and *nāmarūpa*.[55]

I have suggested that *nāmarūpa* is not being defined in terms of the five *khandhas*; but there are metaphorical parallels between the two: they both represent the identity of the individual. We have seen that it is only in later Pali material that *nāmarūpa* is defined as representing the *khandhas*. Maybe this definition was the only way the exegetes of the formula knew how to convey individuality. The definition of *nāma* given in the *Sutta Piṭaka*, that it is *vedanā*, *saññā*, *cetanā*, *phassa* and *manasikāra*, is an odd one for several reasons. First and most obviously, *vedanā* and *phassa* are both subsequent links in the *paṭiccasamuppāda* formula, and *cetanā* is represented by *saṃkhāra* (and *taṇhā*). Second, it is surprising that *manasikāra*, which is usually interpreted as meaning mental attention or concentration, finds a place at a time when the individual is as yet undeveloped. Even if one understands it more generally, as 'activity of the mind', it seems premature to put this before other more basic psychological faculties. Third, and similarly, it is unlikely that *saññā* as we have defined it could have a place prior to the senses, sensory contact and *vedanā*: apperception is directly involved with sensory input, and conception (the cognitive, not the physiological, kind) is a relatively sophisticated psychological process. Perhaps this is another occasion when the author(s) of these passages did not really know how adequately to define the term, a suggestion which is borne out by the fact that the commentary on such passages does not explain why this sequence of five terms is used in the definition of *nāma* but merely transposes them into a classification in terms of the *khandhas*.

That *nāmarūpa* represents individuality is interestingly suggested in a passage in the *Sutta Nipāta* which relates it to *papañca*. The passage states:

> Having understood *nāmarūpa* as manifoldness, which is the root of both subjective and objective disease, he is completely released from bondage to the root of all disease.[56]

I suggest *roga*, disease, is being used in this passage as a synonym for *dukkha*. The root of *dukkha* is thoughts of 'I' and 'mine', from which root grows *papañca*, the process of making manifold, or attributing independent existence to, what is not manifold or independently existing. Attributing independent existence to oneself and attributing independent existence to what is external to oneself are equally relevant, hence the two terms *ajjhattaṃ* and *bahiddhā*. That *nāmarūpa* can refer to external objects will be discussed below, but the point here is that an individual's *saṃsāric* existence, the identity of which is represented by *nāmarūpa*, is caused by failure to see that one does not exist independently. As such, *nāmarūpa* is *papañca*: one's (false) manifoldness.

In his paper "Some Fundamental Concepts of Buddhist Psychology", and in Chapter VI of his *The Origins of Indian Psychology*, Reat discusses at some length the term *nāmarūpa* in the Pali canon.[57] He suggests that it should be understood as "a comprehensive designation of the individuality of a perceived thing".[58] While "designation of individuality" appears similar to the way I have suggested *nāmarūpa* should be understood, Reat's suggestion is different in one very significant respect which in my opinion is not supported by the canonical material. This difference is represented by the fact that he refers to the designation of the individuality "of a perceived thing". He states that:

> There is no indication in the *suttas* that the first four links of the standard enumeration of *paṭiccasamuppāda*, culminating in the phrase '*viññāṇa* conditions *nāmarūpa*', are to be construed as confined to an explanation of rebirth. Instead, the conditioning of *nāmarūpa* by *viññāṇa* refers to the arising of any instance of consciousness.[59]

In the case of the individual, the analysis into *khandhas* is actually an analysis of consciousness as experienced, Reat states: given sufficient conditions for the arising of consciousness, "the five aggregates are brought into the picture as an analysis of that consciousness".[60] He goes on to suggest that "just as consciousness does not arise without an object, so does an object not arise without consciousness", and states that while "there is little evidence of an abstract interpretation of the elements [the standard definition of *rūpa* – 'object'] in the *suttas* themselves ... there is also little to suggest that they posit an independently existing material world".[61] Elsewhere he puts this point more emphatically: "... according to early Buddhist psychology, there are no 'external' objects as such, but only apparent objects based on the objectivization of certain aspects of consciousness."[62]

Reat bases this conclusion that early Buddhism is idealistic on two canonical passages. First, he refers to a passage in the *Mahāhatthipadopamasutta* in the *Majjhima Nikāya*.[63] This, Reat states, supports his claim that the analysis of the human being into five *khandhas* is actually an analysis of consciousness as experienced. In fact the *Sutta* is ambiguous, and Reat's conclusion is not the only one that can be drawn from it. The *Sutta* starts by defining *dukkha* as the five *upādānakkhandhā*. It goes on to give the detailed description of each of the *cattāro mahābhūtā* as they relate to the human body that has been referred to above in chapter I. Then comes the passage in the Sutta which is relevant to us here. It begins by giving an analogy: just as space that is enclosed by stakes, creepers, grass and clay is known as a dwelling, so a space that is enclosed by bones, sinews, flesh and skin is known as a body.[64] The *Sutta* goes on to state that for there to be an appearance of a corresponding kind of consciousness,[65] there has to be one of the internal senses 'intact' (or functional), its corresponding external object within range, and appropriate attention or concentration.[66] The form of the Pali is the same for all the senses. The *Sutta* then states that whatever is *rūpa*, *vedanā*, *saññā*, *saṃkhāra* and *viññāṇa* that comes to be in this way is included in the *khandha* corresponding to each of those five analyses.[67]

The precise meaning of this passage is not immediately clear. First, the analogy of the dwelling place and the body does not seem to have any connection either with what precedes it or with what follows and may be, as Reat suggests, a corruption in the text.[68] In any event, it may be ignored in this discussion. According to Reat, the rest of the passage states that "*rūpa*, as a *khandha* ... come[s] into existence on the basis of the functioning of consciousness".[69] In my opinion, however, it does no more than state in the first instance that consciousness is consciousness *of*, as already discussed in chapter V: for consciousness to arise there has to be internal sense organ, corresponding external object within range, and the appropriate attention (*samannāhāro* – literally the coming together of the two). And second, in what follows the *Sutta* is stating that it is by means of this process of the arising of 'consciousness of' that one analyses one's experience according to *khandhas*: as human beings, our experience is conscious, and all our analyses are therefore by means of the subjective cognitive process. Reat's claim that the analysis into *khandhas* is actually an analysis of consciousness as experienced suggests that all the *khandhas* are (merely) different types of consciousness. This suggestion is not supported elsewhere in the *Sutta Piṭaka*, and in my opinion one should interpret this passage as stating that the analysis into *khandhas* is an analysis of experience as we are conscious *of* it. Such an interpretation does not have the implication that consciousness is the *stuff* of the *khandhas*, and it is in accord with the context of the *Sutta* as a whole: the detailed description of the *cattāro mahābhūtā* is classified as the *rūpakkhandha* by means of being conscious of it: without being conscious of it there could be no analysis of it. Though Reat is correct in stating that "consciousness does not arise without an object", there is no evidence that he is also correct in stating that "an object does not arise without consciousness".

The second passage on which Reat bases his idealistic interpretation is in the *Dīgha Nikāya*, where the consciousness of an *arahant* is being discussed and it is stated that the four elements cease when *viññāṇa* ceases. Long and short, fine and coarse, pure and impure also cease, and name and form cease without trace.[70]

In my opinion, Reat is mistaken in interpreting this passage as evidence that an idealistic ontology is posited in the *Sutta Piṭaka*. I referred above to a passage in the *Udāna* which states that 'that condition wherein is not earth nor water nor fire nor air' is Nirvana.[71] I also pointed out that this need not, and indeed should not, be interpreted ontologically: the four elements are relevant to *saṃsāric* perception, not to Nirvana. Similarly, *arahant*ship is stated to be the cessation of *nāmarūpa* in the sense that it represents freedom from rebirth: Enlightenment means that there is no further coming to be as an individual.[72] At the death of an *arahant*, *viññāṇa*, along with all the other constituents of the human being, also ceases. And since human life is primarily characterised by consciousness (human beings are conscious beings), the cessation of an individual's consciousness for the final time represents the cessation for that individual of all the other things which characterise *saṃsāric* existence. In the *Sutta Nipāta* this is expressed by stating that the cessation of consciousness is the cessation of the arising of *dukkha*.[73] None of this implies, however, that human existence is a product of that individual's consciousness (in the idealistic sense). Indeed the same *Sutta Nipāta* passage states that the cessation of each and every link in the *paṭiccasamuppāda* formula represents the cessation of the arising of *dukkha*, using the same form of Pali words as that quoted for *viññāṇa*, but with the relevant link of the formula in its place. What this is stating is that bondage to *saṃsāric* existence (*dukkha*) ceases for an individual when Enlightenment is attained. Subsequent death is the cessation of all the links of the *paṭiccasamuppāda* formula, so the cessation of any of them also represents the cessation of the arising of *dukkha*, not just the cessation of *viññāṇa*. But since human life is conscious, *viññāṇanirodha* is an appropriate term to use to signify an *arahant*'s ending of *saṃsāric* existence.

Reat does not account for the first two links in the twelvefold version of the *paṭiccasamuppāda* formula: *avijjā* and *saṃkhārā*. Indeed, though he suggests that the first four parts of the formula are applicable to any instance of consciousness, he does not again mention them. Nor does he mention the subsequent links in the formula. As I argued above in chapter IV, there is no evidence to suggest that anything other than individual sentient beings is volitionally formed. And the *paṭiccasamuppāda* formula is given in terms which clearly apply specifically to the individual. I do not, therefore, think that there is sufficient reason to conclude, as Reat does, that the term *nāmarūpa* in the *paṭiccasamuppāda* formula refers to the 'comprehensive designation of the individuality of a perceived thing'. Rather, it refers to the comprehensive designation of the individuality of a human being according to his or her ignorance and formative activities (*avijjā* and *saṃkhārā*). I stated above in chapter IV that *saṃkhāra* as the second link in the *paṭiccasamuppāda* formula is the individualising faculty in the sense of being the formative principle which distinguishes individual A from individual B. *Nāmarūpa* represents the point at which that individual, having become associated with the potential for being conscious, acquires identity in terms of name and form.

I have referred several times to the formula which is given in the *Sutta Piṭaka* to illustrate the cognitive process, particularly in the sections on the *saññā* and *viññāṇa khandhas*. It states that (visual) consciousness arises because of eye and visible object; contact occurs when there is a combination of the three; feelings are caused by contact; that which one feels one apperceives; that which one apperceives one reasons about and causes to become manifold.[74] This is of interest to Reat since it begins with *viññāṇa*, and he discusses it at some length.[75] He treats both this formula and the *paṭiccasamuppāda* formula as descriptions of processes of consciousness. They are each, therefore, in his view, open to interpretation in the light of the other. Thus because the formula describing the cognitive process states that *saññā* arises from feelings, one can assume that "the arising of *saññā* is implied in the standard formula of *paṭiccasamuppāda* by the arising of *vedanā* conditioned by *phassa*".[76] Similarly, he argues, because *nāmarūpa* and *viññāṇa* are mutually conditioning in the ninefold version of the *paṭiccasamuppāda* formula in the *Mahānidāna Suttanta* of the *Dīgha Nikāya*, one can assume that *nāmarūpa* is represented in the formula of cognition by the presence of a sense (he does not explicitly account for the corresponding sense objects but he may have intended to include them), with *nāma* referring to *manas* (and possibly *dhammā*), and *rūpa* referring to the other senses (and possibly their objects). It is in this way, Reat states, that *nāma* and *rūpa* give rise to *adhivacana* and *paṭighasamphassa* respectively.[77]

In my opinion the two formulas have different purposes and describe different processes. On the one hand, the *paṭiccasamuppāda* formula is not describing the arising of consciousness and it is therefore inappropriate to attempt to establish a mini version of the cognitive process in the middle of it. It is possible to see that the persistent arising of the individual's cognitive process, which is based on a false notion of self (i.e. ignorance) and its consequent craving, signifies the continuation of the individual's *saṃsāric* existence as described in the *paṭiccasamuppāda* formula. This is explicitly stated in the *Brahmajāla Sutta*, where the (erroneous) views being refuted are stated to originate with sensations (that is, *phassa*), which give rise to feelings, craving, and so on, which represent bondage.[78] But this is an explanation that such cognitive activity is *saṃsāric* activity which leads to further *saṃsāric* existence, not a description of the ontological status of the cognitive activity itself. And on the other hand, it is not appropriate to prefix the cognitive formula with *nāmarūpa* in the sense in which it is used in the *paṭiccasamuppāda* formula (as Reat understands such use). Even if the objects involved in the cognitive process have their own name-and-form, a point which is discussed in the next paragraph, those objects are not themselves conditioned by *avijjā*, *saṃkhārā* and/or *viññāṇa*. Thus these two formulas are not open to the kind of manipulation suggested by Reat.

As already mentioned, it might be the case that the term *nāmarūpa* could mean the name and form of things other than the human being. In the *Saṃyutta Nikāya* we read of 'external' (*bahiddhā*) *nāmarūpa*,[79] and in the *Sutta Nipāta* it states that a seeing man will see *nāmarūpa*.[80] It might therefore be appropriate for the term to be understood to have two applications: in its most common context, the *paṭiccasamuppāda* formula, it refers to the name and form of the individual human being; in other contexts it refers to the name and form of any objects. The texts do not suggest that in the latter case such an object is dependent on *viññāṇa* for its existence. From descriptions of the cognitive process, however, we know that our perception and apperception of any such object are so dependent.

To sum up, we have seen that the term *nāmarūpa* is commonly understood by scholars of Buddhism to mean 'mind and body', and that the later Theravāda tradition has also understood it in such a way. I have suggested, however, that such an interpretation is incompatible with the main context in which *nāmarūpa* is found in the canonical material. A more meaningful understanding of the term is that it refers to the individualising, or abstract identity, of the human being (or other sentient being) in terms of name and form: dependent on the ignorance, formative activities and subsequent consciousness of a given life, that life has conceptual and formational individuality.

Notes

1. RV. X.71.1.
2. Bṛ. Up. 3.2.12f: *Yājñavalkya, yatrāyaṃ puruṣo mriyate, kim enaṃ na jahātīti? Nāma iti, anantaṃ vai nāma.*
3. In Sanskrit, *nāman* would be the correct form here. But because in the following discussion both Pali and Sanskrit are referred to, I will use the form *nāma* in the interest of clarity.
4. Śat. Br. XI.2.3.3.
5. Śat. Br. XI.2.3.4F: *Te haite brahmaṇo mahatī abhve … te haite brahmaṇo mahatī yakṣe.*
6. Bṛ. Up. 1.4.7; cf also Ch. Up. 6.3, 8.14.
7. Bṛ. Up. 1.6.1–3.
8. *Atha karmaṇām ātmety etad eṣām uktham.*
9. *Nāmarūpe satyam.*
10. *Teṣāṃ nāmnāṃ vāg ity etad eṣām uktham, ato hi sarvāṇi nāmāny uttiṣṭhanti … atha rūpāṇām cakṣur iti etad eṣām uktham, ato hi sarvāṇi rūpāṇy uttiṣṭhanti.*
11. This is discussed by Wayman (1984, p.620), who refers to Louis Renou's *Études sur le Vocabulaire du Rgveda*, Première Série, p.12.
12. Renou, 1958, pp.13f.
13. Ibid., pp.14f.
14. Dhs 617.
15. Aung (trans.) *Compendium of Philosophy*, 1963, p.272.

16. Abh.K.B. 1.10a.
17. Wayman, 1984, p.620.
18. Reat, 1987, p.15.
19. Muṇḍ. Up. III.2.8: *Yathā nadyas syandamānās samudre 'staṃ gacchanti nāmarūpe vihāya, tathā vidvān nāmarūpād vimuktaḥ parāt paraṃ puruṣam upaiti divyam.*
20. For example, Radhakrishnan, 1988, p.172; C. A. F. Rhys Davids, 1914, p.23f; Johansson, 1969, p.78; E. J. Thomas, 1951, pp.63ff.
21. cf. Collins, 1982, p.203f and p.212; Thomas, 1951, p.79.
22. DN.I.223, III.212; AN.I.83.
23. Miln p.49: *Aññamaññūpanissitā ... ekato va uppajjanti.*
24. SN.I.13, 35: *Yattha nāmañca rūpañca asesam uparujjhati*; cf. also DN.I.223.
25. Sn 1100; cf. also Sn 1037. PED suggests that *nāmakāya* is used as a synonym for *nāmarūpa* at Sn 1074. I do not agree. Nor does the translator for the PTS, K.R.Norman (*The Group of Discourses*, 1992, p.120), who translates *nāmakāya* as "mental body", in the sense of 'body/ group of mental faculties'.
26. Vism p.438f: ... *catunnaṃ arūpakkhandhānaṃ vavatthāpane paññā ayaṃ nāma vavatthāpanapaññā; yā rūpakkhandhassa vavatthāpane paññā, ayaṃ rūpavavatthāpanapaññā ti.*
27. Vism p.593f: *Evaṃ anekasatehi suttantehi nāmarūpam eva dīpitaṃ, na satto, na puggalo ... paramatthato pana nāmarūpamattam eva atthī.*
28. Of these two texts, the former is considerably earlier (*c.* second century CE) than the latter (*c.* eleventh century CE).
29. *Rūpakāyo rūpakkhandho, nāmakāyo cattāro arūpino khandhā. Netti Pakaraṇa* 41; *Abhidhammatha Saṅgaha* VIII.14; DhA IV.100. The Pali in the latter puts the same thing differently: *Tattha sabbaso ti sabbasmiṃ pi vedanādīnaṃ catunnaṃ rūpakkhandhassa cā ti pañcannaṃ khandhānaṃ vasena pavatte nāmarūpe.*
30. DN.II.56: *Nāmarūpa-paccayā viññāṇaṃ, viññāṇa-paccayā nāmarūpaṃ*; their mutual dependency is also stated at SN.II.104, 113.
31. DN.II.64: *Nāmarūpaṃ saha viññāṇena.*
32. DN.II.63. Uniquely, the *paṭiccasamuppāda* formula given at *Vibhaṅga* p.138 states that *viññāṇa* is the condition for the arising of *nāma* alone, which in turn is the condition for the arising of the senses, contact and so on. The commentary on this passage states that this is intended to cover the cases of beings without bodies (*Sammohavinodanī* p.174).
33. SN.III.61: *Nāmarūpasamudayā viññāṇasamudayo, nāmarūpanirodhā viññāṇanirodho.*
34. Vism p.558: *Nāman ti ... vedanādayo tayo khandhā; rūpan ti cattāri mahābhūtāni catunnañca mahābhūtānaṃ upādāya rūpaṃ.*
35. This version of the formula is also found at DN.II.32; SN.II.104f, 113.
36. MN.I.53; SN.II.3f; *Paṭis* p.183: *Vedanā saññā cetanā phasso manasikāro, idaṃ vuccat' āvuso nāmaṃ; cattāri ca mahābhūtāni catunnañ ca mahābhūtānaṃ upādāya rūpaṃ, idaṃ vuccat' āvuso rūpaṃ; iti idañ ca nāmaṃ idañ ca rūpaṃ idaṃ vuccati' āvuso nāmarūpaṃ.*
37. MA.I.221: *Vedanā ti vedanākhandho; saññā ti saññākhandho; cetanā phasso manasikāro ti saṃkhārakkhandha.*
38. Reat, 1987, p.17.
39. DN.II.62ff.
40. *Yehi Ānanda ākārehi yehi liṅgehi yehi nimittehi yehi uddesehi nāmakāyassa paññatti hoti, tesu ākāresu tesu liṅgesu tesu nimittesu tesu uddesesu assati, api nu kho rūpakāye adhivacanasamphasso paññāyethāti? No h' etaṃ bhante.*
41. *Yehi Ānanda ākārehi yehi liṅgehi yehi nimittehi yehi uddesehi rūpakāyassa paññatti hoti, tesu ākāresu tesu liṅgesu tesu nimittesu tesu uddesesu asati, api nu kho nāmakāye paṭighasamphasso paññāyethāti? No h' etaṃ bhante.*
42. *Yehi Ānanda ākārehi yehi liṅgehi yehi nimittehi yehi uddesehi nāmakāyassa ca rūpakāyassa ca paññatti hoti, tesu ākāresu tesu liṅgesu tesu nimittesu tesu uddesesu asati, api nu kho adhivacanasamphasso vā paṭighasamphasso vā paññāyethāti? No h' etaṃ bhante.*
43. *Yehi Ānanda ākārehi yehi liṅgehi yehi nimittehi yehi uddesehi nāmarūpassa paññatti hoti, tesu ākāresu tesu liṅgesu tesu nimittesu tesu uddesesu asati, api nu kho phasso paññāyethāti? No h'etaṃ bhante.*
44. Reynolds suggests (1976, p.378) that the term *nāmakāya* in the passage being discussed here is a synonym for the *manomaya* body. In my opinion, he is mistaken. I do not think the term *kāya* in the compound *nāmakāya* in this context is intended to be taken literally as 'body' but in its more generic sense of 'aggregate'. *Manomaya* is discussed in chapter VII.

45. *Rūpasaññānaṃ samatikkamā paṭighasaññānaṃ atthaṅgamā.*
46. AN.IV.426f: *Tad eva nāma cakkhuṃ bhavissati, te rūpā tañ cāyatanaṃ no paṭisaṃvedissati; tad eva nāma sotaṃ bhavissati, te saddā tañ cāyatanaṃ no paṭisaṃvedissati; tad eva nāma ghānaṃ bhavissati, te gandhā tañ cāyatanaṃ no paṭisaṃvedissati;* and so on.
47. *Mahāniddesa* p.127: *Nāman ti saṃkhā samaññā paññatti lokavohāro nāmaṃ nāmakammaṃ nāmadheyyaṃ nirutti byañjanaṃ abhilāpo.*
48. Thomas (1951, p.65) mentions different Buddhist schools which divided the formula into three existences; Collins (1982, p.203f) gives different divisions of the formula. cf. also Nyāṇatiloka, 1980, p.159, who gives the standard Theravāda division.
49. cf., for example, Collins, 1982, p.212; Thomas, 1951, p.79.
50. This 'descent' has been discussed in chapter v.
51. SN.III.61.
52. AN.I.176.
53. *Channaṃ bhikkhave dhātūnaṃ upādāya gabbhassāvakkanti hoti okkantiyā sati nāmarūpaṃ, nāmarūpapaccayā saḷāyatanaṃ, saḷāyatanapaccayā phasso, passapaccayā vedanā ... idaṃ dukkhan ti paññāpemi.*
54. SN.II.28, 95; MN.III.63.
55. A different sequence giving the events of conception and birth is given at MN.I.265f. The context in which is is given does not affect my discussion here.
56. Sn 530: *Anuvicca papañca nāmarūpaṃ ajjhattaṃ bahiddhā ca rogamūlaṃ sabbarogamūlabandhanā pamutto.*
57. Reat 1987 and 1990.
58. Reat, 1987, p.18.
59. Ibid., p.17.
60. Ibid., p.20.
61. Ibid.
62. Ibid., p.317.
63. MN.I.185ff.
64. MN.I.190f: *Seyyathā pi āvuso kaṭṭhañ ca paṭicca valliñ ca paṭicca tiṇañ ca paṭicca mattikañ ca paṭicca ākāso parivārito agāran t' eva saṅkhaṃ gacchati, evam eva kho āvuso aṭṭhiṃ ca paṭicca nahāruñ ca paṭicca maṃsañ ca paṭicca cammañ ca paṭicca ākāso parivārito rūpan t' eva saṅkhaṃ gacchati.*
65. Though *bhāga* literally means 'portion' or 'section', it makes more sense to translate it here as 'kind' because *viññāṇa* is defined as being of six kinds according to the six senses.
66. *Yato ca kho āvuso ajjhattikañ – c' eva cakkhuṃ aparibhinnaṃ hoti bāhirā ca rūpā āpāthaṃ āgacchanti tajjo ca samannāhāro hoti, evaṃ tajjassa viññāṇabhāgassa pātubhāvo hoti.*
67. *Yaṃ tathābhūtassa rūpaṃ taṃ rūpupādānakkhandhe saṅgahaṃ gacchati, yā tathābhūtassa vedanā sā vedanupādānakkhandhe saṅgahaṃ gacchati, yā tathābhūtassa saññā sā saññupādānakkhandhe saṅgahaṃ gacchati, ye tathābhūtassa saṃkhārā te saṃkhārupādānakkhandhe saṅgahaṃ gacchanti, yaṃ tathābhūtassa viññāṇaṃ taṃ viññāṇupādānakkhandhe saṅgahaṃ gacchati.*
68. Reat, 1987, p.20.
69. Ibid.
70. DN.I.223: *Viññāṇaṃ anidassanaṃ anantaṃ sabbato pabhaṃ* (*pabhaṃ* as a variant reading for *pahaṃ* here is referred to in chapter v). *Ettha āpo ca paṭhavī tejo vāyo na gādhati, ettha dīghañ ca rassañ ca anuṃ thūlaṃ subhāsubhaṃ, ettha nāmañ ca rūpañ ca asesaṃ uparujjhati, viññāṇassa nirodhena etth' etaṃ uparujjhatīti.*
71. *Udāna* VIII.1.
72. SN.I.13, 35.
73. Sn 734: *Viññāṇassa nirodhena n' atthi dukkhassa sambhavo.*
74. MN.I.111.
75. Reat, 1991, 314ff.
76. Ibid., p.314.
77. Ibid., p.316. This seems not dissimilar to the mind-body understanding of *nāmarūpa* Reat is attempting to get away from.
78. DN.I.44.
79. SN.II.24.
80. Sn 909: *Passaṃ naro dakkhiti nāmarūpaṃ.*

CHAPTER VII

Manomaya

Introduction

In the introduction I made the point that many of the key terms which we have to consider in order to understand the early Buddhist analysis of the person, and to gain some insight into the psychological processes of the human being, are used in different contexts in the *Sutta Piṭaka* with quite different meanings. We have seen evidence of this problem in almost every chapter. Of the terms with which we are concerned, one of the most difficult to understand precisely is *manas*. I have already discussed this term in two very different contexts in which it is found. The first was as a sense, when I referred to it as *manodhātu*, discussed in chapter I. We saw there that in that context its precise meaning and function were not clearly defined and that many passages had to be considered together in order to extract some degree of clarity. The second context was *manas* in the sense both of mind in general and of thinking, which I discussed in relation to the terms *citta* and *viññāṇa*. We now come to a third use of *manas*, *manomaya*.

Manomaya is one of the most obscure terms found in the Pali canon. Not only can the term can be understood in grammatically different ways but it is also found in many different contexts, some of which suggest it has a metaphorical as well as a more literal meaning. I shall discuss the two implications separately, but we shall see that the metaphorical meaning is in fact suggested by the more literal use of the term. Leaving aside for the present the metaphorical meaning, in all but one of the contexts which will be discussed here, the term *manas* refers to mind in general rather than *manas* as a sense (*manodhātu*). But the grammatical ambiguity arises because not only does *maya* have different meanings, but as a *tappurisa* compound it can be taken as a genitive, locative or instrumental. *Maya* can mean 'consisting of', 'made' or 'originating'. So, if taken as a genitive *tappurisa*, the compound can mean 'consisting of/made of the mind'; 'originating in the mind' if taken as a locative *tappurisa*; or 'made by the mind' if taken as an instrumental. In effect the locative and instrumental have the same meaning: that the mind is the cause of something else coming to be. The genitive meaning, on the other hand, indicates that the stuff of something is the mind, and its concern with *what* something is means that it is an ontological interpretation of the compound. Both of these meanings of *manomaya* are given in the *Pali English Dictionary*,[1] and both are used by translators.[2] In understanding the term *manomaya* one needs to consider the implication of these two possible meanings.

The point has already been made, especially in the Introduction and in chapter v, that it is important to distinguish between what something is made *of*, and *how* it is made: whether a passage is concerned with the former or the latter. In the *Sutta Piṭaka*, I have suggested, the prime concern is with understanding how *saṃsāric* existence operates so that one can understand how to achieve liberation from the cycle of rebirth. Even those analyses which appear to offer an explanation of what there is, and the analysis of the person into *khandhas* is a good example, are intended to assist in understanding how the human being should be understood to function, rather than simply as a separate 'self'. There is no suggestion that the analysis has any ultimate ontological significance: rather, it is notable that insofar as the analysis of the human being into *khandhas* is concerned with the 'what' of the human being, it is 'what' in the sense of structure rather than substance that matters; and we have seen that all the *khandhas* are to be understood as processes. To achieve liberation it is more important to understand, for example, that the processes which we think of as the substance of the body are subject to decay and dissolution, thus emphasising the body's lack of permanence, than what that substance is. This point is the subject of one of the stock expressions in Pali: "This is my physical body, made up of the four great elements... and the very nature of it is impermanence, it is subject to erosion, abrasion, decay and breaking up".[3] And it is also notable that in the analysis of the *rūpakkhandha* non-corporeal bodily processes are given equal emphasis to the more concrete aspects of the body, as we have seen.

I will discuss the term *manomaya* in four different contexts. First, I will consider the first line of the first and second verses of the *Dhammapada*. In this context the main question which arises is whether or not *manomaya* is being used to indicate a particular ontology. The context also shows the extent to which Buddhist teachings are concerned with the power of the mind. Second, I shall briefly refer to *manomaya* in an unusual context where it refers specifically to *manas* as a sense and not to 'mind' in general. We shall nevertheless see that here too it is the power of the mind that is being referred to, if in a different way. Third, I will discuss its use as a metaphorical synonym for the *rūpadhātu* level in Buddhist cosmology and how this corresponds to a *saṃsāric* mode of existence. In order to understand its use in this context, I will also discuss the fact that in the *Sutta Piṭaka* there is no explicit or implicit ontological discontinuity between what one conventionally thinks of as body and mind, *rūpa* and *arūpa*. On the contrary, we shall see that the absence of discontinuity directly corresponds to the way in which cosmological levels metaphorically represent an individual's spiritual progress. Lastly, I will discuss *manomaya* in its most well-known context, that of the ability of those who have attained a certain level of meditation to create a *manomaya* body. By extension from its meaning 'mind-made', *manomaya* in this context is sometimes interpreted as 'formed by the magic power of the mind, magically formed'.[4] And again one of the main points which arises from this context is the power of the mind in Buddhist teachings. We shall see that in the concept of *manomaya* these two points, the absence of ontological discontinuity between body and mind, and the power of the mind, are linked. We saw in the section on *manas* in chapter v how closely thinking is associated with volitions and we saw the role they both play in the cyclic causal nexus. In much of this chapter that association becomes merged and I have not distinguished between volitions and thinking: to do so would be too tediously pedantic and difficult to read. What is meant here is the collective power of the causal nexus as a whole.

In the discussion of the third and fourth contexts in which *manomaya* is found, I shall refer repeatedly to the fact that the concepts with which we are dealing are not exclusively Buddhist. I shall also preface my remarks by a brief discussion of the terms *manomaya* and *vijñānamaya* (literally 'consciousness-made') in the *Upaniṣads*. A more comprehensive comparison between these concepts as they are understood in Buddhism and as they occur elsewhere would no doubt be a fruitful area for more extensive research: many of the concepts are found in other Indian traditions, and the concept of the mind-made body is also a phenomenon found outside India. What distinguishes the Buddhist context from the others, however, is the combination of the Buddha's teaching that karma is volition with his teaching that the path to liberation consists in the purification of the mind. It is clear in the Buddhist material that the acquisition and use of a *manomaya* body is associated with attaining a certain level on the spiritual path. In the *Upaniṣads*, by contrast, this point is far from clear.

First, then, I will consider *manomaya* as it is found in the first line of each of the first two verses of the *Dhammapada*. Here *manas* in the term *manomaya* is used in association with *dhammā*, which is potentially confusing in view of the association elsewhere in Pali material of the terms *manas* and *dhammā* as sense and sense object. As sense and sense object, these two terms were discussed in chapter I. In the *Dhammapada* however, both terms are being used in their generic sense: *manas* is being used as 'mind' in general, and *dhammā* is being used as it is in the *tilakkhaṇa* formula, discussed in chapter IV. When these terms are used generically, the precise meaning of the passage has to be determined from the context. The line in question literally means something like: "Phenomena are the result of mind (or are preceded by mind), have mind as their best, are mind-made".[5] In isolation, this sentence might be construed as positing an idealistic ontology, that the phenomena which comprise the world as we know it, *dhammā*, are nothing but the mind: the external world is magically created by the mind and consists of mind. There is an alternative way of interpreting this line, however, which is, in my opinion, the accurate one. To understand this, we must look at the rest of the two verses in question. In full, the Pali is:

> *Manopubbaṅgamā dhammā manoseṭṭhā manomayā,*
> *manasā ce paduṭṭhena bhāsati vā karoti vā*
> *tato naṃ dukkham anveti cakkaṃ va vahato padaṃ.*
>
> *Manopubbaṅgamā dhammā manoseṭṭhā manomayā,*
> *manasā ce pasannena bhāsati vā karoti vā*
> *tato naṃ sukham anveti chāyā va anapāyinī.*

Excluding the first lines of these verses, a translation of the rest of them is:

> If a man speaks or acts with a wicked mind, sorrow follows him as a wheel follows the foot of a draught [animal]... if a man speaks or acts with a pure mind, happiness follows him as a shadow always follows [him].

The point of these sentences is that one reaps the consequences of one's actions: just as a wheel which is set in motion by a footed beast follows the actions of the foot, and just as a shadow always follows the actions of a man, in just such a way one's future experience is determined by one's speech and actions now. And one's speech and actions are qualitatively conditioned by whether one's *mind* is wicked or good. This corresponds to the Buddha's definition of karma to which I have already referred: "Karma is volition: having willed, one acts by means of body, speech and thought". The whole of the first chapter of the *Dhammapada* is concerned with this teaching: that one reaps as one sows, and that sowing is qualitatively determined by intention.

I mentioned in chapter IV that when used in a non-technical sense 'mind' (whatever term is being used) indicates general mental activity. So the first lines of the first two verses in fact have the following meaning: *dhammā* are an individual's experiences – everything, in fact, that is a part of the individual's life. And qualitatively those experiences follow from one's mental activity: *manopubbaṅgamā*; it is mental activity which principally governs the nature of the life: *manoseṭṭhā*; and it is in mental activity that what follows originates: *manomaya*. To interpret this sentence ontologically is completely to ignore the context in which it is found and to divorce it from the subject matter of the entire chapter. To convey the meaning of *manas* in this context accurately, it is better to translate it as a verbal noun, denoting the activity or process of the mind: 'thinking'.[6] In English this gives us a less ambiguous sentence: "The individual's experiences are preceded by thinking, have thinking as their best, originate in thinking". It is the reification of *manas* as 'mind' which tends to mislead here.

There is a similar passage in the *Aṅguttara Nikāya* which states:

> Whatever states (*dhammā*) are unwholesome, participate in unwholesomeness, are associated with unwholesomeness, all such things are preceded by thinking. One's thinking arises as the first of those states: the unwholesome states follow. Whatever states are wholesome, participate in wholesomeness, are associated with wholesomeness, all such things are preceded by thinking. One's thinking arises as the first of those states: the wholesome states follow.[7]

Once again, this illustrates the role thinking plays in the karmic process. We saw some similar contexts above in the section on *manas* in chapter v where *manas* was associated with the activity of the mind.

In chapter iv, I referred to a passage which stated that one's future rebirth can be influenced by one's volitions.[8] I suggested there that it was illustrating the binding power of volitions. The first two verses of the *Dhammapada*, and the *Aṅguttara Nikāya* passage which we are discussing here, also serve to illustrate the same power. But here it is referred to in more general terms as originating in the mind, or being the magical power of the mind, *manomaya*, rather than as *cetanā* or *saṃkhārā*. And here the power is discussed with direct reference to its ethical dimension and can be summed up by stating that good experiences originate in a wholesome mind and, conversely, bad experiences originate in an unwholesome mind.

The second context in which *manomaya* occurs is when it is used to imply *saṃsāric* perception, or the mundane life of *saṃsāra*, in contrast to the *lokuttara* nature of liberation. Such a context is found in the *Saḷāyatana Saṃyutta* of the *Saṃyutta Nikāya*, and here *saṃsāric* perception is linked to *manas* as the sixth sense (i.e. *manodhātu*). The context is a teaching on the six senses (referred to as *phassāyatanā*). Untamed, unguarded, unwatched and unrestrained, they are the bearers of ill. Conversely, when they are well tamed, well guarded, well watched and well restrained, they are the bearers of happiness.[9] The text proceeds to give examples of the dangers to which a *bhikkhu* is subjected by each of the senses and in what sense they should be guarded. Through the eye, for example, there is the danger of finding the appearance of things delightful or disgusting, and one therefore has to restrain one's desire for sights which are delightful. Similarly, one has to restrain one's tendency to be led astray by sweet sounds. When it comes to *manodhātu*, the Pali states:

> *Papañcasaññā itarītarā narā,*
> *papañcayantā upayanti saññino*
> *manomayaṃ gehasitañca sabbaṃ*
> *panujja nekkhammasitam irīyati.*[10]

This verse was discussed in chapter III with reference to the term *papañca*. It means:

> Men who have conceptions of manifoldness of some kind go on separating things when apperceiving; but [eventually] he [a *bhikkhu*] drives out everything that is mind-made and to do with the mundane life and proceeds to a life of renunciation.

The term *manomaya* here clearly refers to the fact that all *saṃsāric* phenomena are processed by the *manodhātu*. In other words, the subjective experience of the mundane life is conditioned by (*maya*) the mind (*manas*). And the *bhikkhu* is to detach himself from such mundane life and turn himself instead to the *lokuttara* life which will lead to liberation.

This context in which *manomaya* is found appears different from the one discussed above because here the term *manomaya* has been attached to the incoming raw data of *saṃsāric* experience and not the thinking process as such: the former data precede discursive thought, and the latter might be described as the mind's *processing of* that data. But this passage gives us a clear indication of the link between *manodhātu* and the mental processes in general; and it suggests that the power of the mind in fact operates through every level of the mental processes as a whole, from *manodhātu* to thinking or volitions. We have seen in chapter I that the need for the senses to be guarded does not mean that it is in the senses themselves that unwanted volitions originate. But *manodhātu* is the door through which *saṃsāra* is subjectively experienced. It is for this reason that experience acquires the epithet *manomaya*, and also for this reason *manodhātu* can be understood as the source, as it were, of the volitional process which determines one's future lives.

There is, nevertheless, one further point which needs to be made concerning this context in which the term *manomaya* is found. We have seen that even liberating insight involves the use of the mind and we have also seen that liberating insight has to be known: in one context identifying such insight was referred to as the highest function of the *saññākhandha*. This would seem to suggest that the turning of the mind towards *lokuttara* rather than mundane things does not mean that the activity of *manodhātu* ceases completely but that it would have some supra-sensory activity such as was suggested in chapter I. So the reference in this *Saḷāyatana Saṃyutta* context to the driving out of that which is mind-made is intended to be figurative rather than literal. As with the teaching about the other senses, the point is that one should be on one's guard not to be entranced by *saṃsāric* experiences, but should instead be concerned with that which is conducive to liberation. One might put this point differently and say that the power of the mind is to be reorientated.[11] This process was implied in chapter IV where we saw that volitions can be used to eradicate other volitions.

The third context in which I will discuss *manomaya* is when it is used as an abstract synonym for the cosmological level of the *rūpadhātu*. I will also consider the relationship between *rūpa* and *arūpa* and the significance of this relationship for the subject of this chapter. This is closely linked with the fourth of the contexts in which I will discuss *manomaya*, which is when it refers to the ability of those who have mastered a certain level of meditation to create what is called a *manomaya* body deliberately. First, though, a brief outline of the way in which relevant subjects are understood in *Vedic* material, mainly the early *Upaniṣads*, is helpful by way of background.

I have already referred in this chapter to the place in Buddhist teachings of the power of the mind, and I shall return to this point in the discussion below on the remaining two contexts in which *manomaya* is found in canonical material. The concept of the power of the mind was not new in the Buddha's teachings, however. It is alluded to in the Hymn of Creation in the *Ṛg Veda*, for example, where desire (or volition) is stated to be the first seed of the mind.[12] The power of the mind is the motivating factor in the *pariṇāmavāda* of chapter VI of the *Chāndogya Upaniṣad*, where Being creates the universe by thinking "Would that I were many, let me procreate myself".[13] And in many other *Upaniṣadic* cosmogonies the mind plays an instrumental role.[14]

The way these *Upaniṣadic* references to the power of the mind are expressed serves to emphasise the point made above that the reification of the term 'mind' can be misleading. In the *Upaniṣads* as in the Buddhist material the power of the mind originates in the process of thinking, or willing. This important point underlies my use of the expression 'the power of the mind' throughout this chapter.

In spite of the fact that the mind plays such an important cosmogonic role in *Vedic* material, the Brahmanical religion recorded in those *Vedic* texts is usually understood to be based on ritual actions. Indeed, the rationale of the *Vedic* sacrificial religion was that the universe and all individuals depended for continued existence, and the way in which they continued to exist, on the correct performance of ritual actions. To this day, the orthodox Brahmanical tradition teaches that such ritual actions are crucial to the nature of one's future existence. In this causal process there is little or no ethical dimension as we know it. When Yājñavalkya states "One becomes good by good action, bad by bad action",[15] this refers to the fact that the details of the physical (and verbal) actions must be performed correctly. If they are not, bad (i.e. wrong) results will follow. In another passage where Yājñavalkya gives the same teaching, however, we also see the suggestion that it is the power of the mind which determines one's future rebirth. He states first: "As one acts and behaves, so one becomes. The doer of good becomes good, the doer of bad becomes bad".[16] He goes on to state:

> Some say that a person is made by desire. As is one's desire, so is one's intention (*kratu*); as is one's intention, so one performs actions; as is the action he performs, so he becomes.[17]

In spite of the introduction of the term 'desire', there is still no implication of any moral teaching here. As Collins puts it:

> 'Desire' here should not be taken in the general moral sense with which we are familiar...; rather it is that concentrated attention within the sacrificial ritual, focussed on the desired object of sacrifice, which was held to be a necessary condition of attaining it.[18]

What Yājñavalkya does in using the term 'desire' is explicitly to suggest that the power of the mind is instrumental in obtaining the object of the sacrifice.[19]

More usually in *Vedic* material, and in classical Indian religions which are based on the *Upaniṣads*, this power of the mind is associated with knowledge rather than intention in the sense of volitions. Knowledge of a thing gives power over it, and the importance of knowledge underlies the sacrificial rationale: it is knowledge which gives the ritual actions their power. The way this was thought to work in the early sacrificial religion is discussed in some detail by Collins, and I need not go into it here.[20] What is of interest to us here is the early suggestion that knowledge of something through meditation can have a transformative effect on the individual meditator. The principle is found as early as the *Śatapatha Brāhmaṇa*, which states: "One becomes whatever one meditates on".[21] And it is referred to in an early *Upaniṣadic* passage on meditation, where Gārgya instructs Ajātaśatru as follows:

> Verily, I meditate on him [Brahman] as a likeness. He who meditates on him in this way, to him comes what is like, not what is unlike; from him arises what is like him.[22]

The suggestion that one becomes what one meditates on is also of cosmological significance. The *Upaniṣads* teach that Brahman is everything. So it follows that if one meditates on Brahman one becomes identified with everything. This is generally expressed in the microcosmic/macrocosmic formula that *ātman* is Brahman, and knowledge (in the sense of experience) of this constitutes liberation. One passage in the *Bṛhadāraṇyaka Upaniṣad* identifies *ātman*/Brahman with all things. It states: "The self (*ātman*)is indeed Brahman; it is consciousness-made, mind-made and breath-made".[23] The passage continues: "[The self] is sight-made, hearing-made, earth-made, water-made, air-made, space-made, light- and no-light-made ... made of all".[24] This passage clearly indicates an absence of ontological discontinuity between the different things of (or by) which one is made and implies that in identifying with Brahman one identifies with everything.

The first three of the things of/by which one is made according to this *Bṛhadāraṇyaka Upaniṣad* passage, that one is consciousness-made (*vijñānamaya*), mind-made (*manomaya*) and breath-made (*prāṇamaya*), are referred to elsewhere in the *Upaniṣads* in a way which suggests that they constitute a threefold analysis of the levels of human existence. The *Taittirīya Upaniṣad* states that one has as it were three layers of bodily existence. First, it states: "Breath is the life of all beings", and this life is referred to as the "bodily self".[25] This is not so far-fetched if one recalls that breathing is part of the *rūpakkhandha*, and that *vāyu* is one of the primary characteristics of *rūpa*. One might suggest that (together with heat) it is the least dense mode of *rūpa* itself. The similarity between *Upaniṣadic* descriptions of the *prāṇas* and the canonical description of the element *vāyu* was discussed in chapter 1. The *Taittirīya Upaniṣad* goes on:

> Verily, different from and within that which is breath-made is a self which is mind-made. By that [mind-made self] this [bodily self] is filled. This, verily, has the form of a person; according to that [bodily] personal form is this [mind-made self] with the form of a person.[26]

Of the third level, the text states:

> Verily, different from and within that [self] which is mind-made is a self which is consciousness-made. By that [consciousness-made self] is this [mind-made self] filled. This, verily, has the form of a person; according to that [mind-made self's] personal form is this [consciousness-made self] with the form of a person.[27]

This is a clear reference to one's existence at different levels of density and subtlety, ranging from bodily or solid existence through other existences which have form but are without solidity. This is supported by a more general passage in the *Chāndogya Upaniṣad*, which states that food (*anna*), water (*āpo*) and heat (*tejo*) exist in three modes: coarse (*sthaviṣṭha*), medium (*madhyama*) and subtlest (*aṇiṣṭha*).[28] It is from this passage that Śaṅkara concludes that everything is threefold in this way.[29] We shall see below that in Buddhism the teaching that the path to liberation is a progressive purification of the mind corresponds clearly to cosmological levels which can be defined according to degrees of density or subtlety. In corresponding to an intermediate subtle level of cosmological existence, *manomaya* therefore also corresponds to an intermediate stage on the path to liberation. Though we have seen in the *Bṛhadāraṇyaka Upaniṣad* passage above that there is no ontological discontinuity between these and other levels or aspects of existence, the teaching in the *Upaniṣads* is completely unsystematic, and it is unclear whether any comparable correspondence in terms of 'levels' in both microcosm and macrocosm can be made. From the little evidence there is, it seems more likely that the three *Upaniṣadic* bodies co-exist at all times and the range between dense and subtle represents the range between the outer, empirical, self and the inner, 'real', self. In principle, this is suggested by the emphasis in the *Upaniṣads* on the 'inner controller' and the 'self within the heart'. It is also more specifically suggested in another passage in the *Bṛhadāraṇyaka Upaniṣad*. In answer to the question "Which is the self?", it states:

> The person [self] is the consciousness-made [self] which is among the breaths [that is, the bodily self, according to the *Taittirīya Upaniṣad* passage quoted above]; it is the light within the heart.[30]

The *Upaniṣad* goes on to state: "There is an intermediate third state, that of being in sleep [or dream]".[31] In this context, the term *manomaya* is not used to describe the intermediate level of sleep/dream, but three levels are nevertheless indicated. There is a lengthy description of the freedom in the sleep/dream state to do whatever one wishes.[32] This is remarkably similar to descriptions of the abilities acquired by the Buddhist who creates a *manomaya* body, as we shall see. Though in classical Indian thought dreams are not considered to be delusions or unreal (except insofar as any or all of *saṃsāric* perception is), they are not an ability or mode of existence which is acquired with spiritual progress. It might, however, be that the dream state is used to exemplify the creative power of the mind, in which case it could correspond to the existence in a *manomaya* body of a Buddhist *bhikkhu* who has achieved a certain level of meditation.

That the dream state is being used as an analogy for a level at which one exists seems more likely in view of the fact that the *Upaniṣads* give an alternative threefold analysis of the individual. This is the bodily self (*śarīra*), the dream self (*svapna ātma*) and the self in (dreamless) sleep (*suptaḥ* ... *svapnaṃ na vijānāti*).[33] These are three levels of the empirical self, and they act as the bearer of the deathless, bodiless (real) self.[34] Here the dream state might suggest a level at which the power of the mind is able to act creatively. This state is not unreal, but nor does it constitute absolute reality: it is an intermediate state, between the physical body and the cessation of (*saṃsāric*) mental activity, symbolised by dreamless sleep.

Explicit reference to the fact that there is a subtle self or body is rare in the early *Upaniṣads*. So far as I am aware, the term *liṅga śarīra*, for example, occurs only once in the early *Upaniṣads*.[35] It occurs more (though it is still not common) in later *Upaniṣads*,[36] and it is frequently used by Śaṅkara in his commentaries on the *Upaniṣads*. In the early *Upaniṣads*, it is the terms *manomaya* and *vijñānamaya* (and possibly dreams) which suggest the subtle self. But the theory of the subtle self and its constitution is not well developed in the early *Upaniṣads*, and where these terms occur they often do not fit the threefold model suggested above in the passages cited from the *Taittirīya* and *Bṛhadāraṇyaka Upaniṣads*. Two passages seem to invert the levels of *manomaya* and *vijñānamaya* suggested above. For example, *manomaya* (not *vijñānamaya*) is used elsewhere in the *Bṛhadāraṇyaka Upaniṣad* in a passage which states: "This person who is mind-made is of the nature of light, is real, is within the heart ...".[37] And in another passage in the same *Upaniṣad*, *vijñānamaya* (not *manomaya*) is used of the mode of a person when he falls asleep. Then, the passage states, he functions as a "consciousness-made person".[38] Here it is the consciousness-made person who can do whatever he pleases in dreams:

> When he moves about in dreams, these are his worlds: then he becomes as it were a great king, as it were a great brahman. He as it were enters high and low. As a great king can move around in his country as he pleases taking [with him] his people, so also here this [consciousness-made person], taking with him his breaths, moves about in his own body as he pleases.[39]

Elsewhere, it is the *prāṇas* which appear to be the subtle self.[40]

In his translation of the principal *Upaniṣads*, Radhakrishnan states: "In the dream state the self is identified with the subtle body",[41] but he does not give any textual references to support this statement. And we do not know whether he assumes that the concept of the subtle body incorporates both *manomaya* and *vijñānamaya* bodies. Another passage in the *Bṛhadāraṇyaka Upaniṣad* adds to the confusion when it states that the subtle self has *manas* "attached to it" (*nisaktaṃ*).[42] In his commentary on this passage, Śaṅkara ignores the implication of *niṣaktam* and states: "the subtle body is called mind because mind is the principal factor of the subtle body".[43] Śaṅkara clearly identifies the *manomaya* body with the subtle body. But the context of this passage does not indicate that this is the dream-body. The passage discusses what happens to someone when they die and are reborn. It states that the subtle self "comes again from that world to this world for [fresh] work".[44] This is another passage where *manomaya* is used where one might expect to find *vijñānamaya*. The situation is further complicated by the fact that in his *bhāṣya* on the *Chāndogya Upaniṣad*, Śaṅkara identifies the *prāṇa śarīra* with the subtle body.[45]

From all these references, we can conclude that though there is some evidence in the *Upaniṣads* that the individual exists on three levels of density, this evidence is far from clear, and there are many confusing or contradictory references. The three levels seem to co-exist for all people and do not appear to be acquired through the power of the mind, or meditation. Through meditation one can, however, become identified with whatever one meditates on, and it appears that there is no ontological discontinuity between levels of existence.

I turn now to a consideration of *manomaya* in the third and fourth contexts in which it is found in the *Sutta Piṭaka*. The main concern of this book has been an investigation of the fivefold analysis of the human being into *khandhas*. We have seen that these are divided into one *rūpakkhandha*, which is the living body of the individual, and four *arūpakkhandhas*, which collectively represent the mental faculties of the individual. Though when considered together this analysis appears to conform to the convention that the individual comprises body and mind, in Buddhism, this apparent dualism does not have the ontological significance it usually carries in dualistic religions or philosophies. As I have already mentioned, the distinction between the bodily and the mental *khandhas* in Buddhism is not intended to suggest that human beings consist of two ontologically distinct substances, one physical and the other mental. A later Buddhist school, the Yogācāra, interpreted this absence of distinction in an ontological sense: to mean that 'all is mind'. In my opinion this conclusion cannot be drawn from the material in the *Sutta Piṭaka*. It has been a constant theme of this book that the teaching of early Buddhism is not concerned with offering an ontological analysis as such: it is concerned with offering whatever information and guidance are necessary to enable people to achieve liberating insight and so escape the cycle of *saṃsāric* existence. Such teaching does not include an analysis of whether the actual stuff of anything is mind (whatever that might be) or anything else. It does, however, include information concerning the nature of things, or the mode in which things exist. This teaching is contained in the metaphysics implicit in the *tilakkhaṇa* formula and the doctrine of *paṭiccasamuppāda*. From these, we know that all things are dependently originated and as such are impermanent, unsatisfactory and do not occur as (separate/independent) 'selves'.[46]

This means that what it is important to understand for the purposes of liberating insight is that whether something is physical or mental it is of precisely the same nature. Whether it be solid or liquid, apperceived or conceived, it is equally dependently originated. This is why Buddhist meditation exercises, such as those described in the *Satipaṭṭhāna Suttas,* include as objects for meditation the body itself, thoughts, feelings, and abstract conceptual factors such as doctrinal teachings.[47] The exercises are to be similarly practised in each case and the point of each of them is the same: the realisation that none of these things should be thought of in terms of their separateness or selfhood, subjectively or objectively. We have also discussed what appear to be widely differing constituents of the human being: the physical body as described in passages about the *rūpakkhandha,* ideas as described in passages about the *saññākhandha*, and volitions as a product of the *saṃkhārakkhandha*, for example. In spite of the apparent differences between them, all of these are *saṃkhāras* in the metaphysical sense: they are all conditioned. One might suggest, therefore, that insofar as our experience leads us to think in terms of the substance of things, all we can know about them from Buddhist teachings is that we experience a variation in the degree of density and/or in the behaviour of similarly conditioned phenomena. *What* the phenomena are, in the ultimate sense, is irrelevant to attaining liberating insight. Even the four *mahābhūtā* can be understood in such a way: it is hardly credible, for example, that the solid parts of the body literally consist of earth, *paṭhavī*. The point is their solidity or extension. And the same is true for fluidity (*āpo*), heat (*tejo*) and motion (*vāyo*): these abstract meanings are more relevant than the literal meanings of these terms (water, fire and wind). These primary constituents of *rūpa* are not types of substance, but constitute different modes or states which come together as derived *rūpa*. And all of these primary constituents of the *rūpakkhandha* are *saṃkhāras*: the more detailed information refers to their position on what Johansson calls the "spectrum of density or solidity".[48] All phenomena on the spectrum could also be called different modes of reality. In Buddhism, all *saṃkhāras*, whether solid or abstract, are different modes of reality: none is more real than any of the others.[49] This is perhaps easier for us to grasp in view of the discovery in modern physics that matter is a gross form of energy. And the analogy of ice, water and steam also illustrates the absence of ontological discontinuity between different modes of existing on the spectrum of density.

This spectrum is reflected in Buddhist cosmology which, though it is only fully evolved in the commentarial tradition and in the *Visuddhimagga* of Buddhaghosa, is unsystematically present in the canon. Briefly, this is divided into three spheres: the sphere of desire (*kāmadhātu*), the sphere of form (*rūpadhātu*) and the sphere of formlessness (*arūpadhātu*). The first and third of these spheres have various complex levels.[50] The first, the *kāmadhātu*, is comprised of the various heavens and hells in which beings are reborn in what in Buddhist terms are gross *rūpa* bodies. The middle sphere, the *rūpadhātu*, is the level at which live certain beings (often called *devas*) which have subtle *rūpa* bodies. The third sphere, the *arūpadhātu*, is stratified according to the more rarified levels of meditation which are attained by advanced disciples. It is inhabited by those who died just before gaining liberating insight; they dwell at an appropriate level of pure meditation and at this stage they are formless.

Gombrich calls the *arūpadhātu* "an elaborate spacial metaphor for spiritual progress".[51] In fact one might say that all three of the *dhātus* are spacial metaphors for spiritual progress. The *kāmadhātu* is inhabited by those whose actions are still impure or 'gross' enough to keep them in the cyclic world of sensual desire: it correlates with the gross physical body. Though the *rūpadhātu* is inhabited by the *devas* mentioned above, who derive from Mahā Brahmā,[52] it is also inhabited by those who have performed an important service or who have achieved a certain level of meditation. And though such individuals possess a *rūpa* body, there is canonical evidence that it is subtle *rūpa*: as it were mid-way between gross *rūpa* and the formlessness of the *arūpa* level. In the fourth point raised in this chapter we shall also see that this subtle body, which is called *manomaya*, can also be acquired or created by some individuals who still inhabit the *kāmadhātu*, and that the ability to create such a body is acquired on the spiritual path.[53] The metaphor of the spiritual path underlines the continuity between the spheres. And just as for Buddhists the path represents the progressive purification of the mind, so the spheres represent corresponding degrees of density or subtlety.[54] It is notable that just as liberation means the cessation of *saṃsāric* existence, so the achievement of insight itself does not have a corresponding cosmological stratum.

Collins discusses the relation between Buddhist cosmology and psychology, calling it psychological cosmology.[55] He tabulates the cosmological spheres of early Buddhism and correlates them with meditative levels.[56] This has been mentioned in chapter v. The correspondence between cosmology and psychology, and the lack of ontological discontinuity, is again evidenced by the fact that experience of a certain meditative level identifies the subject with that level of reality, enabling the meditator to manipulate it. We have also seen a somewhat different, and spiritually humble, example of this principle in chapter iii. There, we referred to canonical passages in which *bhikkhus* were encouraged to develop spiritually advantageous 'concepts', such as impermanence and selflessness. This practice would contribute to the *bhikkhu's* realisation of these insights: in experiencing the psychological ideas he eventually identifies with them cosmologically.

The psychological/cosmological transmutation which comes about through meditation is the same as the rationale behind the practice of classical yoga,[57] and we saw examples of this process above in the *Śatapatha Brāhmaṇa* and the *Bṛhadāraṇyaka Upaniṣad*. In these three examples, the transmutation of the meditator is different from that in Buddhism. In them, the point is to become the same as the stuff on which one is meditating (usually Brahman); in Buddhism, the point is to experience what is meant by selflessness. The former imply an ontological transmutation, of what one is. The latter is an epistemic transmutation, to know how one operates. In stating only that one realises *how* one is, Buddhist teachings leave unanswered the question of whether one thereby becomes identified with everything.

The term *dhātu*, which we have just seen used to refer to cosmological levels, is used elsewhere in the *Sutta Piṭaka* to refer to a classification of the four *mahābhūtā*, (earth (*paṭhavī*), water (*āpo*), wind (*vāyu*) and fire (*tejo*)), plus space (*ākāsa*) and consciousness (*viññāṇa*).[58] One can see that here, too, there is a progression from the grossest or densest element to the subtlest. And their classification together as elements indicates their congruity in all other respects: consciousnessness is not categorically distinct from earth. The fact that there are no category distinctions is further emphasised in this *Sutta*, which is called the *Bahudhātuka Sutta*, when the term *dhātu* is applied in like manner to processes such as the senses, to abstract notions such as comfort and discomfort, happiness and unhappiness, harmfulness and harmlessness, and to the three cosmological realms, as well as to the six elements just mentioned.[59]

There is in the *Sutta Piṭaka* an alternative threefold division of the degrees of density of phenomena to that of the cosmological *dhātus*, and it is here that we find the term *manomaya* introduced in this context. In the *Poṭṭhapāda Sutta* of the *Dīgha Nikāya*, the Buddha explains to Poṭṭhapāda that there are three modes in which an individual (*atta-paṭilābha*) can exist in *saṃsāra*.[60] The term I have translated 'an individual', *atta-paṭilābha*, is uncommon and its meaning is not generally established. It literally means 'the taking on of a self'. The commentary glosses it as *attabhāva*.[61] The term *attabhāva*, which literally means 'becoming a self', has several meanings, given by the *Critical Pali Dictionary* as follows:

> 1. (abstract) existence of a soul ... 2. The existence as an individual, proper nature; but most frequently concrete: a living being, or its bodily form, person, personality, i.e. the various appearance of the *attā*, opp. the continual existence of the *attā*... (among words denoting 'body').[62]

In the context found here, it must surely have the meaning of existence as an individual in *saṃsāra*, which is, in effect, existence as a conventional self, because the three terms *oḷārika*, *manomaya* and *arūpa* undoubtedly refer respectively to gross and subtle form, and to absence of form. The commentary glosses the three as corresponding to *kāmabhava*, *rūpabhava* and *arūpabhava* respectively.[63] This would preclude the possibility of *attabhāva* having the more concrete meaning of 'body'. So here *manomaya* has a metaphorical meaning which corresponds to the cosmological level of the *rūpadhātu*: it is existence at a level which is between that of gross *rūpa*, which corresponds to the *kāmadhātu*, and that of formlessness, which corresponds to the *arūpadhātu*. It is existence as it were at the intermediate level of subtle *rūpa*, the *rūpadhātu*. In the *Sutta*, the Buddha explains that the first has form, is characterised by the four great elements, and is nourished by solid food. The second also has form, but it originates in the mind; here, one has all the limbs of a (gross) physical body and has supernormal senses. The third is without form and originates at conceptual levels.[64]

We see from the Pali that in this passage the three modes of existence all relate to the *atta-paṭilābha*. Indeed, the Buddha explicitly states that he teaches a doctrine which leads to the abandoning of the conventional notion of selfhood in *each* of these existences.[65] They therefore might be said to represent the degrees of density in which one can have *saṃsāric* existence. And once again the absence of discontinuity between gross, subtle and formless is emphasised.

We noted above that in Buddhism the *arūpadhātu* is a spacial metaphor for spiritual progress, and I suggested that all the cosmological levels could be considered in the same way. This is supported in the commentary on the *Poṭṭhapāda Sutta* passage, where spiritual progress, by way of the attainment of certain levels of meditation, is clearly linked with the three spheres. Significantly, we also see from the Pali that the cosmological term *brahmaloka* is explicitly identified with meditational levels. The commentary states that *kāmabhava* refers to those who live at any of the levels between hell and a certain type of god (the *devas*) by taking on a gross (*oḷārika*) *rūpa* body.[66] *Rūpabhava* refers to those who live with a subtle *rūpa* (*manomaya*) body, and this level corresponds to a range of spiritual attainments from the first *jhāna* level right up to the highest *brahmaloka* level of meditation. *Arūpabhava* refers to those who live with an *arūpa* body, and this level corresponds to meditational attainments ranging from the *brahmaloka* known as the sphere of infinite space up to the *brahmaloka* known as the sphere which is neither conceptual nor non-conceptual.[67]

The *Brahmajāla Sutta* suggests that the intermediate level is also called the 'sphere of radiance'.[68] It states that beings here are "mind-made and radiating light from themselves".[69] I referred to this passage in chapter v and suggested there that as individuals progress on the spiritual path, so they are increasingly described in terms of light and radiance. It would appear that this radiance is apparent at the intermediate level of *manomaya*: the lightness which results from spiritual progress corresponds to the subtlety (or lightness) of the level at which one exists.

The clearest canonical reference to the distinction between *rūpa* and *arūpa devas* and their association with psycho-cosmological levels is found in the *Majjhima Nikāya*. Those *devas* which are *rūpa* are described as *manomaya* and those which are *arūpa* are described as *saññāmaya*.[70] In discussing this passage in chapter III, it was suggested that though the passage itself is not concerned to make clear whether or not such gods actually exist, the description indicates the difference between gods which have form, which can be apperceived, and gods without form, which can only be conceived of. Elsewhere in the *Sutta Piṭaka*, however, the existence of all such *devas* is taken for granted, and this passage serves to confirm the point that bodies which are *manomaya* do not consist *of* the mind, but have form, *rūpa*, which is created *by* the mind. *Arūpa* gods, on the other hand, exist at a level which can only be referred to as abstract, and correspond to *arūpa* levels of meditation. Like the commentary on the *Poṭṭhapāda Sutta*, the commentary on this passage also confirms that the subtle *manomaya* body of the *rūpa deva* requires a certain meditative state to have been achieved in the same way that existence at the level of the *arūpa deva* does. *Rūpa* and *arūpa devas*, it states, are the product of the *rūpa* and *arūpa jhānas* respectively.[71] Here the attainment of a certain (unspecified in the commentary) *rūpajjhāna* is the prerequisite for the creation of a mind-made *rūpa deva*; and the attainment of a certain (again unspecified) *arūpajjhāna* is the prerequisite for the existence of an abstract or conceptual *arūpa deva*.

In the *Aṅguttara Nikāya* there is another passage which connects *deva* levels with meditational attainment and spiritual progress. Here, Sāriputta is relating to the *bhikkhu* Udāyin that if a *bhikkhu* who has achieved the meditative level of *saññāvedayitanirodha* does not subsequently achieve liberation (*no aññaṃ ārādheyya*: literally, 'does not accomplish wisdom') while in this life (*diṭṭhe va dhamme*: literally, 'in a visible condition'), he will be reborn higher than (*atikamma*: literally, 'go beyond') the *deva* community which feed on solid food and live (*upapanno*: literally, 'arise') in a mind-made body.[72] The prerequisites are that the *bhikkhu* shall have completely achieved morality, concentration and wisdom, and shall have entered and emerged from the state of *saññāvedayitanirodha*.[73] Three times Sāriputta relates to Udāyin that this is so.[74] When Udāyin repeatedly refuses to believe him, Sāriputta appeals to the Buddha, who asks Udāyin who he thinks has a mind-made body.[75] Udāyin replies that it is those *devas* who are formless and conceptual, which, the Buddha states, is the word of an ignorant fool.[76] Sāriputta was right: if a *bhikkhu* has achieved morality, concentration and wisdom and has entered and emerged from *saññāvedayitanirodha*, but nevertheless does not achieve liberating insight, he will be reborn with a mind-made body at a level higher than the community of *rūpa devas* who feed on solid food.

This passage seems to suggest that the *manomaya*, or *rūpadhātu*, level is complex (in the same way the *kāmadhatu* and *arūpadhātu* levels are): there are both those *devas* who feed on solid food, and a higher, or perhaps more subtle, level beyond that. In stating that those who have experienced *saññāvedayitanirodha* go to the *rūpadhātu*, it is possible that Sāriputta is referring to those who have experienced *saññāvedayitanirodha* without first experiencing the *arūpajjānas*, since those who are proficient in the *arūpajjhānas* would be reborn in the *arūpadhātu*. Udāyin perhaps does presume that one who has experienced *saññāvedayitanirodha* has also first experienced the *arūpajjhānas*, but misuses the term *manomaya*. In any event, Udāyin is told he is an ignorant fool to confuse the two levels of *manomaya* and *arūpadhātu*.

The implication of this passage is that even if a *bhikkhu* has attained the highest meditational level of *saññāvedayitanirodha*, the next rebirth will be in the *rūpadhātu* unless he has experienced the *arūpajjhānas*. And we also see from the passage that there is the added proviso that the meditational achievement is accompanied by the proper following of the Eightfold Path (summed up in the three terms *sīla*, *samādhi* and *paññā*). This is a further indication of the link between rebirth and spiritual progress: the *bhikkhu* must be spiritually accomplished in all respects. Only if he is accomplished in this way does meditational attainment achieve a corresponding future level of existence if he falls short of liberating insight.

Elsewhere we read that the process can be reversed: those with a subtle body can revert to having a solid body if they feast on the taste of the earth and feed on it and are nourished by it for a long time; to the extent that they thus feed, their bodies become solid.[77] This passage is part of the *Aggañña Suttanta*, and describes how the world begins to re-evolve.[78] From its unevolved state the process is one of gradual solidification. The final stage is when, tasting the earth with their fingers, the subtle beings are overcome by the taste and this brings about desire.[79] Here we have a figurative account of the way in which false notions of separate selfhood, which are the corner-stone of the ignorance upon which desire is based according to Buddhist teachings, bring about solidification: and it is precisely the opposite of the process of liberation. Though the *Sutta* is concerned with the genesis of the social order and not with a regression in the progress of an individual, it supports the point being made in this chapter that ignorance corresponds to solidity and insight corresponds, according its degree, to subtlety or formlessness.

We read in the *Satipaṭṭhāna Sutta* that in the practice of *sati* on one's state of mind (*citta*), one of the states of mind that one might have achieved is that of having "become great" (*mahaggata*).[80] The commentary on this states that this means that one has experienced the *jhānas*, either *rūpa* or *arūpa*. At the level of the *kāmadhātu*, one's mental state is one of not having become great.[81] This suggests that the experience of meditation makes the individual subtler in a way which is described as the mind expanding. This clearly fits with the suggestion that the process is one of liberation: the metaphor is that at its most dense or ignorant level, existence is contracted or restricted; at its most subtle level, it expands to the point where it is free from restriction. This point was suggested in chapter v.

In the *Aṅguttara Nikāya* there is a passage which clearly indicates that the term *rūpa* used in connection with the term *manomaya* refers to subtle (not gross) *rūpa*. The passage states that Kakudha, a personal attendant of Mahāmoggallāna, has just died and been reborn with a mind-made body. The form of the mind-made body is such that it fills two or three villages in Magadha.[82] In this instance, one can clearly infer that the *rūpa* of Kakudha's body is subtle because the text goes on to state that in spite of its size it does not cause harm either to himself or to others.[83] In this rebirth, Kakudha is a *deva*, the text states.[84] There is no explicit mention in this passage that Kakudha has achieved an appropriate level of meditation. We cannot, therefore, tell whether this achievement has been taken for granted, or whether his service as Mahāmogallāna's personal attendant is sufficient for the attainment of a spiritually advanced rebirth.

To sum up the third point in this chapter, *manomaya* is found in the *Sutta Piṭaka* in contexts which show that it represents the cosmological level of the *rūpadhātu*, which is the intermediate level between gross *rūpa* and formlessness, characterised by subtle *rūpa*. The stratification of the cosmological levels in turn corresponds to spiritual progress: the spectrum ranging from the most dense form level to the level of formlessness parallels the disciple's progress from ignorance to insight. Being at an intermediate level on the spectrum of density, the attainment of a *manomaya* existence represents an intermediate level of spiritual progress.

The fourth of my contexts for discussing *manomaya* is when it refers to the ability of those who have mastered a certain level of meditation to create a mind-made body. As the attainment of a certain meditational level in one life results in rebirth at the *rūpadhātu,* or *manomaya,* level in a subsequent life, a *bhikkhu* may come to understand this link and use it to affect the mode in which he exists in his present birth. He learns the principle of this at an early stage in his meditative practice. We read, for example, that in the first *jhāna*, which arises from detachment (*vivekaja*), a *bhikkhu* "drenches, saturates, permeates and suffuses this same body with the happiness[85] and joy which arise from detachment; there is no part of this whole body which is not filled with the happiness and joy which arise from detachment".[86] From this passage, we see that in meditation the *bhikkhu* is able to affect his body. At more advanced levels of meditation, he is able deliberately to create a subtle body while he is living in a gross *rūpa* body. This ability is described in the *Sāmaññaphala Sutta* of the *Dīgha Nikāya.* The *bhikkhu* must have attained what is referred to as the meditative level of the fourth *jhāna* (elsewhere called the fourth *rūpajjhāna*), which is characterised by equanimity and purity of mindfulness, and is without pleasure or pain.[87] In some contexts in the Pali canon, the four *rūpajjhānas* precede four *arūpajjhānas*, and one has to be proficient in all eight *jhānas* before liberating insight can be achieved.[88] But in this *Dīgha Nikāya* passage, it is clear that the fourth *rūpajjhāna* represents the culmination of meditative practice, and insight is attained from this level. Prior to liberating insight, however, the *bhikkhu* progressively acquires various other insights and powers. Each of these is enumerated in the text and will be discussed shortly.

According to this *Sutta*, the first result of attaining the fourth *jhāna* is that the *bhikkhu* is able to purify his mind sufficiently to see clearly the relationship between his body and his consciousness: this passage was referred to in chapter v. With his mind so purified, the text states, he is then able to "apply and bend down his thoughts to the magic creation of a mind-made body" and "from this body, he magically creates another mind-made body, having form and all the [corresponding] limbs and parts and with supernormal senses (*ahīnindriyaṃ*)".[89] According to the *Critical Pali Dictionary*, *ahīnindriyaṃ* means 'without defect of any (sense)-faculty'.[90] Buddhaghosa suggests that it has this meaning when he glosses the term in two places as *paripuṇṇindriya*[91] and *avikal-indriya.*[92] I have used the term 'supernormal' because if the context is concerned with a magically created mind-made body then it would seem likely that such perfected senses would also in some sense be 'supernormal'. We shall see below that the use of supernormal (*dibba* - 'divine') senses is referred to in this passage, and if the ability to behave in such a way is acquired at a relatively advanced stage of the spiritual path then perhaps what is to us supernormal is in fact an indication that the senses are perfected. In support of this interpretation, we read elsewhere that a *bhikkhu* who attains the meditative state of *saññāvedayitanirodha* has senses which are "quite purified".[93]

There follow three analogies which imply that the mind-made body looks identical to the *bhikkhu's* existing body. The first is the pulling of a reed from its sheath: one knows that the two are separate from each other but they precisely fit together or correspond to each other. The point of the second and third analogies is the same as the first: a sword and its scabbard and a snake and its slough.[94] The form of the Pali is the same for the sword (*asi*) and scabbard (*kosi*), and the slough (*karaṇḍa*) and the snake (*ahi*).

A possibility which arises from these analogies is that they might also be an indication that the creating of a mind-made body is of spiritual significance: that it is an ability which is acquired when a certain advanced stage on the path to liberation is attained. Eliade points out that the image of the snake and its cast skin, for example, is one of the oldest symbols indicating initiation, or mystical death and resurrection, and is found in Brahmanical literature.[95] In the *Sāmaññāphala Sutta*, the acquisition of various magical or supernormal powers (*iddhis*) and insights, which culminate in liberating insight, follows the stage at which the *bhikkhu* is able to create the *manomaya* body. As such, the process might have metaphorical symbolism as a rite of passage or initiation to the level at which the soteriologically advanced stages of the *bhikkhu's* progress along the path take place. This might be more plausible if one understands the creating of a *manomaya* body as a 'subtlising' process, not as *another* body, as I suggest below. Alternatively, the analogies might just indicate the close relationship between the bodies, such as we saw described in the *Taittirīya Upaniṣad*, where the three levels of bodies were said to 'fill' each other, indicating that they normally occupy the same space.

As well as the fact that the mind-made body looks identical to the *bhikkhu's* existing physical body, this passage tells us that it also has form, it is *rūpa*. The variety in the modes of reality to which we have already referred gives us some indication that this mind-made body, though it has form, might differ in nature from our physical bodies. We have also seen that the Brahmanical religion recorded in the *Upaniṣads* accepted the existence of an individual's 'subtle body' (*manomaya, vijñānamaya* or *liṅga śarīra*). And we have concluded above that rebirth at the psycho-cosmological level of *manomaya* means having a subtle *rūpa* body. It is likely, therefore, that in this context also the created body is a subtle body. Because the mind-made body referred to in the *Sāmaññaphala Sutta* has form, however, we know that it is not merely a concept that the *bhikkhu* creates: its level of reality is *rūpa* rather than *arūpa*, even if it is subtle *rūpa*.[96] Its existence, therefore, is not *in* the mind or *of* the mind, but it is a body created *by* the power of the mind. In some way the *bhikkhu's* mind is able to manipulate *rūpa* to create a subtle body in exactly the same form as the gross body.

The phenomenon of deliberately creating a body is not unique to Buddhism, or even to the Indian tradition as a whole. In his book, *Yoga: Immortality and Freedom*, Eliade discusses the phenomenon of the transmutation of substance in tantric yoga and in Western alchemy.[97] Both practices involve the manipulation of matter by the power of the mind. And both involve the transmutation of the flesh into a subtle body. For alchemists it is a 'body of glory'; for yogins it is a divine body (*divya-deha*), called a 'diamond body' by Vajrayānists and a 'perfect body' (*siddha-deha*) by Haṭha yogins.[98] In the light of our discussion above, we can see the likely significance of the fact that in the *Sāmaññaphala Sutta* passage the meditative level attained by the *bhikkhu* who creates the *manomaya* body is stated to be the most rarified of the *rūpajjhānas* and not an *arūpajjhāna*. In attaining the level of subtle *rūpa*, he is able to identify with and manipulate it: his mind has the power to create a subtle body. If we relate this to our discussion above of *manomaya* as it corresponds to the cosmological level of *rūpadhātu*, then were this *bhikkhu* to die having attained this meditative level, he would be reborn as a *deva* in the *rūpadhātu*. The difference here is that in remaining alive, he is able to create the same mode of existence deliberately.

This relationship between the mind and the body is referred to in the *Iddhipāda Saṃyutta*, where Ānanda asks the Buddha if he knows he will reach the *brahmaloka* in his mind-made body by means of his psychic power (*iddhi*), and the Buddha replies that he does.[99] Ānanda then questions the Buddha in exactly the same way if he knows he will reach the *brahmaloka* in his body made of the four great elements by means of his psychic power, and the Buddha again answers in the affirmative. This ability to do the same thing with both bodies, the Buddha goes on to state, is because the *tathāgata* concentrates the body in the mind and concentrates the mind in the body: in his body he enters and abides in the conception (*saññā*: that is, he visualises) of bliss and lightness so that his body is lighter, softer, more plastic and more radiant.[100] What this passage means is that in meditation the *tathāgata* identifies body and mind. This does not mean that he identifies *with* body and mind, but that he identifies them as of like nature. And being of like nature, only differing in degree of density, both can be manipulated in the same way.[101]

Johansson states of this passage that it illustrates the way "a material body may become less heavy and solid through meditation and by not identifying oneself with it".[102] He goes on to state that "the idea is probably that the mind (*citta*) is thin and light; by mixing it well with the body the combination will become less heavy. Concentration in itself is a force, and concentration on lightness is apt to reduce the weight of the body".[103] The *Iddhipāda Saṃyutta* itself does not state that the lighter body comes about because one does not identify oneself with it, but this is implicit in the fact that the subtle body is acquired at a certain level of spiritual insight: one can assume that it follows from this that progress has been made in the liberating task of ceasing falsely to identify with one's empirical body. Johansson's second and third sentences miss this point, however. It is not a question of mixing light mind with heavy body and producing something in between. The point is that greater degrees of insight correspond to less dense levels of reality, so one no longer exists at the more dense levels. At the more dense levels of *rūpa*, the mind is correspondingly dense or ignorant; as one progresses, *both* one's mind and one's body become less dense. Concentration is indeed a force, but its task is to clarify (lighten) the *mind*: and the state in which one has bodily existence follows from this. When one has consciously understood this fact through spiritual progress, and crucially through the attainment of advanced stages of meditation, one is able to direct the mind to manipulating the more dense levels of reality. The *tathāgata* is Enlightened, and his complete understanding of the process enables him to identify body and mind in meditation and have mastery over both.

That one comes to understand the link between spiritual progress and the density of the body is dramatically exemplified in a passage in the *Saḷāyatana Saṃyutta*.[104] This passage relates the death of Upasena. Instead of his body being subject to the normal process of decay after death, it is spontaneously scattered like a handful of chaff.[105] The reason for this, the text states, is that Upasena had for a long time removed any concept of 'I' or 'mine'.[106] This clearly indicates the link between conscious identification with one's empirical existence, which in Buddhist terms is tantamount to the most basic (or dense) ignorance, and the continuing of one's gross material body. Conversely, no longer having any false notions of 'I' represents insight, or en-light-enment, which means that one's body is correspondingly light. And in this passage Upasena knows in advance that when he dies his body will spontaneously dissipate in this way: it is he who announces that this will happen. He instructs other *bhikkhus* to lift this body onto a couch and take it outside before it is spontaneously scattered like a handful of chaff.[107]

In this use of the term *manomaya*, then, yet again the power of the mind is being referred to. This time there is no explicit link with an ethical dimension, as we saw in the *Dhammapada*: the link is, rather, with the achievement of an advanced stage on the spiritual path. But it is nevertheless cardinal to Buddhist teaching that in order to achieve spiritual progress ethical issues must first be dealt with. So what we see here is the way the power of the mind continues to determine one's *saṃsāric* existence at advanced stages on the path. And at a certain advanced stage, the mind can be deliberately used in a creative manner to manipulate *rūpa*. We saw above that the *saṃkhārakkhandha* volitionally constructs every *khandha* in which one experiences a future life. What we are considering here is the implication of that. If liberation has been achieved through the mind (and the terms *paññā*- and *ceto-vimutta* clearly refer to the centrality of the role of the mind in liberating insight), those future lives are *not* experienced and the bodies are *not* formed. And if the presence or absence of major congenital abnormalities of the body is karmically determined, as suggested in chapter 1, and if karma is volition, then one can see an even more direct link between the mind and the physical body. Though one is unaware of it, it is the mind that is the power or creative force behind not only the condition of one's body but also its very existence. Furthermore, we have seen above in a reference to the *Aggañña Sutta* that desire (or volition, the power of the mind) is instrumental in the solidification of re-evolving beings. In Buddhism such solidification might symbolically indicate ignorance, but it nevertheless also indicates the creative power of the mind in a manner which echoes the way human beings originate according to the *Vedic* cosmogonies I have mentioned. This point is implicit in the second Noble Truth. It states that the arising of *dukkha* is dependent on desire (*taṇhā*). Elsewhere, *dukkha* is defined as the five *khandhas*, or *saṃsāric* existence. So it follows that the meaning of the second Noble Truth is precisely the point made in this paragraph: that volitions are the instrumental factor in bringing about future bodily rebirths in *saṃsāra*.

In considering the creative power of the mind in Buddhism in this way, we illustrate even more strongly the absence of discontinuity between gross and subtle form, and formlessness, *rūpa* and *arūpa*. And according to the *Sāmaññaphala Sutta,* a *bhikkhu* is able, when he has attained the highest level of meditation and purified his mind appropriately, deliberately to create another body with his mind. It could be that having achieved a stage where karma is no longer the medium through which the power of the mind works, he is able to utilise that power *intention*-ally: he 'applies and bends down the mind' (*cittaṃ abhinīharati abhininnāmeti*) to creating a mind-made body (*manomayaṃ kāyaṃ abhinimmināya*).

The *Sāmaññaphala Sutta* continues with a description of other things the *bhikkhu* is able to do at this stage, and from this description we can see other ways in which it is claimed that the power of the mind is able to manipulate *rūpa*. First, he is able to practise the various *iddhis*, or supernormal powers: the *bhikkhu* has the ability to become many when he is one, and then to become one again; he can be be either clearly visible or indiscernible; he goes unobstructed[108] to the other side of a wall, a fence or a mountain as if through air; he enters and emerges from the ground as if it were water; he walks on water without sinking[109] as if it were the ground; he travels cross-legged in the air like a bird on the wing; even the moon and the sun, with such potency and majesty, he touches and grasps with his hand; with his body he reaches even to the *brahmaloka*.[110] In effect, he can make himself into anything he wishes. The *Sutta* gives the analogy of a skilled potter or his apprentice being able to make or create out of well prepared clay any shape of bowl he likes, or an ivory carver out of ivory, or a goldsmith out of gold.[111]

The *iddhis*, also called magic or psychic powers, are a pan-Indian phenomenon and pre-date Buddhism. The Buddha seems not only to have taken it for granted that such powers exist, but, as we see here from the

Sāmaññaphala Sutta, he teaches that they are acquired as part of the meditative process.[112] The *Suttas* also refer to the development of the *iddhipādas*, the 'bases of supernormal power'.[113] There are four bases: resolution (*chanda*), energy (*viriya*), thought (or ?concentration) (*citta*) and investigation (*vīmaṃsā*). One might suggest from these four that the collective purpose of developing the *iddhipādas* is the focussing of the power of the mind. In the *Aṅguttara Nikāya*, the Buddha is stated to have identified disciples according to their specific mastery of such powers: Mahā Moggallāna is most skilled in the psychic powers, and Culla-panthaka is most skilled at the creating of a mind-made body, for example.[114]

It is stated elsewhere that the *iddhis* are either worldly (*āmisa*) or in accord with *dhamma* (sometimes called 'spiritual').[115] In the *Vinaya* the *iddhis* described here are called *puthujjanika iddhi* and these are contrasted with the three knowledges (*tisso vijjā*) and the divine sight (*dibba cakkhuṃ*), which are considered desirable for a disciple to acquire.[116] In the *Kevaḍḍha Sutta* the Buddha explicitly states that he is concerned about, ashamed of and detests the special psychic powers because he sees danger in the practice of them.[117] For the Buddha, the real wonder or miracle is education.[118] He explains that this begins with exercises in reasoning (*vitakka* and *manasikāra*) and proceeds through the entire range of teachings he has given, culminating in the realisation of the Four Truths and the destruction of the *āsavas*.[119] There are also strict rules in the *Vinaya* about inappropriate practice of the *iddhis*: the display of *iddhis* beyond the capacity of ordinary men is prohibited,[120] and a *bhikkhu* who falsely claims possession of such powers expels himself from the *Saṅgha*.[121] There are, however, several references in canonical material to the use of *iddhis* in contexts where they are considered acceptable. The several references to the practice of disappearing from one place and reappearing in another is a good example, and one which the Buddha himself practises.[122] In the *Kevaḍḍha Sutta*, this 'magical' form of transport is explicitly associated with the power of the mind: "Then, Kevaḍḍha, the *bhikkhu* attained such a level (*rūpa*) of concentration that, when his mind was completely concentrated, the way leading to the *devas* appeared [to him]".[123] Later in the same *Sutta*, the *bhikkhu* uses the same technique when moving to the next *devaloka*.[124] The *Mahāparinibbāna Sutta* also relates that the Buddha magically transports both himself and his following of disciples across a river.[125]

The concern of the Buddha about the practice of the *iddhis* and the presence of the rules in the *Vinaya* together suggest that the distinction between these two types of *iddhi*, worldly or in accord with *dhamma*, is considered of great importance. Concern about abuse of the *iddhis* probably reflects the fact that such powers were abused by some who perhaps were believed to practise certain meditations specifically in order to acquire the more sensational powers. In India such people became known as *siddhas*, the same term used for the powers themselves in the Yoga tradition. In Patañjali's

Yoga Sūtras, the whole of chapter III is concerned with the supernormal powers.[126] Patañjali's teaching is complex, but indicates that though the yogin acquires such powers the real power is achieved through *samādhi*, not through the *siddhis*, and the practice of the *siddhis* can hinder liberating insight, defined as right *samādhi*.[127] So though such people could perform things which lay people could not, such practices alone neither indicate their spiritual accomplishments nor contribute to their eventual liberation. The teaching of the Buddha is thought by scholars to pre-date that of classical yoga, but the Buddha's opinion that the abuse of the powers is dangerous as well as not being in accord with *dhamma* is highly likely to have been for the reason given by Patañjali: his concern was always with whatever is conducive to liberation.

From the level of the fourth *jhāna*, there are several other things the *bhikkhu* is also able to do. These are all conducive to insight and constitute what are called the superknowledges (*abhiññā*) which are in accord with *dhamma*. In summary, he is able to use his divine hearing (*dibba sotadhātu*) (no doubt one of the supernormal senses) to hear both celestial and human sounds whether far or near. In similar manner, he is able to grasp fully with his own mind the minds of other beings and men and to know accurately the state of those other minds; whether they are angry, steadfast or attentive, for example. He is able to recall accurately any number of his own former places of existence (or former lives) and he can use his divine sight, *dibba cakkhu* (another of the supernormal senses), to see beings passing from one life to another. He sees the way in which the qualitative nature of their activities has given rise to the condition in which they were reborn. Finally, the *bhikkhu* is able to understand and root out the *āsavas*. He understands as it really is the fact of unsatisfactoriness, the origin and cessation of unsatisfactoriness, and the path leading to the cessation of unsatisfactoriness (the four Noble Truths). Likewise, he understands the *āsavas* of sensual desire (*kāma*), the desire for continued existence (*bhavāsava*) and ignorance (*avijjā*) as they really are, and is able to eradicate them. Knowing he is liberated, he realises the cycle of rebirth has been destroyed, the holy life has been fulfilled, he has done what had to be done: after this life there will be no further life.[128]

Of all of these supernormal abilities, only one, the creation of the body, is specifically stated to be *manomaya*. But just as the mind-made body required that the *bhikkhu*, having achieved the stated meditative level, 'apply and bend-down his mind' in order to create such a body, so in the description of every single one of the other abilities, it clearly states that first the *bhikkhu* has to apply and bend-down his mind.[129] The difference seems to be that the body is *created* by the mind whereas the other supernormal abilities are *activities* of the mind: in the former case, the mind *produces* something; in the latter case the mind *does* something. And though it is not explicitly stated in the text, it would appear that it is the mind-made body which is subsequently directed by the mind to perform the *iddhis*, use its divine hearing and seeing, have insight into the minds of others, and recall former existences, and ultimately eradicate the *āsavas*. This is perhaps more likely in view of the fact that the *iddhis* are the only one of the supernormal abilities referred to in this and other similar passages which are stated to be 'worldly' powers; all of the others are in accord with *dhamma* and conducive to insight. The former, as we have noted, are not specifically Buddhist; the latter are. As such, the supernormal abilities might be said to be supramundane (*lokuttara*) activities, possibly requiring a more subtle, or rarified, bodily vehicle. The *iddhis* are the only supernormal abilities which involve any external movement of the mind-made body. All the others are internal or subjective supernormal activities. So it might be that in the latter cases the mind-made body is not separate from the normal body, but is constituted as if the reed were still in its sheath, the sword in its scabbard, and so on. Thus in such circumstances the mind-made body could be thought of as some sort of 'subtlising', or 'sensitising' of the body and its faculties. This suggestion would fit well with the correspondence between developing the clarity of the mind and the density of the body, discussed earlier.

The term *manomaya*, then, in the context of the ability to direct the mind to the creating of a 'mind-made' body is another illustration of the centrality of the power of the mind in Buddhist teachings. Just as from the Buddha's teaching that karma is intention it follows that the power of the mind creates and shapes our very existences, so at certain meditative levels that intention can be consciously directed to the creating of a body with certain faculties conducive to insight, such as supernormal senses. The key difference is that the former seems to us to happen 'automatically': we are not conscious that our existence originates in the mind. The latter is the deliberate creation of a body. There is also a difference in the quality of the *rūpa* with which the bodies are constituted when the mind itself has advanced to a certain stage on the spiritual path. Our 'normal' bodies are gross *rūpa*, whereas the mind-made body is subtle *rūpa*. This is true whether the *manomaya* body is one in which one is reborn as a result of having attained a certain level of meditation in a previous life, or whether the *manomaya* body is deliberately created in this life. The implication of both is that the clarifying of the mind which is achieved on the path to liberation results in a corresponding subtlising of the body. It is in this sense that the metaphorical meaning of *manomaya* is suggested by its literal meaning: the metaphorical meaning represents an intermediate psycho-cosmological level which corresponds to the fact that a certain degree of spiritual advancement has to have been achieved for the deliberate creation of something 'originating in the mind', the literal meaning of *manomaya*.

If we compare the concepts discussed in the last two points in this chapter as they are found in the *Sutta Piṭaka* with similar concepts in *Upaniṣadic* material, we see that there are some close similarities between them. In both traditions, the power of the mind plays a central role. According to both traditions, the practice of meditation harnesses that power in a way which transforms the meditating subject. Both traditions state that the individual exists at different levels of density or subtlety, and that there is no ontological discontinuity between the levels. We have seen that in the Buddhist material the metaphor of the spiritual path clearly underlies the continuity between the levels of existence. And as the Buddha's teaching states that the path represents the progressive purification of the mind, so the levels of existence represent corresponding degrees of density or subtlety. In the *Upaniṣads*, this correspondence cannot be made in the same way. Though the material is far from clear, one can, however, suggest that there is a correspondence which differs only because liberation in the two traditions is understood differently. The material in the *Upaniṣads* suggests that the different dense and subtle bodies, or modes of existence, co-exist. It suggests that they represent the range between the outer, empirical, self and the inner, 'real', self. These are all simultaneously present in the life of the individual, whose task it is to identify with the real self rather than the empirical self. In Buddhism, the liberating process consists, rather, of progressing from ignorance to insight, which corresponds to the 'subtlising' of one's body. In the *Upaniṣads* one has to realise what is already the case; in Buddhism, to make a process happen. In both traditions, the goal is achieved by progressively identifying with less dense levels of existence.

The contexts in which the power of the mind has been discussed in this chapter have dwelt in particular on its power in relation to the body. We have seen that the very existence of the body in *saṃsāra* originates in the volitional activity of the mind. And the mode of existence of the body corresponds directly to the spiritual progress of the individual, which in Buddhism is the progress from ignorance to insight: from density to light. This leads me to my final chapter, in which I will discuss the attitude towards the body in early Buddhism. We shall see that it is unjustifiably held responsible for many of the activities of the mind.

Notes

1. PED, p.521.
2. *Dialogues*, I, p.30, 47f, etc. uses 'made of mind'; Ñāṇamoli, in his translation of the *Visuddhimagga*, translates it as 'mind-made', which corresponds to an instrumental interpretation of the term (*The Path of Purification*, 1964, p.443f).
3. For example at DN.I.76: *Ayaṃ kho me kāyo rūpī cātum-mahābhūtiko ... anicc' ucchādana-parimaddana-bhedana-viddhaṃsana-dhammo.*
4. PED, p.521.
5. *Dhammapada* 1 and 2: *Manopubbaṅgamā dhammā manoseṭṭhā manomayā.*
6. 'Thinking' is meant here in a non-technical sense (i.e. not equating *manas* with *vitakka* or any other more overtly discursive term), merely to convey the point being made.

7. AN.I.11: *Ye keci bhikkhave dhammā akusalā akusalabhāgiyā akusalapakkhikā sabbe te manopubbaṅgamā. Mano tesaṃ dhammānaṃ paṭhamaṃ uppajjati anvad eva akusalā dhammā ti. Ye keci bhikkhave dhammā kusalā kusalabhāgiyā kusalapakkhikā sabbe te manopubbaṅgamā. Mano tesaṃ dhammānaṃ paṭhamaṃ uppajjati anvad eva kusalā dhammā ti.*
8. MN.III.99.
9. SN.IV.70: *Adantā aguttā arakkhitā asaṃvutā dukkhādhivāhā ... Sudantā suguttā surakkhitā susaṃvutā sukhādhivāhā.*
10. SN.IV.71.
11. We are reminded of the passage referred to above in the discussion on *manas* in chapter v which describes liberation in terms of not paying attention to any outward sign but paying attention to the signless realm: *Sabbanimittānañ ca amanasikāro, animittāya ca dhātuyā manasikāro* (MN.I.296).
12. *Ṛg Veda* X.129.4: *Kāmas tad agre sam avartatādhi, manaso retaḥ prathamaṃ yad āsīt.*
13. Ch. Up. VI.2.3: *Tad aikṣata bahu syām prajāyeyeti.*
14. For example, Bṛ.Up.1.2.1, 1.4.1f, 1.4.17; Ait. Up. 1.1.1.
15. Bṛ. Up. III.2.13: *Puṇyo vai puṇyena karmaṇā bhavati, pāpaḥ pāpeneti.*
16. Bṛ. Up. IV.4.5: *Yathākārī yathācārī, tathā bhavati. Sādhukārī sādhur bhavati, pāpakārī pāpo bhavati.*
17. Ibid.: *Athau khalv āhuḥ kāmamaya evāyam puruṣa iti. Sa yathākāmo bhavati, tat kratur bhavati; yat kratur bhavati, tat karma kurute; yat karma kurute, tat abhisampadyate.* cf. Ch. Up. III.14.1: *Yathā-kratur asminl loke puruṣo bhavati tathetaḥ pretya bhavati, sa kratuṃ kurvīta.* cf. also Ch. Up. VIII.2.2.
18. Collins, 1982, p.58. Collins discusses the development of the doctrine of rebirth in the *Vedic* material in considerable detail. cf. also Jayatilleke, 1949, p.220.
19. Reat (1990, p.111f) also discusses the power of the mind in the sacrificial ritual described in the *Ṛg Veda.*
20. Collins (1982, p.58ff) discusses the earlier background to this central teaching of the *Upaniṣads.*
21. Śat. Br. X.V.2.20: *Taṃ yathā yathopāsate tad eva bhavati.*
22. Bṛ. Up. II.1.8: *Pratirūpa iti vā aham etam upāsa iti, sa ya etam evam upāste, pratirūpaṃ haivainam upagacchati, nāpratirūpam, atho pratirūpo 'smāj jāyate.* The whole of this chapter teaches that one becomes what one meditates on.
23. Bṛ. Up. IV.4.5: *Sa vā ayam ātmā brahma; vijñānamayo manomayaḥ prāṇamaya.*
24. Ibid.: *Cakṣurmayaḥ śrotamayaḥ pṛthivīmaya āpomayo vāyumaya ākāśamayas tejomayo 'tejomaya ... sarvamayaḥ.* cf. also Bṛ. Up. III.7.3-23.
25. Tait. Up. II.3.1: *Prāṇo hi bhūtānām āyu ... tasyaiṣa eva śarīra ātmā.*
26. Ibid.: *Tasmād vā etasmāt prāṇamayād anyo 'ntara ātmā manomaya. Tenaiṣa pūrṇaḥ. Sa vā eṣa puruṣa-vidha eva; tasya puruṣa-vidhatām anv ayaṃ puruṣa-vidha.*
27. Tait. Up. II.4.1: *Tasmād vā etasmān manomayād anyo 'ntara ātmā vijñānamaya. Tenaiṣa pūrṇa. Sa vā eṣa puruṣa-vidha eva, tasya puruṣa vidhatām anv ayaṃ puruṣa-vidha.*
28. Ch. Up. VI.5.1-4.
29. Ch. Up. *Bhāṣya* p.421: *Sarvasya trivṛt-kṛta-tva.*
30. Bṛ. Up. IV.3.7: *Katama ātmeti? Yo' yaṃ vijñānamayaḥ prāṇesu hṛdy antarjyotiḥ puruṣaḥ.* The expression *prājñātmā* is substituted for *vijñānamaya puruṣa* at Bṛ. Up. IV.3.35, but the context indicates the same phenomenon is being referred to.
31. Bṛ. Up. IV.3.9: *Sandhyaṃ tṛtīyaṃ svapna-sthānam.*
32. Bṛ. Up. IV.3.9-IV.3.34.
33. For example, at Ch. Up. VIII.9–11.
34. Ch. Up. VIII.12.1: *Tad asyāmṛtasyāśarīrasyātmano 'dhiṣṭhānam.*
35. Bṛ. Up. IV.4.6.
36. For example, at Śvet. Up. 1.18; Maitrī Up. 6.10; 6.19.
37. Bṛ. Up. V.6.1: *Manomayo 'yaṃ puruṣaḥ bhāḥ satyaḥ tasminn antar-hṛdaye ... .*
38. Bṛ. Up. II.1.17: *Vijñāna-mayaḥ puruṣa.*
39. Bṛ. Up. II.1.18: *Sa yatraitaya svapnāyācarati, te hāsya lokāḥ: tad uteva mahārājo bhavati, uteva mahā-brāhmaṇaḥ. Uteva uccāvacaṃ nigacchati. Sa yadā mahārājo jānapadān gṛhītvā sve janapade yathā-kāmaṃ parivarteta, evam evaiṣa etat prāṇān gṛhītvā sve śarīre yathā-kāmaṃ parivartate.*
40. For example, Bṛ. Up. IV.4.2.
41. Radhakrishnan, 1953, p.253.
42. Bṛ. Up. IV.4.6: *Liṅgaṃ mano yatra niṣaktam asya.*
43. Bṛ. Up. *Bhāṣya*, p. 855: *Manaḥ pradhānatvāl liṅgasya mano liṅgam ity ucyate.*

44. Bṛ. Up. IV.4.6: *Tasmāl lokāt punar aiti asmai lokāya karmaṇe.*
45. Ch. Up. *Bhāṣya* p.204 (Commentary on Ch. Up. III.14.2): *Prāṇa-śarīraḥ prāṇo liṅgātmā.*
46. Nirvana is stated to be unconditioned (*asaṃkhataṃ*) (*Udāna* VIII.3). Though we know from the third line of the *tilakkhaṇa* formula that this does not mean it is or has an independently existing self (*sabbe dhammā anattā*), the fact that it is unconditioned suggests that it is not subject to dependent origination. The *paṭiccasamuppāda* doctrine explains *saṃsāric* experience, however, so this question does not affect the points I am making in this chapter, which are also concerned with experience in *saṃsāra*. The way selflessness is attributed to Nirvana is discussed in the Conclusion.
47. MN.I.55ff; DN.II.290ff.
48. Johansson, 1979, p.37.
49. Johansson discusses the absence of discontinuity between the gross and the subtle, *rūpa* and *arūpa*, in his book *The Dynamic Psychology of Early Buddhism* (1979, *passim*).
50. Gombrich, 1975, p.133ff explains these in much more detail than it is necessary for me to go into here. cf. also Thomas, 1951, p.111f.
51. Ibid., p.134.
52. Ibid., p.135, presumably written with the *Aggañña Suttanta* in mind.
53. Reynolds (1976, p.381f) shows how the *rūpadhātu* corresponds to the Buddha's *dhammakāya* in the late Theravāda and Mahāyāna traditions, and states that the notion of a *dhammakāya* evolved from references to the *manomaya* body.
54. We see a parallel in the colloquial English usage of terms such as 'dense' and 'thick' to refer to one end of the spectrum of intelligence and 'bright' and 'clear' to refer to the other end.
55. Collins, 1982, p.215ff.
56. Ibid., p.217. cf. also Nārada, 1979, p.40f.
57. Eliade, 1973, p.88.
58. MN.III.62.
59. MN.III.62f.
60. DN.I.195: *Tayo kho 'me Poṭṭhapāda atta-paṭilābhā, oḷāriko atta-paṭilābho, manomayo atta-paṭilābho, arūpo atta-paṭilābho.*
61. DA.II.380: *Tattha atta-paṭilābho ti attabhāva-paṭilābho.*
62. CPD s.v. *attabhāva.*
63. DA.II.380.
64. *Katamo ca Poṭṭhapāda oḷāriko atta-paṭilābho? Rūpī cātummahābhūtiko kabaliṅkārāhāra-bhakkho, ayaṃ oḷāriko atta-paṭilābho. Katamo manomayo atta-paṭilābho? Rūpī manomayo sabbaṅga-paccaṅgī ahīnindriyo, ayaṃ manomayo atta-paṭilābho. Katamo ca arūpo atta-paṭilābho? Arūpī saññāmayo, ayaṃ arūpo atta-paṭilābho.* The term *ahīnindriyo*, which I have paraphrased as supernormal senses, is discussed below.
65. DN.I.195f: *Oḷārikassa (manomayassa/arūpassa) kho ahaṃ Poṭṭhapāda atta-paṭilābhassa pahānāya dhammaṃ desemi.*
66. Surprisingly (in view of the widely accepted Ascension of Jesus Christ), Westerners often find it odd that gods can have gross *rūpa* bodies. But this is a common pan-Indian phenomenon and is explicitly referred to in the *Sutta Piṭaka* at, for example, DN.I.34. It is, perhaps, made easier to understand from the context we are discussing here: during the gradual progression through the stages on the spiritual path, there comes a point when an individual has advanced sufficiently to be known as a 'god'. This point comes when he or she still has a gross *rūpa* body.
67. DA.II.380: *Oḷārik' attabhāva-paṭilābhena avīcito paṭṭhāya paranimmita-vasavatti-pariyosānaṃ kāma-bhavaṃ dassesi; manomaya-attabhāva-paṭilābhena paṭhama-jjhāna-bhūmito paṭṭhāya akaniṭṭha-brahmaloka-pariyosānaṃ rūpa-bhavaṃ dassesi; arūp'attabhāva-paṭilābhena akās' ānañc' āyatana-brahmalokato paṭṭhāya neva saññā-n' āsaññ' āyatana-brahmaloka-pariyosānaṃ arūpa-bhavaṃ dassesi.*
68. DN.I.17: *Loko ābhassaro.*
69. *Manomayā … sayaṃ-pabhā.*
70. MN.I.410: *Devā rūpino manomayā … devā arūpino saññāmayā.*
71. MA.III.122: *Jhānacittamayā … arūpajjhānasaññāya saññāmayā.*
72. AN.III.192: *Kabaliṅkārāhārabhakkhānaṃ devānaṃ sahavyataṃ aññataraṃ manomayaṃ kāyaṃ upapanno.*
73. *Sīlasampanno samādhisampanno paññāsampanno saññāvedayitanirodhaṃ samāpajjeyya pi vuṭṭhaheyya pi.*

74. *Atth' etaṃ ṭhānan ti.*
75. AN.III.194: *Kaṃ pana tvaṃ Udāyi manomayakāyaṃ paccesī ti?* In the PTS edition of the *Aṅguttara Nikāya*, this sentence reads as follows: *Kaṃ pana tvaṃ Udāyi manomayaṃ kāyaṃ paccesī ti?* This would have to be translated "What, Udāyin, do you think a mind-made body is?". Though it is a small point, I have chosen to emend the Pali to give a *bahuvrīhi* compound, *manomayakāyaṃ*, which both accords with the use of *kaṃ* and makes more sense in the context.
76. *Ye te bhante devā arūpino saññāmayā ... bālassa avyattassa bhaṇitaṃ.*
77. DN.III.86: *Atha kho te ... sattā rasa-paṭhaviṃ paribhuñjantā tam-bhakkhā tad-āhārā ciraṃ dīgham addhānaṃ aṭṭhaṃsu. Yathā yathā kho te sattā rasa-paṭhaviṃ paribhuñjantā tam-bhakkhā tad-āhārā ciraṃ dīgham addhānaṃ aṭṭhaṃsu, tathā tathā tesaṃ sattānaṃ kharattañ c'eva kāyasmiṃ okkami.*
78. DN.III.84: *Ayaṃ loko vivaṭṭati.*
79. DN.III.85: *Tassa rasa-paṭhaviṃ aṅguliyā sāyato acchādesi, taṇhā c' assa okkami.*
80. MN.I.59.
81. MA.I.280: *Mahaggatam ti rūpārūpāvacaraṃ; amahaggatan ti kāmāvacaraṃ.*
82. AN.III.122: *Tena kho pana samayena Kakudho nāma Koliyaputto āyasmato Mahāmoggallānassa upaṭṭhāko adhunā kālakato aññataraṃ manomayaṃ kāyaṃ upapanno, tassa evarūpo attabhāvapaṭilābho hoti, seyyathā pi nāma dve vā tīṇi vā māgadhikāni gāmakkhettāni.*
83. *So tena attabhāvapaṭilābhena n'eva attānaṃ no paraṃ vyābādheti.*
84. *Kakudho devaputto.*
85. *Sukha*, the opposite of *dukkha*. As a synonym for Nirvana, its meaning is not happiness in the affective sense, but refers to the absence of the dis-ease that is *dukkha*.
86. MN.I.276: *So imam eva kāyaṃ vivekajena pītisukhena abhisandeti parisandeti paripūreti parippharati; nāssa kiñci sabbāvato kāyassa vivekajena pītisukhena apphutaṃ hoti.*
87. DN.I.75: *Adukkhaṃ asukhaṃ upekhāsati-pārisuddhiṃ catutthajjhānaṃ.*
88. The eight *jhānas* correspond to the eight *vimokkhā*, and can be followed by a ninth attainment, *saññāvedayitanirodha*, what PED calls "trance" (PED, p.286). This was referred to in chapter IV. Whether the *jhānas* are thought to be fourfold or eightfold, insight is separate from them: they are the means to the end and not the end in itself. It was because they made the *jhānas* themselves the aim of their teaching that the Buddha rejected the doctrines of two of his teachers, Āḷāra Kāḷāma and Uddaka Rāmaputta (cf. MN.I.164f).
89. DN.I.77: *Manomayaṃ kāyaṃ abhinimmināya cittaṃ abhinīharati abhininnāmeti ... So imamhā kāyā aññaṃ kāyaṃ abhinimmināti rūpiṃ manomayaṃ sabbaṅga-paccaṅgiṃ ahīnindriyaṃ.* cf. also MN.II.17f.
90. CPD, s.v. *ahīnindriya*. PED (p.65) suggests that *ahīnindriya* is probably an inferior reading for *abhinindriya*, which it suggests comes near in meaning to **abhiññindriya*. CPD rejects this as a misreading.
91. DA.I.120.
92. DA.I.222.
93. MN.I.296: *Indriyāni vippasannāni.*
94. DN.I.77: *Seyyathā pi puriso muñjamhā isīkaṃ pavāheyya. Tassa evam assa: 'Ayaṃ muñjo ayaṃ isīkā, añño muñjo aññā-isīkā, muñjamhā tv eva isīkā pavāḷhā ti'.*
95. Eliade, 1973, p.165, referring to *Jaiminīya Brāhmaṇa* II, 134, etc.
96. Again terminology makes the situation confusing: we have seen in chapter I that *rūpa* is defined as consisting of the four elements, of which *paṭhavī* is one. It would have made it easier for us to grasp the notion of subtle body had a term other than *rūpa* been used. The point really is that the subtle body is not just conceptual. We have also seen the use of the term *rūpa* in another context in which it is without solidity in chapter VI.
97. Eliade, 1973, p.274ff.
98. Eliade, 1973, p.274. *Siddha* is the term used for the various powers acquired by the yogin, but it literally means 'perfection'.
99. SN.V.282: *Abhijānāti nu kho bhante bhagavā iddhiyā manomayena kāyena brahmalokaṃ upasaṃkamitā ti?... Abhijānāmi khvāham Ānanda iddhiyā manomayena kāyena brahmalokam upasaṃkamitā ti.*
100. SN.V.283: *Yasmiṃ Ānanda samaye tathāgato kāyam pi citte samādahati cittam pi ca kāye samādahati; sukhasaññañca lahusaññañca kāye okkamitvā viharati, tasmiṃ Ānanda samaye tathāgatassa kāyo lahutaro ceva hoti mudutaro ca kammaniyataro ca pabhassarataro ca.*
101. cf. Bṛ. Up. VI.2.15.
102. Johansson, 1979, p.38.

103. Ibid.
104. SN.IV.40f.
105. SN.IV.41: *Atha kho āyasmato Upasenassa kāyo tatth'eva vikiri seyyathāpi bhusamuṭṭhī ti.*
106. Ibid.: *Tathā hi panāyasmato Upasenassa dīgharattam ahaṃkāra-mamaṃkāra-mānānusayā susamūhatā.*
107. SN.IV.40: *Etha me āvuso imaṃ kāyaṃ mañcakam āropetvā bahiddhā nīharatha purāyam kāyo idheva vikirati seyyathāpi bhusamuṭṭhīti.*
108. *Asajjamāno*: literally, this means unattached, or not clinging, so it might be that the *bhikkhu* is able to do the things described because he has achieved a state where he is detached.
109. *Abhijjamāno*: literally, without breaking through.
110. DN.I.78: *So aneka-vihitaṃ iddhi-vidhaṃ paccanubhoti: eko pi hutvā bahudhā hoti, bahudhā pi hutvā eko hoti, āvibhāvaṃ tiro-bhāvaṃ tiro-kuḍḍaṃ tiro-pākāraṃ tiro-pabbataṃ asajjamāno gacchati seyyathā pi ākāse, paṭhavīyā pi ummujja nimmujjaṃ karoti seyyathā pi paṭhaviyaṃ, udake pi abhijjamāno gacchati seyyathā pi paṭhaviyaṃ, ākāse pi pallaṅkena kamati seyyathā pi pakkhī sakuṇo, ime pi candima-suriye evaṃ mahiddhike evaṃ mahānubhāve pāṇinā parimasati parimajjati, yāva brahma-lokā pi kāyena va saṃvatteti.*
111. *Seyyathā pi dakkho kumbha-kāro vā kumbhakārantevāsī vā suparikammakatāya mattikāya yaṃ yad eva bhājana-vikatiṃ ākaṅkheyya taṃ tad eva kareyya abhinipphādeyya* (and the form is the same for ivory (*danta*) and gold (*suvaṇṇa*)).
112. T.W. Rhys Davids comments on this in his introduction to the *Kevaḍḍha Sutta* in his translation of *Dīgha Nikāya*, Vol. I (*Dialogues*, I, p.272).
113. DN.II.103, 115; MN.I.103, II.11. They are also discussed at length in *Paṭis* II.205ff.
114. AN.I.24: *Etad aggaṃ bhikkhave mama sāvakānaṃ bhikkūnaṃ iddhimantānaṃ yadidaṃ Mahā Moggallāno ... manomayaṃ kāyaṃ abhinimminantānaṃ yadidaṃ Culla-panthako.*
115. AN.I.93: *Dve 'mā bhikkhave iddhiyo. Katamā dve? Āmisa-iddhi ca dhamma-iddhi ca.* DN.III.112 contrasts *ariya* and *no-ariya iddhi.*
116. Vin.II.183.
117. DN.I.213: *Imaṃ kho ahaṃ Kevaḍḍha iddhi-pāṭihāriye ādīnavaṃ sampassamāno iddhi-pāṭihāriyena aṭṭiyāmi harāyāmi jigucchāmi.*
118. *Anusāsani-pāṭihāriyaṃ.*
119. DN.I.214ff.
120. Vin.II.112.
121. Vin.III.91.
122. I am indebted to Mark Allon for the following references (as well as several others used in this chapter): DN.II.50 (the Buddha); DN.I.222, DN.II.37, 40, 46f, 181, 239f, 253–4 (other buddhas, *bhikkhus* or *devas* - including Brahmā, who travels between *lokas* in this way).
123. DN.I.215: *Atha kho so Kevaḍḍha bhikkhu tathā-rūpaṃ samādhiṃ samāpajji yathā samāhite citte devayāniyo maggo pātur ahosi.*
124. DN.I.220.
125. DN.II.89. In a personal communication, Mark Allon informs me that similar examples of the Buddha making use of various *iddhis* are found more frequently in the Buddhist Sanskrit version of the *Mahāparinirvāṇa Sūtra.*
126. Woods, 1914, p.203ff.
127. Ibid., p.265.
128. DN.I.84: *Vimuttasmiṃ vimuttam iti ñāṇaṃ hoti, khīṇā jāti vusitaṃ brahmacariyaṃ kataṃ karaṇīyaṃ nāparaṃ itthattāyāti pajānāti.*
129. *Cittaṃ abhinīharati abhininnāmeti.*

CHAPTER VIII

The Attitude towards the Body

Our subject in this chapter is the attitude towards the human body in Pali Buddhism. We shall see that in the canonical material this attitude is primarily analytical, but that it changes to being openly negative by the time of Buddhaghosa. This change in attitude is important for two main reasons. First, it diverges from the doctrinal teaching on the relationship between body and mind; and second, it is likely to distort meditation exercises which use the body as the meditational subject. Theravāda Buddhism is spreading in Western countries at the same time as the attitude towards the body is enjoying what one might call a high profile in Western culture. If a view about the body which is fundamentally different from the canonical position is disseminated in the West as representing 'the Theravāda Buddhist view', then this misleads body-conscious Western Buddhists and non-Buddhists alike.

A further word needs to be said here about the expressions 'body and mind' and 'the attitude towards the body'. In the foregoing discussion of the analysis of the human being into *khandhas*, and particularly in chapter VII, we have seen that though the *khandha* of the body is largely dense or solid and the mental *khandhas* are formless, there is nevertheless no ontological distinction between them: whether or not they involve the constituents of *rūpa,* they all represent the occurrence of different processes or events on a spectrum of possible modes of existence. It follows that the terms 'body' and 'mind' might misleadingly suggest some sort of Cartesian dualism, especially to a Western reader. They might also mistakenly be interpreted as denoting two opposing objects rather than a combination of processes or events. But the fact is that as ordinary people we do tend to substantialise body and mind, and our *saṃsāric* experience of *rūpa* and *arūpa* is that they are qualitatively different. As Griffiths puts it: "The mental and the physical are categories of event which are phenomenologically irreducibly different".[1] Ice and steam give us a good analogy to illustrate the situation. There is no ontological discontinuity between these different states in which the same chemical combination of hydrogen and oxygen occurs. Phenomenologically, however, this is far from obvious: each is qualitatively distinct from the other and our experience of each of them is irreducibly different. We have to have some knowledge of chemistry to know the true relationship between them. Similarly, the absence of ontological discontinuity between, and the real nature of, the human processes are insights which are only realised as one progresses on the path to liberation. Conventionally, we continue to think of the body and mind as two distinct aspects of ourselves. It is with this conventional dualism that we are concerned in this chapter.

This book has been primarily concerned with the constitution of the human being as it appears to have been understood by the compilers of the *Sutta Piṭaka* of the Pali canon. I have also in some places drawn on the Pali *Abhidhamma*, the commentarial material, most of which is believed to have been compiled by Buddhaghosa in the fifth century CE, and Buddhaghosa's own work, the *Visuddhimagga*. The *Abhidhamma*, the commentaries and the *Visuddhimagga* together form a highly influential corpus of written material which has become the foundation of Theravāda Buddhism. Buddhaghosa's writings in particular have been so influential as to have become the determinant of the orthodox Theravāda position on virtually every point of religious concern. Buddhaghosa himself, however, claims merely to have been an exegete of the canonical material upon which the commentaries are based and to which there are numerous references in his *Visuddhimagga*. This claim is extremely important for Theravāda Buddhists: the Pali canon has always been, and remains to this day, the canonical heart of Theravāda Buddhism. Those who accept the teachings of Buddhaghosa believe they are adhering to the teachings contained in canonical material.[2]

Theravāda Buddhism is often, one might say commonly, understood to have a negative attitude towards the human body. Though there are what appear to be negative statements about the body in the canonical material, we shall see in this chapter that this negative attitude has largely been promulgated by Buddhaghosa, both in his *Visuddhimagga* and in the commentaries on the Pali canon: in spite of his exegetical claims, Buddhaghosa's writing is in fact significantly different in this respect from canonical material. The statements in the canonical material and the increasingly negative attitude towards the body will be discussed in the light of the canonical analysis of the human being which has been the main subject of this book. I shall consider whether there is any constitutional or doctrinal basis for a negative attitude towards the body, and discuss possible reasons for the presence of negative statements in the canon. We shall also see that some translations of the Pali canon have been responsible for introducing negativity towards the body where none exists in the Pali. Other translators of what appear to be negative statements in the canon have failed sufficiently to consider the context in which certain Pali words have been used. The result of this is that the English versions sound more negative than the contexts warrant.

In discussing first the attitude towards the human body in the canonical material, we have to consider an apparent paradox. On the one hand, we can see in the Pali Canon statements about the body which appear to be distinctly negative. We read, for example, that the body is a 'heap of corruption' (*pūtisaṇḍa*),[3] that bodily functions are 'impure' (*asuci*),[4] and that only a completely deluded (or ignorant) fool would think of the body as beautiful.[5] A passage in the *Aṅguttara Nikāya* describes the body as a boil (*gaṇḍo*), which has nine open wounds (*nava vaṇamukhāni*), nine natural openings (*nava abhedanamukhāni*). Whatever oozes out from them is impure (*asuci*), bad-smelling (*duggandhaṃ*) and loathsome (*jegucchiyaṃ*).[6]

In the *Khandha Saṃyutta* we read that it is one's body that leads one astray, at least as much as the other parts of our fivefold psychophysical make-up (that is, the four *khandhas* other than the body). We are told, for example, that "[Our] teacher, sir, is one who speaks of the control of desire and passion ... in the body, in feelings, in apperception, in the volitional constituent, in consciousness".[7] Another passage states that we are to "... get rid of that desire and passion which are in the body, feelings, apperception, the volitional constituent, consciousness".[8] Such statements are particularly relevant since passion and desire are the very source of karmic bondage in Buddhism, as we are told in the second Noble Truth and as has been further demonstrated in previous chapters.

Apart from canonical statements which attribute passion and desire in like measure to all the *khandhas*, from some translations of Pali texts it seems that it is the body alone which leads us astray. For example, in a Pali Text Society translation of the *Sutta Nipāta*, we read that it is from the body that "passion and hatred have their origin", and thoughts which "toss up the mind" arise from the body.[9] And in Müller's translation of *Dhammapada* 202 and 203 he states: "there is no pain like the body" and "the body is the greatest of pains".[10] The importance of such translations should not be underestimated as they are widely disseminated as representing the canon of Theravāda Buddhism and as such are source books for students and believers alike.

On the other hand, the other side of the paradox is that it is cardinal to Buddhism that karmic consequences accruing to any particular individual are entirely dependent on his or her mental volitions. I have already referred above to the definition of karma in the Pali canon as volition, and that it is having willed that one acts through body, speech and mind.[11] This is central to the Buddha's message, and indeed is precisely what distinguished his teaching from that of other Indian religions of his time: in interpreting action (karma) as volition, he uniquely ethicised the law of karma. From this it is clear that the Buddha qualitatively distinguished volitions from the body so far as the function of the law of karma is concerned, in spite of the fact that volitions and body are equally impermanent and conditioned in their constitution and are not ontologically distinct, as we have seen in chapter VII.

In that chapter, I also referred to the power of the mind in a more general sense, and two points emerged there which are relevant here. First, not only is it volitions (*taṇhā*, according to the second Noble Truth[12]) which condition our future existences (*dukkha*), but it is also volitions which keep us on the cycle of rebirth in *saṃsāra* at all: because of, and conditioned by, one's ignorance, such volitions bind us to the cycle of becoming. And second, we saw that the spiritual path according to Buddhist teachings is a gradual clarifying of the mind, and that progress along this path corresponds to the level of density at which one exists in any given life.

In view of the centrality of the role of ignorance and volitions in influencing one's mode of existence, it seems *prima facie* unlikely that it is from the body that passion, desire and hatred, all of which are in themselves volitions which arise because of ignorance, originate. Indeed, we have discussed in some detail already that such volitions are directed towards something by the *saṃkhārakkhandha*. But we have not yet specifically considered the attitude towards the body according to the *Sutta Piṭaka*. And in view of the presence of what appear to be distinctly negative statements about the body in this material, we shall now turn to a consideration of the early attitude towards the human body.

The analysis of the human being into five constituent parts, the *khandhas*, was given by the Buddha in order to illustrate how one should understand the experience of individuality in terms of selflessness. Our study of this analysis has perhaps led us to a position where we can see that one can look at it in two ways: first, one can see that the different *khandhas* are each responsible for specific and different aspects of the human being, and second, one can see that they are all nevertheless interdependent and mutually conditioning: it is *together* that they produce the psychophysical continuum of an 'individual'. I shall treat these two aspects, the distinctiveness and the interrelatedness of the *khandhas*, separately.

In considering first their distinctiveness, I shall draw on canonical descriptions of the practice of *sati*, mindfulness. This practice is particularly relevant here because, first, the subjects on which the mindfulness meditation is to be practised include the body and volitions, and each subject is distinguished from the other in the meditation exercises, emphasising their distinctiveness, and, second, because mindfulness is a meditational practice which is so important in Pali Buddhism that it has two *Suttas* and a *Saṃyutta* entirely devoted to describing its techniques: the *Satipaṭṭhāna Sutta* and the *Mahāsatipaṭṭhāna Suttanta*, in the *Majjhima Nikāya* and *Dīgha Nikāya* respectively, and the *Satipaṭṭhāna Saṃyutta* in the *Saṃyutta Nikāya*.[13] At the beginning and end of the *Suttas*, the practice of *sati* is described as follows:

> There is a way, *bhikkhus*, leading to [only] one destination, for the purification of beings, for the transcending of grief and lamentation, for the cessation of unsatisfactoriness and misery, for the attaining of the [right] path, for the realising of *nibbāna*; this [way] is the four foundations of mindfulness.[14]

Likewise, in the *Satipaṭṭhāna Saṃyutta*, we read: "The four foundations of mindfulness, if cultivated and developed, are conducive to complete indifference, passionlessness, cessation, tranquility, highest knowledge, complete enlightenment, to *nibbāna*".[15] The text goes on to state: "Whoever neglects the four foundations of mindfulness also neglects the noble path which is the way to the complete destruction of unsatisfactoriness".[16]

The four bases, or meditational objects, for the mindfulness exercises are the body (*kāya*), feelings (*vedanā*), states of mind or thoughts (*citta*) and abstract mental objects (*dhammā*). We shall see that in this context volitions are included in the general term *citta*. According to the sources which describe the practice of *sati* in detail, all four of these are to be practised in precisely the same way. But we nevertheless read in the *Aṅguttara Nikāya* that mindfulness concerning the body (*kāyagatā sati*) is sufficient in itself for the attaining of Nirvana.[17] We shall see from the more detailed descriptions of *sati* that the point is to achieve liberating insight into selflessness. The practice of all four of the exercises is advocated, but insight can be gained simply by meditating on the body. It is interesting to recall here that according to Buddhist tradition, it was observing the impermanent nature of the human body, through seeing in turn an ill person, an old person and a corpse, that prompted the *bodhisatta* Gotama to go forth from home on the journey that was to lead to his Enlightenment.

The *Satipaṭṭhāna Suttas* contain detailed descriptions of the method to be followed in the mindfulness exercises. All procedures are first of all to be followed using the *bhikkhu's* own (*ajjhattaṃ*) body, feelings, states of mind and abstract mental objects as the object of meditation. Then, the same procedures are to be followed on external (*bahiddhā*) body, feelings, states of mind and abstract mental objects. In this context, the term *bahiddhā* refers not just to what is 'external' to oneself in general, as it did in descriptions of the *rūpakkhandha* (and the use here of *kāya*, not *rūpa*, for 'body' probably reflects this), but to the body, feelings, states of mind and abstract mental objects of someone else.[18] With regard to the body, the *bhikkhu* is first of all to centre his attention on the body *qua* body, and not on the feelings or anything else he might associate with the body but which are the subject of another specific mindfulness exercise. The techniques are essentially identical for the other three meditational subjects mentioned above, and in this way each of the subjects of meditation is considered to be distinct from the others. With regard to the body, we read (and the form is the same for the other subjects of meditation):

> In this [exercise], *bhikkhus*, a *bhikkhu* proceeds contemplating the body *qua* body, ardent (i.e. conscientious), attentive and mindful, in order to remove [himself] from the covetousness and misery (*abhijjhādomanassaṃ*) in the world.[19]

I have translated *abhijjhādomanassaṃ* as 'covetousness and misery', but the term clearly refers to desire, which binds one to *saṃsāra* (*saṃsāra* is indicated by 'in the world' – *loka*), and to *dukkha*, the unsatisfactoriness with which *saṃsāra* is associated. So one might paraphrase the last part of the sentence as: "in order to remove [himself] from desire and unsatisfactoriness, which are associated with *saṃsāra*". Precisely this is the purpose of the meditation.

In the meditation exercise on the body, the *bhikkhu* then concentrates in turn on different aspects of the body, such as breathing, posture, the standard list of bodily parts, and functions (walking, sitting down) and so on. He also meditates on a corpse in progressive states of decomposition, which the texts describe in considerable detail. The *bhikkhu* trains himself (*sikkhati*) to 'experience' (*paṭisaṃ√vid*) each object of meditation very precisely, excluding every thought other than that it is a part of the body. In this way the *bhikkhu* establishes that while the body, or part thereof, exists, he also becomes aware of and observes its impersonal nature: there is nothing about it which constitutes separate selfhood. The *Suttas* state:

> ... his mindfulness is present precisely to the extent necessary for knowledge, sufficient for mindfulness, and he proceeds unattached, not grasping [i.e. identifying with] anything in the world.[20]

The attitude of detached observation required for this exercise is suggested by Nyanaponika when he states that a *bhikkhu* meditates on each object "without reacting to them by deed, speech or mental comment".[21] The commentary confirms that the purpose of the meditation exercise is to gain insight into selflessness when it glosses 'not grasping anything in the world' as: "he does not grasp at [false notions] such as having a soul, or thinking 'this is my self' of anything in the world, whether it be the body or any of the other *khandhas*".[22]

The *Suttas* also strongly imply in these exercises that there is nothing about any particular part, or condition, of the body that is intrinsically desirable or repugnant: be it breathing or posture, hair or pus, a young body or a rotting corpse, a *bhikkhu* is merely to *observe* it quite free from any connotation. The purpose of such mindfulness exercises is so to concentrate on each specific subject of meditation that there follows clear comprehension of its precise nature, which is that it is impersonal and conditioned. The exercise is purely analytical, and in experiencing each of the objects of meditation in this way as distinct from each other, a *bhikkhu* understands that there is nothing *inherently* disgusting, or hateful, or desirable, or anything else about the body; nor is there anything *inherently* desirable or repugnant about pleasurable or painful feelings.

Desire (*sarāga citta*; lit: 'a state of mind with desire') and hatred (*dosa*), along with other volitions, are meditated on as part of the mindfulness exercise on *citta*, the third of the four objects described in the *Satipaṭṭhāna Suttas*.[23] In this exercise the *bhikkhu* observes and understands (*pajānāti*) every state of mind he experiences. Included here are volitions, such as those just mentioned, and whether or not he has experienced certain levels of meditation (*jhāna*). This is expressed by his meditating on whether he has experienced a state of mind that "has become great" or "has not become great", (*mahaggataṃ, amahaggataṃ*). I referred to these terms in chapter VII. They are glossed in the commentary as indicating that he has been associated through meditation with the subtle and formless cosmological levels and the gross material level respectively.[24] In understanding other states of mind, the *bhikkhu* is also able to see to what extent he has gained insight. He sees, for example, whether or not his state of mind has other states of mind "superior to it", whether or not it is "composed" (in the sense of having equilibrium), and whether or not it is "liberated".[25]

Again, as with the other exercises which comprise the four foundations of the practice of mindfulness, the *bhikkhu* does this "precisely to the extent necessary for knowledge, sufficient for mindfulness" so that "he proceeds unattached, not grasping anything in the world".[26] Understanding his state of mind not only enables him to understand his progress on the path to liberation, but also allows him to see that any volitional activity is directed *towards* the body or feelings or abstract mental objects *by* certain mental states. By separately meditating on the body *qua* body, on feelings *qua* feelings, and so on, the *bhikkhu* sees that volitional activity need not accompany those constituents of the human being: they originate in mental states because of lack of insight.

So our consideration of the key meditation exercise, *sati*, which concentrates on the distinctiveness of the five *khandhas*, clearly indicates that in the Pali *Nikāyas* the attitude towards the body that the *bhikkhu* is to adopt is one of analytical observation. Such analytical observation is conducive to gaining insight into impermanence and selflessness. It also suggests that there is no foundation for stating that the body is the origin of passion, hatred and thoughts which toss up the mind.

I turn now to discussing the question of the attitude towards the body and the origin of passion, hatred and thoughts which toss up the mind in the light of the interrelatedness of the *khandhas*. In view of the many references I have made to the way in which the *khandhas* work together, this discussion need only be brief. As already stated, it is *together* that one is to understand the *khandhas* as aspects of the psychophysical continuum called an 'individual'. Each of the *khandhas*, and part thereof, has precisely the same conditioned (*saṃkhata*) status, and as such is characterised by impermanence (*aniccatā*), unsatisfactoriness (*dukkhatā*) and impersonality (*anattatā*), the 'three characteristics' of the *tilakkhaṇa* formula. They are unsatisfactory precisely because they are impermanent, or transitory, and impermanent in that they do not exist independently. Their very lack of independently existing identity is the most fundamental aspect of their interrelatedness. This interrelatedness is emphasised by the fact that the *khandhas* are collectively defined by the Buddha as what constitutes *dukkha*.[27]

Given that it is as individual human beings, or, one might say, as individual bundles of *khandhas*, that we experience conditioned, *saṃsāric*, existence, this is essentially the meaning of the first Noble Truth.

It has already become clear to us in earlier chapters on each of the *khandhas* in turn that they are mutually dependent in their functioning. One of the passages which describes the cognitive process, to which I have referred several times, is probably the best example of such mutual dependency:

> Visual consciousness arises because of eye and visible form; contact [occurs] when there is a combination of the three; feelings are caused by contact; that which one feels, one apperceives… .[28]

Here we can clearly see that the operation of the sense involves the *rūpakkhandha*, awareness is the function of the *viññāṇakkhandha*, feelings are classified as the *vedanākhandha*, and apperception is an aspect of the *saññākhandha*.

A particularly notable point which arises from this passage, apart from the fact that it obviously confirms that the *khandhas* are interrelated, is that both feelings and apperception can arise without any involvement of the *saṃkhārakkhandha*. We saw from the description of the analytical meditation exercise above that volitions are separate from the body and feelings. Here, likewise, in a passage which serves to illustrate the interconnectedness of the *khandhas* rather than that they are separate, we have a canonical passage which indicates that the presence of a feeling, be it physical or mental, agreeable or disagreeable, is *not* dependent on there being a concomitant volition concerning it.[29] I will return to this point.

We can now see more clearly that it is misleading to say that volitions such as passion, hatred and thoughts which toss up the mind arise from the body. The body is indeed present in the arising of feelings, but it is completely unactivated, as it were, unless the cognitive ('mental') faculties of awareness, apperception and feeling are simultaneously present: and it is towards this combination of functioning *khandhas* that volitions are subsequently directed. The fact that the *khandhas* function together, however, does serve to explain the presence in the canon of those statements cited above which advocate the driving out of desire and passion from all five of the *khandhas*. Furthermore, desire and passion arise because of ignorance regarding the selflessness of *all* things, and the reference to the driving out of desire and passion in each of the *khandhas* can be understood to mean that this selflessness has to be understood in every one of the *khandhas*. But we nevertheless know from the analysis of the human being given in the *khandha* formula that volitions actually originate in the *saṃkhārakkhandha*: though we might apparently experience volitions within the body itself, they have mentality rather than corporeality as their source. So we can state quite specifically that all karmic effects, which in Buddhism axiomatically arise from passions and desires, are produced by the *saṃkhārakkhandha* and do not originate from the body, the *rūpakkhandha*. This understanding of the body's role does not suggest that a negative attitude towards it is appropriate. From the teaching given in the *Sutta Piṭaka,* it would seem that the attitude towards the body should be neither negative nor positive: one is to have a purely analytical attitude towards one's body.

In view of this doctrinal position, why do we also find canonical statements which appear to refer to the body negatively? Why is there the apparent paradox mentioned above? Before addressing the specific quotations to which I referred above, I will suggest a few possible general reasons for the presence in the canon of what appear to be negative references towards the body.

The first and most obvious reason is the Brahmanical and *śramaṇa* milieu in which Buddhist teachings were first promulgated. Some of these traditions taught that the body and its secretions were polluting, and many advocated physical asceticism and the mortification of the body. The practice of overtly subjugating the body to physical duress, combined with the view that it is polluting, indicate that the body was considered to have a negative effect on one's chances of salvation. In the Pali canon itself, apart from a very few exceptions, the Buddha taught that extreme physical asceticism and self-denial were unnecessary. Indeed, they were potentially as misleading as indulgence: what is required is the Middle Way. The texts tell us that the Buddha himself, while still the *bodhisatta* Gotama, spent six years as a wandering ascetic, subjecting his body to extremes of heat, cold, hunger, thirst, and so on. It was not until he realised the futility of such behaviour from the soteriological point of view, and relinquished it, that he was able to become Enlightened.[30] If, however, the negative view was widespread, then it is likely that some of the people who were converted to the teaching of the Buddha were influenced by this earlier attitude.

Second, Buddhist teachings allow room for what one might call a 'healthily negative' attitude towards the body. This is represented by the Buddha's reaction to his observation of the human body as it is when old, diseased and dead before he went forth from home, mentioned above. And its relevance is to the impersonality which lies at the heart of the Buddha's teaching. Insight into this impersonality is liberating knowledge itself, and ignorance of it is what binds us to *saṃsāric* existence. If one has a slightly sceptical, or detached, attitude towards one's body, one is less likely falsely to identify with it.

That having been said, we *do* tend to identify with our bodies. And this leads us to the third possible reason for negative statements about the body in the *Sutta Piṭaka*. Faced with the Buddha's teaching that we are to realise that all things are impermanent, unsatisfactory and impersonal, one might instinctively apply this teaching to the body rather than to mental processes, at least initially. Our experience is of a mind which is ever-changing, flickering here and there constantly. But our bodies seem relatively permanent to us, and we intuitively identify to some degree with them.

That we also identify other people to some degree with *their* bodies is clearly illustrated in a well-known story in the *Mahāparinibbāna Sutta*. We read there that Ānanda, the Buddha's closest friend and disciple, remained, in spite of his advanced wisdom, so attached to the physical presence of the Buddha that he did not achieve Enlightenment until after the Buddha died and Ānanda was able to eliminate this attachment once and for all.[31] It is precisely in order to avoid this kind of mistake that the mindfulness exercises are to be practised both on one's own *and* on someone else's body.

The Buddha himself acknowledged the apparently greater permanence of the body. It is related in the *Nidāna Saṃyutta* of the *Saṃyutta Nikāya* that the Buddha stated that anyone looking for something permanent and lasting would do better to try the body, which lasts up to a hundred years, than the mind, which changes every moment.[32] For anyone struggling against false notions of permanence, what more obvious object is there on which they can both concentrate their efforts and also subsequently vent their frustrations than the body?

My final suggestion draws on the link between the mind and the body that we saw in the last chapter. There, it became clear that it is volitions that in effect cause the body to arise in successive lives. At its simplest, this is because the volitions which constitute karmic activity arise because of ignorance: and karmic activity leads to rebirth in another body. We also saw in that chapter the way in which the density of the body corresponds to degrees of ignorance. It was suggested that the density of the body in which a given existence takes place can reflect the spiritual progress of the individual. It might be, therefore, that in the spiritual struggle from ignorance to insight, the psychology of the situation tends to be inverted and the physical body, which is the most dense form of *rūpa* with which one can be reborn, is psychologically held responsible for ignorance rather than recognising that in reality the causal process is the reverse: the body represents the 'impurity' of the *mind*; it is not impure itself. This psychological reversal of the causal process might be even more likely because (with very few exceptions) Enlightenment is achieved while in the physical body. So what one might call the full extent of the spectrum of density can be experienced by an individual in one lifetime: the dense level of the physical body is present even when formless levels of meditation are experienced. With such great contrast, the most dense levels might attract negative associations even for a *bhikkhu* who is at a relatively advanced level of insight.

For any or all of these reasons the *bhikkhus* themselves might have been predisposed, even unconsciously, towards making negative statements about the body. In turning now to the quotations from the canon which I cited above, however, we also see that in some cases a deeper consideration of their context shows them to be less negative about the body than at first appears.

The statement that "only an ignorant fool would regard it [the body] as beautiful" can perhaps be explained as follows: anyone ignorant as to the real nature of the body, who has not cultivated the foundations of mindfulness in order to see it as it really is, has not analysed it into its constituents. Such a person has not perceived the body merely and precisely *qua* body, but has a view of the body which is meta-physical, or what some modern writers might call 'holistic'. In Buddhist doctrinal terms, what this means is that such a person still erroneously identifies in some way with his or her body. Because there is no room for such a view in the process of cultivating the penetrating analysis of the bodily complex necessary for liberating insight, and because anyone who *has* cultivated such insight is considered wise, anyone holding such a view might be deemed a fool, certainly from a relative point of view; and the more so because it is only from the holistic point of view that the body could possibly be considered beautiful: its constituent parts, activities and functions are merely parts, activities and functions.

In the reference to the body being a "heap of corruption", the Pali term translated here is *pūtisaṇḍa*. *Pūti* is also sometimes used with *kāya* and sometimes with *sandeha*.[33] All such expressions refer to the body. Other meanings of the word *pūti*, apart from corruption, include 'putrid', 'rotten' or 'decayed'. While the description 'heap of corruption, rottenness or decay' appears *prima facie* to be unequivocally negative about the body, in fact what such a term is doing is serving to emphasise the body's impermanence, rather than that one should feel negative about it. This interpretation is confirmed by the fact that *pūtisaṇḍa* is found in contexts which include other terms such as *bhindana*, which means 'breaking up, brittle, falling into ruin', and *pabhaṅgu*, which means 'brittle, easily destroyed, perishable'.[34] And in one passage which uses the term *pūtikāya*, the context is explicitly intended to illustrate impermanence: after describing the body as *pūti*, the Buddha asks Vakkali: "As to this, what do you think, Vakkali: is the body permanent or impermanent?"[35]

I also referred above to the presence in the Pali canon of statements that the body is 'impure'. There are many Pali words for impure, but the ones most frequently found in connection with bodily functions are *asuci* and *asubha*. *Asuci* is used in a passage in the *Aṅguttara Nikāya* to which I referred above which describes the body as a boil from whose nine openings impurity (*asuci*), stench and loathsomeness ooze out.[36] To refer to purity in such a context clearly overlooks the meaning of purity in Buddhist doctrinal terms. The Buddha teaches that salvation is obtained by progressing from ignorance to insight. His prescription for how to achieve insight is given in terms of following a path which can also be described as a process of purification. This, indeed, is how Buddhaghosa understands it, and he accordingly called his seminal work the *Visuddhimagga*: 'The Path to Purity'. The path to purity cannot, however, be understood to mean that a disciple is to overcome or avoid the body or its functions and secretions because they are impure in the way suggested in the passage quoted above from the *Aṅguttara Nikāya*. As we have seen, the psycho-cosmological status of the body in relation to the spiritual path represents the state of the *mind*: purity is a metaphor for the degree to which one has achieved insight, and is not associated with the body *qua* body. Doctrinally, in ethicising the law of karma, the Buddha taught that defilement was moral or psychological. Only indirectly is this connected with the physical body insofar as one's body is one of the channels for one's intention, or will to act, as we have seen in the definition of karma, and in the ethical triad of *kāya*, *vacas* and *citta* or *manas*. According to the Buddha's teaching, impurity, or defilement, comes from unwholesome (*akusala*) states of mind. In Buddhist teachings the term for wholesome (*kusala*) implies karmic neutrality or spiritually beneficial states of mind.[37]

A passage in the *Sutta Nipāta* illustrates the doctrinal understanding of impurity. It states that some people think one can avoid all tainted fare (*āmagandhaṃ*) if one only eats certain foods which have been properly prepared: "Eating what is well-made, well prepared, given by others, pure, outstanding ... thinking 'Tainted fare is not appropriate for me'...".[38] This view was widely accepted in the Brahmanical and *śramaṇa* milieu in which the Buddha taught. The *Sutta* continues, however, with the Buddha's teaching that what pollutes us are activities which are harmful to others, such as killing (*pāṇātipāta*), stealing (*theyya*), telling lies (*musāvāda*), adultery (*paradārasevanā*),[39] or volitions which are based on ignorance and which are karmically binding, such as greed (*giddhā*), anger (*kodha*), arrogance (*mada*),[40] and so on. The *Sutta* summarises the uselessness of external or ritual practices (in particular Brahmanical and *śramaṇa* ones) in the cause of purity:

> Not the flesh of fish, nor fasting, nor nakedness, nor shaven head, matted hair, dirt, nor rough animal skins, nor observance of the fire ceremony, nor even the many penances there are in the world for (gaining) immortality, nor hymns nor oblations, nor the performance of sacrifices at the proper season, purify a man... .[41]

Though bodily functions are not explicitly referred to here, it is clear from the context that it would be erroneous to think that they are polluting. Rather, the *Sutta* goes on to state:

> One should wander guarded in the appertures (of the sense organs), with one's sense-faculties conquered, standing firm in the doctrine, delighting in uprightness and mildness. Gone beyond attachment, with all miseries eliminated, a wise man does not cling to things seen or heard.[42]

Here we have an unequivocal statement that what should concern a disciple is following the doctrinal path. The purpose is to go beyond attachment. And the implication of this passage is not only that it is not the body or its functions that are polluting, but that even to dwell on the question of whether bodily functions might be polluting constitutes clinging to things seen. The Buddha teaches that the true struggle should be within oneself: it is a moral and psychological struggle which should be directed towards the overcoming of clinging, which is itself a particularly unwholesome state of mind.

I have suggested above that the presence in the canonical material of negative statements about the body might be because, however unconsciously, the body was psychologically held responsible for ignorance. At least in theory, this might account for references to the body being impure. The metaphor associating density, ignorance and impurity is, however, a sophisticated one, and in my opinion it is more likely that the term 'impure', when used in connection with the body and its functions, is present in the canon as a result of the Brahmanical background in which the teaching took root. This is clearly the case when there is an explicit association of impurity with bodily secretions. The effect of the underlying metaphor is more likely merely to have predisposed the collators of the material to including such doctrinally inconsistent expressions.

I will return below to the reference to the body's nine oozing openings when we consider Buddhaghosa's attitude towards the body. But if we look now at the context of this passage, we see that the body is first described according to the stock phrase that it is made up of the four elements and begotten of mother and father. I have referred to this passage before, and the point of it is contained in what follows: that the body is impermanent, subject to erosion and decay, is perishable and subject to destruction.[43] In Pali, it concludes: *Tasmā ti ha bhikkhave imasmiṃ kāye nibbindathā ti*. E. M. Hare, in his translation for the Pali Text Society, translates this sentence: "Wherefore, monks, be ye disgusted with this body".[44] It is equally philologically correct, and in my opinion more appropriate both in this specific context and in the wider context of Buddhist teachings as a whole, to translate it: "So, monks, be indifferent towards (or dis-enchanted with) your body".[45] The purpose of this passage is not to encourage *bhikkhus* to feel disgust towards their impure bodies but to discourage them from seeking anything permanent in, or identifying with, their bodies. The terms in which the description of the body itself is couched are surely the result of non-Buddhist, and certainly non-doctrinal, influence.

There is in the canonical material, both in the *Saṃyutta Nikāya*[46] and in the *Vinaya*,[47] an important story which illustrates the way in which certain early *bhikkhus* disastrously failed to understand both the meaning of purity and also the fact that meditating on the body is intended to give insight into its impermanence. We read that the Buddha:

> ... talked to the *bhikkhus* in many ways on the subject of impurity (*asubha*). He spoke in praise of what is impure; he spoke in praise of the contemplation of what is impure; he spoke again and again in praise of the stage of meditation on what is impure.[48]

The *bhikkhus* go away to meditate on what is impure, and the text implies that the principal subject they used was their bodies. It states:

> They dwelt intent upon the practice of contemplating what is impure in different ways. They were troubled by their own bodies, ashamed of them, loathing them.[49]

The *Vinaya* version of the story gives an analogy to describe the depth of their revulsion:

> It is as if a woman or a man when young and delicate and fond of dressing up, having washed their hair, would be troubled, ashamed and full of loathing because they had the corpse of a snake or of a dog or of a man hung around their neck.[50]

It continues: "So these *bhikkhus*, being troubled by their own bodies, ashamed of them, and loathing them, by themselves deprived themselves of life and deprived each other of life".[51] Both the *Vinaya* and the *Saṃyutta Nikāya* accounts record that a great many *bhikkhus* either killed themselves, or were killed by another at their own request, for this reason.[52]

According to the *Vinaya,* when the Buddha learns of what has been done, he is extremely angry with them. He states: "*Bhikkhus*, it is not suitable for these *bhikkhus*, it is not fit, it is not proper, it is not worthy of a disciple, it is not good, it should not be done".[53] He then gave the following instruction: "Whatever *bhikkhu* intentionally deprives a human being of life, or who seeks to be a knife-bearer,[54] he is defeated, he is not one of the community".[55] This instruction is the third of the *pārājika* rules, the breaking of which means that a *bhikkhu* has expelled himself from the *Saṅgha*: his discipleship is 'defeated'.

Because of the disastrous nature of the episode which followed the *bhikkhus'* misunderstanding of the teaching on impurity, it is unsurprising that one should read at the end of the *Saṃyutta* account that Ānanda said to the Buddha: "It would be a good thing, Lord, if you would explain [the teaching] in another way, so that the community of *bhikkhus* might be established in knowledge".[56] This plea, and indeed the episode as a whole, perhaps indicates the difficulty *bhikkhus* had in understanding that the purpose of meditating on impurity (or unloveliness) is to realise its impermanence.[57]

I turn now to the translations I cited. In Norman's translation of *Sutta Nipāta* 271, we read that passion, hatred and thoughts which toss up the mind arise from the body. The word 'body' has been supplied by the translator: it is not present in the Pali at all, which reads: *Rāgo ca doso ca itonidānā, aratī ratī lomahaṃso itojā, ito samuṭṭhāya manovitakkā kumārakā dhaṅkam iv'ossajanti.* Norman translates the verse as follows: "'From this (body) passion and hatred have their origin. From this (body) aversion and delight and excitement are born. Arising from this (body) thoughts toss up the mind, as young boys toss up a (captive) crow."[58] At the front of his translation, Norman states: "Words in round brackets are those which need to be supplied in the English translation, although not found in the original Pali". The key word in the Pali, to which Norman feels it necessary to add the English word 'body', is *ito*, literally 'from this'.

The context is that the *yakkha* Sūciloma has asked the Buddha, in order to test whether he is a real ascetic or just looks like one, where passion and hatred have their origin. Immediately following on from the verse quoted above, we read: *Snehajā attasambhūtā nigrodhasseva khandhajā.* Norman translates this: "(They are) born from affection, arisen from oneself, like the trunk-born (shoots) of the banyan tree."[59] In an earlier edition of his translation, Norman gives an alternative rendering at the end of the story, translating *ito* as "from within".[60] In the context of Sūciloma's question and the subsequent verse, this would seem to me to be far preferable to, and one might say more accurate than, "from this body". The commentary glosses *ito* as *attabhāvato*. I cited the different meanings of the term *attabhāva*, as given in the *Critical Pali Dictionary*, in chapter VII. We saw that it has a variety of meanings ranging from 'soul' in an abstract sense, the conventional individuality experienced by an unenlightened person, represented concretely by the five *khandhas*, and sometimes it can mean body. In later material it is sometimes used when either the body or the five *khandhas* are erroneously taken in the sense 'this is my self'.[61] In Buddhist Sanskrit, *ātmabhāva* is used for 'body'; but this is in conjunction with *pratilambha*, again meaning bodily existence in its broad sense.[62] From the context in which we find it here, the most likely of all these meanings is, in my opinion, that of a conventional being, which is also its most frequent meaning. Nor does the context support the translation of *ito* in the earlier text as "from this body".

In Müller's translation of *Dhammapada* 202 and 203, he states: "there is no pain like the body" and "the body is the greatest of pains".[63] The Pali sentences from which these translations have been made are, respectively, as follows: *n'atthi khandhādisā dukkhā* and *saṃkhārā paramā dukkhā.* The first of these is clearly repeating the Buddha's definition that the *khandhas* are what constitute *dukkha.* With regard to the second, *saṃkhāra* does have a multitude of meanings, and on occasion means bodily existence in its broad sense. But it never means 'body' in the sense of 'corporeality'. So what this sentence is saying is that the greatest *dukkha* is *saṃsāric* existence, which is precisely the content of the first Noble Truth. Bateson makes the same mistake in his article on "The body-Buddhism" in the *Encyclopedia of Religion and Ethics* when he states "the body is the sphere of suffering" and "... the body is the origin of suffering".[64]

The Pali word *nibbidā* is often found in contexts in the canon which refer to the human body. We saw it above in the *Aṅguttara Nikāya* passage about the impermanence of the body. The way *nibbidā* is translated frequently tends to further the view that the early Buddhist attitude towards the body was negative. *Nibbidā* can mean 'disgust', 'revulsion', 'indifference' or 'disenchantment'.[65] In contexts where it must mean 'indifference' or 'disenchantment', translating it as 'disgust' or 'revulsion' is highly misleading. In the Pali Text Society translation of Volume V of the *Saṃyutta Nikāya*, for example, a translation by Woodward includes the following: "These seven limbs of wisdom ... conduce to downright revulsion (*ekantanibbidāya*), to dispassion, to cessation, to calm, to full comprehension, to the wisdom, to *Nibbāna*".[66] *Nibbidā* frequently occurs in this phrase, and in my opinion it cannot here mean anything other than 'indifference' or 'dis-enchantment': 'downright revulsion', directed towards the body or anything else, would be a karmically unwholesome, and therefore binding, volition quite inappropriate for a *bhikkhu* at this stage of the path. To use the words from another of Woodward's translations, it would be one of the "evil, unprofitable states which come to be because of wrong views".[67] Even if one were to understand the qualities referred to in this sentence, disgust or indifference, dispassion, cessation, calm, full comprehension, wisdom, Nirvana, as being qualities which are acquired sequentially, it seems highly improbable to me that disgust would immediately precede so many other qualities which are more associated with detachment. Woodward repeats the translation of *nibbidā* as "downright revulsion" throughout his translations for the Pali Text Society.[68] E. M. Hare translates *nibbidā* in the same context as "complete disgust"[69] or as "complete weariness".[70] T. W. Rhys Davids, however, translates it as "detachment".[71]

There are a multitude of similar examples of translations which are misleading about the attitude towards the body, but these will suffice to make my point. Scholarly works other than translations can be just as misleading in statements about the body, possibly because they have relied on the translations.

We can now reconcile the apparent paradox referred to above in summing up the attitude towards the human body found in the canonical material. We have seen that the doctrinal position according to the Buddha's teaching is that the attitude towards the body should be analytical. This correlates with his teaching that karma is volition: it is one's state of mind, not one's body, which is the source of desire, hatred and other karmically binding states which determine the nature of one's future rebirth(s). The presence in the canon of statements which appear to be negative about the body is probably the result of outside influence or doctrinal confusion which arises because of the demands of the spiritual struggle. Many such statements are in any case not as negative as they at first appear if read in their context or if translated more appropriately.

I turn now to consider Buddhaghosa's attitude towards the human body. My examples are mainly drawn from Buddhaghosa's *Visuddhimagga*, but I will also refer to the commentaries, which are believed to have been compiled by him. Many people composed the material Buddhaghosa included in the commentaries, however, and I have already acknowledged that he can hardly have been the only one to write in such a way. Nevertheless, the *Visuddhimagga* is consistently and exaggeratedly negative about the body. I can only choose a few examples here.

I start with an example of the difference between the canonical material and the commentaries. Though it is a relatively minor example, it nevertheless clearly illustrates the difference between simple analysis, which is found in the former, and descriptive value which is added in the latter. I referred in chapter 1 to the standard list of the constituents of the human body which is found in several places in the Pali canon. The list of thirty-one parts (or thirty-two when the brain is added), which is invariably given without comment, is as follows:

> There are in this body head-hairs, body-hairs, nails, teeth, skin, flesh, sinews, bones, bone-marrow, kidneys, heart, liver, membranes, spleen, lungs, intestines, mesentery, stomach, excrement, bile, phlegm, pus, blood, sweat, fat, tears, serum, saliva, mucus, synovic fluid, urine (brain).

It is this list which is used in the *Satipaṭṭhāna* exercise on parts of the body, which clearly illustrates the extent to which each and every part is to be observed in the same objective light as part of the analytical meditational exercise. This is regardless of whether it is, say, a tooth, or mucus or pus. In itself, each part has nothing that is to be regarded with anything other than complete neutrality. In the commentary on this list, however, qualitative words are added, so the body and its constituent parts are described as 'vile' (*kucchita*), 'impure' (*asubha* and *asuci*), and 'loathsome' (*jegucchā*).[72]

In the section of the *Visuddhimagga* which describes the practice of mindfulness on the body, not only does Buddhaghosa give a substantial description (as opposed to an analysis) of each of the parts of the body to be meditated upon, but he also introduces many negative adjectives which are not in the canonical material. Thus just of mere head hairs we read that they are subject to a "fivefold repulsiveness" (*pañcadhā paṭikūlato*), as to colour (*vaṇṇa*), shape (*saṇṭhāna*), odour (*gandha*), habitat (*āsaya*) and location (*okāsa*).[73] As a specimen from a lengthy passage, I quote:

> Head hairs are repulsive in colour as well as in shape, odour, habitat and location... Just as a baby's excrement, as to its colour, is the colour of turmeric and, as to its shape, is the shape of a piece of turmeric root, and just as the bloated carcase of a black dog thrown on a rubbish heap, as to its

> colour, is the colour of a ripe palmyra fruit and, as to its shape, is the shape of a [mandoline-shaped] drum left face down, and its fangs are like jasmine buds, and so even if both these are not directly repulsive in colour and shape, still their odour is directly repulsive, so too, even if head hairs are not directly repulsive in colour and shape, still their odour is directly repulsive.[74]

Other similes used in this passage are village sewage (*gāmanissanda*), a dunghill *(gūtharāsi)* and a charnel ground (*susāna*).[75]

Buddhaghosa uses the body in the chapter of the *Visuddhimagga* where the meditation subject is loathsomeness or impurity, *asubha*. He sums up his lengthy description of the body's nature by quoting some verses:

> Fools cannot in their folly tell;
> They take the body to be fair,
> And soon get caught in Evil's snare
> Nor can escape its painful spell.
>
> But since the wise have thus laid bare
> This filthy body's nature, so,
> be it alive or dead, they know
> There is no beauty lurking there.

For this is said:

> This filthy body stinks outright
> Like ordure, like a privy's site;
> This body men that have insight
> Condemn, is object of a fool's delight.
>
> A tumour where nine holes abide
> Wrapped in a coat of clammy hide
> And trickling filth on every side
> Polluting the air with stenches far and wide.
>
> If it perchance should come about
> That what is inside it came out,
> Surely a man would need a knout
> With which to put the crows and dogs to rout.[76]

The passage concludes:

> So a capable *bhikkhu* should apprehend the sign wherever the aspect of foulness is manifest, whether in a living body or in a dead one, and he should make the meditation subject reach absorption.[77]

Even allowing for poetic licence, this passage is in striking contrast to the canonical analysis by which a *bhikkhu* also arrives at the conclusion that there is nothing inherently desirable about the body.

Buddhaghosa is traditionally thought to have been born a brahmin. I think this is almost certainly true, judging from the terminology he uses in describing the body. So far as I am aware, his concern is not with the origin of volitions such as passion and hatred but with the physical aspects of the body. One further example will serve here: a section of Buddhaghosa's description of the body's nature. The description begins relatively objectively, but becomes wonderfully lurid as it goes on:

> This is the body's nature: it is a collection of over three hundred bones, jointed by one hundred and eighty joints, bound together by nine hundred sinews, plastered over with nine hundred pieces of flesh, enveloped in the moist inner skin, enclosed in the outer cuticle, with orifices here and there, constantly dribbling and trickling like a grease pot, inhabited by a community of worms, the home of disease, the basis of painful states, perpetually oozing from the nine orifices like a chronic open carbuncle, from both of whose eyes eye-filth trickles, from whose ears ear-filth, from whose nostrils snot, from whose mouth food and bile and phlegm and blood, from whose lower outlets excrement and urine, and from whose ninety-nine thousand pores the broth of stale sweat seeps, with bluebottles and their like buzzing round it, which when untended with tooth sticks and mouth-washing and head-anointing and bathing and underclothing and dressing would, judged by the universal repulsiveness of the body, make even a king, if he wandered from village to village with his hair in its natural wild disorder, no different from a flower-scavenger or an outcaste or what you will. So there is no distinction between a king's body and an outcaste's in so far as its impure stinking nauseating repulsiveness is concerned.[78]

If this is Buddhaghosa's apology for Buddhism against the caste system of the Brahmanical religion (which is based on a complex structure of purity and pollution), in my opinion it fails dismally! What we read here is riddled with concern about the polluting effects of bodily secretions, and, in my view, it is nothing more than the Brahmanisation of Buddhist hermeneutics.

Further on in the same passage, we read the following:

> So men delight in women and women in men without perceiving the true nature of [the body's] characteristic foulness, masked by adventitious adornment. But in the ultimate sense there is no place here even the size of an atom fit to lust after.[79]

Buddhism certainly teaches that lust, or desire in general, is misplaced. But *not* because the body is foul. It is misplaced because insight into the transient nature of all things brings the knowledge that what one is desiring is momentary, impermanent, and therefore unsatisfactory. Like the *bhikkhus* who committed suicide, Buddhaghosa appears to have missed this point altogether, even though it is implicit in the teaching given consequent to the earlier episode. What he appears to be doing once again is Brahmanising Buddhist teaching.[80]

I return to the point made twice above that one can be aware of one's body and sensations without having any concomitant volition. It is fundamental to a *bhikkhu's* progress on the path to liberating insight that he achieves *indifference*, or *detachment*. It is nonsensical in a Buddhist context to cultivate antipathy, towards the body or anything else. Because of the presence in the canon of descriptions of *asubha bhāvanā*, it is sometimes argued that revulsion can be used as a meditational tool or catalyst for a *bhikkhu*. But we have seen above that the term *asubha* is used in contexts where the point is to understand impermanence, not that one should be disgusted: what the *bhikkhu* is aiming for is indifference. And any meditation on the *bhikkhu*'s own feeling or mental state of disgust would be for the same purpose. Not only does this follow from the doctrinal teaching of freedom from all volitions, but it is explicitly stated in several places in the *Sutta Piṭaka*. We read in the *Dīgha Nikāya*, for example, that a *bhikkhu* who "lives detached from sensual pleasures, detached from unwholesome conditions" experiences ease (*sukha*, the opposite of *dukkha*).[81] In the *Brāhmaṇa Saṃyutta* in the *Saṃyutta Nikāya,* which redefines what a brahmin is, it states that a brahmin is one who has "cast out both wickedness and merit.[82]

In the third *jhāna*, a *bhikkhu* "pervades, drenches, permeates and suffuses his body with *sukha* without associating it with pleasure".[83] Elsewhere we read that a *bhikkhu* is to reach a point where:

> his mind is immovable, his body is immovable, [he is] inwardly well established, well released. If he is aware with his mind of an attractive/a repulsive state, he is not affected (*maṅku*; literally, troubled).[84]

Finally, a later text, the *Milindapañha,* states that "*arahants* have neither attraction nor antipathy".[85]

Having an attitude of disgust or revulsion towards anything would constitute a karmically unwholesome, and therefore binding, 'view', just as much as considering something to be beautiful and/or desirable; and the *bhikkhu* has to see through and transcend all views and attain a karmically neutral position. We have seen this point borne out in the canonical descriptions of meditation: there is nothing in them which is designed to induce any specific negative (or positive) attitude; merely a detached observation of what is. The question of gender is also relevant here. To have a positive or negative attitude towards the male or female would be just as much a karmically binding view; and the point is to be neutral. So one might say that doctrinally or philosophically there is no room for sexism in early Buddhism. The link between sexism and the attitude towards the human body is the subject of Wilson's paper "The Female Body as a Source of Horror and Insight in Post-Aśokan Buddhism".[86] Wilson establishes and extensively discusses the antipathy towards the body in commentarial literature. She concentrates her study on the *Dhammapadaṭṭhakathā*, but also draws widely on other commentaries and on Buddhist Sanskrit texts. She seeks to illustrate that the negativity is largely directed towards women's bodies, representing the ultimate dis-enchantment for male *bhikkhus*. The examples she gives are certainly negative about the female body. But I am not convinced, as Wilson is, that such passages necessarily reflect mysogyny on the part of the authors. Though institutionalised Buddhism, as part of Indian culture, was undoubtedly patriarchal, and though such patriarchy is not doctrinally defensible, the use of women's bodies to illustrate impermanence might merely reflect the fact that the texts were mostly composed by and for men and that the sexual instinct is the most difficult desire to eradicate. In my opinion the most important point of Wilson's paper is that the degree of negativity towards the body in later, non-canonical, literature has considerably increased. In concentrating on possible mysogyny in the texts, however, Wilson misses the point that such negativity is non-doctrinal. It indicates a lack of understanding on the part of the authors of the later material that meditating on the body is for the purpose of understanding its impermanence. Through such understanding, a *bhikkhu* is able to be detached either from identifying with it or desiring it.

Because the cultivation of indifference, or detachment, is so central to understanding Buddhist teaching, in my opinion Buddhaghosa (and others writing in a similar tone) does a grave disservice to Buddhism in writing as he does about the body. He goes far beyond merely commenting on the canon, and his elaborate reinterpretations result in a teaching which bears little relation to that contained in the original material.

We have seen clearly that it is not from the body itself that the karmically binding passions and desires arise. We have seen too that the point of meditation exercises is to see the human being as it really is, and so to understand that there is nothing towards which any volition is justifiable: so one might say that there is nothing either desirable or repulsive about the body but thinking makes it so. All volition is due to ignorance concerning the fundamental impersonality of all phenomena, physical or mental. It is for this reason that the *paṭiccasamuppāda* formula, which the Buddha taught in order that others might understand how the human being continues to be reborn, while ultimately circular rather than linear, is described in canonical texts as beginning with ignorance.[87] Put differently, volitions have mentality rather than corporeality as their constitutional source, and ignorance as their psychological source. According to the Pali canon there is little or no room in Buddhism for a negative attitude towards the body, and the negative terminology used by Buddhaghosa widely diverges from the original material. The earliest Buddhist attitude towards the body is neither positive nor negative: it is analytical.

Notes

1. Griffiths, 1986, p.112.
2. I recognise that Buddhaghosa cannot single handedly have introduced the attitude recorded here and that there will have been (possibly many) others prior to him with a similar view. But it is he who has been of primary influence on the tradition as a whole, and such important figures attract the brunt of any subsequent criticism or disagreement. In spite of my criticism of and disagreement with him as stated in this chapter, I of course do not presume to suggest that his eminence as a Buddhist leader and thinker is in any way unjustified.
3. *Dhammapada* 148. This translation is used both by Müller in SBE Vol X, and by Radhakrishnan.
4. For example, Sn 197, 205.
5. Sn 199: *Subhato naṃ maññatī bālo avijjāya purakkhato.*
6. AN.IV.386: *Tato yaṃ kiñci paggghareyya, asuci yeva pagghareyya, duggandhaṃ yeva pagghareyya, jegucchiyaṃ yeva pagghareyya.*
7. SN.III.7: *Rūpe kho āvuso chandarāgavinayakkhāyī satthā vedanāya saññāya saṃkhāresu viññāṇe.*
8. SN.III.27: *Rūpasmiṃ (vedanāya/saññāya/saṃkhāresu/viññāṇasmiṃ) chandarāgo taṃ pajahatha.*
9. Norman (trans.), *The Group of Discourses* (1992), p.30.
10. SBE Vol. X.
11. AN.III.415.
12. For example, at DN.II.308.
13. MN.I, *sutta* 10; DN.II. *sutta* 22; SN.V.141ff.
14. MN.I.55f, 63; DN.II.290, 315: *Ekāyano ayaṃ bhikkhave maggo sattānaṃ visuddhiyā sokapariddavānaṃ samatikkamāya dukkhadomanassānaṃ atthagamāya ñāyassa adhigamāya nibbānassa sacchikiriyāya; yadidaṃ cattāro satipaṭṭhānā.*
15. SN.V.179: *Cattāro me bhikkhave satipaṭṭhānā bhāvitā bahulīkatā ekantanibbidāya virāgāya nirodhāya upasamāya abhiññāya sambodhāya nibbānāya saṃvattanti.*
16. SN.V.179: *Yesaṃ kesañci bhikkhave cattāro satipaṭṭhānā viraddhā, viraddho tesaṃ ariyo maggo sammādukkhakkhayagāmī.* cf. also SN.V.182, 294. Gethin (1992, p.30ff) discusses the term *satipaṭṭhāna*, and how best to translate it, in great detail.
17. AN.I.43: *Ekadhammo bhikkhave bhāvito bahulīkato mahato … vijjāvimuttiphalasacchikiriyāya … kāyagatā sati.* cf. also *Milindapañha* 248, 336.
18. The commentaries state that *ajjhattaṃ* means *attano* and *bahiddhā* means *parassa* (MA.I.249; DA.III.765).
19. MN.I.56; DN.II.290: *Idha bhikkhave bhikkhu kāye kāyānupassī viharati ātāpī sampajāno satimā vineyya loke abhijjhādomanassaṃ.*
20. MN.I.56; DN.II.292: … *assa sati paccupaṭṭhitā hoti yāvad eva ñāṇamattāya patissatimattāya, anissito ca viharati na ca kiñci loke upādiyati.*
21. Nyanaponika, 1986, p.3.
22. MA.I.250; DA.III.766: *Lokasmiṃ kiñci rūpam vā - pe - viññāṇaṃ vā ayaṃ me attā vā attanīyam vā ti na gaṇhāti.*
23. MN.I.59; DN.II.299.
24. MA.I.280; DA.III.776: *Mahaggatam ti rūpārūpāvacaraṃ. Amahaggatan ti kāmāvacaraṃ.*
25. MN.I.59; DN.II.299: *Sa-uttaraṃ … anuttaraṃ pajānāti, samāhitaṃ … asamāhitaṃ pajānāti, vimuttaṃ … avimuttaṃ pajānāti.*
26. MN.I.60; DN.II.300.
27. SN.V.421: *Saṃkhittena pañc' upādānakkhandhā dukkhā*; SN.III.158: *Katamañ ca bhikkhave dukkhaṃ? Pañc' upādānakkhandhā ti 'ssa vacanīyaṃ.*
28. MN.I.111f: *Cakkhuñ c' āvuso paṭicca rūpe ca uppajjati cakkhuviññāṇaṃ, tiṇṇaṃ saṅgati phasso, phassapaccayā vedanā, yaṃ vedeti taṃ sañjānāti* … .
29. As we have seen, there are what one might call the 'underlying' *saṃkhāras*, which function as the 'fuel' of continued existence in *saṃsāra*. What need not function in the example discussed here is the *saṃkhārakkhandha* in the sense of conscious volitions.
30. This is related in the *Ariyapariyesana Sutta*, MN.I.160ff.
31. DN.II.142ff.
32. SN.II.94f.

33. SN.I.131; MN.II.65; SN.I.131, III.120.
34. SN.I.131: *Iminā pūtikāyena bhindanena pabhaṅgunā* ... ; *Dhammapada* 148: *bhijjati pūtisandeho.*
35. SN.III.120: ... *iminā pūtikāyena* ... *Taṃ kiṃ maññāsi Vakkali: rūpaṃ niccaṃ vā aniccaṃ vā ti?.* The use of *rūpa* and not *kāya* in the second part of this passage is not, in my opinion, significant: impermanence is, after all, an attribute of all aspects of *rūpa*, not just the body. Nor do I consider that the fact that the teaching given to Vakkali in this passage is usually considered to be *ad hominem* affects the point I am making here.
36. AN.IV.386.
37. By extension, the term *kusala* has the sense of 'skilful', referring to spiritually beneficial activites. This was extensively developed by Mahāyāna Buddhism where the frequently used expression 'skill in means' (Sanskrit: *upāya kauśalya*) refers to activities which are beneficial either to one's own spiritual progress or, in the case of a *bodhisattva*, in the assisting of others to salvation. This led to the suggestion by some Mahāyāna Buddhists that the Buddha's life as Gotama and his early teaching were but part of his *upāya kauśalya* to help all beings out of *saṃsāra* in a way they could understand at that time, the later form of them being superior or more complete.
38. Sn 240–1: *Yad añhamāno sukataṃ suniṭṭhaṃ parehi dinnaṃ payataṃ paṇītaṃ* ... *paribhuñjamāno* ... *na āmagandho mama kappatī ti.* 'Tainted fare' is Norman's translation (*The Group of Discourses*, 1992, p.27).
39. Sn 242.
40. Sn 243, 248, 245. A lengthy description in the *Saṃyutta Nikāya* of what each stage of the noble Eightfold Path means refers to qualities similar to those in the *Sutta Nipāta* passage discussed here (SN.V.8ff). cf. also *Dhammapada*, chapter XXVI (383ff).
41. Sn 249: *Na macchamaṃsaṃ nānāsakattaṃ na naggiyaṃ muṇḍiyaṃ jaṭā jallaṃ kharājināni nāggihuttass' upasevanā va yā ye vā pi loke amarā bahū tapā mantāhutī yañña-m-utūpasevanā sodhenti maccaṃ* .... I have followed Norman's translation. I shall refer to his use of round brackets below.
42. Sn 250: *Sotesu gutto vijitindriyo care dhamme ṭhito ajjavamaddave rato saṅgatigo sabbadukkhappahīno na lippati diṭṭhasutesu dhīro.* I have followed Norman's translation except for relocating 'One should wander' at the beginning of the verse for easier reading.
43. AN.IV.386: *Aniccucchādana-parimaddana-bhedana-viddaṃsanadhamma.*
44. GS.IV.258.
45. I will discuss the term *nibbidā* below.
46. SN.V.320.
47. Vin.III.68f.
48. Vin.III.68; SN.V.320f: *Tena kho pana samayena bhagavā bhikkhūnaṃ anekapariyāyena asubhakathaṃ katheti. Asubhāya vaṇṇaṃ bhāsati; asubhabhāvanāya vaṇṇaṃ bhāsati; ādissa ādissa asubhasamāpattiyā vaṇṇaṃ bhāsati. Asubha* can also be translated as 'what is not beautiful' (Woodward's translation of SN.V.320 uses 'unlovely': KS.V.284). This translation has the same implication of impermanence as 'impure' does.
49. *Te anekākāravokāraṃ asubhabhāvanānuyogaṃ anuyuttā viharanti, te sakena kāyena aṭṭiyanti jarāyanti jigucchanti.*
50. Vin.III.68: *Seyyathāpi nāma itthi vā puriso vā daharo yuvā maṇḍanakajātiko sīsaṃ nhāto ahikuṇapena vā kukkurakuṇapena vā manussakuṇapena vā kaṇṭhe āsattena aṭṭiyeyya harāyeyya jiguccheyya.*
51. *Evam eva te bhikkhū sakena kāyena aṭṭiyantā harāyantā jigucchantā attanāpi attānaṃ jīvitā voropenti aññamaññaṃ pi jīvitā voropenti.*
52. Vin.III.69f; SN.V.321.
53. Vin.III.71: *Vigarahi buddho bhagavā. Ananucchaviyaṃ bhikkhave tesaṃ bhikkhūnaṃ ananulomikaṃ appaṭirūpaṃ assāmaṇakaṃ akappiyaṃ akaraṇīyaṃ.*
54. *Satthahāraka*: bringing a knife so that a *bhikkhu* can kill himself.
55. Ibid.: *Yo pana bhikkhu sañcicca manussaviggahaṃ jīvitā voropeyya satthahārakaṃ vāssa pariyeseyya, ayaṃ pi pārājiko hoti asaṃvāso 'ti.*
56. SN.V.321: *Sādhu bhante bhagavā aññaṃ pariyāyam ācikkhatu tathā yathāyaṃ bhikkhusaṅgho aññāya saṇṭhaheyya ti.*
57. There are other accounts of *bhikkhus* committing suicide in the *Sutta Piṭaka* (for example at SN.I.120f; SN.III.123f), but they are not attributable to misunderstanding the nature of the body. The purpose of such passages, and the *Vinaya* passage discussed here, may have been primarily to indicate that one should not commit suicide. This does not, however, invalidate the point I have made.
58. Norman (trans.), 1992, p.30.

59. Ibid.
60. Norman (trans.), 1984, p.47.
61. This is discussed in Collins, 1982, p.156f.
62. PED, p.22.
63. SBE Vol. X, p.54.
64. ERE, Vol.II, p.759.
65. The Sanskrit equivalent of *nibbidā* is *nirveda*, from *nir√vid*. Monier Williams gives as alternative meanings for *nirveda*: "complete indifference, disregard of worldly objects… loathing, disgust for…" (p.557). For *nibbidā*, PED gives: "disgust with worldly life, tedium, aversion, indifference, disenchantment" (p.365).
66. SN.V.82: *Satt'ime bhikkhave bojjhaṅgā bhāvitā bahulīkatā ekantanibbidāya virāgāya nirodhāya upasamāya abhiññāya sambodhāya nibbānāya saṃvattanti.*
67. GS.V.153.
68. For example, at KS.V.158, 227, 316; GS.V.152, 153.
69. GS.III.68.
70. GS.IV.97.
71. *Dialogues*, I.255.
72. *Paramatthajotikā* p.38f.
73. Vism, p.249.
74. I have followed Ñāṇamoli's translation, *The Path of Purification* (henceforth referred to as *Path*), p.269 of Vism, p.249f: *Kesā nām' ete vaṇṇato pi paṭikūlā, saṇṭhānato pi gandhato pi āsayato pi okāsato pi paṭikūlā … Yathā hi daharassa kumārassa vaccaṃ vaṇṇato haliddivaṇṇaṃ, saṇṭhānato [pi] haliddipiṇḍasaṇṭhānaṃ, sankāraṭṭhāne chaḍḍitañ ca uddhumātaka-kāḷasunakhasarīraṃ vaṇṇato tālapakkavaṇṇaṃ, saṇṭhānato vaṭṭhetvā vissaṭṭhamudiṅgasaṇṭhānaṃ, dāṭhā pi 'ssa sumanamakuḷasadisā ti ubhayam pi vaṇṇasaṇṭhānato siyā appaṭikūlaṃ, gandhena pana paṭikūlam eva, evaṃ kesā pi siyuṃ vaṇṇasaṇṭhānato appaṭikūla, gandhena pana paṭikūlā yevā ti.*
75. Vism, p.250.
76. I have followed Ñāṇamoli's rather quaint but effective translation (*Path*, p.202f.) of Vism, p.196:

    Imaṃ hi subhato kāyaṃ gahetvā tattha mucchitā
    bālā karontā pāpāni; dukkhā na parimuccare.

    Tasmā passeyya medhāvī jīvito vā mattassa vā
    sabhāvaṃ pūtikāyassa subhabhāvena vajjitaṃ

    Vuttaṃ h'etaṃ:

    Duggandho asucikāyo kuṇapo ukkarūpamo
    nindito cakkhubhūtehi kāyo bālābhinandito.

    Allacammapaṭicchanno navadvāro mahāvaṇo
    samantato paggharati, asuci pūtigandhiyo.

    Sace imassa kāyassa anto bāhirako siyā
    daṇḍaṃ nūna gahetvāna kāke soṇe nivāraye ti.

77. Ñāṇamoli, *Path*, p.203, translating Vism, p.196: *Tasmā dabbajātikena bhikkhunā jīvamānasarīraṃ vā hotu matasarīraṃ vā, yattha yattha asubhākāro paññāyati, tattha tatth' eva nimittaṃ gahetvā kammaṭṭhānaṃ appanaṃ pāpetabban ti.*
78. Ñāṇamoli, *Path*, p.201f, translating Vism, p.195: *Pakatiyā pana idaṃ sarīraṃ nāma atirekatisata-aṭṭhikasamussayaṃ asītisatasandhisanghaṭitaṃ navanahārusata-nibaddhaṃ navamaṃsapesisatānulittaṃ, allamanussacammapariyonaddhaṃ chaviyā paṭicchannaṃ, chiddāvachiddaṃ medakathālikā viya niccuggharitapaggharitaṃ, kimisaṅghanisevitaṃ rogānaṃ āyatanaṃ, dukkhadhammānaṃ vatthuparibhinna-purāṇagaṇḍo viya navahi vaṇamukhehi satatavissandanaṃ, yassa ubhohi akkhīhi akkhigūthako paggharati, kaṇṇabilehi kaṇṇagūthako, nāsapuṭehi siṅghāṇikā, mukhato āhārapittasemharudhirāni, adho-dvārehi uccārapassāvā, navanavutiyā lomakūpasahassehi asucisedayūso paggharati, nīlamakkhikādayo samparivārenti, yaṃ dantakaṭṭhamukhadhovana-sīsamakkhana-nahāna-nivāsana-pārupanādīhi apaṭijaggitvā, yathā-jāto va pharusavippakiṇṇakeso hutvā gāmena gāmaṃ vicaranto rājā pi puppha-chaḍḍakacaṇḍālādisu aññataro pi samasarīrapaṭikūlatāya nibbiseso hoti, evaṃ asuciduggandhajegucchapaṭikūlatāya nibbiseso hoti, evaṃ asuciduggandhajegucchapaṭikūlatāya rañño vā caṇḍālassa vā sarīre vemattaṃ nāma natthi.*

79. Ñāṇamoli, *Path*, p.202, translating Vism, p.195: *Tato iminā āgantukena alaṅkārena paṭicchannattā tad assa asubhalakkhaṇaṃ asañjānantā purisā itthīsu, itthiyo ca purisesu ratiṃ karonti. Paramatthato pan' ettha rañjitabbakayuttaṭṭhānaṃ nāma aṇumattam pi natthi.*
80. Damien Keown, in his article "Morality in the Visuddhimagga" (1983), states that Buddhaghosa's treatment of Buddhist ethics in the *Visuddhimagga* is far more concerned with practices than with intentions. This would seem to support my point.
81. DN.II.214: *Asaṃsaṭṭho viharati kāmehi, asaṃsaṭṭtho akusalehi dhammehi. Tassa asaṃsaṭṭhassa kāmehi asaṃsaṭṭhassa akusalehi dhammehi uppajjati sukhaṃ.*
82. SN.I.182: *Yo 'dha puññān ca pāpañ ca bāhitvā.*
83. DN.I.75: *Evam eva kho mahārāja bhikkhu imam eva kāyaṃ nippītikena sukhena abhisandeti parisandeti paripūreti parippharati.*
84. SN.V.74: *Tassa ṭhito va kāyo hoti ṭhitaṃ cittam ajjhattaṃ susaṇṭhitaṃ suvimuttaṃ. Manasā kho pan'eva dhammaṃ viññāya manāpaṃ/amanāpaṃ na maṅku hoti.*
85. Miln 44: *N'atthi mahārāja arahato anunayo vā paṭigho vā.*
86. Wilson, 1995.
87. cf. AN.I.177, where *dukkhasamudaya* is explained according to the *paṭiccasamuppāda* formula, beginning with *avijjā*, rather than the more usual *taṇhā*.

Conclusion

I STATED IN THE INTRODUCTION that three of the key doctrines taught by the Buddha, the four Noble Truths, the *paṭiccasamuppāda* formula and the *khandha* analysis, were all concerned with the human being and *saṃsāric* existence. This, I stated, suggested to me the importance the Buddha attaches to understanding the constitution of the human being and prompted the orientation of my research. I also referred in the Introduction to the fact that there is no suggestion in the *Sutta Piṭaka* that the Buddha had any concern with ontological matters; on the contrary, he dismisses all ontological questions as irrelevant and/or misleading. When applied to the human being, this means that in the early Pali material contained in the *Sutta Piṭaka* we do not find information concerning what we are comprised of, but only how we work. We have seen that the constitution of the human being is understood and taught by the Buddha in terms of processes and events. Here I wish to bring together these two points: the emphasis on the human being and the absence of concern with ontological matters.

First, I have considered in some detail several ambiguous passages which some scholars have interpreted as positing an idealistic ontology, in the perhaps somewhat limited sense that 'everything is (merely) made of the mind' (whatever that is). In each case I have suggested that the passages can be interpreted in another, non-idealistic (and, indeed, non-ontological) way, and that in my opinion this alternative interpretation is more likely to be correct. In introducing the Buddha's lack of interest in ontological questions, I based my comments primarily on canonical passages which state that he refused to answer such questions. And I also stated that I did not want to counter one suggested ontology, usually the idealism as described, with another. But the further point I would like to make here is that any implicit ontology, if there is such a thing in the *Sutta Piṭaka*, needs to allow for the centrality of the human condition to the Buddha's teachings. For the Buddha, the one basic truth is the reality of suffering. This, indeed, is the first Noble Truth, and is the *raison d'être* of the Eightfold Path to liberation. In idealistic systems suffering is sometimes said to be a delusion. There is no possibility that the Buddha's teaching contained in the *Sutta Piṭaka* can be interpreted as saying that suffering is just a delusion. Though he never discusses whether the world is real, his concern to teach, and his emphasis on alleviating the human condition by offering release from suffering, presuppose that there really are human beings who really can learn how to bring an end to *saṃsāric* existence. Though he is not interested in ontological questions, he most emphatically is a humanist.

Second, the centrality of the human being in the Buddha's teachings does not preclude the possibility that there are other sorts of beings existing in different sorts of ways, ways which are what we might call 'subtle', and certainly not obeying the laws of matter as they are conventionally understood. Of relevance here is the suggestion by Buddhist modernists that the Buddha anticipated modern physics, which explains that all matter is energy. In its emphasis on how things are rather than what things are the Buddha's teaching allows for beings to exist in an infinite number of ways in a manner not incompatible with this modern law of physics. To mix the terminologies of Buddhism and physics, such beings might be thought of as 'bundles of energies' (*khandhas*), manifesting at different degrees of density, brought together as conditioned by the power or fuel (energy) of volitions.

Third, and finally, I stated in the Introduction that one of the ways in which the Buddha's teaching diverged from that contained in the *Upaniṣads* is that he taught that the macrocosmic/microcosmic correspondence was not one of ontological identity but that all things are dependently originated. This book has perhaps shown how central this teaching is for an understanding of the constitution of the human being. I also referred to the fact that many scholars have approached the subject of the human being in early Buddhism by discussing the doctrine of *anattā*. We saw that this is often considered to be the central doctrine of early Buddhism and that it tends to be understood as a denial of any kind of soul or self. I would like to suggest here that the doctrine of *anattā* is not intended to be a denial of being as is implied in the English 'there is no self'. Rather, it is no different from the doctrine of *paṭiccasamuppāda* and is therefore simply intended to indicate *how* things are.[1]

We have seen that everything within the cycle of *saṃsāra* is conditioned or constructed, *saṃkhata*. This is another way of expressing the doctrine of dependent origination: all things are dependently originated. From these two teachings, it *follows* that there is nothing in *saṃsāric* existence that is permanent. And it follows further from this that there is no independently existing or permanent entity which one might call a self or soul. Therefore, though the prime concern of these two teachings focusses on the way things exist rather than what exists, they might also be called a doctrine of *anattā*. Nirvana is also (implicitly) included in the doctrine of *anattā*: *sabbe dhammā anattā* is the last line in the *tilakkhaṇa* formula. But the inclusion of Nirvana is also not intended literally as a denial of being. Rather, Nirvana is selfless both because it is the experience of ceasing to project the separateness of selfhood onto oneself and everything else and also in the sense that it is an epistemic experience. This means that thinking in terms of self *or of there being no self* is making a category mistake. None of the Buddha's teachings is actually concerned with what is, *or with what is not.* The fundamental error is simply thinking in any such terms since they are all missing the point that the way things (really) exist does not correspond to the notion of separateness that is implicit in the confirmation *and in the denial* of selfhood. As the Buddha puts it: understanding dependent origination means one will no longer ask questions about *individual* (i.e. separate) existence in *saṃsāra*, past, future, or present, such as "Am I, *or am I not*? What am I? How am I? This 'being' that is 'I', where has it come from, where will it go?"[2] Though the doctrine of *anattā* appears to convey an overriding concern to make ontological denials, I suggest that if one takes this term at face value it can act as something of a red herring in one's attempt to understand the constitution of the human being.

Notes

1. See my paper "*Anattā:* A Different Approach" for an extensive discussion of this suggestion.
2. SN.II.27: … *ahaṃ nu kho smi, na nu kho smi; kiṃ nu kho smi; kathaṃ nu kho smi; ahaṃ nu kho satto kuto āgato so kuhiṃgāmī bhavissatī ti.*

Bibliography

Primary Sources

I have used the Pali Text Society editions of all Pali texts and quote from them by permission of the Pali Text Society which owns the copyright to the works.

Basu, B.D. (ed.) *Sāṃkhya-Pravacana-Sūtraṃ with the Vṛtti of Aniruddha.* Allahabad: Sudhindranath Vasu, 1915.

Limaye, V.P. and Vadekar, R.D. *Eighteen Principal Upaniṣads* Vol. I. Poona: Vaidika Saṃśodhana Maṇḍala, 1958.

Müller, M. (ed.) *Ṛg Veda Saṃhitā* Vols. I and II (2nd ed.). London: Trübner & Co., 1877.

Röer, E. (ed.) *Bṛhadāraṇyaka Upaniṣad with the Commentary of Śaṅkara Ācārya and the gloss of Ānanda Giri.* Calcutta: Asiatic Society of Bengal, 1849.

———. *Chāndogya Upaniṣad with the Commentary of Śaṅkara Ācārya.* Calcutta: Asiatic Society of Bengal, 1850.

———. *Śatapatha-Brāḥmaṇa.* Bombay: Gangavishnu Shrikrishnadass, 1940.

Vasubandhu *Abhidharmakośa and Bhāṣya.* Varanasi: Bauddha Bharati Publications, 1981.

Secondary Sources and Translations

Aronson, H. B. *Love and sympathy in Theravāda Buddhism.* Delhi: Motilal Banarsidass, 1980.

Aung, S. Z. & Rhys Davids, C. A. F. (trans.) *Points of Controversy.* London: PTS, 1915.

Aung, S. Z. (trans.) *Compendium of Philosophy* (revised and edited by C. A. F. Rhys Davids). London: PTS, (repr.), 1963.

Bareau, A. *Les Sectes Bouddhiques du Petite Véhicule.* Saigon: École Française d'Extrême Orient, 1955.

Batchelor, S. "Existence, Enlightenment and Suicide: the Dilemma of Nanavira Thera" Unpublished paper given at *The Buddhist Forum* at SOAS, December 1993 (publication forthcoming).

Bateson, J. H. "The Body (Buddhist)" in Hastings, J. (ed.) *The Encyclopedia of Religion and Ethics* Vol. II. London: T. & T. Clark, 1908.

Bhattacharya, K. *"Upadhi, upādi* et *upādāna*", *Mélanges d'Indianisme à la mémoire de Louis Renou*. Paris: 1968.

———. *L'Ātman-Brahman dans le Bouddhisme Ancien*. Paris: 1973.

———. "*Diṭṭhaṃ, Sutaṃ, Mutaṃ, Viññātaṃ*" in S. Balasoorya (*et al.*) (eds.) *Buddhist Studies in Honour of Walpola Rahula*. London: 1980.

Bodhi, Bhikkhu "*Khandha* and *Upādānakkhandha*" in *Pali Buddhist Review* Vol. I, No.1, 1976, pp. 91–102.

Bloomfield, M. *A Vedic Concordance*. Cambridge, MA: Harvard University Press, 1906.

Böhtlingk, O. & Roth, R. *Sanskrit-Wörterbuch*. St. Petersburg: Kaiserlichen Akademie der Wissenschaften, 1858.

Bunnag, J. *Buddhist Monk, Buddhist Layman*. Cambridge: CUP, 1973.

Carrithers, M. *The Forest Monks of Laṅkā*. New Delhi: OUP, 1983.

Carter, J. R. *Dhamma: A Study of a Religious Concept*. Tokyo: Hokuseido Press, 1978.

Chalmers, Lord (trans.) *Further Dialogues of the Buddha* Vol. II (SBB Vol. VI). London: OUP, 1927.

Collins, S. *Selfless Persons*. Cambridge: CUP, 1982.

———. "Indian Ideas of Mind" in Gregory, R.L. (ed.) *The Oxford Companion to the Mind*. London: OUP, 1987.

———. *The Body in Theravāda Buddhist Monasticism* Unpublished paper given at 'The Body: A Colloquium on Comparative Spirituality' at Lancaster University, 1987.

———. "*Nirvāṇa*, Time, and Narrative" in *History of Religions* Spring 1992.

Copleston, F.C. *Aquinas*. London: Penguin, 1955.

Conze, E. *Buddhist Thought in India*. London: 1962.

———. *Buddhism – Its Essence and Development*. Oxford: (repr.) 1974.

Cousins, L.S. "The *Paṭṭhāna* and the Development of the *Theravādin Abhidhamma*" in *JPTS* Centenary Volume, 1981.

———. "Pali Oral Literature" in Denwood, P. and Piatigorsky, A. (eds.) *Buddhist Studies: Ancient and Modern*. London: Curzon, 1983.

———. "The 'Five Points' and the Origins of the Buddhist Schools" in Skorupski, T. (ed.) *The Buddhist Forum* Vol. II. London: SOAS, 1991.

Dasgupta, S. *A History of Indian Philosophy* 5 vols. Delhi: Motilal Banarsidass, (repr.), 1975.

de Silva, P. *An Introduction to Buddhist Psychology*. London: Macmillan Press, 1979.

Eggeling, J. (trans.) *Śatapatha Brāhmaṇa* (of the *Mādhyandina* School) SBE Vol. XLIV. Delhi: Motilal Banarsidass, (repr.), 1963.

Eliade, M. *Yoga: Immortality and Freedom* (2nd ed.). Princeton: Princeton University Press, (repr.), 1973.

Falk, M. *Nāma Rūpa and Dharma Rūpa*. Calcutta: University of Calcutta Press, 1943.

Filliozat, J. "The Psychological Discoveries of Buddhism" in *University of Ceylon Review* Vol. XIII 1955, pp.69–82.

Franke, R. O. (trans.) *Dīghanikāya*. Göttingen: Vandenhoech & Ruprecht, 1913.

Frauwallner, E. *The Earliest Vinaya and the Beginnings of Buddhist Literature*. Rome: Serie Orientale Roma VIII, 1956.

———. *History of Indian Philosophy* Vol. I (trans. V. M. Bedekar). Delhi: Motilal Banarsidass, (repr.), 1984.

Geiger, M. & W. *Pāli Dhamma*. Munich: Verlag der Bayerischen Wissenschaften, 1920.

Gethin, R. M. L. "The Five *Khandhas*: their treatment in the *Nikāyas* and early Buddhism" in *Journal of Indian Philosophy*, 14, 1986 pp.35–53.

———. *The Buddhist Path to Awakening: a Study of the Bodhi-Pakkhiyā Dhammā*. Leiden: E. J. Brill, 1992.

Gombrich, R. F. *Precept and Practice*. Oxford: Clarendon Press, 1971.

———. "Ancient Indian Cosmology" in Blacker, C. & Loewe, M. (eds.) *Ancient Cosmologies*. London: George Allen & Unwin, 1975.

———. "Notes on the Brahmanical Background to Buddhist Ethics" in Dhammapala, G. (*et al.*) (eds.) *Buddhist Studies in Honour of Hammalava Saddhātissa*. Sri Lanka: Buddhist Research Library Trust, 1984.

———. *Theravāda Buddhism: A Social History from Ancient Benares to Modern Colombo*. London: Routledge & Kegan Paul, 1988.

———. *How Buddhism began: the Conditioned Genesis of the Early Teachings*. The Louis H. Jordan Lectures in Comparative Religion given at SOAS 1994, (publication forthcoming).

Gonda, J. *Loka: World and Heaven in the Veda*. Amsterdam: N.V. Noord Hollandsche Uitgevers Maatschappij, 1966.

Griffiths, P. J. *On Being Mindless*. Illinois: Open Court, 1986.

———. "Pure Consciousness and Indian Buddhism" in R. K. C. Forman (ed.) *The Problem of Pure Consciousness*. London: OUP, 1990.

Hamilton, Sue *The Body in Early Buddhism* Unpublished M.Phil thesis, University of Oxford 1990.

———. "From Buddha to Buddhaghosa: changing attitudes towards the human body in Theravāda Buddhism" in Jane-Marie Law (ed.) *Religious Reflections on the Human Body*. Indiana University Press, 1995.

———. "*Anattā*: A Different Approach" in *The Middle Way*, Vol. 70, 1, May 1995.

Hare, E. M. (trans.) *Gradual Sayings* Vol. III (repr. 1988), Vol. IV (repr. 1989). Oxford: PTS.

Harvey, P. *The Selfless Mind: Personality, Consciousness and Nirvana in Early Buddhism*. London: Curzon Press, 1995.

———. "The Mind-body relationship in Pāli Buddhism: a philosophical investigation". Unpublished paper given at the Tenth Conference of the International Association of Buddhist Studies. Paris: July 1991.

Horner, I. B. *The Early Buddhist Theory of Man Perfected*. London: Williams & Northgate, 1936.

———. (trans.) *The Book of the Discipline* Vol. I. London: PTS, (repr.), 1982.

———. (trans.) *Middle Length Sayings* Vol. I (repr. 1987), Vol. II (repr. (repr. 1989). London and Oxford: PTS.

Hume, R. E. (trans.) *The Thirteen Principal Upanishads* (2nd ed.). Delhi: Oxford University Press, (repr.), 1985.

Jacobi, H. "Cosmogony and Cosmology (Indian)" in Hastings, J. (ed.) *Encyclopedia of Religion and Ethics* Vol. IV. London: T. & T. Clark, 1908.

James, W. *The Varieties of Religious Experience*. New York: The Modern Library, 1929.

Jayasuriya, W. F. *The Psychology and Philosophy of Buddhism*. Colombo: YMBA Press, 1963.

Jayatilleke, K. N. "Some Problems of Translation and Interpretation(1)" in *University of Ceylon Review* Vol. VII 1949 pp. 208–225.

———. *Early Buddhist Theory of Knowledge*. London: George Allen & Unwin, 1963.

Johansson, R. E. A "*Citta, mano, viññāṇa* – a Psychosemantic Investigation" in *University of Ceylon Review* Vol. 23 nos 1 & 2 April–Oct 1965 pp. 165–215.

———. *The Psychology of Nirvana*. London: George Allen & Unwin, 1969.

———. *The Dynamic Psychology of Early Buddhism*. Oxford: Curzon Press, 1979.

Johnston, E. H. (ed. and trans.) *Aśvaghoṣa's Buddhacarita* (or *Acts of the Buddha*). Delhi: Motilal Banarsidass (repr.), 1978.

Kalupahana, D. J. *A History of Buddhist Philosophy*. Honolulu: University of Hawaii Press, 1992.

———. "Consciousness" in Dhirasekera, J. (ed.) *Encyclopedia of Buddhism* Vol. IV. Government of Sri Lanka, 1979.

Karunadasa, Y. *The Buddhist Analysis of Matter*. Colombo Department of Cultural Affairs, 1967.

Karunaratna, W. S. "*Cetanā*" and "*Citta*" in Dhirasekera, J. (ed.) *Encyclopedia of Buddhism* Vol. IV. Government of Sri Lanka, 1979.

Keith, A. B. *Buddhist Philosophy in India and Ceylon.* Oxford: Clarendon Press, 1923.

Keown, D. "Morality in the *Visuddhimagga*" in *Journal of the International Association of Buddhist Studies* Vol. 6, I, 1983.

Law, B. C. (trans.) *Designation of Human Types.* London: PTS, 1922.

Lamotte, E. *Histoire du Bouddhisme Indien.* Louvain: Publications Universitaires, 1958.

———. *Le Traité de la grande vertu de Sagesse de Nāgārjuna.* Louvain: Publications Universitaires, 1980.

McDermott, J. P. "Karma and Rebirth in Early Buddhism" in O'Flaherty, W. (ed.) *Karma and Rebirth in Classical Indian Traditions.* London: University of California Press, 1980.

MacDonell, A. A. *A Vedic Reader.* Oxford: Clarendon Press, (repr.), 1928.

Mādhavānanda, Swāmī (trans.) *Bṛhadāraṇyaka Upaniṣad with the Commentary of Śankarācārya* (3rd ed.). Almora: Advaita Ashrama, 1950.

Malalasekera, G. P. *The Buddha and His Teachings.* Buddhist Council of Ceylon, 1957.

Malkani, G. R. "The Conception of Reality as Dynamic" in *Proceedings of the Indian Philosophical Congress* 1953 pp. 179–197.

Manné, J. "Categories of *Sutta* in the Pāli *Nikāyas* and their Implications for our Appreciation of the Buddhist teaching and Literature" in *JPTS* XV. Oxford, 1990.

Masefield, P. "How 'noble' is the Ariyan Eightfold Path?" in Connolly, P. (ed.) *Perspectives on Indian Religion.* Delhi: Sri Satguru Publications, 1986.

Matthews, B. "Notes on the Concept of the Will in Early Buddhism" in *Sri Lanka Journal of the Humanities.* December 1975, no 12, pp. 152–60.

Monier-Williams, M. *A Sanskrit-English Dictionary.* Delhi: Motilal Banarsidass, (repr.), 1986.

Müller, F. Max (trans.) *The Dhammapada* SBE Vol. X. Oxford: Clarendon Press, 1881.

Ñāṇamoli, Bhikkhu (trans.) *The Minor Readings* and *The Illustrator of Ultimate Meaning.* London: PTS, 1960.

———. *The Guide.* London: PTS, 1962.

———. *The Path of Purification* (2nd ed.). Colombo: A. Semage, 1964.

———. *The Path of Discrimination.* Oxford: PTS, (repr.), 1991.

Ñāṇananda, Bhikkhu *Concept and Reality in Early Buddhist Thought.* Sri Lanka: Buddhist Publication Society, (repr.), 1986.

Ñānavīra Thera *Clearing the Path.* Colombo: Path Press, 1987.

Nārada, Le Ven *La Doctrine Bouddhique de la Re-naissance* (trans. Migot, A.). Paris: Librairie D'Amérique et d'Orient, 1979.

Nārada, U. (trans.) *Discourse on Elements*. London: PTS, 1962.

Norman, K. R. (trans.) *The Group of Discourses*. London: PTS, 1984.

———. *The Group of Discourses* Vol. II. Oxford: PTS, 1992.

———. "An Epithet of Nibbāna" in *Upadhyaya Commemoration* Vol. I, 1987, pp.23–31.

Nyanaponika, Bhikkhu *Abhidhamma Studies*. Colombo: Frewin & Co., 1949.

———. *The Power of Mindfulness*. Kandy: Buddhist Publication Society, (repr.), 1986 (Wheel Series no 121/122).

Nyāṇatiloka *Guide through the Abhidhamma Piṭaka*. Colombo: Bauddha Sāhitya Sabhā, 1957.

———. *Buddhist Dictionary* (4th ed.). Kandy: Buddhist Publication Society, 1980.

Oldenberg, H. *Buddha: his life, his doctrine, his order* (translated from the German by William Hoey). London: Williams and Norgate, 1882.

Pande, G.C. *Studies in the Origins of Buddhism* (3rd ed.). Delhi: Motilal Banarsidass, 1983.

Paṭhamakyaw Ashin Thiṭṭhila (trans.) *The Book of Analysis*. London: PTS, 1969.

Pe Maung Tin and Rhys Davids, C. A. F. (trans.) *The Expositor* Vols. I, II. London: PTS, (repr.), 1976.

Pérez-Remón, J. *Self and Non-Self in Early Buddhism*. The Hague: Mouton Publishers, 1980.

Pieris, A. "The notions of *Citta, Attā and Attabhāva* in the Pāli Exegetical writings" in S. Balasoorya (*et al.*) (eds.) *Buddhist Studies in Honour of Walpola Rahula*. London: Gordon Fraser, 1980.

Pio, E. *Buddhist Psychology: A Modern Perspective*. New Delhi: Abhinav Publications, 1988.

Piyananda, D. "The Concept of Mind in Early Buddhism" PhD. thesis, The Catholic University of America, 1974.

Radhakrishnan, S. (trans.) *The Principal Upaniṣads*. London: George Allen & Unwin, 1953.

———. *The Dhammapada*. Madras: OUP, (repr.), 1988.

Rahula, W. *Zen and the Taming of the Bull*. London: Gordon Fraser, 1978.

———. *What the Buddha Taught*. London: Gordon Fraser, (repr.), 1985.

Reat, N. R. "Some Fundamental Concepts of Buddhist Psychology" in *Religion* 17, 1987, pp.15–28.

———. *Origins of Indian Psychology*. California: Asian Humanities Press, 1990.

Renou, L. *Études sur le Vocabulaire du Rgveda; première série*. Pondichéry: Institut Français d'Indologie, 1958.

Reynolds, F. "The Several Bodies of Buddha: Reflections on a Neglected Aspect of *Theravāda* Tradition" in *History of Religions* Vol. 16.1, 1976–77, pp.374–389.

Rhys Davids, C. A. F. "On the Will in Buddhism" in *Journal of the Royal Asiatic Society*, pt 1 January 1898, pp.47–59.

———. *Buddhist Psychology*. London: G. Bell & Son, 1914.

———. *The Birth of Indian Psychology and its Development in Buddhism*. London: Luzac, 1936.

———. "Towards a History of the Skandha-Doctrine" in *Indian Culture* Vol. III, 1937, pp. 405-11; 653–62.

———. (trans.) *Kindred Sayings* Vol. I (repr. 1989), Vol. II (repr. 1990). Oxford: PTS.

———. (trans.) *A Buddhist Manual of Psychological Ethics* (3rd ed.). London: PTS, (repr.), 1974.

Rhys Davids, T. W. (trans.) *Dialogues of the Buddha* Parts I, II & III (SBB Vols. II (repr. 1923), III (repr. 1977) and IV (repr. 1921)). London: OUP.

———. and Stede, W. (eds.) *Pali English Dictionary*. London: PTS, (repr.), 1986.

Ruegg, D. S. *La Théorie du Tathāgatagarbha et du Gotra*. Paris: École Française d'Extrême Orient, 1969.

Skilling, P. "*Vimuttimagga* and Abhayagiri: the Form-Aggregate according to the *Saṃskṛtāsaṃskṛta-viniścaya*" in *JPTS* Vol. XX, 1994, pp. 171–210.

Smart, N. "Creation, persons and the Meaning of Life" in R. Ruddock (ed.) *Six Approaches to the Person*. London: Routledge & Kegan Paul, 1972.

———. "Living Liberation" in E. Sharpe (ed.) *Man and His Salvation*. Manchester University Press, 1974.

Soma Thera, *The Way of Mindfulness* (5th ed.). Kandy: Buddhist Publication Society, 1981.

Thomas, E. J. *The History of Buddhist Thought*. London: Routledge & Kegan Paul, (repr.),1951.

———. *The Life of the Buddha as Legend and History* (3rd ed.). London: Routledge and Kegan Paul, 1949.

Trenckner, V. (ed.) *Critical Pali Dictionary*. Copenhagen: Royal Danish Academy of Sciences and Letters, 1924–1981.

U Ba Kyaw (trans.) *Elucidation of the Intrinsic Meaning*. London: PTS, 1980.

Verdu, A. *Early Buddhist Philosophy*. Washington DC: University Press of America, 1979.

Warder, A. K. *Indian Buddhism.* Delhi: Motilal Banarsidass, 1970.

———. *Introduction to Pali* (2nd ed.). London: PTS, 1984.

Wayman, A. "Regarding the translation of the Buddhist terms *saññā/saṃjñā, viññāṇa/vijñāna*" in Wijesekera, O. H. de A. (ed.) *Malalasekera Commemoration Volume.* Columbo: The Malalasekera Commemoration Volume Editorial Committee, 1976.

———. "A Study of the *Vedāntic* and Buddhist Theory of *Nāma-rūpa*" in Hercus, L.A. (*et al.*) (eds.) *Indological and Buddhist Studies* (2nd ed.). Delhi: Srī Satguru Publications, 1984.

Welch, H. *The Practice of Chinese Buddhism.* Cambridge, MA: Harvard University Press, 1967.

Whitney, W. D. *The Roots, Verb-Forms and Primary Derivatives of the Sanskrit Language.* Leipzig: Breitkopf & Härtel, 1885.

Wijesekera, O. H. de A. "The Concept of *Viññāṇa* in *Theravāda* Buddhism" in *Journal of the American Oriental Society* Vol. 84, July-September 1964, pp. 254–259.

Williams, P.M. "Nāgārjuna: Selections from the *Mādhyamakakārikā*, together with excerpts from the commentaries" in *The Middle Way* Vol. 52, 1977, pp.72–123.

———. *Mahāyāna Buddhism: the Doctrinal Foundations.* London: Routledge, 1989.

———. "Non-Conceptuality, Critical Reasoning and Religious Experience. Some Tibetan Buddhist Discussions" in M.McGhee (ed.) *Philosophy, Religion and the Spiritual Life.* Cambridge: CUP, 1992.

Wilson, E. "The Female Body as a Source of Horror and Insight in Post-Aśokan Buddhism" in Jane-Marie Law (ed.) *Religious Reflections on the Human Body.* Indiana University Press, 1995.

Woods, J. H. *The Yoga-System of Patañjali.* Harvard University Press, 1914.

Woodward, F. L. (trans.) *Gradual Sayings* Vol. I (repr. 1989), Vol. II (repr. 1992), Vol. V (repr. 1986). London and Oxford: PTS.

———. *Kindred Sayings* Vol. III (repr. 1975), Vol. IV (repr. 1980), Vol. V (repr. 1990). London and Oxford: PTS.

———. *Minor Anthologies* Part II. London: OUP, 1935.

Zaehner, R. C. (trans.) *The Bhagavadgītā.* Oxford: OUP, 1969.

Zürcher, E. *Buddhism: its Origin and Spread in Words, Maps and Pictures.* London: Routledge & Kegan Paul, 1962.

Zysk, K. G. *Asceticism and Healing in Ancient India.* Oxford: OUP, 1991.

Short Glossary

anattā Selflessness. The Buddha taught that all things are dependently originated (see *paṭiccasamuppāda*): nothing occurs independently or separately, but, rather, all things occur because of/conditioned by other things. It is erroneous, then, to attribute separate, independent self-hood onto anything, either subjectively or objectively: this is not 'how things really are' (see *yathābhūtaṃ*). Seeing 'things as they really are' (that is, that they are 'selfless' in this sense) constitutes the cessation of ignorance, or Enlightenment (*q.v.*).

arahant The term used to indicate an Enlightened person (literally: 'worthy one'). According to the early Buddhist texts, the experience of attaining Enlightenment (*q.v.*) is the same for all people as it was for the Buddha.

ariyasāvaka Literally 'disciple who is noble', this term refers to those who have made considerable progress on the spiritual path, hence they are also referred to as 'advanced disciples'.

āsava The *āsavas* are the fundamentally binding (to *saṃsāra*, *q.v.*) aspects of what it means to be a human being, needing to be eradicated if one is to achieve Enlightenment (*q.v.*). Three or four *āsavas* are referred to: all/any sensual desire(s), the desire for continued existence, ignorance, and (when four are mentioned) 'views'. Underpinning all of them is the basic error of separateness (see *anattā*, *q.v.*): all desires presuppose a separate desirer; continued existence presupposes identity in terms of separateness; ignorance is the (normal *saṃsāric*) state of not seeing that things are really selfless, and therefore not separate; and 'views' are held by a 'separate' self about something perceived (erroneously) also to be separate (thus separateness is presupposed both subjectively and objectively). The *āsavas* are so deep seated in the human psyche that they are described as needing to be 'rooted out', which achievement is co-terminous with Enlightenment.

bhikkhu A (male) member of a Buddhist monastic community. By extension, a disciple following the path taught by the Buddha. Members of female communities are called *bhikkhunī*. Males and females can experience Enlightenment (*q.v.*).

dhamma Most commonly, this term is used to refer to the teachings of the Buddha as a whole: he taught 'the *dhamma*'. It also means the Truth, in the sense that the Truth represents 'things as they really are' (see *yathābhūtaṃ*), and what he taught was a means whereby one might experience that. *Dhamma* is also used as a generic term to refer to all knowable things, and is a way of saying 'everything'.

dukkha Often translated 'suffering', but 'unsatisfactoriness' less misleadingly conveys its meaning. It is the term that was used by the Buddha in the first Noble Truth (*q.v.*) to describe the principal characteristic of human existence in *saṃsāra* (*q.v.*). It relates to the impermanence (and hence ultimate unsatisfactoriness) of all things in *saṃsāra*. It can most accurately be understood if it is borne in mind that this is a truth statement, not a value judgement.

Enlightenment On experiencing Nirvana (*q.v.*), one is Enlightened: one 'sees things as they really are' (see *yathābhūtaṃ*), thus experiencing the cessation of ignorance. The word 'buddha' literally means awake, the analogy being that ignorance corresponds to sleep and Enlightenment/Nirvana corresponds to 'waking up' to 'how things really are'. In Buddhism, the (gradual) eradication of ignorance (one follows a progressive path over many lives) is referred to as acquiring 'insight'.

jhāna Literally meditation. In Buddhism (and in other Indian religions), a common kind of meditation is said to be stratified into 'levels', meaning levels of experience and/or insight that are characterised in certain ways, and it is to such levels that *jhāna* refers. In the Pali texts, sometimes four and sometimes eight *jhānas* (levels of meditation) are referred to. When eight are referred to, these are usually sub-divided as to four *rūpajjhānas* and four *arūpajjhānas*. *Rūpa* and *arūpa* mean 'form' and 'formless' respectively. According to the Buddha, even experiencing the highest of such meditational levels does not in itself constitute insight into 'things as they really are' (see *yathābhūtaṃ*/Nirvana). It is this insight that distinguishes Buddhist forms of meditation from others.

karma Literally 'action', karma more specifically means (in Indian religions as a whole) that actions have consequences. The Buddha taught that the consequential aspect of any action (put into effect through thought, word or deed) lies in the intention behind it.

lokuttara Literally 'above the world', this term refers both to those who have made spiritual progress beyond the merely mundane/ordinary level of the *putthujana* (*q.v.*), and to anything associated with advanced (supramundane) stages of the path.

Nirvana The goal to which human beings can aspire, according to the Buddha, is the cessation of the unsatisfactoriness (*dukkha, q.v.*) which characterises the human condition (*saṃsāra, q.v.*). The experience of such cessation (*dukkhanirodha*) is known as Nirvana. Nirvana literally means 'blowing out', and refers to the blowing out (cessation) of the fuel which causes the continuity of unsatisfactoriness. According to the second Noble Truth (*q.v.*), the fuel is craving or desire, often further subdivided into the three 'fires' (fuel) of greed, hatred (together the affective aspect of the fuel) and ignorance (the cognitive aspect of the fuel). After experiencing Nirvana, one will no longer be reborn in *saṃsāra*.

Noble Truths In his 'first sermon', the Buddha taught four 'Noble Truths': that the human condition is characterised by unsatisfactoriness (*dukkha, q.v.*); that *dukkha* is caused by cravings; that there can be cessation of *dukkha* (*dukkhanirodha*, a synonym for Nirvana, *q.v.*); and a way to achieve such cessation (the Noble Eightfold Path).

paṭiccasamuppāda Dependent origination. The Buddha taught that all things, of whatever nature (physical, mental, abstract, concrete, subjective or objective – all things), that are or can be experienced in *saṃsāra* (*q.v.*) are dependently originated. As such, nothing occurs independently or separately. It follows from this that the attribution of separate, independent self-hood to oneself or anyone or anything else is erroneous (see *anattā*).

puthujjana By contrast with *ariyasāvaka* (*q.v.*), *puthujjana* refers to 'ordinary' or 'ignorant' (ordinarily ignorant) people who have not made progress on the spiritual path to insight.

saṃsāra In Buddhism (and other Indian religions), all living beings are thought to experience a series of lives (reincarnation/rebirth). *Saṃsāra*, which literally means 'going round', is the term used to indicate this cyclic experience, and by extension is often used to refer to 'life on earth' or the human condition as a whole. (According to Buddhist/Indian cosmology, it is not limited to life on earth as such, and also applies to non-human living beings: rebirth can be at a variety of cosmological levels and in a variety of forms.) The experience of Nirvana (*q.v.*) means one will no longer be reborn, and is thus the 'opposite' of *saṃsāra*. Neither term should be understood spacially. They indicate different states of being: the former subject to rebirths, the latter not.

saṅgha The Buddhist community. Sometimes the term refers to the community of all Buddhists, but more usually it refers specifically to the monastic community, the members of which are called *bhikkhus* (*q.v.*).

sukha A synonym for Nirvana (*q.v.*), and the opposite of *dukkha* (*q.v.*). Literally, *sukha* means 'bliss' (contrasted with 'suffering'/*dukkha*). It is not, however, an affective state of bliss (i.e. pleasure/happiness) but more profoundly refers to the cessation of the unsatisfactoriness which characterises the human condition. In particular, this refers to the 'ease' which corresponds to the absence of the 'dis-ease' of ignorance.

tathāgata An epithet of the Buddha, and by extension a term for any Enlightened (*q.v.*) person. The term, virtually untranslatable, means something like 'thus-gone', referring to the absence/cessation of separate individuality experienced when one sees that 'things as they really are' (see *yathābhūtaṃ*) are selfless (see *anattā*) in the sense of being not separately identifiable.

yathābhūtaṃ Literally 'things as they are', this important term refers to the Buddha's teaching that the cessation of ignorance (the cognitive aspect of the 'fuel' which causes continued existence in *saṃsāra* (*q.v.*)) is 'seeing things as they really are'. Such experience is the equivalent of Nirvana (*q.v.*). It follows that a key feature of human experience in *saṃsāra* is that one does *not* 'see things as they really are'.

General Index

Index of Textual Sources